The Man
Behind the Guns

Other books by EDWARD G. LONGACRE

From Union Stars to Top Hat:
A Biography of the
Extraordinary General James Harrison Wilson

Mounted Raids of the Civil War

The Man
Behind the Guns

A Biography
of
General Henry Jackson Hunt,

Chief of Artillery,
Army of the Potomac

Edward G. Longacre

South Brunswick and New York: A. S. Barnes and Company
London: Thomas Yoseloff Ltd

A. S. Barnes and Co., Inc.
Cranbury, New Jersey 08512

Thomas Yoseloff Ltd
Magdalen House
136–148 Tooley Street
London SE1 2TT, England

Library of Congress Cataloging in Publication Data

Longacre, Edward G   1946–
    The man behind the guns.

        Bibliography: p.
1. Hunt, Henry Jackson, 1819–1889. 2. United
States. Army—Biography. 3. Generals—United
States—Biography. 4. United States—History—
Civil War, 1861–1865—Regimental histories—Army of
the Potomac. 5. United States. Army. Army of the
                    Potomac. I. Title.
E467.1.H89L66   973.7′3′0924 [B]   76-10885
              ISBN 0-498-01656-0

PRINTED IN THE UNITED STATES OF AMERICA

to
Smooth, Zip, Moose,
D.O.M., French, Head Jock,
and the other remnants of the "Benton Zoo"

Contents

Acknowledgments

During much of my research I have been fortunate to enjoy the assistance of General Hunt's great-grandson, Commander J. Conway Hunt, United States Navy (retired), and the general's great-grandnephew, Mr. Frederick Drum Hunt, both of Washington, D.C. To both gentlemen, who furnished copies of many of the general's papers and diary entries, plus photographs of him, his second wife, and their children, as well as genealogical information on the Hunt family, I owe a great debt of gratitude.

Others who furnished assistance include: Mrs. Yolanda Marin de Hartnett and Miss Joan Di Donato of the War Library, Pennsylvania Commandery, Military Order of the Loyal Legion of the United States; Dale Floyd of the Old Military Division, National Archives; Charles F. Cooney, Division of Manuscripts, Library of Congress; Dr. Richard J. Sommers, Curator of Manuscripts, United States Army Military History Research Collection, Army War College; Gary Christopher, Manuscripts Department, Historical Society of Pennsylvania; Kenneth Rapp, Assistant Archivist, United States Military Academy Archives; Mrs. Marie T. Capps, Manuscripts Librarian, United States Military Academy Library; Mrs. Rebecca Ladenheim and Mrs. Mary VandenBerge of the Government Publications Department, Free Library of Philadelphia; Mrs. Karen Avenick, Interlibrary Loan Desk, La Salle College Library; and Mrs. Tillie Clement and Mrs. Gladys Bewley, of the Haddonfield (New Jersey) Free Library.

For running down various obscure facts, as well as for furnishing rare books of incalculable value in my research, I should also like to thank Mrs. Martha Matheny, of the South Carolina Historical Society; and Mr. Wayne Maxson, Interlibrary Loan Service, Temple University Library.

Special notes of gratitude must go to Mrs. Esmond A. Grosz of New Orleans, Louisiana and Mrs. Murray Preston of Chevy Chase, Maryland for providing information on the family of General Hunt's first wife, the De Russys; and to Mrs. Georgie Hayes McClerkin of Washington, D.C. for furnishing similar material pertaining to the Craigs, the family of the General's second wife.

9

An even more special note of appreciation goes to Dr. Russell F. Weigley, Department of History, Temple University, whose guidance has been of substantial value to me and whose solicitude kept me on the payroll as a teaching assistant at Temple long enough to finish this book.

Finally, I thank my father, Edgar Thorp Longacre, for assistance too apparent and at the same time too obscure to be specified.

Introduction

No doubt the story is apocryphal,[1] but it endures because it seems to ring so true:

In the midst of battle—perhaps in middle Virginia, or perhaps in lower Maryland or southern Pennsylvania—the Federal Army of the Potomac and the Confederate Army of Northern Virginia were locked in a fierce artillery duel. Cannon on both sides had unlimbered and were belching fire as fast as their gunners could load and aim, yank lanyards, sponge bores, and reload. One Union battery was particularly busy, its young captain shouting frantic orders to fire and fire again, foregoing adequate sighting between rounds.

From out of the powder smoke rode on officer on a pale horse—a gaunt, grizzled man with a full beard, clad in a dust-covered tunic, a silver star on his shoulder straps, and a faded sash of scarlet around his waist: the uniform of a brigadier general of artillery. Oblivious to his coming, the captain called for even more rapid discharges of his guns—until the general dismounted, strode to his side, laid a gloved hand on his shoulder, and spun him about. General Henry Jackson Hunt, commander of artillery of the Army of the Potomac jabbed an accusing finger at the nearest gun and shouted above the din:

"Young man, are you aware that every shot you fire costs the government two dollars and sixty-seven cents?"

Whatever the degree of its authenticity, the anecdote captures some of Henry Hunt's more notable traits. A frugal, conservative, no-nonsense artillerist, he deplored excessive expenditure of ammunition: "the besetting sin of some of our commanders." His precise, inspired, energetic, and highly effective use of light field batteries won him the reputation as his era's foremost authority on the art and science of gunnery. Thanks to his keen eye for terrain, his consistent coolheadedness under fire, and his unchallenged grasp of technical data, the artillery of the main Federal army in the eastern theater attained a prominence not equalled by any other branch of the service on either side. Even his adversaries testified to the results of Hunt's guidance: "Give me Confederate infantry and Union artillery," asserted rebel General D.H. Hill, "and I'll whip the world!"

The widespread praise that Hunt garnered from comrades as well as

11

from opponents is amply documented in dozens of commanders' reports recommending him for the highest honors the army could bestow. He won unqualified praise from above in every battle in which he served.

Yet the modern-day student of American history either knows Hunt not at all or only vaguely. Today's historians invariably echo the praise that Hunt had won so often in his own time, some even stating that he, almost singlehandedly, won the war for the Union. But few relate any information to make the man come alive as a person, rather than merely making him a symbol of Federal military prowess. He has never before received a biographer's consideration; nor has he been the subject of any scholarly study whatsoever during the last several years. Some full-length studies of campaigns in which he conspicuously participated omit mention of his name altogether.

Less-worthy colleagues have fared much better. For choice, Union General Benjamin F. Butler, almost universally adjudged a gross incompetent, has been the focus of a half-dozen biographies released during the past two decades. Many other incompetents, who won no battles except via tongue or pen, bask contentedly in the light of history, while able soldiers like Hunt thrash about in the swamp of historical neglect.

Conceivably, Hunt's fate owes a great deal to the nature of the service branch with which he was intimately associated throughout his career. While dozens of latter-day studies have recounted details of Civil War infantry and cavalry operations, a bare handful have discussed in adequate depth the contributions rendered by cannoneers—both Union and Confederate.

There may be simple explanations for this. A specialty arm, an amalgam of science, higher mathematics, and mechanical engineering, based on a highly technical body of literature, the art of the artillerist may appear to historians as too complex and too esoteric for popular consumption. Certainly Hunt, as a master artillerist—thus a highly proficient technician as well as a born soldier—has similarly been disregarded.

It would appear that few artillery commanders of the Civil War era were effective self-promoters. Hunt himself was as ambitious and as desirous of renown as any other soldier of the Union, supremely self-confident and vastly proud of his capabilities—justly so. Yet by nature he was also quiet and introspective, performing his duties without flamboyance. Furthermore, had he possessed the desire and the knack for advancing his own career, he lacked an effective showcase for his talents. It was his fate to serve in an army that seemed to regard artillery generals as behind-the-lines administrators first, last, and always: an attitude that later historians also adopted.

Additionally, Hunt never sought to ingratiate himself with those who might have advanced his standing. In fact, he alienated those superiors (and they were legion) who did not appreciate his brutal candor. By the same token, a prickly temper, unleashed whenever his highly sensitive pride was sore, antagonized a good many of his peers and resulted in a number of unseemly controversies, rivalries, and feuds that lowered his status in the eyes of the high command. Like the cannon he controlled, he could rarely do his job without discharging fire and fury, no matter who stood in his path.

At the same time, he was a steadfast friend to those whom he considered worthy of esteem and fraternity; and, in general, he was a discerning judge of character. When he gave his trust and comradeship to another, no threat of man or God—not War Department black-listing nor the wrath of the general in chief—could force him to withdraw his support. The most obvious case of such fidelity was Hunt's vocal admiration for George B. McClellan, with whom he remained close long after it became politically unwise to do so. Here, of course, as in several other cases, the dictates of Hunt's own conscience worked to his severe disadvantage.

As suggested by his staunch alliance with McClellan, much of Hunt's wartime travail and perhaps also his lack of historical prominence resulted from his naive indifference toward national politics. In an army whose lifeblood was only as rich as its political vitality, whose fortunes seemed every bit as dependent upon affairs in Washington City as on the battlefield, Hunt displayed a studied contempt for things political—at least when such conflicted with his unwavering conception of military responsibility. When he did make forays into the political realm, he almost invariably retreated with painful wounds. It is not too pat to trace his Civil War plight to a single root: his identity as a devout Democrat in an army sustained by the patronage of a Republican administration seeking to repress civil rebellion.

Another reason for Hunt's historical neglect relates directly to his fidelity to the artillery. By remaining in that arm while so many of his wartime and peacetime colleagues transferred to other branches of the service, he perpetuated his inability to receive rank, prestige, authority, and salary commensurate with his duties and responsibilities.

During his three-year tenure as chief of artillery of "Mr. Lincoln's Army," Hunt commanded the equivalent of a full-size army corps, but which, to reduce administrative headaches and expenditures, was never designated or treated as such. For example, at Gettysburg, where he reached the apex of his career, he commanded sixty-five batteries, 364 cannon, over eight thousand officers and men, and more than seven thousand animals, plus dozens of ammunition and baggage trains. Thus he was both an administrator and a front-line commander. Yet, not then, or ever after, did he win the full rank of major general, though every infantry and cavalry corps commander—many in charge of far fewer troops than he—did.

Because Hunt's sprawling command was fragmented and attached to infantry and cavalry for battle-line service, he not only lost immediate control over it but was relegated to the status of an aide on the staff of the commander of the army. For the first year and a half of the war he was a colonel; afterward a brigadier general of volunteers; and, finally, on the eve of the conflict's final campaign, he was made a major general—but only by brevet, or honorary title. This honor did not even allow him to receive the salary due an officer of that grade, or to use his new title for official duties—benefits that officers of brevet rank had received earlier in the war.

Many times infantry and cavalry chiefs asked that Hunt be assigned to them; that he might command a brigade or division; a full major generalship would accompany the latter. Had he been permitted to accept, he would probably have finished the war as a formally acknowledged corps commander, and perhaps as a major general in the Regular Army as well as in the volunteer service—attainments that accrued to several officers far inferior to him in terms of solid military contributions. But Hunt's artillery expertise was deemed so vital to the welfare of the Army of the Potomac that he was never permitted to take up other duties. Thus he forfeited rank, recognition, and pay, to his everlasting detriment. In the post-Civil War army he reverted to his old grade of lieutenant colonel, while many former artillery subordinates, who had won higher rank in the volunteers after transferring to infantry or cavalry commands, were assigned to duty over his head, according to the seniority given them by their wartime promotions.

Perhaps the most distressing aspect of Hunt's fidelity was the pay he had lost from the army's unwillingness to bestow upon him proper rank. After the war he calculated that, by failing to name him a major general, the War Department had cost him 47,402 dollars in pay and emoluments through four years of conflict. Additional pay losses resulted from this same fidelity. His command was so vast and, due to its attachment to other arms, so scattered that he required an extensive personal staff to oversee its administration. However, the army would grant him no more than a few aides, since it virtually considered Hunt himself a staff officer. This meant that on most occasions his highest-ranking subordinates would have to leave their batteries and ride great distances to his headquarters to submit certain reports, often necessitating their spending the night as his guests, which in turn required Hunt to delve into his own purse to defray the cost of their board and lodging.

Almost as often, foreign military observers and other visitors at army headquarters were fobbed off on him by billeting them to the artillery command. The aggregate expense for entertaining both his own officers and a steady influx of guests amounted to two thousand dollars over and above Hunt's yearly allowances. The irony in this was emphasized in 1884 by a Congressman promoting a bill to retire Hunt as a major general, thereby granting him an adequate pension: "In other words, he served his country in a position of the greatest responsibility and peril and paid $2,000 a year for the privilege. . . ." But the bill was killed by presidential veto.[2]

A final reason for the apathy with which history has treated Hunt was his own failure to leave a body of memoirs. This was not due to a lack of literary talent; he was regarded in his own time as one of America's finest writers on technical and historical subjects pertaining to the army in general and the American artillery in particular. He was also a skilled author of popular history; his three-article overview of the Gettysburg campaign, published in the 1880s in *Century Magazine* and reprinted in *Battles and Leaders of the Civil War*, still stands as a clear, concise, and vivid primary source on that crucial struggle.

Hunt neglected to enshrine himself in literature for two principal reasons: first, he detested the sort of egotistical self-indulgence that figured prominently in the published reminiscences of many of his Civil War colleagues; second, he never found the time to write anything but short articles, and those only at infrequent intervals. Because his government failed to provide him with an adequate living wage, even in retirement, he was forced to hold steady employment until the time of his death in 1889 at age sixty-nine. In fact, he knew such economic hardship in retirement that he applied for the post of governor at the Washington, D.C. Soldiers's Home because it furnished living quarters in addition to a small salary—he could no longer support himself, his wife, and four underage children while also paying the mortgage and upkeep on their private home. He remained active in the discharge of his many responsibilities at the home through his final four years, though wracked by afflictions such as rheumatism, gout, and migraine headaches, the severity of which would have incapacitated many younger men.

Though no memoir writer, Hunt had a deep appreciation for history, and obviously hungered for the recognition and appreciation not granted him in proper measure during his lifetime. He carefully preserved many of his private and official papers, plus those wartime journals in which he had penned graphic and intriguing accounts of service in the field. In fact, later in life, in an apparent effort to guide—perhaps to manipulate—the hand of the historian, Hunt, in many journal entries, appended marginal explanations (sometimes purely in hindsight) of wartime decisions, courses of action, and involvement in various events. Thus, consciously or not, and like many other Civil War commanders, he seems to have made a concerted attempt to explain away some of his more controversial acts of omission and commission. For this reason, therefore, his papers must be used carefully, lest they entrap a historian or critic in error, half-truth, or untruth.

Even so, what Henry Hunt has left behind constitutes an engaging legacy of fact and conjecture about the men and events in seminal periods of American history, placing many of them in a new and compelling perspective. Much of it also provides a running account of some of the saddest injustices ever suffered by an American at the hands of his own army. Yet, through it all, the historian finds no betrayal of bitterness, no violent recriminations, no acid prose in which Hunt bewails his fate.

One might have expected otherwise of a man with so keen a sense of pride and so brittle a temper, in view of the dismaying number of hardships he encountered in the discharge of his ordained duties. But whatever qualities Henry Jackson Hunt may have possessed, he seems to have had absolutely no capacity for self-pity.

The Man
Behind the Guns

General Hunt's great ability in organizing artillery and handling it on the field of battle, justly entitle him to be considered the greatest American artilleryman.

Allen J. Greer,
The Field Artillery Journal

1

A Soldier Born and Bred

From his earliest days, he lived in a military environment. As the son and grandson of officers—and, in adolescence, an orphan adopted by a military community—he seemed predestined to assume the soldier's life.

This family tradition encompassed far more than three generations. By 1819, when Henry Jackson Hunt was born, it already extended almost two centuries into the past. In fact, the family's earliest American progenitor was a man of the sword—more accurately, of the cannon—and a nobleman to boot. Colonel William Hunt, commander of artillery in the Royal English Army, had been knighted at thirty-three by his sovereign, Prince Rupert, in reward for distinguished service during the civil war against the forces of Cromwell and Parliament.

Sir William's service was not uniformly rewarding. After gallant participation in the defense of the stronghold of York, he found himself a member of those forces soundly defeated in July 1664 at Marston Moor.[1] With the Royal Army in chaos, Rupert fleeing his realm, and Parliament on the verge of seizing crucial power, William took counsel with his own better judgment and decided it was time to seek a new life elsewhere: as far from England as possible. In the words of his biographer, he cropped his long hair "and laid aside his fine dress as well as his title." Under the name of a deceased cousin, he took ship for America, departing his native land soon after receiving an ironic tribute from his enemy. In recognition of Sir William's prowess as artillerist, prowess that had won him the right to add a cannon symbol to his family coat of arms, Cromwell had placed a substantial price on his head.[2]

Much to the chagrin of the future lord protector, William Hunt made good his escape—in 1645, settling in Weymouth, colony of Massachusetts Bay. There he married twice, survived both wives, raised a prodigious family, and established a new reputation for love of things genteel and gentle: this he bequeathed to later generations, which abounded with clergymen and scholars, including several graduates of Harvard College.[3]

19

Engraving of Gen. Henry J. Hunt (COURTESY, MR. FREDERICK D. HUNT, WASHINGTON, D.C.)

Yet it proved impossible to stifle the more combative instincts in the Hunt bloodline. Sir William's great-great-grandson, Thomas V. Hunt, born in Watertown, Massachusetts in 1754, returned the family interest to the battlefield. And Thomas passed this renewal of tradition to his grandson, Henry Jackson Hunt.

The American Revolution gave Thomas his first experience in soldiering. In April 1775 he joined the patriot cause by enlisting as a sergeant in Captain Craft's company of Bay State Minutemen. He received his baptism of battle at Lexington and Concord later that same month. Thereafter, he served as an ensign in a regiment of Massachusetts infantry, as a lieutenant in Colonel Henry Jackson's Additional Continental Regiment, and as a captain when storming the enemy-held garrison at Stony Point, New York, under "Mad Anthony" Wayne in July of 1779. In that victorious assault, Thomas was desperately wounded by a British bayonet.[4]

After lengthy convalescence, he returned to the colors. In January '81 he transferred to the Ninth Massachusetts Volunteers, serving therein through much of the Yorktown campaign, in which, that October, he suffered a second wound. After another recuperation, Thomas participated in the final weeks of the conflict, serving under his old mentor, General Jackson. During this period he broke bread with such personages as Alexander Hamilton, Baron Friedrich Wilhelm von Steuben, and the Marquis de Lafayette. Upon occasion he also enjoyed the privilege of being present at the side of George Washington.[5]

At the close of the conflict, while the victorious Continentals disbanded, Thomas, a young officer of recognized talent, opted to remain in uniform. In June 1784—by which time the nation's army numbered all of 775 officers and men—[6]he left the ranks and returned to Massachusetts only long enough to court, win, and marry a Waltham girl, Eunice Wellington, who in time would bear him twelve children, including eight sons. Soon after the wedding, Thomas marched back into the field.

The balance of his career was varied, colorful, and successful. At thirty-seven he became a captain in the Second United States Infantry; trekked westward in 1791 during General Arthur St. Clair's ill-starred foray against the Miami Indians; trudged homeward in defeat; and returned to exact revenge under Anthony Wayne at Fallen Timbers, late in '94. Afterward, the army established new outposts in the wilderness; and Thomas, now a major in the First Infantry, took command at Fort Defiance, and then at a garrison named after his ranking commander, in what is now Indiana. It was at Fort Wayne that Thomas's fifth son, who would father the most famous Hunt of all, came into the world in 1799.[7]

Upward rose Thomas—to lieutenant colonel in 1802, and to full colonel, in command of the First, two years later. In July 1805, by virtue of his newly won eagles, he was appointed first commander of Cantonment Belle Fontaine, on the south bank of the Missouri River, not far from where it touches the Father of Waters and flows hard by a meager settlement named St. Louis.[8] There the colonel lived out his allotted years, shooting Indians, fighting floodtide and yellow fever, and shaking hands with the wandering Lewis and Clark.[9]

His death in August 1808 and that of his wife three months later made orphans of eleven surviving children. Thomas's eldest son, first in the family to wear the name Henry Jackson Hunt in honor of his father's revolutionary-war commander, became father surrogate, distributing brothers and sisters to relatives and family friends. The children were dispersed far and wide, "scattered to the four winds of Heaven," as the fourth son, John Elliott Hunt, later recalled.[10]

It was John who proved the most enterprising and successful of the brood: pioneer settler of the same Maumee Valley that his father had helped rid of hostiles; postmaster of Maumee and then Toledo, Ohio; an executive in a local mercantile house; and a member of the Ohio Senate.[11] This prominence would open doors for his brother Samuel's eldest son, whom John would raise through adolescence.

At first, brother Sam seemed destined to forge a career in the army at least as prominent as John's in civil life. Thanks to his father's distinguished service record, he was provided with an appointment to West Point, class of 1818. At the military academy, however, he displayed less than the scholar's aptitude. Midway through his term of study he dropped out to marry Julia Herrick, daughter of a Plattsburgh, New York physician and a member of the landed gentry. Like his father before him, Samuel afterward headed west, wife at his side. Though not an academy graduate, he had been appointed from civil life a lieutenant in the Third United States Infantry.[12]

An early death would prevent Samuel from attaining higher rank. Still, he was permitted time to father four children, three of whom would survive childhood.

His firstborn inherited the name of Colonel Thomas Hunt's revered superior. Henry Jackson Hunt came into the world on 14 September 1819 at Detroit Barracks on Lake St. Clair, Michigan Territory, during his father's garrison service on the Upper Lakes. The other surviving children were Lewis Cass Hunt (named for Thomas Hunt's favorite subordinate at Fort Defiance), born 23 February 1824 at Fort Howard, Green Bay; and a lone daughter, Julia Herrick Hunt. From complications attending Julia's birth, her mother would ultimately die on the frontier.[13]

The most significant period in Lieutenant Sam Hunt's brief military career began with his transfer south from garrison duty on the lakes in mid-1826. The journey carried him, his as yet intact family, and the rest of his regiment, led by Brevet Brigadier General Henry H. Leavenworth, down the network of waterways toward the Great American Desert, where new posts were to be built.[14] Many years later Sam's oldest son, only seven years of age during the trip, snatched up random memories of the journey:

> . . . the boats were cordelled [towed by the men] up the portage. There they were unloaded and the cargoes packed across to the Wisconsin. My memory is that they called the distance three miles. The boats were then hauled across the land and reloaded, the passengers, (women and children) walked. We then re-embarked and floated down the Wisconsin and the Mississippi to St. Louis. . . . I remember perfectly that a large body of Indians stopped us on the way. I think they were Winnebagoes. I remember that Colonel Leavenworth held a council with them, and my impression is that they objected to our passing through their country.

No matter; the Winnebagos were ignored and the voyage did not end till the travelers reached St. Louis. There, in Thomas Hunt's old bailiwick, Samuel and his colleagues constructed Camp Adams on the west bank of the Mississippi. Renamed, soon afterward, the Jefferson Barracks, the post superseded Belle Fontaine as the principal garrison in that district.

For the Hunts, life at Jefferson Barracks proved deadly. Already young Lewis was suffering from chronic intestinal ills, and his mother, debilitated by the just-ended rigorous journey, died later that year. Thus, early in 1827, when a mission to establish another garrison (this to guard the Santa Fe Trail) got under way, Sam Hunt joined it with a brood of motherless children at his side.

Via keelboats, four companies of the Third, and their dependents, floated up the Missouri, clambering onto its left bank not far from the mouth of the Little Platte River. Nearby, in the wilds of what three decades later would be named the Kansas Territory, the soldiers again set to work in fatigue parties. This time they began work on a large cantonment destined to become perhaps the most famous American post in the Southwest. As leader of the expedition that founded it, Colonel Leavenworth gave it his name.

While construction proceeded, the Hunts lived in a large tent, later in a bark hut, still later in a log cabin, before being able to move into garrison quarters.[15] Such crude lodging ensured them of a hard life come winter; still, the summer of '27 exacted the heaviest toll among the troops. When the warm weather came, half of the garrison died, and with them many civilians, including Samuel's second-born son.

At the height of the epidemic, while Sam Hunt and his infant daughter remained at the fort, Henry and Lewis were sent to live among foster parents just across the river in Liberty, Clay County, Missouri. There, under constant medical care, Lewis partially recovered his health, though he would suffer recurring symptoms for the remainder of his life. And there, for the next one and a half years, both boys received their first formal schooling.[16]

During that time, health and sanitation at Leavenworth continued to worsen. Finally, in the spring of 1829, the cantonment was temporarily evacuated, its personnel ordered back to Jefferson Barracks via steamboat. Rejoining their father and sister at the fort, Henry and Lewis accompanied their return to St. Louis.

Samuel had once been a hearty and exuberant young man, "independent," as his eldest son recalled, "and given to practical jokes." But by now he was melancholy, borne down by the loss of wife and son. Weakened by this and other hardships and tragedies, he fell prey to the very sickness that he had fled Cantonment Leavenworth to elude, and in September 1829 was buried beside his wife at the little cemetery at Jefferson Barracks.[17]

Thus a second generation of Hunt children had been orphaned in the wilderness. For a time the trio was adopted by military families in St. Louis; then, like their father, uncles, and aunts, were parcelled out to other relatives. Julia and Lewis were sent to live with their Uncle Henry in Detroit, where he ran a business and served as a colonel in the Michigan territorial militia. There and thereabouts they received further education; later, Lewis matriculated at Ohio's Kenyon College.[18]

The eldest did not go to Michigan; Henry was sent to northwestern Ohio to live in the home of his Uncle John. In that more civilized environment, it was thought that he might more easily find answers to the educational, social, and professional questions soon to confront him.

Though only ten, Henry was mature and self-reliant because conditions had compelled him to be. This was fortunate; his enforced parting from the remnants of his immediate family would have proved a much greater ordeal to one of average emotional strength.

*   *   *

He left no recollection of his life in Ohio, but it may be assumed that he required much time to adjust to the new type of lifestyle that the area dictated for him. Certainly in Maumee City, under his uncle's guidance, he devoted the bulk of his time to absorbing a common-school education. In doing so he was preparing for a quest toward an inevitable goal.

The circumstances of his residence in the Maumee Valley must have strengthened his resolve to be a military man. There, as in the considerably wilder tracts farther west, the art of soldiering was accorded general popularity, for it possessed an obvious and valuable utility. Northwestern Ohio was not the forest primeval or the Great American Desert, but neither was it New York City; by no means was its every acre pacified and settled. Many corners of the region had been wrested from Indians only temporarily; others not at all. The military establishment that sought to guard those areas was looked upon with the highest esteem by those who required its protection. For much the same reason, local militia were well regarded, and military titles went to civilians as well as homegrown warriors—thus John Elliott Hunt's informal designation as "General" Hunt, as result of his community prominence.

At this juncture, in fact, esteem of things and men military seemed a national quality. The nation's standing army was quite small by later standards: fewer than seven thousand in the aggregate. But in 1833 the government would increase it, and would increase it further three years later, until it reached an 1837 peak of 12,449.[19] The concept of a young country on the rise necessitated an expanding army to safeguard national power. In such an atmosphere, the profession of arms took on great appeal as well as value.

At an early stage Henry decided to follow his father's lead by craving an education at the military academy. Unlike his father, he vowed to leave West Point with diploma and commission in hand. Fortunately, John Hunt's political connections were as good as the very best, extending as they did to Secretary (of War) Lewis Cass: a relative by marriage as well as the son of Colonel Thomas Hunt's favorite executive officer.[20] Primarily through this contact, young Henry received the appointment he coveted; and, though shy of the normal age requirement of sixteen, he prepared to enter West Point, class of 1839.

In his middle teens Henry was not the classic model of military material, at least not in appearance. He was of medium height, but a slender frame made him look much taller. His face was thin, low-jawed, with high cheekbones and a beak of a nose. Effects of childhood ills contracted on the frontier still marked him: he was easy prey for respiratory afflictions and was totally deaf in his left ear.[21] His lack of physical coordination kept him a gawky youth, though a deeply tanned and almost leathery-looking face, added to his self-reliant bent, gave him a visible maturity beyond his years. When he spoke, however, that mature aspect was somewhat diminished by a high-pitched voice and a noticeable lisp.

In certain areas of dress and deportment, he reflected the circumstances of his upbringing. Indifferent toward stylish attire, he favored functional clothing, were it rumpled or soiled. He wore his hair long and full, sometimes to the point of shagginess. In demeanor he was fiercely independent—an obvious legacy of his frontier childhood. He had the pioneer's confidence in self and faith and perseverance in hard work on roads to success. He reflected it at the outset of his West Point career, determined to master every intellectual and disciplinary subtlety of his chosen profession.

Without doubt, the road lying ahead would prove steep, rocky, and sometimes treacherous. But Colonel Thomas Hunt and Lieutenant Samuel Hunt had negotiated the terrain without loss of heart; like-minded kin could do no less.

* * *

Despite taking a vow of success, the young plebe found that he would not collect a brilliant scholastic record at West Point. The precise, orderly mind that he had long wished to develop would not completely take form, no matter how hard he persevered. Still, certain inherent skills would stand him in good stead through much of his coursework, including most of the mathematics subjects. And, despite his childhood ills, his constitution would enable him to meet most of the academy's physical demands. He simply hoped that other demands, scholastic and disciplinary, would not pose unwieldy burdens.

During the June encampment that preceded his first year of study—his fourth class year—he was introduced to the formal business of soldiering, and adapted to it readily enough. Though far from an extrovert, he also won a number of friends among the cadet corps. But, though the quality of the coursework that he had begun in September was low by academy standards of even a few years later, some subjects, such as European and classical languages, brought him difficulty. In his initial year he did well enough in his strongest areas, winning decent grades in algebra and trigonometry, as well as satisfactory marks in descriptive geometry. Thus, although less proficient in French, his overall performance was sufficient to rank him sixteenth in a class of fifty-eight.[22]

In some respects, his first year at the Point provided a violent shock. Along the Upper Hudson he encountered, off grounds, a great deal more civilian apathy and antipathy toward soldiering as a profession than he had experienced either on the Kansas frontier or in the Maumee Valley. This atmosphere was reflective of political stances assumed in Washington City. The philosophy of the man in the White House, Andy Jackson, had reached out to influence those who lived in close proximity to military institutions such as the academy: that philosophy seemed to bode ill for the future of West Point and for the military as a profession.

Though a renowned soldier, Jackson was self-taught, and was thus suspicious of the foundations on which a tutorial agency such as the academy had been built. To him (as also, it seemed, to Secretary Cass) West Point appeared an elitest institution whose faculty and administrative personnel, pretenders to nobility, worked at cross-purposes to the spirit of national egalitarianism that pervaded Jacksonian politics. Thus the West Point of the 1830s had come under widespread suspicion as an extension of aristocratic privilege. Its primary evil, its critics felt, was its insistence that soldiering was not only a way of life but a profession in the deepest meaning of that term, complete with a rich tradition from which it drew a historical perspective of itself, and founded upon a body of detailed technical literature. Many who felt like Jackson and Cass asserted that the future of America's armed might lay in the militia rather than in a professional army. So believed Thomas Jefferson, during whose administration the academy had come into being—primarily as a training school for militia officers.

This view would gain many new adherents in the not too-distant future, when a seemingly endless war against Florida's Seminole Indians got under way. Its frustrating longevity, without a commensurate degree of conspicuous success, would lead the nation to question anew the very utility of a standing army of so-called professionals. Then, too, there were many who believed that not even militiamen should be educated at the academy, where even they might likely become contaminated by its aristocratic leanings. Better that militia officers be schooled at more democratically oriented civilian institutions.[23] With such prevailing attitudes, the future of West Point seemed very much in doubt.

All of these arguments infuriated Cadet Hunt, who vigorously denied their validity. He had seen firsthand the value of and the need for a highly trained Regular Army, when living under its protection on the frontier. To dismantle the single institution capable of raising the army's efficiency and discipline to their uppermost levels was—or should be—unthinkable.

Some nine years later he would reflect upon his academy training and return the same verdict:

> The West Point Academy furnishes a solid foundation on which to build a military education and it is the duty of every officer to turn the knowledge so liberally bestowed upon him by the government to the very

best account . . . [or] the Army will fall back in character towards the old times when idleness, ignorance, brutality and debauchery, were the almost necessary, or at least the most usual characteristics of the officers and the soldiers.[24]

In the end, despite the hostility of the Jacksonians, the academy would endure. So would Cadet Hunt. He would endure because of a determination to find a comfortable "home" in the profession in whose utility he had such faith. By the end of his first year, he had already won a firm fraternal niche in the corps of cadets, having become close to a number of young men who, in later life, would grasp abiding fame in uniform; from the class of 1839: Henry W. Halleck, E.R.S. Canby, Edward O.C. Ord—and the cohort who, until his untimely death in 1862, would remain Hunt's closest friend: Isaac I. Stevens of Massachusetts, a brilliant student destined to graduate at the head of the class.[25]

He also ingratiated himself with a few upperclassmen, and in the near future would make friends with others. Several of these were also fated to achieve soldierly fame in the years ahead; from the class of 1836: Montgomery C. Meigs and Thomas West Sherman; from the class of '37: William H. French, John Sedgwick, Braxton Bragg, and Lewis G. Arnold; and among the class of '38: William F. Barry, Pierre G.T. Beauregard, Irvin McDowell, William H. Hardee, Edward Johnson, and Henry H. Sibley.[26] Of course, Hunt would have been stunned in disbelief if told that a quarter of a century hence he would wage war against a goodly percentage of these fellow cadets.

Such companions in turn bestowed upon Hunt trust, esteem, and fraternity. But they couched their regard in gentle sarcasm. Aware that the rumpled young cadet from the wilderness looked anything but cherubic, they dubbed him "Cupid."[27] The irony in this appellation could hardly have escaped its bearer.

Nor did the young cadet remain aloof from his instructors and administrators. He came to form an especial esteem for a few, including the academy's superintendent, Major René E. De Russy. Two years before, from his chores in the Corps of Engineers, the major had been called to West Point to succeed Major Sylvanus Thayer, whose alleged elitist proclivities had antagonized the man in the White House. De Russy possessed considerable administrative skill and energy, as well as much more tact than his predecessor—qualities that would later elevate him to the command of his corps. Hunt's cordial relations with him were considerably strengthened by his friendship with De Russy's son, Gustavus, who, though failing to graduate, was for a time a member of the class of '39.

Though usually only in the strict pupil-teacher sense, Hunt forged close ties with instructors such as Dennis Hart Mahan, the military and civil engineering genius who taught West Point's most highly regarded courses; as well as with the aloof and highly formal artilleryman, Albert E. Church, whose inherent mechanical skill guided his teaching of mathematics.[28]

Lieutenant Church was probably one of the instructors who instilled in Hunt an interest in cannon employment and the supervision of same. A like stimulus was provided by one of the most promising artillerists at West Point: Lieutenant Robert Anderson, assistant professor; later, full professor of tactics pertaining to that arm. Anderson's growing reputation would be much increased by the 1839 publication of a tactical artillery treatise, which he would translate from the French, with modifications for its adaptation to American needs. Quite incidentally, the renown brought to him by this publication, and later ones in the same field, would be overshadowed by the notoriety received when commanding a fort in the harbor of Charleston, South Carolina, in April 1861—a fort bombarded by hostile secessionists who sought civil war.[29]

Perhaps it was inevitable that Hunt should have been drawn toward artillery service; the academy in the middle and late 1830s was pervaded by a decided artillery influence. A large percentage of its faculty and administrative personnel (including its commandant of cadets) had served with cannon units in permanent fortifications, as well as in the field, during the Black Hawk War of 1832 and the early stages of the current conflict in Florida. When in 1838 Major Richard Delafield succeeded De Russy as superintendent, this influence would further be bolstered.[30] Himself an engineer officer, Delafield would nevertheless give artillery instruction wider curricular attention: an artillery "laboratory" would be set up, and practice with lightweight and mobile cannon would receive new impetus. For these and other reasons, by the time Cadet Hunt was set to take the artillery drill courses in his third, second, and first class years, he would be motivated by a desire to learn as many of the nuances of that service arm as humanly possible.

Despite the pleasure brought to him by his interest in the art and science of gunnery and pyrotechny, his third-class year was a period of frustration and worry: it was a period of academic danger. It was due to no great lack of effort. He worked diligently all the while, his classroom studies consuming at least eight hours per day, from 7:00 A.M. till 1:00 P.M. and again from two till four in the afternoon. Outside class, he spent much additional time poring over texts and classroom notes on geometry, integral and differential calculus, practical surveying, geography, grammar and rhetoric, mechanical drawing, and, once again, French[31]. The thoroughness with which he strove to master those subjects innately difficult for him was indicated by greatly improved marks in geography and French. By the end of the year such grades nearly matched those he received in his math courses.

But his greatest danger came from the various disciplinary infractions for which he was adjudged guilty. The seventy-two demerits given him for such offenses during his plebe year fell twenty-six short of the total he received during his third class year. The increment, affecting as it did his overall scholastic standing, threatened to play hob with his class rank.[32]

During his second class year, his disciplinary record worsened. Soon it neared a point at which it posed a decided threat to his continuance at the academy. Likewise, his academic record suffered; the grades he received in physics, chemistry, drawing, astronomy, optics, and electricity were quite a bit lower than those he had won in the pure mathematics courses the year before. But his everlengthening delinquency list still constituted his greatest enemy.[33]

A glance at that list provides some curious particulars. It seems to indicate a studied attempt to circumvent or flout the rigid moral code that in the 1830s stood as one of the academy's most notable characteristics. During his second class year, for example, he was continually on report for tardiness in answering roll calls; for loitering in areas off limits to cadets; for sleeping through reveille; and for similar infractions. His attitude toward dress remained highly casual: many demerits were accrued to him for having his "Coat out of order at guard mounting"; for "Shoes out of order at drill"; for wearing no vest at inspections; and for allowing his hair to grow long and unkempt more than a few times. Inspecting officers noted that he was habitually neglectful of hanging up his uniform and keeping his quarters neat. Additionally, he earned black marks for pranks: tossing bucketfulls of water down the halls of the cadet dorms and bursting into laughter while in the ranks on the drill plain.

Demerits for more-serious infractions also came his way. The strictest academy rules were the observance of lights-out and the prohibition of stimulants in quarters. On several occasions Hunt defied such rules, smoking cigars and chewing tobacco after hours in his room. More frequently he was reported for using profane language at cadet gatherings.

It may seem difficult to reconcile such a disciplinary record with Hunt's lifestyle during his later career, the most obvious characteristics of which were the dignity, courtliness, and decorous formality with which he performed his duties—always the gentleman in uniform, a soldier of the old school.

But even in those later years, beneath a rigid exterior, Hunt often played the rowdy—indulging a zest for practical jokes, bawdy verse, good liquor, and poker sessions. All were facets of a personality formed on the frontier—a life of wilderness license, boisterousness, and exuberance. His defiance of an inflexible academy ethic, puritanical in nature, was a case of reversion to type.

His disciplinary problems mounted for quite some time. From his entrance to West Point in mid-1835 until the same point in 1837, he had acquired 170 demerits. During his second class year—September '37 to June '38—he amassed that same amount plus ten. It was but twenty demerits shy of the total that meant instant dismissal.[34] Coupled with his declining academic average, this, at the close of his next-to-last year at the Point, lowered him to twenty-sixth position in a pared-down class of thirty-three.

He must have been acutely aware that continuing troubles of this sort would seriously hamper his prospects for securing a desirable service appointment should he survive to graduate. During his last year, he made great efforts to mend his ways at last, slashing his demerits and showing renewed strength in almost all coursework.

His determination endured long enough. When he received his coveted diploma on 21 June 1839,[35] his final class standing reflected this spirit: he had finished nineteenth in a thirty-one-member class.

Therefore, though by no means owning the most distinguished cadet record in academy annals, he could at least embark on his chosen profession— as a second lieutenant of artillery—with the satisfaction of knowing that he had closed out his scholastic career on the upgrade.

2

The Hardships of Fidelity

A cursory glance backward would seem to indicate that Lieutenant Hunt had chosen to enter a branch of the service that offered him a singularly frustrating career. As the American artillery moved into its sixty-fifth year, almost as many years of hardship and aggravation lay behind it.

Artillery's troubles stemmed from its nebulous identity within the army's organizational system. For centuries, European armies had regarded this arm as a special branch of the service, combining the functions of combat duty with those of administration and supply. For various reasons, this precedent had never been adopted by the American high command. Since its formal organization in 1775, the United States artillery had been considered solely an arm of the line, its functions exclusively military. To handle its administrative concerns and to supply it with matériel, an Ordnance Department had been organized and maintained.[1]

Too often this arrangement had failed to yield beneficial results. This was so primarily because the apparent functions of artillery and ordnance had a disconcerting tendency to overlap. Only once, and for just a brief period, had this undesirable situation been relieved, when from 1821 to 1832 artillery and ordnance had been merged. Considering their status made inferior by consolidation, ordnance officers had lobbied vocally and successfully for its termination, despite artillerists' objections. Thus, for seven years prior to Hunt's graduation from the academy, the ordnance and artillery had again been separate entities, with high-ranking officers in each clashing time and again in authority conflicts.

By this arrangement, artillery had much the worse of it. In the main, the ordnance establishment—as a War Department bureau—had a formally designated chief, capable of overseeing all functions of the arm and furthering its interests in the capital. Artillery had no appointed chief, no one to coordinate its myriad duties or effectively organize its struggle to preserve its rightful privileges and responsibilities.[2]

This undesirable situation and others of similar character had resulted

31

from artillery's anomalous position as an arm of the line. In battle, it could not stand alone—unlike infantry or mounted troops; it served only in concert with those other arms, except when handling garrison or siege duties. Thus it was considered something of an auxiliary branch of the service and was deemed, from above, in no great need of supervision by one of its own.

Treated in this way, artillery had gradually lost its tactical identity. For all intents, artillery of years past meant heavy artillery, or foot artillery. On stationary duty, cannoneers manned the guns of seacoast or inland forts. When they took the field, precisely because few lightweight, mobile cannon had been produced, its people served with the infantry, armed with muskets.

By 1839, several attempts had been made to effect changes. In April 1808 Congress had authorized the raising of the first regiment wholly composed of light artillery.[3] This innovation and others proposed at the same time came about as result of the Napoleonic wars—then in progress across the ocean; if America were to find herself involved in such an international conflict, she would have to overhaul and streamline all branches of her armed forces. But some months after the first light company was equipped with mobile cannon and enough horses to pull them, Secretary (of War) William Eustis had decided that the expense of maintaining the animals was prohibitive. Eventually the single company was dismounted, and, though eight other companies of the "light artillery regiment" were duly recruited, they remained light artillery only in name.

And yet, before it lost its horses, the light company attracted much favorable attention, especially because of its remarkable ability to maintain a fleet six miles per hour on the march. Still, not until 1821 did Congress respond to such acclaim, and then very cautiously. That March it passed legislation designed to equip as light artillery one company in each of the four cannon regiments then in existence.[4]

Again, these units remained light artillery only in name. Not for seventeen years was the law implemented, and then only because a far-sighted and energetic secretary of war, Joel R. Poinsett, had come to power. Beginning in 1838 he forced the Congress to carry out the terms of the law that it had allowed to atrophy for almost two decades. The four companies eventually were mounted—each given three 6-pounder guns and one 12-pounder howitzer; every cannon hauled by a four-horse team. Later each company would be permitted to mount two additional guns.[5] Three of the units were known simply as "mounted artillery," their cannoneers, when on the march, riding atop ammunition chests carried on wheeled caissons and limbers, also pulled by the teams. The fourth company—the first to be mounted under Poinsett's directive—was termed "horse artillery," or "flying artillery." Designed to accompany and support either dragoons or cavalry, the members of this unit rode their own horses instead of caissons and limbers.

During his tenure in office, Secretary Poinsett instituted various other artillery reforms, impanelling commissions to study improved processes of cannon manufacture, increasing the size of the artillery regiments, and organizing an artillery instructional camp within a much larger school of practice. The school, known as "Camp Washington," was set up outside Trenton, New Jersey, one month before Cadet Hunt became Lieutenant Hunt, There, for the dissemination of the latest in artillery procedures, were sent all of the companies mounted by Poinsett's decree.[6]

The war secretary's efforts soon garnered new prominence for the light artillery. Then, too, Brevet Major Samuel Ringgold, whose Company C of the Third Artillery was the newly created horse-artillery unit, was not only a capable soldier but an enterprising promoter of his arm's interests. Through his skill at public relations, the War Department and Congress soon began to think about giving horses to other cannon companies.

Therefore, Henry Hunt was joining the artillery at a time of ferment and high promise, despite its checkered past.

To be sure, many distressing conditions still plagued the arm: it lacked a titular head; and it suffered from Ordnance Department interference—the latter's failure to develop durable lightweight cannon, accurate to distances beyond half a mile; from a bewildering plethora of gun calibres and models; and from poor quality projectiles, fuzes, and other artillery implements.

Even those woes did not tell all. Artillery also experienced a chronic shortage of field-grade officers (those whose rank entitled them to command more than a single company), and lacked a comprehensive body of tactics (even Anderson's 1839 treatise would require revision to tailor its French model to the peculiar needs of American light artillery). Finally, the arm was burdened by drawbacks common to all branches of the midnineteenth-century army: low pay, slow promotions, poor-quality rations, and deteriorating morale.[7]

A realist, Hunt recognized all of this. He vowed to persevere anyway. He sensed, with men such as Poinsett and Ringgold in power, and others of similar caliber likely to follow in their wake, that the artillery's renaissance was not far away. As did many of his academy classmates, he believed that artillery was the coming trend. An early association with it might assure him a rewarding, perhaps even a glorious, career.

* * *

His initial orders, received in mid-August, posted him to a typical heavy-artillery unit: Company F of the Second Regiment.[8] Doubtless he was disappointed; he had been an enthusiastic proponent of mounted artillery since his first exposure to it at West Point. But he recognized that almost every artillerist desired to fill the few positions open in the mounted units. As a newborn subaltern in an army in which seniority ruled all, he stood no chance of gaining his preferment.

Some circumstances of his first tour of duty must have compensated him for such chagrin. The posting did return him to the site of his birth: Detroit, the largest city in the infant state of Michigan. There he took up duties in a garrison that his grandfather had commanded shortly after its surrender by England to the American forces in 1796—the same fort at which Hunt's father had served a quarter of a century later. In addition to this opportunity to renew a family association with Detroit Barracks, Hunt found it a place of consequential activity, for it served as the headquarters of the regimental commander, Colonel James Bankhead, as well as being the home of Company B of the Second and Company F. Finally, there Hunt was reunited with one of his closest acquaintances among the upperclassmen at West Point: Lewis G. Arnold. The class-of-'37 graduate was in temporary command of F Company by virtue of a recent promotion to first lieutenant and the absence of its captain on detached duty in St. Louis.

But Hunt had little opportunity to acquaint himself thoroughly with Arnold's executive officer, Lieutenant Francis Woodbridge; with Colonel Bankhead; with the bulk of Company F's enlisted personnel; or even with the routine duties of garrison life. Barely six weeks after he arrived in Michigan, he learned that the colonel had decided to transfer his quarters, as well as both his companies, to upper New York State; once there, to join the rest of the once widely scattered regiment in a Canadian border watch.[9]

Thus Lieutenant Hunt repacked his recently unpacked belongings, and with his new comrades took ship over the Great Lakes toward the city and post of Buffalo, where the journey ended in the middle of October; and there, under Colonel Bankhead—and also at nearby Fort Niagara under Captain C.S. Merchant—the Second Artillery was to spend the better part of two years.[10]

Hunt's first extensive duty tour found him observing a tract of disputed land that had seen violent rioting for several months. Citizens of Montreal and other cities in Lower Canada had rebelled against the oppressive rule of British colonial administrators. The rebels, dubbing themselves "Sons of Liberty"—namesakes of American patriot groups of the prerevolutionary period—had clashed time and again with Canadian Regulars, spilling and shedding blood along a wide arc north of the border. The Regulars had succeeded in chasing the surviving rebels into the States, where reports now had them organizing to reclaim their native land by an invasion of force.[11]

In all probability Hunt approved of the Sons of Liberty, though for his own reasons. He had inherited an anti-British bias from his grandfather and father, which motivated him to hope that some provocative border incident would openly involve his country in the Canadian civil strife. Such involvement, he believed, could end only in American conquest and possession of her neighbor to the north. He would profess similar sentiments during the Oregon-Canada controversy that would again threaten war between the two countries in the early and middle 1840s.

About this present conflict, Hunt's government did not seem to share his sentiments; neither did many of his fellow officers. Wrote one: "The United

States government was determined fully to enforce the neutrality laws, while a class of scatter-brained, irresponsible men, on and near the frontier, seemed to be as fully determined to involve the two governments in trouble."[12]

Because more-reasonable and conciliatory spirits prevailed, Company F and her comrades stood inactive along the border until Canada's Regulars quenched the last spark of rebellion.[13] The American observers' time was occupied by service along both the Niagara River and, from September 1840 to August 1841, the northeastern edge of Lake Ontario, at Madison Barracks, in Sacket's Harbor, New York.

While still on the Niagara frontier, Hunt made the acquaintance of an officer, fated to exercise a heavy influence on the early stages of Hunt's career. Late in 1839 another component of the Second Artillery joined F Company at Buffalo Barracks—Company A, commanded by a New York native, First Lieutenant James Duncan (USMA 1834). A veteran of the fighting in Florida—like Lieutenants Arnold and Woodbridge—Duncan was lanky, with a thin, kind-looking face, made even leaner by frizzy sidewhiskers that extended to his jawbone. Such features, compounded by a sharp, long nose and a wide forehead, crowned by thinning hair, left him with a far from handsome appearance. Still, he commanded attention and admiration from a wide array of colleagues, primarily because of the renown he had won as officer in charge of one of the four companies mounted by Secretary (of War) Poinsett. Duncan was returning to garrison duty after three months' service at the prestigious instructional camp near Trenton; he wore his accolades easily and stylishly.[14] In a brief time, young Hunt decided that Duncan was his model of officership. In turn, the older officer took a positive interest in Hunt's career.

With other superiors as well, Hunt got along very well indeed. Also, he experienced no great difficulty in establishing rapport with those under his rule. A major factor in his easy transition to a life of command was the democratic spirit given him by formative years with the frontier army. He had not lost that peculiar trait generally termed the "common touch." He could be formal and even stiffish in the performance of his duties, sufficiently so to satisfy the spit-and-polish votaries among the garrison's officer corps. Off duty he was sufficiently casual and easygoing to win a host of comrades who shunned formality except on the parade ground.

Never would he grow haughty or condescending to any man in the ranks— not to the rawest, most insignificant recruit in his command. More than forty years hence he would still be characterized in these terms: "He possesses in a high degree," wrote one erstwhile colleague in 1882, "chivalrous rectitude, frankness, dignity and kindness which grace and enforce stern discipline without rendering it hateful to his subordinates." Another would speak of Hunt's "genial sympathy" even toward "men of low estate."[15]

Certain other traits stood as peculiarly expressive of his personal code of behavior. Perhaps the most obvious was a straightforwardness and candor in all affairs—military or civil. A man of insoluble integrity, he rarely hesitated to advance the truth as he beheld it, and never adhered to the popular course simply because of that popularity. He never temporized or truckled, never consciously compromised his principles, never stifled his moral judgment for fear of consequences. He would often be accused of stubbornness, of hardheaded willfullness, of an overly frequent tendency to declaim against stupidity or malice within high circles of command. Just as often he would be criticized as lacking even rudimentary forms of tact and prudence. But even if some confused or misattributed his motives, no one would ever indict him for a streak of viciousness. The cruel bent that some military critics have deemed proper, even desirable, in a top-level field commander was never a facet of the Hunt ethos.

All of which helps explain why those soldiers who served under him did his bidding without resentment and with alacrity. Such men may have chuckled at some of his fancied eccentricities and physical features, including his gaunt, sharp-boned face, Roman nose, and rather dull complexion (one young officer would later describe it as "the color of an old drum-head").[16] They may also have joked about his strident voice and lisp and the rumpled appearance he seemed to present even in full-dress uniform. But it is probably true that most, if not all, of them genuinely liked the man. Thus would yet another observer assert:

> There was probably no officer in the United States army who was more popular with both officers and men than . . . Hunt. Modest, unassuming, warm-hearted, and just to all, he was indeed the true type of a soldier and gentleman.[17]

* * *

Early in August of 1841 Lieutenant Hunt, now in his third year in the officer corps, took ship up the Erie Canal with the rest of his company for a new field of duty.[18] Later that month F Company found itself at a recently reconstructed garrison whose foundations had been laid in the 1790s: Fort Adams, on Brenton Point, Rhode Island, where it commanded the entrance to Narragansett Bay and the adjacent harbor of Newport. A spacious pentagonal structure of masonry, it ranked second in size only to Fort Monroe, off Hampton Roads, Virginia.

The rebirth of Fort Adams had begun in 1838, and the project was well advanced by Hunt's arrival.[19] The work was progressing under immediate supervision of a young engineer lieutenant who happened to be Hunt's bosom friend: Isaac Stevens. The reunion of the two classmates came at an important juncture. Barely three weeks afterward, Hunt served as an attendant while Stevens wed his long-time sweetheart, Margaret Hazard, the ceremony held at the fortress.[20] Afterward, not unnaturally, Hunt saw a great deal less of his companion than he wished, Stevens and his bride moving into the married-officers' quarters.

Hunt was also bereft of other close allies. Lieutenant Duncan and A Company had been dispatched to Fort Hamilton, still other close acquaintances of Hunt accompanying Duncan. Hunt assuaged the pain occasioned by such losses by writing regularly to friends far and near. Among his closest correspondents were, of course, the members of his immediate family, including Uncle John in Maumee City; brother Lewis, now an employee of a New Orleans commission house but soon to obtain an unexpected appointment to West Point, class of 1847;[21] and sister Julia, now living with relatives in the East. Others to whom he wrote and from whom he received replies included Duncan and West Point classmates and upperclassmen of previous acquaintance—among them, William F. Barry, William French, and John Sedgwick. He also kept in touch with his academy superintendent, writing now-Lieutenant Colonel De Russy at his current post at Fort Monroe.

Even with such wide-ranging correspondence, he must have been given too many idle hours, for he voluntarily added the duties of acting garrison quartermaster to his regular company chores.[22] This quickly multiplied his writing efforts, for he found it necessary to stay in constant touch with the office of the quartermaster general in Washington, concerning matters ranging from funds for the transport of ordnance stores to the provisioning of fuel for the winter months. At times the increased workload became onerous, but he seemed to thrive on extra duty; incidentally, he did not mind at all the accompanying salary boost.

While serving in his new capacity, Hunt twice ran afoul of his superiors, revealing certain characteristics that would bring him much grief in years ahead. In mid-November of 1842, the post commander, Brevet Colonel A.C.W. Fanning, saw fit to reprimand him for allowing an unauthorized subordinate to submit some requisitions in Hunt's name. Hunt, who had endorsed the procedure as entirely justified, was stung by what he considered an undeserved rebuke. Snatching up pen and paper, he addressed to his superior a terse response, remarking that Fanning himself had resorted to the same practice on numerous occasions and broadly implying that for him to accuse another of wrongdoing in similar circumstances was tantamount to hypocrisy.[23]

Whether or not bowing to his subordinate's logic, Fanning allowed Hunt's impertinence to pass. But the incident demonstrated the swiftness and boldness with which Hunt would attempt to salve abraded pride. Until the close of his career, he would not tolerate what he saw as unfair criticism, but would be apt to join battle by retaliating with criticism of his own.

A second episode that brought his pride under attack while at Fort Adams occurred approximately at the same time. By late '42, Hunt was also the acting commissary of subsistence at the garrison. That November another second lieutenant, who had been posted to Adams some weeks earlier, suddenly pressed a claim to Hunt's position, citing a year of seniority over him and written authorization from regimental headquarters relative to that seniority. Since he had professed no such title during his initial weeks at the fort, his behavior sent Hunt into a rage. In a pet, the acting commissary chief complained to Colonel Bankhead, asserting that the usurper's written authorization had cast aspersions on Hunt's competency in the position. Remonstrating against the pay loss that would accompany his relief, he angrily added that the newcomer had not voiced his claim until after Hunt had disposed of an unusually burdensome spate of commissary paperwork. Not receiving satisfaction from Bankhead's headquarters, Hunt went over his commander's head by addressing a plea directly to Washington.

His perseverance won out. Three weeks later the commissary general himself overruled Bankhead and kept Hunt in power, noting that he had performed his various chores "to my entire satisfaction."[24]

His pride again soothed, the victor turned gracious and cordial to the vanquished. It is perhaps well that he did; for, in the not too-distant future, his opponent, Lieutenant William A. Nichols, would become his brother-in-law.

Thus, if Hunt had a prominent failing, it was a failing that hindered a great many men, and perhaps an even greater percentage of soldiers: a highly sensitive pride. There was a paradox in this. Though so unassuming and so casual in outward appearance, as to suggest that he was wholly without vanity, he was, in actuality, highly sensitive to slights, both tangible and imagined. At base, then, he was self-proud—but in a particular sense alone. He was proud of his capabilities and accomplishments—that is, proud of the fruits of intelligence and industry, not of externals, physical talents, and those circumstances of birth and breeding over which men exercise little or no control.

* * *

Hunt's stay at Brenton Point lasted fifteen days longer than two years— one hundred and six tedious weeks of service with heavy artillery that had never been fired in battle, and probably never would be. Not until August of 1843 was he granted a change of scenery, when, with his company and another, he was transferred to Fort Hamilton—one of the garrisons fronting the harbor of New York City. Somewhat less spacious and less picturesque than his home on Narragansett Bay, Fort Hamilton at least placed him in proximity to a lively metropolis and a center of culture. It also returned him to the presence of cherished allies, such as Lieutenant Duncan, and brought him into contact with strangers who in time would become friends equally dear.

One such man won his high regard from their first meeting: Captain Robert Edward Lee of Virginia, the engineer in charge of remodeling the ten-year-old garrison. Of the Virginian, a dozen years his senior, Hunt later recalled: "He was. . . . as fine-looking a man as one would wish to see, of perfect figure and strikingly handsome," as well as quiet and gentlemanly to the highest degree.[25]

Like Duncan's, Lee's character and personality had a decided influence on the young artillerist. Hunt came to relish his visits to the small private residence maintained near the fort by Lee, his wife, their two young sons, and infant daughter. As the result of Lee's pious example, Lieutenant Hunt became, for the only period in his life, a regular churchgoer. As a fellow Episcopalian by family heritage, if not by conscientious practice, Hunt was impelled to attend the little garrison chapel at which Lee served as vestryman. Soon he could even be found spending an evening in Lee's presence, listening respectfully as the older man expounded on theology. In particular, Hunt recalled the quiet humor with which Lee warned him against the dissentious evils of Puseyism, an Episcopal "High Church" movement that many of their acquaintances considered too deeply tainted by the excesses of Romanism. Alluding to the cattiness of the local representatives of the High Church faction, Lee punned sarcastically about "Pussyism." "Beware of Pussyism," he said. "Pussyism is always bad, and may lead to unChristian feeling; therefore beware of Pussyism!"[26]

The frequency with which Hunt attended church at Fort Hamilton is probably an indication of how boring his service was there. As weeks became months, he grew highly restive in New York harbor, his lively surroundings notwithstanding, and fretted that his career would provide him with nothing but the same apparently valueless routine that he had already endured in Rhode Island and upper New York State: drilling his men for active campaigning that might never come—or which, should it materialize, would see them all serving as glorified infantrymen. Thus the high hopes he had originally entertained about artillery reform and rehabilitation were slowly, but steadily dying. Some of his acquaintances had already left the ranks for the more apparent blandishments of civil life, continuing a trend that had begun in 1836 when the unpopularity of the endless struggle in the Florida swamps had prompted fully one-fifth of the army's commissioned officers to tender their resignations. Perhaps his only recourse was to follow that trend.[27]

Then, between early 1844 and the close of '45, it seemed that the Oregon border troubles would rescue him. His family's old friend and patron, Lewis Cass, now a senator from Michigan, was leading a nationwide fight to establish claim to Oregon's territorial border at latitude 54° 40', fully aware that the British government would never countenance the plan. For a time, President James Polk seemed in harmony with the militants, and long before the crisis reached its peak, Lieutenant Hunt was excitedly writing a friend:

We are getting into a fuss here about the Oregon question. I hope that it may lead to a war that will drive the d——d inveterate mercenaries from our continent. I go in for it and hope that once engaged it may be continued as long as men or means can be found or until England loses not only Oregon but the Canadas.[28]

It was not to be. Early in '46 the Congress at last initiated formal debate over the controversy, and eventually supported the more moderate claims advanced by forces such as those led by a Missouri politico who had secured the entrance of Lewis Hunt to West Point: Senator Thomas Hart Benton. That June saw the signing of a treaty by which the United States and Britain fixed the northern extremity of the disputed territory at the 49° line. Afterward, Lieutenant Hunt could only damn Congressional faint-heartedness.[29]

Perhaps foreseeing this dismal outcome, he steadily grew more disgruntled at Fort Hamilton. Not long after professing a desire to see war against the "inveterate mercenaries" of Europe, he wrote a long letter to his friend Duncan, who had returned to Fort Adams, in which he revealed the depth of his depression.

Specifically, he was concerned about recent rumors that Congress was again preparing to slash the size of the peacetime army, by lowering junior officers' salaries so drastically that many would have to resign. Two years before, the legislators had enacted a similar law, despite the already growing stack of officers' resignations, reducing the armed forces to 7,890 officers and men. Each artillery regiment had been seriously affected, losing seventeen enlisted men per company and being forced to cut each unit's complement of guns from six to four.

In 1843, on the other hand, the adjutant general had announced his firm belief that a great many more than the 3,656 artillerists then in the ranks were required to work the thirty-five permanent forts and thirty-one frontier outposts maintained by the army. Deaf to such assertions, Congress had formed retrenchment committees to delve into the desirability of further reduction. Though finally prevailed upon to recommend no personnel cuts, they had called for continued economizing in areas of "extra expenditures,"[30] such as that which now troubled Hunt.

Hunt was already well informed about such pending developments by the time Duncan told him of the latest rumors: "Your statement of the intention to reduce the pay of the army generally did not therefore surprise me," he informed Duncan,

> nor was I much more surprised to hear of differences in the scales of reduction as applied to the staff and line, and to different grades of the same corps. I regret that the reductions are so made as to fall with their heaviest weight on the junior officers; the expenses of the colonel are reduced with his allowances, not so however with the subalterns.

He went on to cite the basis for his chagrin, and in so doing stated his philosophy of the value of the professional soldier:

> The military profession is one that requires as much study, as much thought, and as extensive reading as any other (the mastery indeed of a single branch is the work of a lifetime). It is a profession which, if I may use the expression, is monopolized by the government, and all its

members must draw their support from a common fund [i.e., Congress]. There is not, therefore, that inducement which springs from necessity and competition, nor are there in times of peace those opportunities . . . that are constantly presenting themselves to the lawyer, the physician, the farmer, the mechanic or to the man of any distinct trade or profession. The tendency of such a state of affairs to induce neglect of the higher branches of the profession and even of those duties which are not required from day to day, is obvious. It becomes then a high obligation on the part of every officer to devote such a portion of his resources as his means will admit to the improvement of his military education, and as the science of war, like that of law or any other science is a progressive one, it becomes as much the duty of the officer to keep up with the age in his profession as it is that of the lawyer to keep pace with the changes in the laws. . . . The rate of pay as at present established is scarcely sufficient to allow officers of the junior grades to furnish themselves with the most necessary of those military works which are considered as standard in the profession, and I am much afraid that if to all the other adverse circumstances now operating on the line of the army, the contemplated reductions are added, that the zeal of such officers as look upon their profession as one to which much time, attention and expense are to be devoted, will be . . . effectually quenched.

In the balance of his seven-page missive he noted that, even without the contemplated retrenchment,

The pay of the junior officers will now barely support them and as you know, those who have families have no spare funds. If the pay is reduced to the amount proposed that of a second lieutenant will be $636. per annum, that of a first Lieut. of ten years standing, $756, amounts which scarcely equal the salaries of clerks who have served their employers half the period. These sums look respectably on paper—but they are rather *nominal*, than *real* amounts. A 1st Lieut. of ten years standing may be considered as sufficiently advanced in life to have a family about him; and, if he were stationary in some New England or inland town, $756. would be found sufficient to support his family respectably. But, unfortunately this is not the case. The stations of officers are necessarily at the most expensive positions in the country.

In this same vein:

The frequent changes from post to post prevent any of the economical arrangements so necessary and so usual in a fixed habitation, and subject officers and their families to all the inconveniences, all the troubles, and all the expenses, incident to that pleasant condition commonly known as "living from hand to mouth." And those incidental expenses are by no means small. Independent of the expense of moving his family and effects, the officer is obliged to sacrifice at hasty sales, those few articles of furniture he has been compelled to provide for himself at every post at which he is stationed. . . . A 2nd lieutenant, a widower, now sitting at my side, tells me that in fourteen months of married life he was obliged to move five times by change of posts. Such a state of affairs cannot but be extremely expensive. . . . If I remember aright the much quoted and much admired expression of a great writer was, that "the condition of a soldier should be one of *honorable* poverty." This is true enough. I hope however in applying it to our case, the adjective will not be lost sight of.[31]

It may seem that Hunt's eloquence was wasted, for, in the end, the much-feared paycuts never descended upon the army. Yet, in deciding not to implement such reductions, Congress did nothing to remedy those discomforts and privations that formed so integral a part of the American soldier's life. Few would be ameliorated significantly during the course of Hunt's career—not even the relegation of unmarried officers to the "damp, unhealthy, close, and disagreeable" garrison casemates where artillerymen were compelled to bunk; in which rot and mildew destroyed clothing, food—and health.

* * *

As before, somehow, he endured. In October 1844 he was shuttled to another of the New York harbor posts, Fort Columbus, on Governors Island, where he busied himself by teaching the honorable (and frequently exasperating) trade of soldiering to raw recruits. Returning to regular garrison duty in the fall of '45, he received orders to relocate with his company for the sixth time in his brief career. Again he suffered the attendant financial inconveniences of which he had so feelingly written to Duncan.

His new orders returned him to Narragansett Bay and Newport Harbor. At Fort Adams he spent the next eight months, during which the revived pleasance of his surroundings wore away; he found himself again depressed by an essentially unchanged and unchanging situation.[32]

When not on duty, he sat in his damp and drafty "cave," writing long into the night by oil lamp and candle. He wrote with a sense of futility, but also, paradoxically, with a spirit of hope, as well as with a sense of mission, urged by friends in the ranks to put their common plight into ringing words that might stir into action some new champion of military reform. While he wrote, he listened dully to the melancholy tread of the sentries on the ramparts above; to the night wind blowing through the casemate, threatening to stifle the fragile candle flame; and to the drip of stagnant water from the ceiling, striking the concrete floor with the unending regularity of eternity.

3

Causeways and Orange Groves

Finally, toward the close of 1845, the longing for active duty, which had led Hunt to favor conflict with Britain the year before, had found a new hope for satisfaction. The Republic of Texas, which had won its independence from Mexico nine years before, had recently declared its desire to become part of the United States. Soon after, President Polk and a bevy of influential officials in Washington proclaimed their intention to see Texas's wish granted. But similar to English opposition to the cession of new territory to Oregon, Mexico also resisted Texas's efforts to join the Union. Fearing that a crucial shift of political and geographic power might eventuate, the Mexican government hinted broadly that any attempt to admit Texas as a state would bring open war.

Polk was willing to meet this challenge; so, too, were most of the legislators in Washington City. On 1 March 1845 the Congress resolved overwhelmingly to offer annexation to Texas, and the president quickly endorsed the decision. Enraged, the Mexican government withdrew its ministers from the American capital and began to mobilize for war. Should United States forces occupy Texas in force, or invade territory between the Nueces River and the Rio Grande, which Mexico considered her own, fighting would no doubt commence.

Late in June, shortly before his transfer to Fort Adams, Hunt learned that the sort of overt act that might precipitate a clash of arms had already been ordered. On the fifteenth, Polk had directed the commander of American forces in the Southwest, Brevet Brigadier General Zachery Taylor, to cross into disputed territory near the Rio Grande. Surprisingly, this movement failed to bring war. Believing Mexico's militant stand had been nothing but a bluff, Polk then sent an emissary to Mexico City to bargain for a favorable settlement of the Texas boundary dispute, as well as to offer to purchase other land the United States wished to acquire from her southern neighbor—Upper California and the vast New Mexico Territory.[1] For several months the negotiations hung fire, compelling Hunt and comrades across the land to wait patiently in garrison and camp, one ear attuned to the rumblings down south.

In the end, Mexico refused to deal with the United States. On the sixteenth of January 1846, General Taylor was told to move his four thousand Regulars to the east bank of the Rio Grande—an action that Hunt realized would not be tolerated by the Mexican authorities, their earlier passivity notwithstanding. Anxiously he wrote Lieutenant Duncan, whose mounted company was one of four units from the Second Artillery now in Taylor's army, inquiring of the latest particulars from the scene of action. His friend's replies abounded in expectations of imminent conflict. Even so, Taylor's encroachment did not commence until 8 March.

On 24 April the tension was snapped at last. On the Texas side of the Great River, Mexican horsemen ambushed and wiped out a much smaller contingent of Taylor's dragoons. The shock waves from Texas soon rippled across the nation; on 11 May Polk sent a war message to Congress. A bill of appropriations for the coming conflict passed both Houses by margins even greater than the joint resolution that had brought Texas into the Union.[2]

Rapid mobilization followed. On the first day in June most of the stateside companies in the Second Artillery were ordered to Lower Texas. Hunt was ecstatic: at age twenty-six, after seven years as a soldier, his career was at last to be launched. A second source of pleasure was the realization that war below the border would provide a grand proscenium for the talents of the artillery.

Benefits continued to accumulate. On 18 June, even as Company F was in transit south, he received word of his promotion to first lieutenant.[3] Coming as it did at such a time, it seemed a happy augury.

* * *

His new enthusiasm quickly fled. When in midsummer his unit reached Reynosa, Mexico, across the Rio Grande and a few miles west of Fort Brown, Texas, his mood reverted to gloom. Service in the field did not at first come his way—and when it did come he would see action as a quasi-infantry officer: no cannon had accompanied Company F from Rhode Island. Initially he was only assigned to administrative duties along the border, while his comrades—in fact, most of the regiment—idled among the supply depots of Taylor's army, condemned to wait along the sidelines of the war while, farther south, the decisive action went forward. The frustration of menial duty was bothersome enough, but it was compounded by the lack of sanitation, poor rations, bad water, and amoebic diseases rampant in his camp. Reynosa would provide few fond recollections.[4]

Already a couple of full-scale battles had taken place near his campsite, though prior to his coming. On 8 May—three days before Polk's war message was delivered—Taylor's small command, only 2200 of its members engaged, had whipped twice as many Mexicans at Palo Alto, a few miles above Fort Brown. The following day, fighting at Resaca de la Palma, just below Palo

Alto, saw the Americans again wrest victory from a much larger foe. The two days of conflict had enabled Taylor to enter Mexico proper, the land of many an American expansionist's fondest dreams.

Hunt was highly pleased to learn that Duncan's elite company A—despite jeers from jealous infantrymen—had played a crucial role in both engagements. So too had Ringgold's C of the Third, though the gleaming career of its commander had been ended by a fatal wound at Palo Alto.

In the first battle, Duncan (recently promoted captain) had delivered such a scorching close-range fire against the enemy that his shells had set the prairie grass afire. Later in the fight he had spied a Mexican attempt to circumvent the American left flank, and play havoc with the supply trains in Taylor's rear. With speed born of urgent necessity, the captain limbered up, passed to the rear around a clump of blazing grass, and advanced to within three hundred yards of the flanking column. There he emplaced his guns and raked Mexican foot and mounted troops with a vicious fire, compelling their retreat and winning high praise from Zach Taylor.[5]

At Resaca de la Palma, after Ringgold's erstwhile company had drawn the enemy's artillery fire, enabling Taylor's dragoons to make a safe and successful charge that routed the enemy, the fleeing members of General Mariano Arista's army were harassed and pursued by Duncan's company. The pursuit did not cease until Arista and his soldiers had been chased into and below the Rio Grande.[6]

Now, with Hunt and his cannonless cannoneers ensconced at Reynosa, Taylor's army was nearing the end of a lengthy pause between fighting. Refitting after Resaca de la Palma, Duncan—soon to be named lieutenant colonel by brevet for his gallantry on 8–9 May—was compelled to patch several gaps that battle had torn in his unit. Late in August, Hunt was pleasantly surprised by Duncan's invitation that he join Company A on an attached basis. As an indication of the older officer's regard, it both flattered and overjoyed Hunt. Straightaway he wrote General Taylor, requesting the required permission. But Taylor's adjutant, Major W.W. Bliss, one of Hunt's instructors at West Point, crumpled his hopes: Hunt's services were needed nowhere so sorely as at his present locale; request denied.[7]

Hunt cursed his plight, but could do nothing else. At least the pang of disappointment was somewhat assuaged by his opportunity to stage reunions with old friends in the ranks and to make new ones in all branches of the service. With him in upper Mexico at one time or another were such West Point comrades as fellow artillerymen William French, William Barry, John Sedgwick, William Haskin, Simon Drum, G.A. De Russy, Ambrose Burnside, Richard Rush, Calvin Benjamin, and Braxton Bragg. Among the staff officers, he became acquainted with youngsters such as Cadmus Wilcox and Joseph Hooker. Within the ordnance command he formed an especially close alliance with Benjamin Huger. Of the infantrymen, he came to know Lieutenants Levi Gantt and James Longstreet; and, of the engineer corps, he became acquainted with subalterns like Pierre Beauregard and George B. McClellan (the latter a brilliant youngster from the class of 1846, who had just come south). He was also returned to the presence of other engineers, such as Robert Lee and Isaac Stevens. He was probably happiest to see Stevens, fresh from New England surveying chores. The latter reciprocated, writing his Margaret: "I have seen a good deal of my old friend Hunt the last few days. . . . He is a man I esteem very much, and he is as worthy of it as ever."[8]

Hunt had other diversions than pleasant company to balance his lost opportunity to join Duncan. Chief among them was gambling. In later years he vividly recalled the faro games in Reynosa and elsewhere in Mexico from which he frequently emerged a big winner: "I missed my profession."[9] Some evenings he collected hundreds of dollars for his participation, providing cause for a sound sleep afterward. When free from administrative duties, he also sought pleasure in other minor vices, such as whiskey and cigars, though careful to overindulge at none.

Other more decorous pastimes helped while away his off hours during the long, sweltering summer of 1846. One in which he indulged quite regularly was the careful recording of the most visible deficiencies in artillery administration, with a view to future efforts to obtain their improvement or redress. Some of his observations gave him pause. He was shocked and dismayed, for instance, by the conviction that many ordnance officers considered themselves to be the authority over, not only artillery supply, but tactical artillery employment as well. Such manifestations would later impel him to lodge detailed complaints with the War Department. In one he would claim that during much of the conflict in Mexico the army's cannoneers "earned much but received little credit—for the batteries themselves were in the hands of the Ordnance officers, and care was taken that to them the chief glories of the heavy Artillery should be given." In another letter he would declare: ". . . their employment as artillerists was not only a fraud on the artillery but on the country."[10]

A wholly anomalous command situation was responsible for Hunt's concern about ordnance domination. The very nature of the training that he and his artillery comrades had received rendered suspicion to their ability to carry out the field functions of their arm. Experienced only as foot artillerymen, many had never been taught the rudiments of working the newest models of available cannon. With few light cannon in Mexico, chances were that most gunners would have no opportunity to display their ignorance. But should siege chores fall on them, the men would prove incapable of serving emplaced cannon, forcing the more knowledgeable ordnance people to step in and work the pieces the gunners had supplied, the nuances of which only they seemed to understand.[11]

Fortunately, some pleasant rumors took Hunt's mind from such unhappy speculation. One, prevalent in upper Mexico toward the close of the summer concerned the opening of a second front: this to range inland from the Gulf Coast near the citadel of Vera Cruz. If it proved true, Hunt stood a strong chance of advancing to the seat of war, though he would be forced to travel afoot.

He received the second rumor no less eagerly. Speculation from Washington had the secretary of war, William L. Marcy, entertaining serious thought of mounting additional artillery units for service below the Rio Grande. Hunt took heart: apparently artillery had already found a stage upon which its performance could gain notoriety and official support.

Both of the rumors became fact—and at approximately the same time. The balance of the year saw no decisive development with regard to either, but soon after the first of the year, stasis ended. On 11 February and 3 March, Congress passed legislation authorizing each artillery regiment to add an eleventh and twelfth company, and providing for the mounting of four additional light companies, one from each regiment. One so chosen was E Company of the Third Artillery, once led by Hunt's friend, Braxton Bragg (though this was a mere formality, the unit having served mounted, by special authority, for several months already). The company from Hunt's own regiment selected for this distinction was M—its newest—under Captain James F. Roland.[12]

Less than a week after Congress approved artillery expansion, the first of the widespread rumors also came true. On 9 March a seaborne expedition out of New Orleans—more than ten thousand Regulars and volunteers led by a former artilleryman, Commanding General Winfield Scott—landed all but unopposed at Vera Cruz. At that fortified seaport, fighting on the second front got under way. With "Old Fuss and Feathers" Scott, all six foot four, 250 pounds of him, having thus gained a firm grip on Mexico's eastern coast—plus Zach Taylor's recent overwhelming victory against General Antonio López de Santa Anna's army at Buena Vista—it appeared that the war had already passed its turning point. Continuously successful thus far, the Americans seemed fated to capture the enemy's capital—the City of Mexico— and close out hostilities in one sweeping thrust.[13]

Although most of his comrades looked upon Winfield Scott as the paragon of military genius, fit to rank with the great Washington himself, Lieutenant Hunt had doubts about the commanding general's vaunted abilities. He was also familiar with Scott's prodigious vanity and his penchant for striving for political as well as military glory. Still, he was cheered by the news of Scott's lodgement, for the commencement of this campaign soon resulted in many of Taylor's troops, including F of the Second Artillery, being ordered to Vera Cruz. At last, Hunt moved toward the sound of the fighting.

By the second week in March, he and his unit were positioned outside the walled city on the Gulf Coast, while siege operations moved apace. The Second—at first commanded directly by Colonel Bankhead, then, upon his transfer to detached duty, by Captain Samuel McKenzie—was attached to a division of Regulars of all branches, under one of Scott's ablest lieutenants, Major General William Jenkins Worth. At once, most of the regiment was sent to man the trenches that engineers and fatigue crews had dug south, west, and north of the seaport, cutting off its four thousand defenders from communication with other Mexican troops farther inland.

As Hunt had anticipated, some of his men were assigned to work the heavy-siege guns brought from New Orleans in Scott's fleet of transports. Hunt's worst fears were confirmed when many of the cannoneers proved inadequate to this demand, giving ordnance personnel further opportunity to establish a claim to handling the new-fangled heavy guns.[14] Looking on in disgust, Hunt began to wonder whether the travail he suffered in reaching the front would in fact prove worthwhile.

Service in the rifle pits—under the baking sun, amid thick clouds of dust, and among sand fleas, wood ticks, red bugs, and scorpions—lasted nearly two weeks. Not until 28 March—four days after Scott unleashed a heavy cannonade against the city—did Vera Cruz surrender.[15] Without once having had an opportunity to distinguish himself, Hunt felt barren and unfulfilled by this triumph.

For several days thereafter, Scott kept his bulky army in and around the city, occupying and fortifying the castle of San Juan de Ulúa, firming up his communication and supply lines, and mapping plans for an inland advance to Mexico City. In the meantime, though guarding captured property and prisoners and protecting their own matériel, his soldiers were warned against disturbing the normal flow of life and commerce in Vera Cruz.

Though Hunt found this work trying, he looked forward to the decisive movement that Scott had to make before summer arrived, bringing with it to the coastal lowlands such annual ills as the *vómito,* yellow fever, which might swiftly decimate his ranks.[16]

As earlier, Hunt passed the time inspecting and drilling his men; running errands for his superiors; writing family and friends; dealing poker hands; smoking and drinking. Once again, he also became religious. One particular church visit he would never forget.

On the Sunday following the city's surrender, he left company headquarters to seek out the nearest Catholic church—a passable substitute for the Episcopalian houses of worship impossible to find in his present locale. Entering a little church just outside the city walls, he was surprised to find it occupied not only by a standing crowd of Mexicans but also by several American soldiers, most of whom had probably never before attended a Mass or any other religious service. A glance at a strategically located pew near the front altar told him why the crowd was so large. Seated there, looking most uncomfortable, was General Scott himself, with his entire staff, including Captain Lee and Lieutenant Beauregard. Of the group, only Beauregard was a Catholic, so Hunt surmised that the commanding general was in attendance merely as a goodwill gesture, demonstrating his tolerance of local religious customs.

Though he and his aides wore full-dress uniforms, with sabers and sashes, Scott obviously had not expected the pastor to place him on such conspicuous display, especially considering his ignorance of Catholic ritual. As the Mass progressed, Hunt stood in the rear of the church, rather enjoying the general's discomfiture. Then Captain Lee, at the near end of the pew, saw him and gestured to him, indicating that Hunt should take a place beside him.

Hunt hesitated, especially as he wore a faded and dusty tunic without belt or sash. Still Lee gestured. So he went forward, acutely conscious of his own position as the new center of all eyes. He sat rigidly beside his much more resplendant colleagues, keeping his eyes low throughout the service, not saying a word.

But his ordeal did not end with the Mass—nor did Scott's. In still another gesture of respect, the priest saw that the commanding general was handed a lighted taper; so too each of his staff. Not knowing what this meant, Scott passed his candle to Lieutenant Beauregard; whereupon the priest stubbornly gave him another. By now, embarrassment had turned Scott's ruddy face even redder; and it remained flushed when the pastor led him and his officers to the head of a procession that was soon trailing from the church and into adjacent streets. There all were greeted by curious glances from native and military bystanders, many of whom guffawed and gestured in derision.

Though an unwilling participant in all of this, Hunt was suddenly struck by its ludicrousness. On impulse he leaned forward and whispered to the solemn-visaged Captain Lee, directly ahead of him.

After attempting to ignore the interruption, in hopes of avoiding cause for further embarrassment, Lee finally turned to him: "Well?"

Replied Hunt in a louder whisper: "Captain Lee, I really hope there is no *Pussyism* in all this."

Never had he seen Lee lose his composure. Even now, as Hunt recalled, "his face retained its quiet appearance, but the corners of his eyes and mouth were twitching in the struggle to preserve his gravity."[17]

* * *

By 8 April, when General Scott led his army northwestward from Vera Cruz, Hunt was in sublime spirits. Not only was he leaving behind scenes of dull routine, he was also marching toward active campaigning as a mounted artillerist. Weeks before, Captain Duncan, also a member of Scott's expeditionary force, had launched a second campaign to attach the young subaltern to his company, and this time had succeeded. The transfer constituted the greatest impetus yet given Hunt's career.

Since his transfer to Company A of the Second, he had worked arduously to reacquaint himself with those light-artillery tactics he had not studied since West Point. He had also familiarized himself with Duncan's other subordinates, Lieutenants William Hays and Henry F. Clarke, academy graduates in 1840 and 1843 respectively, thus junior to him in age and experience. Neither was a hard man to get to know or admire; both would remain close friends of his for decades to come.

Getting to know his new weapons was not quite so easy; but by now he had thoroughly oriented himself to the unique qualities of the three 6-pounder guns and the single 12-pounder howitzer in Company A. Each was pulled by a team of four horses—such transport made possible by lightweight carriages and each gun's weight of only 640 pounds. However, as Hunt had by now realized, such light pieces also tended toward fragility and had a severely limited effective range. Thus their mobility was absolutely essential; only by their ability to advance quickly to within six hundred to eight hundred yards of their enemy could they render adequate service on a consistent basis.[18]

Hunt neared his baptism of combat by way of Jalapa—General Scott's immediate objective—a village about sixty miles northwest of Vera Cruz and approximately 140 miles due east of the City of Mexico. Even before the army entered Jalapa, however, fighting was renewed. Amid a mountain pass named Cerro Gordo, a few miles short of the village, thirteen thousand troops under Santa Anna (now the president of Mexico as well as one of its leading generals) sought to block the invaders' path. Battle erupted on 17 April and continued to the next day. But Duncan's company was engaged only slightly; in his first action, Hunt was little more than a spectator in uniform. Even without A Company's help, the nine thousand troops that General Scott committed to battle sent their adversaries whirling in defeat toward their capital.[19] Afterward the anabasis resumed.

Scott, despite twin victories on his ledger, moved cautiously, venturing north, then south, and finally westward from Cerro Gordo, Worth's division in the lead. Such caution proved unnecessary when, without opposition, Worth occupied Jalapa and, twenty-two miles beyond it, the town and castle of Perote. Scott's people laid over for an extended rest in both locations, as well as in the hamlet of Tepeyahaulco, several miles before Perote. Significantly, Duncan's unit was one of those holding the most vulnerable post, in advance at Tepeyahaulco.[20] At all three places the local elevation was sufficient to place the army above the fever-prevalent lowlands.

Hunt welcomed the respite, not alone for siesta opportunities, but for the time permitting him to immerse himself further in mounted-artillery studies. He likewise welcomed a spate of reports received there from other theaters of combat. Almost without exception, they were highly encouraging. In addition to the successful ventures by Taylor and Scott thus far, American efforts to seize and hold New Mexico and Upper California were bearing much fruit. Santa Fe had been occupied the previous August by General Stephen Watts Kearny, following a grueling 850-mile advance across arid tracts with an army of 1,700. With his mounted troops he had thence moved to California and, on 6 December, had won a decisive struggle at San Pascual, not far from San Diego. Later cooperation by an American fleet under

Commodores John Sloat and R.F. Stockton would bring about the complete occupation of all Mexican-claimed territory in California. And shortly before the siege of Vera Cruz began, Colonel Alexander W. Doniphan and 850 troops of all arms had marched south from New Mexico to capture the strategic stronghold of Chihuahua, stamping out enemy resistance in the far-western quarter of Mexico. Finally, all significant ports on Mexico's eastern coast had been seized or neutralized by a fleet under Commodore Matthew Perry. These successes would permit Scott to move against the enemy capital with the assurance that he would face no threat from any direction, except that toward which he was advancing.[21]

It was well into the second week in May before Scott's army rumbled out of Jalapa and vicinity. Now it headed for Puebla, twelve miles away, in the center of the Valley of Mexico: this, Mexico's second city, lay less than one hundred miles from its capital, and was considered a formidable stronghold in its own right. But by the fourteenth, when the invaders drew within sight of the city, Hunt and his comrades learned that Santa Anna's mounted rear guard was in process of withdrawing from Puebla into Mexico City, where the final showdown would take place.[22]

The report, however, proved untrue; and General Scott discovered it so almost too late. On the morning of the fifteenth, as the Americans prepared to take full possession of Puebla, their march was suddenly and mysteriously halted; they were soon directed in a wholly different direction than anticipated. Eventually they found themselves facing 2,500 Mexican cavalrymen, formed for an attack on a broad plain outside the city. Afterward, Hunt was told that young Lieutenant McClellan of the engineers had detected an enemy intent to strike Scott's flank as the Americans marched off into Puebla, their eyes looking elsewhere. Because McClellan had brought timely warning to the commanding general, Scott had had time to turn an about-face and prepare proper resistance. Now, seeing their opportunity for a surprise attack destroyed, the cavalry trotted off toward Mexico City. From this episode grew Hunt's admiration for George McClellan's daring and enterprise.[23]

Occupation of Puebla brought still another rest period: this an extensive one. In mid-August, after weeks of inactivity, punctured by several interofficer feuds centering about or instigated by General Scott, and following unsuccessful attempts by President Polk's special emissary to convince the Mexican government to accept peace terms, the commanding general finally moved directly on Mexico City.

Coming up from the south, the American advance was halted near the capital suburbs of Contreras and Padierna, where fierce fighting erupted on the nineteenth. That day Hunt and Duncan saw little action, though much glory came to briskly engaged artillery associates: Captain Simon Drum, and Lieutenants John B. Magruder and Franklin D. Callender. By the close of that fighting, the decisive portion of which had consumed all of seventeen minutes, the invaders had captured both of the strategically located towns, giving them a formidable foothold on the outskirts of their ultimate objective.

On the twentieth, in a sanguinary struggle several miles farther east, near the hamlet of San Antonio and the river and town of Churubusco, Lieutenant Hunt entered his first full-scale battle. That morning Scott sent General Worth's two brigades against several adjacent fortified positions, in concert with movements by divisions under Major Generals David E. Twiggs and Gideon Pillow.

At the start of the movement, Duncan's company and Colonel John Garland's infantry brigade were thrown out in advance of the rest of Worth's command. Moving to within musketry range of entrenched Mexicans below Churubusco, both units soon came under a shower of shells and balls. Seeking cover, Duncan had Hunt move their four guns to an angle in a long causeway that lined the swamp-bordered Churubusco Road. There the cannoneers unlimbered among some natural shelter that kept them safe from harm, until ordered again to move forward: this time as far as the enemy trenches on Garland's flanks.

Even without artillery support at close range, the infantry had gouged some Mexicans from their works by frequent volleys of musketry. Now, aided by Duncan's heavier cover fire, they chased their opponents from all defenses but one: a fortified chapel on the far right of the no-longer-formidable trench line. But at that church, riflemen and a gun crew, working a heavy artillery piece, menaced the further advance of Garland's brigade and also kept Duncan's men in fear of quick death.[24]

After lengthy observation, Captain Duncan turned to his new second in command and ordered Hunt to move two of their guns around to the rear of the chapel via the main causeway into Churubusco. Hunt did not hesitate for a moment. Following his lead, a pair of Company A's weapons raced to the scene of need, horses galloping furiously along the causeway. When he was within two hundred yards of the church, Hunt swung the cannon to the rear of the edifice, and there unlimbered under another hail of fire from still-determined defenders on the chapel's flanks.

Despite such resistance, Hunt soon had both guns tossing shot and shrapnel into the stronghold. By what General Worth later termed "a fire of astonishing rapidity," Hunt within five minutes silenced the Mexican marksmen in and outside the church, as well as the heavy cannon that had so bedeviled Garland's foot troops.[25] Even when the enemy fled through the streets to the north, he kept up a murderous fire, lacing the survivors' ranks with salvos at close range. Bolstered by such a show of strength, Garland's brigade rushed up to the church from the other side, taking what prisoners remained.[26]

Once the last embers of Mexican resistance had burned out, Duncan rushed to Hunt's side and bestowed high praise for the energetic manner in which he had handled his two-cannon section. The captain later inserted such encomiums into his official report of the engagement, helping the young lieutenant win the first of two brevet promotions to be tendered him for his services in Mexico.

His work well done, Hunt, much pleased by his maiden efforts in front-line combat, retired with the rest of A Company to refit, recuperate, and renew his energies.

* * *

This time he had a relatively brief rest. By the first week in September the push for Mexico City was again in motion, the invaders now angling toward a steep hill a couple of miles southwest of the capital. Atop the rise stood the ancient castle of Chapultepec, crammed to its battlements with armed Mexicans.

The Americans also drove toward a stone foundry, originally a government-run mill, a few hundred yards west of Chapultepec. Five days before Scott's army attacked the latter, a part of it—Worth's division, plus supporting infantry, artillery, and dragoons—was sent to the foundry—El Molino del Rey (the King's Mill)—and to an adjacent edifice with equally tall and thick walls: the Casa Mata. In both buildings, as in the nearby castle, uniformed Mexicans awaited them, lending credence to rumors that the Molino housed a wealth of heavy ordnance being cast for Santa Anna's army.[27]

On his way to his dual objectives, General Worth fragmented his own command and those attached for the occasion, sending a five-hundred-man picked force to storm the enemy positions at the mill, supported by three other infantry outfits and several cannon. One of the artillery units was Duncan's, assigned to guard the left flank of the troops operating against the mill, and thus facing the approximate center of the enemy line. Finally, a brigade of foot troops under Colonel J.S. McIntosh, on Duncan's left, would attempt to penetrate the Mexican defenses at the Casa Mata, on the western side of the mill.

At 3 A.M. on 8 September, the five hundred-man storming party went forward with great verve, covered by Duncan's and Hunt's fire. Despite this support, it was nearly forced into retreat before the three other infantry outfits in that sector rushed up to render crucial aid, enabling the Americans to seize and hold the Mexican center. But when Colonel McIntosh went ahead with his secondary attack on the Casa Mata, against the extreme Mexican right, his men found themselves outflanked by a massive phalanx of gaudily uniformed lancers preparing to crush them in a mounted counterassault.

Duncan and Hunt observed this crisis. Without awaiting orders, they rushed their guns to the threatened sector—cannon, caissons, and limbers, rocking and jouncing over the rutted ground. At a crucial spot on Worth's far left, Hunt unlimbered under a deadly barrage of musket fire, where he received his first battle wounds from two spent bullets. Beside him, Lieutenants Hays and Clarke were also hit, though neither seriously. With

Duncan directing them, all stood their posts long enough to spray the front ranks of mounted Mexicans with canister, the shotgun-effect of which shredded the half-formed attack columns, dissolving all alignment and sending the lancers scrambling rearward in chaos, many of them afoot. Minutes later, Worth's own dragoons were charging past Duncan's guns with drawn sabers to add the finishing touches to the struggle. The Casa Mata was abandoned, as were the lines at El Molino del Rey. The road to Chapultepec lay invitingly clear.[28]

Shrugging off his injuries, Hunt expressed his readiness to make, at once, that last leg of their journey. But General Worth recalled his exhausted troops and, after destroying the military goods stored in both the mill and the Casa, placed his command in camp at Tacubaya, less than a mile to the south. For four days he patched the holes recently cut in his division, while his overworked medical officers ministered to the wounded, including Duncan's trio of subalterns.

On the morning of 12 September, Winfield Scott marched onward to the castle atop the hill—last barrier to the seat of Mexican government and commerce. That barrier fell with great ease, thanks to careful preparation and an all-day cannonade followed by a multipronged assault on the thirteenth, which seized the castle from both south and west after only an hour's struggle. During the fighting Hunt added new weight to his reputation by blasting a Mexican fieldwork at the base of the hill, which had precluded a crucial part of the attack from proceeding. Thanks to his accurately directed fire, the work was abandoned, allowing a South Carolina volunteer infantry regiment in his front to capture the southwestern sector of the Mexican position.[29]

Before morning was done, shouts of victory were rolling along the American line. Wasting no time, now when complete victory was at hand, Scott pushed the rest of his army to Mexico City—Hall of the Montezumas—easily securing the western extension of a pair of causeways that led across vast marshlands into the walled capital. The Chapultepec Causeway gave entrance to the city from the southwest via the Bélen Garita—a huge fortified gate before the walls in that sector. The Tacuba Causeway provided access to Mexico City from due west and led to a second towering gateway: the San Cosme Garita. Scott sent most of Worth's division, A Company of the Second included, along the Tacuba Causeway, while a smaller division of volunteers under Major General John A. Quitman proceeded up the other avenue of approach, over a mile to the south.[30]

In the preliminary stage of the operation, Hunt was separated from his immediate superior. At Worth's directive, Duncan sent him and Lieutenant Clarke, with one 6-pounder gun and the 12-pounder howitzer, plus two caissons, toward the Chapultepec Causeway to assist the left flank of Quitman's command in besting a Mexican fieldwork midway between the elevated thoroughfares.

But by the time the pair of cannon were within Quitman's reach, as Hunt later reported:

I soon found myself under a very severe fire, and seeing it was impossible to take up a more advanced position on the road (to which I was confined by deep ditches on either side) from which I could produce an effect upon the enemy without great risk of shelling our own troops who were in the advance, I halted the section and reported to Gen. Quitman.

The division leader had him set up the cannon in a wide and boggy field about one hundred yards behind the position held by the infantry. But there, too, Hunt found his line of fire blocked by the advancing foot soldiers. With Quitman's approval, he again limbered up and, with the ubiquitous musket balls whistling around him, relocated near the Chapultepec Causeway, 250 yards in advance of a sandbagged American parapet and not far from the enemy position opposing Quitman's drive. From there Hunt found he could enfilade the work; he did so with shell from his howitzer and shrapnel from his 6-pounder. By firing for several minutes with great effect, he enabled Quitman's troops to overrun that part of the line and at last head for the Bélen Garita.

Once this part of the line was secure, Hunt sought further orders from Quitman. One of the division commander's aides, however, mistakenly directed him onto a side road that, to Hunt's surprise, returned him to Duncan and the rest of A Company.[31] Here, on the American left, at any rate, he could furnish General Worth with the same sort of aid he had provided for Quitman.

Such aid was crucially needed on the Tacuba Causeway. While Quitman's volunteers charged the Bélen Gate, Worth's Regulars had been halted far short of the San Cosme Garita by a formidable array of Mexican artillery and entrenched infantry. Thus, late that afternoon, Worth collared Hunt and commanded him to take one gun and blast a gap through a strategically located barricade alongside the Garita. Once past that barrier—which in ironic understatement Captain Duncan called "a troublesome little breastwork" —Worth's men could smash their way through the walls and into the city's inner districts.[32]

Pausing, Hunt peered through gathering darkness and accumulating powder smoke, past the infantrymen huddling on either side of the causeway, and fixed his eyes on the gateway—its ramparts agleam with small-arms' fire. To move forward as Worth desired would be hazardous in the extreme. On the other hand, numerous colleagues had similarly sacrified themselves on this day, including Captain Drum and Lieutenant Benjamin, who had died beside their guns near the Bélen Garita. Knowing that he would be rushing to glory or death, and perhaps both, Hunt ordered Company A's howitzer and an eight-man gun crew forward.

What followed, said Worth, was "a brilliant exhibition of courage and conduct." Up the causeway moved the cannon, while much of the fiercest storm of balls and shell Hunt had yet faced flew around him. At the start, a few of the gunners were hit, one of them toppling dead into the road; but, backed by Lieutenant Clarke, Hunt kept the rest moving forward. When a battery horse fell dead, stalling the movement, Hunt had the gun cut free, and helped manhandle it onward. To his rear, Worth's foot soldiers tried to give him cover fire, but could provide little assistance; the torrent of Mexican lead seemed to increase.[33]

Two hundred yards in front of the main enemy position at the gate was an abandoned Mexican breastwork, the lone source of shelter in the causeway. Miraculously, the crew reached it, though Hunt, Clarke, and two enlisted men were the only ones unwounded. From behind this cover, Hunt ordered others to position and load the howitzer. As soon as shrapnel had been rammed home, Hunt's gunner touched a slow match to the barrel vent. The resulting blast and those that followed broke up the "troublesome little" work that was the focal point of General Worth's concern and frustration, filling the air with splinters, ripped sandbags, and corpses. Though a battery of three Mexican cannon on his flank made Hunt's position precarious, he continued to call for discharges until the breach Worth had desired was sufficiently wide to accomodate attacking infantry. The little gun crew hung on until Worth's foot troops had an opportunity to go forward at full tilt, pouring through the gap Hunt had created and gaining access to the walls of the city.[34] At about the same time, and partially because of this success, Quitman's division gained a similar lodgement at the Bélen Gate.

While Hunt and his colleagues followed Worth's infantry to the garita, the latter employed a tactic they had first used in the battle of Monterey; first, chopping holes in the adobe and soft stone walls with pick axes and crowbars, then flooding through to the streets of Mexico City. Simultaneously, artillerymen attached to Colonel Garland's brigade dismantled some small, mobile mountain howitzers, hauled the parts up to the roofs and towers of buildings just inside the walls, and there reassembled the little cannon. Firing from commanding vantage points, the howitzer crews ensured a complete rout of the enemy and the ultimate collapse of all resistance in the capital.[35]

Only when full darkness came was Hunt permitted to remove his guns and men to the rear. His uniform dark with sweat and coated with grime, his face blackened by powder stains, he was mobbed by officers and men who had witnessed his amazing exploit along the fire-swept causeway. Soon his congratulators included Duncan, Garland, and Worth.

But the most significant praise escaped him. Though commended for gallantry in Worth's and Duncan's reports, too many other officers had comported themselves heroically for Hunt's adventures to retain great prominence. As a result, he later found that in his detailed account of the campaign to Mexico City, published in January 1848, General Scott, though citing the bravery of dozens of subordinates, had neglected to mention so much as the name of Lieutenant Hunt. Though Hunt may have foreseen that his conduct on 13 September would bring him a second brevet—that of major—the knowledge failed to mollify his anger over Scott's unconscionable lapse; and he told the commanding general so in a heated letter. Scott replied in a manner hardly calculated to sooth injured pride: Hunt's feat along the Tacuba Causeway simply "had escaped his recollection."[36]

Hunt was not alone in being so neglected. A few days after the fighting outside Mexico City, a young lieutenant from Garland's brigade sought him out to corroborate some alleged heroics at the height of the action on the thirteenth.

Referring to a Mexican breastwork on the Tacuba Causeway not far from that which Hunt and his howitzer had blasted to fragments, the subaltern asked hopefully: "Didn't you see me go first into that work the other day?"

"Why, no," Hunt told him, a casual acquaintance. "It so happened I didn't see you, though I don't doubt you were in first."

"Well, I *was* first, and here Colonel Garland has made no mention of me!" The fellow shook his head in frustration. "The war is nearly done; so there goes the last chance I ever shall have of military distinction!"

In a sympathetic tone, Hunt told Lieutenant Ulysses Grant that the future might not be so unkind to him as that.[37]

*   *   *

The surrender of the City of Mexico was formally observed on the day following its capture. Afterward, General Scott showed disinterest in pursuing the defenders who, still led by Santa Anna, had escaped via northward trails leading to the village of Guadelupe Hidalgo. The fugitives were so few that the Mexican army was now a shadow of its former size. Recognizing this, officials in Mexico City opened peace negotiations with Scott, despite Santa Anna's avowed desire to fight on. Ultimately the overruled president-general would add his command to others surrendered to the invaders.

While negotiations progressed, Duncan's company, with other elements of the army not stationed in the capital, returned south to Tacubaya—the site of General Scott's headquarters—where they received a well-earned rest. Cognizant that the war was ended, but that forging a peace might prove almost as long an ordeal, Duncan's people spent much of their early days in camp making their new residence as comfortable as possible. Their estimation of future events proved prophetic, for when autumn came the army was still in and around Mexico City. Winter found them there as well, as did the new year, 1848.

Despite the change in seasons, the Mexican climate held mild, and, at Tacubaya, Lieutenant Hunt enjoyed it considerably. He had established his personal retreat in a large hacienda on the outskirts of the village, amid lavish gardens and a picturesque orange grove in full blossom. When off duty, he basked under the sun, was caressed by cool breezes, watched hummingbirds flit about the groves, partook of the ripe fruit that surrounded him, and sipped mescal and tequila. The total effect of his sumptuous habitation more than quieted the pains of those wounds now scarring over.

Hunt's stay in his orange grove was made still more pleasant by frequent visits from old friends such as Lee,[38] Barry, French, Wilcox, De Russy, Bragg, and Stevens. It is conceivable that he also enjoyed an opportunity to see his brother Lewis, who had graduated thirty-third in the thirty-eight-man West Point class of '47, and was now a full-fledged lieutenant in the Fourth Infantry. Unlike his highly acclaimed sibling, however, he had arrived in Mexico too late to see action in the decisive campaigning.

Only one notable incident brought a note of displeasure to Hunt's lovely hacienda. That winter another squabble broke out within the high echelon of command, involving Scott in a bitter controversy with Generals Worth and Pillow as to whose ability the successful battles of August and September were primarily attributable. Brevet Lieutenant Colonel Duncan imprudently involved himself in the feud by asserting that the credit properly belonged to Worth; even worse, he told the newspapers so. Furious, publicity-conscious Scott arrested him—and Worth and Pillow as well. When he learned the news, Hunt leapt to his company commander's defense, but could do nothing to secure his release from custody.[39] Before the controversy died out late in the winter, resulting in the jailed trio being set free, Hunt's regard for the commanding general of the army had reached its nadir.

Still, with this single exception, life amid the orange trees and hummingbirds of Tacubaya would remain one of Hunt's most pleasant experiences. In later years he would recall with undiminished fondness the warmth and beauty of his hacienda, and the camaraderie he enjoyed there over card games and drinking bouts, and during long, lazy conversations under the sun. Never again would war be so kind to him.

4

Triumphs and Tragedies

Hunt's sabbatical at Tacubaya ended in June 1848 when he joined most of Scott's army in boarding transports at Vera Cruz to sail for home. The peace negotiations had in fact taken longer to resolve than had the battle action of the war; for eight and a half months the terms of Mexico's capitulation had remained in a diplomatic limbo, until finally ratified by both Washington and Mexico City. According to the final agreement, Mexico would sell, for a pittance, 525,000 square miles of that land in southern Texas, Upper California, and the New Mexico Territory for which American jingoists had long hungered.

At once, life in the postwar army gave Hunt headaches. No sooner had Company A reached New Orleans than it lost its horses, as did all but three of the light companies—the result of a new War Department economy campaign. Hunt remonstrated against this policy, but on this occasion did so without the influential support of Colonel Duncan, who recently had been promoted inspector-general of the army and had been sent on tours of posts in far-off locales. Hunt's lone voice was not heeded in Washington. A mounted unit in name only, Company A was sent to Fort Columbus, New York; and from there, three months later, to Fort McHenry in Baltimore Harbor, where in September 1814 Francis Scott Key had composed a stirring ode by dawn's early light.

In both New York and Baltimore, Hunt spent anxious weeks inquiring about the future status of his unit, and taking soundings of the national attitude toward the military. His latter findings gave him even greater concern than those regarding his company. Appropriations cuts recently voted by Congress and vocally approved by civilians in all walks of life reflected, he believed, a renewed national bias against his profession. At length, he concluded that he and his colleagues had been basely used by their country, supported during a war fought for political gain and territorial conquest, then crippled and shuffled into semioblivion at dozens of inade-quately furnished garrisons.

Brevet Major Henry J. Hunt, c. 1850 (COURTESY, LIBRARY OF CONGRESS)

His gloom dissipated slightly in November, soon after taking station at Fort McHenry. There Duncan's company was returned its horses, as were the three other original light units. Later rumors had an additional quartet of companies about to be remounted, too. These reports began to materialize as fact the following April.

But such a rush to redress past wrongs would be of fairly short duration. Early in 1851 Secretary (of War) Charles M. Conrad would yet again "de-horse" all but two of these eight companies, declaring mounted artillery "utterly useless" in peacetime and overly expensive to maintain. As per his ruling, Duncan's company would lose its animals for the second time in three years.[1]

Even before the second dismounting, however, Lieutenant Hunt had cause for gloom. Since his return from Mexico he had served as commander *pro tem* of Company A; but after July 1849 he held that position on a permanent basis. That month, in his final weeks of service at Fort McHenry, he received the sad intelligence of Colonel Duncan's death. Having survived combat on so many fields, the inspector-general had succumbed to yellow fever while on a duty tour of plague-swept Mobile, Alabama.[2]

The loss of both an esteemed commander and an intimate friend left Hunt bereaved for a lengthy period, his spirits further lowered by the army's inconsistent attitude toward the maintainence of so vital a force as her mounted artillery.

He was finally lifted from his melancholy by some pleasant and memorable features of his next tour of duty: Fort Monroe, from mid-1849 to December 1852. At Hampton Roads, on the tip of the Virginia peninsula, he was brought together with old friends, including his respected West Point mentor, Lieutenant Colonel De Russy. The engineer officer had been at Fort Monroe for the past three years, ever since relinquishing his academy post, constructing works for the garrison as well as at nearby Fort Calhoun. Now one of the ranking executives of the Corps of Engineers, he would head that prestigious arm a decade hence.

Most of the colonel's family was with him at Hampton Roads, including his pretty nineteen-year-old daughter, Emily.[3] Accepting frequent invitations to dine and socialize with the De Russys, Hunt soon found himself powerfully attracted to the young girl, sister of his West Point chum, Gustavus (another of Emily's brothers had been a mate of Lewis Hunt in the academy class of '47). Soon Hunt found himself reevaluating his bachelor status. At age thirty, he certainly should have been mature enough to accept the responsibilities of married life. Thanks to the increased pay and emoluments accompanying his recent brevet promotions—considerably bolstered by his dice and card winnings from Mexico—he could afford to support a wife and family, though in nothing approaching luxury. So deciding, he was soon seriously courting Emily. Her parents voiced no objection.

Like his father before him, Hunt made his engagement brief. In December of '51 he travelled to the De Russy ancestral home in Plattsburgh, New York; and there, on the eighteenth of that month, was joined to Emily in wedlock.[4] The ceremony and the wedding trip, at the height of the holiday season, were joyous events, though the latter was short as well. By the first week in the New Year, bride and groom had returned to Fort Monroe, moving into the married-officers' quarters. At last Hunt had escaped the dark, drafty caves of his bachelor years, as well as the loneliness that pervaded them.

* * *

His service on the peninsula affected his life in a second significant manner. Despite his months in Baltimore harbor, he considered this duty tour his first true exposure to life in the South. It proved wholly agreeable. He came to form a high opinion of the majority of Virginians, renowned for their hospitality, elegant breeding, sense of history and tradition, and lively interest in things military. He was also captivated by the local scenery, and, perhaps with a view to future settlement there as a civilian, purchased some property in Norfolk.

At bottom he shared extensive common ground with Virginians and their neighbors farther south. He was innately sympathetic toward several of the political aims and grievances publicized by their states' rights activists. Already the nation had begun to tremble from shock waves unleashed by that political and cultural controversy, partially as result of recent efforts by Washington politicos to determine the territorial status of land acquired from Mexico. Though Hunt doubted that the political antagonisms dividing the country would expand to dangerous proportions, he agreed that the controversy was growing louder, thanks largely to Northerners' attempts to tip the scales of political power by legislating most of the Mexican acquisition closed to the growth of slavery.

Hunt was no wild-eyed bigot. He did not believe that the black race should be doomed to a life of perpetual servitude, contrary to the gist of the impassioned utterances of some of his Virginia hosts. Not himself of a mind to own slaves, he had had little exposure to them, especially during his formative years on the frontier. But neither did he consider the black man inherently equal to the white. On balance, he undoubtably considered the peculiar institution a problem for the South herself to remedy, and waxed confident that if left to her own devices, the South would do so in proper time by legislating the practice out of existence.

Still, Hunt was firmly opposed to secession from the Federal Union—a concept some Southerners had termed their only recourse in the face of Northern antagonism toward their way of life. Ten years later, he would be called on to back his belief with a willingness to wage war against erstwhile friends below the Mason-Dixon Line. At that time, precisely because of the kinship he had developed in the 1850s toward Southerners and their lifestyle, he would have to resolve a painful conflict of sympathies.

* * *

Within a week after Secretary Conrad decreed that for a second time Company A and five of her sister units had to give up their horses, Hunt put into print an angry denunciation of War Office insensitivity toward military innovation. In a lengthy diatribe addressed to the secretary himself, he presented a cogent and yet comprehensive summary of administrative apathy and neglect. Though seeking to aid all branches of the service, Hunt's anger had particular reference to the various means by which the artillery had been misused and emasculated over the years. He inveighed most strongly against the continuing efforts of ordnance officers to take over the employment as well as the supply of the artillery, to the extent of seeking to supplant cannoneers at seacoast and inland garrisons across the country.[5]

His words provoked no early reforms. Yet, from this point on, Hunt renewed and redoubled his efforts to gain public recognition and War Department redress of artillery's lengthy and lengthening list of grievances. He had curtailed earlier efforts in this vein when war with Mexico broke out, and his skills as an agitator had since atrophied. But now, spurred by the encouragement of like-minded reformers, such as his friend Brevet Captain Isaac Stevens, Hunt contributed memorandum after memorandum on the subject.[6] Stevens, now in charge of the Coast Survey Office in Washington, had sufficient influence to see them widely circulated throughout the War Department.

Hunt's favorite proposals—including a new merger of the ordnance and artillery into an agency that would restore rightful responsibilities and privileges to each; the shelving of Congressional plans for further troop reductions; and the reopening of an artillery instruction school (Camp Washington had closed during the Mexican War)—all brought predictable responses. Ordnance executives labelled him an obstructionary and a crank.[7] Legislators who favored military retrenchment to please like-minded constituencies attacked him as a foe of governmental economizing. Other, more thoughtful recipients of his writings, not just artillerists, welcomed his proposals for change and provided him with new ones.

Though gratified by the nature of this response, both pro and con, Hunt found that the fruits of his efforts were few. He did have a few near misses. The most significant of these occurred in March of 1852 when he witnessed the creation of a bill that had eventuated from his efforts to appoint a chief of artillery,[8] with power to enhance the cohesiveness and efficiency of the arm. The measure, sponsored by James Shields of Illinois, chairman of the Senate Military Committee, was finally defeated by what Hunt vaguely termed "official opposition."[9] But by then, at least, his struggle for reform had brought him a widespread reputation as the ablest soldier-defender of artillery's value and good name.

In December of '52, Hunt and his wife—their lives recently brightened by the birth of their first child, a daughter, who had received her mother's name—were sent to Fort Moultrie, in the harbor of Charleston, South Carolina. There Hunt was separated from Company A and took command of another unit, by virtue of his three-month-old promotion to the full grade of captain. The assignment, coming on the heels of newly won fame as the artillery spokesman, seemed to herald an imminent upswing in his career.

Though of course pained by his enforced departure from Hays, Clarke, and his other comrades in Duncan's old company, Hunt realized that his late commander's name would always adhere to that unit, no matter how hard he tried to make it his own; a fresh start might allow him to attain company command solely in his own right, and perhaps make over a unit in his own name and style. To be sure, he was gratified by the new friendships he had cemented in Charleston when succeeding another recently deceased but less-famous commander, Brevet Major James Roland, who had been in charge of Company M of the Second Artillery.[10] Such friendships extended to a pair of second lieutenants destined to serve at his side for the next nine years: Edward R. Platt and James Thompson. He was also pleased to meet the noncoms and enlisted men under his authority, whose military caliber he valued from the start. Still another aspect of his new tour of duty sat well with him: he was glad once again to be stationed among Southerners, of whose hospitality he would partake anew on a frequent basis, especially in the armories and clubrooms to which officers of the city's several militia outfits would invite him.

On the other hand, the circumstance reportedly behind his coming to Charleston, in company with several hundred other troops of all arms, seemed ominous. The Wilmot Proviso of 1847 and the compromise measures of 1850, the terms of which forbade slavery in most of the land won from Mexico, had incensed many in the Deep South. South Carolinians had recently held a statewide convention in Charleston to air local opinion about possible secession from the Union. An alarmed War Department had dispatched troops to reinforce strategic government garrisons in the state.[11]

The climate of affairs led Hunt to reevaluate the violent capabilities of the states' rights conflict. In the end, he maintained one overriding belief: though still in sympathy with many aspects of the South's political plight, he wholeheartedly disapproved of the ordinances adopted by the Charleston convention, especially those affirming that secession was a legal right of the states and "fully justified by violations of the Constitution" (which implicitly sanctioned slavery). After so declaiming, the delegates had overwhelmingly voted to remain in the Union. Hunt was nevertheless disturbed to note they had done so "for reasons of expediency alone."[12]

Because of the intensifying political crisis, plus the return of yellow fever in the summer of 1853, Hunt and Emily were glad to be sent elsewhere that June. He was particularly pleased by the nature of his new orders, which directed Company M to Fort Washita, Indian Territory, not far from the northeastern border of Texas. Jefferson Davis, Mississippi-bred successor to War Secretary Conrad, had ordered M and two other light companies remounted and placed on frontier duty as instructional units. He had done so principally because of the continuing efforts of Senator Shields to restore the light artillery to its proper status under the law. At Hunt's dogged urging, the senator had secured a small Congressional appropriation for the express purpose of returning all de-horsed companies to their pre-1852 standing.[13] Thus, indirectly at least, Hunt could claim credit for the present turnabout of circumstances.

After a month-long trip down the Atlantic and Gulf Coasts, thence up the Mississippi River, Hunt, wife, and daughter, plus the rest of M Company and its dependents, enjoyed a lengthy stopover at Fort Smith, Arkansas, communications center of the Southwest. At Fort Smith the unit drew horses and light 6- and 12-pounder cannon, as well as caissons, limbers, carriages, harnesses, and a travelling forge.[14] After an interval filled with a crash course to break in new recruits and the reacquaintance of veterans to the complexities of mounted drill, the company trekked overland to Fort Washita, 150 miles to the southwest, near the confluence of the garrison's namesake stream and the much broader Red River. On the left bank of the Washita River, Hunt was rudely introduced to the harsh reality of garrison duty on the frontier of the 1850s.

The post was a shambles. Though built only eleven years before to protect settlers and domesticated Indians from nomadic hostiles, the garrison looked ancient. The roofs on all of its limestone buildings were dilapidated and leaky; its hospital unfit for use; its stables "insufficient and unsuitable for the accommodation of artillery horses"; its storehouses "utterly unfit"; and its magazine located in "a very unsafe position."[15] Moreover, it lacked a granary, workshops, and a gunhouse. If such was Jefferson Davis's concept of a fit place to employ mounted artillery, the man was either ignorant, deluded, or malicious; certainly he was no champion of military efficiency.

Service in the Indian Territory presented Hunt with a few compensatory experiences. In brief time he came to cherish the lovely vistas and the handsome, rugged topography of this stretch of God's country. Here he also established enduring ties with a number of subalterns sent to study light-artillery tactics under his tutelage, and renewed friendships with officers temporarily stationed in the territory, including Robert Lee (now the lieutenant colonel of the Second United States Dragoons), Joseph E. Johnston, William Barry—and Brevet Lieutenant Colonel Braxton Bragg, whose six-gun C Company of the Third Artillery (once the personal command of

Major Ringgold, patron saint of the horse artillery) was condemned in 1854 to the same fate as Hunt's unit. Here, too, in April of 1855, Hunt's firstborn son, Henry, Jr., came into the family, delivered in the more adequately furnished hospital at nearby Fort Arbuckle.[16]

Even so, unhappy hours seemed to predominate. Hunt's and Bragg's splendidly appointed companies slowly crumbled into disrepair before their eyes, lacking as they did the most rudimentary maintenance facilities. Though Hunt stayed on at the post, Bragg, in disgust, resigned his commission in January 1856, crying that the "finest battery I ever saw was destroyed in two years at a cost of $100,000."[17] Of even greater impact on Hunt's personal well-being, complications attending the birth of Henry, Jr. had left his wife weak and ailing, conditions worsened by the lack of specialized medical care available on the frontier.

In an apparent effort to deflect his attention from those concerns, Hunt threw himself into his instructional work. Even before Bragg's resignation, however, he discovered himself for several periods of time, not only in command of his company, but also of the garrison. Burdened with such a heavy administrative workload, he found that the amount of time that could be devoted to his tutorial duties was significantly diminished. As a result, he devised a drill system that was to have far-reaching influence on the army's tactics, as well as training.

He felt that his pupils could grasp this simplified drill quickly enough to leave him sufficient time for other chores. It substituted blocks of men— eight for a foot-artillery company, ten per each mounted unit—for one individual soldier, which for rank and file formation was designated by all drill manuals to be the basic unit for evolutions on the parade ground. In time it was discovered that this deceptively simple feature made the drill adaptable to infantry and cavalry service as well.

Those officers who witnessed the implementation of Hunt's idea were amazed by the resultant economy of troop movement, as well as by the shortened study time it permitted. Barry and Johnston were particularly enthusiastic about the system and urged Hunt to adapt it for battle maneuvering as well as for parade-ground training. Hunt was so encouraged that he took a furlough to spend full time refining and expanding his model, as well as developing a new and simplified system of spoken commands to complement it.

At length, he sought to interest the high command in the system. Yet the War Department, perhaps because of his reputation as an agitator and iconoclast, rejected his so-called "gun-detachment" concept, deeming the alteration of present drill procedures unnecessary. A few years later Hunt offered it to Colonel Philip St. George Cooke, then revising mounted tactics under War Department auspices, but Cooke vetoed its applicability to cavalry useage. Not until 1860 would Hunt find an opportunity to put his idea into print and into action on a wide-scale basis.

Later still, two controversies would spring up as a result of the new system. When revising its own artillery tactics in 1863, the French Army would adopt much of it without crediting Hunt's authorship.[18] And four years afterward, Brevet Major General Emory Upton—who had received his early training as an artillerist under Hunt—would also appropriate Hunt's model without authorization. Upton would slightly modify it to embrace his own conception of infantry tactics, founded on maneuvers by sets of four soldiers—a natural extension of Hunt's gun-detachment principle.[19]

Hunt would feel that, in addition to plagiarizing, Upton had botched his theft: ". . . he did not comprehend the principle itself or at least the extent and value of its application." He would also blast Upton's "ridiculous system of commands."[20] More than a few times he would consider legal action against the younger officer, but would be prevented from following through because of Upton's powerful allies in the War Department, as well as by the lack of funds to cover court costs.[21] Thus, until the end of his days, he would brood over the unhappy truth that the 1867 revised tactics had brought Emory Upton the national renown that their true creator never received.

* * *

Personal tragedies multiplied as 1856 drew to a close. During the past year, Emily's health had badly deteriorated. By October Hunt feared for her survival; and, that same month, came harsh news which he had nevertheless anticipated. Because its guns and equipment had been disabled by constant use on the practice field without needed upkeep, Company M was again ordered unhorsed. Along with G Company of the Fourth Artillery, another unit gone to seed on the frontier, Hunt's command would return to Fort Monroe, there to serve as a unit of instruction for seacoast and garrison service only.[22]

Soon afterward Hunt received an opportunity to tell Jeff Davis exactly what he thought of the irresponsible training program that had ruined Company M. The following month Special Orders #134 directed him, upon his arrival at Fort Monroe, to repair alone to Washington. In the capital he was to take a seat on a board convened to amend the system of instruction for field artillery.[23]

With mounted cannon units disintegrating all about him, Hunt might ordinarily have found bitter humor in this assignment. But there was nothing humorous in the trip east—a journey rendered thoroughly somber by his wife's continuing debility. Reluctantly, he left her and the children in the care of the De Russys at Fort Monroe. He then hastened to the capital, though hardly in a mood to focus full attention on the job awaiting him.

It is not known whether Hunt made use of his chance to unburden himself of rage and frustration in the presence of the War Secretary. It is known that, as per orders, he joined the two other principals on the panel of artillery experts, William Barry and William H. French, and, despite the distractions that vied for his attention farther south, got down to work.

At bottom, the trio found themselves pressed to evolve consistency, cogency, clarity, and efficiency from a tangle of older drill systems and various War Department suggestions for a modern one. Specifically, they had to provide a workable replacement for Robert Anderson's 1839 text, which following its revising in 1845 by Major Ringgold had remained the accepted manual for all forms of light artillery.[24] Only after long, laborious months of evaluating, adapting, modifying, and revising historically accepted modes of instruction would Hunt, Barry and French produce the sort of results that would justify the wisdom behind their selection for this task.

The work was completed in two extended sessions: from November 1856 to September 1857; and from September 1858 to March 1860. The year-long interlude embraced a period during which the presence elsewhere of all three was deemed vital. By the time the panel was formally dissolved, it had devised principles to guide what were known as the "School of the Piece," "of the Section" (a two-cannon detachment of a company), and "of the Battery" (heretofore an infrequently used term designating a mounted-artillery company). Such principles had been a part of earlier texts, however, and in somewhat the same form. The board's unique contribution, according to one artillery historian, was the degree to which it went beyond the scope of precedent: ". . . far exceeding in breadth of design and completeness of execution anything of a similar nature that had been given the artillery arm."

This historian continues:

> The features wherein the instruction of 1860 was superior to its predecessors consisted in articles on organization, matériel, and the service of artillery in campaign, presenting a philosophical and instructive *exposé* of the general principles underlying the formation, discipline, and service, both in peace and war, of an efficient field artillery. . . . [Also] the equipment of a battery, both in personnel and matériel; and its management, both as a school for subalterns and under all circumstances of war, marches, transportation, encampment, and conduct in action, were fully and clearly laid down with many practical suggestions—the result of experience in the field.[25]

The cornerstone upon which the tactical wing of this vast and impressive structure was built was the gun-detachment principle devised by Hunt at Fort Washita. Though much of the credit for its development would eventually elude him, Hunt could later take satisfaction from knowing that his system saw wide acceptance during America's pivotal war. In March 1860 the War Department approved the revised tactics for general use by

the army; and under its authority they were published later that year by
J.B. Lippincott & Company of Philadelphia, entitled: *Instruction for Field
Artillery.* The popularity accorded the work—as well as that of a French-based
supplemental text, *Evolutions of Field Batteries of Artillery,* translated soon
afterward by Major Anderson[26]—would ensure that during the national
hostilities of 1861–65 both Union and Confederate artillerists would make
wide useage of the revised tactics. Of Hunt's, Barry's, and French's work,
another historian has declared:

> The appearance, on the eve of war, of this system of instruction, was
> a most opportune circumstance; it was no mere work of the scissors.
> Major Hunt and his worthy coadjutors . . . here gave to the Army that
> which was both original and practically useful.[27]

Hunt, however, did not spend quite as much time on the revision
board as did his collaborators. He missed several weeks of labor toward
the end of its first session when called from Washington in mid-May 1857
by the most painful news of his adulthood: his wife was dead. On the
twelfth, Emily had succumbed at Fort Monroe to the long-range effects of
those childbirth complications that had plagued her for two years.

He had foreseen this end. Still he was unprepared to accept the
anguished realization that her loss had cast him and his motherless children
adrift. Painfully he made his way south to place Emily to rest in the De
Russy family plot at St. John's Episcopal Church in Hampton, Virginia,
where her youngest brother, John, had been sleeping for almost two years.

Appreciating his subsequent plight, the De Russys came to his aid.
They agreed to continue to care for their five-year-old granddaughter and
two-year-old grandson for an indefinite period—at least until Hunt could
sort out the complexities of his situation.[28]

Being in a frame of mind not conducive to renewing work on tactics
revision, he was spared that ordeal. That summer the high command once
again saw fit to remount Company M. This time it would receive its horses
and guns at Fort Leavenworth and, there, fight Indians and white guerrillas
terrorizing the Kansas-Nebraska-Missouri territory. Hunt would accompany
his unit.

With no great enthusiasm, even at the thought of rejoining a mounted
command, he and M Company embarked together from Hampton Roads
for their new place of duty, via ship, horseback, and stagecoach. Hunt's mood
was the inevitable result of loneliness. Though heading west in company
of so many familiar faces, it somehow seemed that he was travelling alone.

* * *

By 13 September 1857 he had returned to the garrison whose founding
he had observed as a child of seven.[29] But Leavenworth—now also the name
of a boom town a few miles from the post—was no longer the same as his

memory had it. As a primary jumping-off point for settlers travelling farther west via the Santa Fe and Oregon Trails, the fort had expanded to huge proportions. The size of its garrison force had grown commensurately; now it was the home of elements from the Second and Fourth Artillery, the Sixth Infantry, and the Second Dragoons (the latter, with executive officer Lee in temporary command, arrived there at approximately the same time as Hunt's company). A far cry from its situation in 1827, the fort stood in the midst of civilization, lying but thirty miles above one of the West's great population centers: the City of Kansas.[30]

Soon after reaching the post, Company M received new hardware: four spanking-new smoothbore brass cannon, light 12-pounders of the "Napoleon" model, recently adopted for army use by administrators in Washington. Developed in France under the patronage of Emperor Napoleon III, who had given it his name, the piece was lightweight and highly mobile, and had an effective range of more than half a mile, with a theoretical range of twice that far. Technically a hybrid, it combined some features of the gun with some of the howitzer, proving capable of the range and accuracy of the former and the higher-angled fire of the latter. It could fire solid shot, shell, shrapnel, and canister with reliability and ease, and was an especially deadly weapon when hurling canister, shotgunlike, at distances under three hundred yards.[31] In time it would win Hunt's acclaim as the best all-around field piece of his era.

At Fort Leavenworth, Company M's commander found himself more frequently occupied in coaching his men on the drill plain than in running down marauding Indians or breaking up bands of violent proslaveryites and abolitionists who, over the past couple of years, had clashed time and again up and down the state. Ironically, however, an opportunity for military service eventually came his way from a distant locale.

Some nine hundred miles westward, in the Valley of the Great Salt Lake, Mormons who had settled the Utah Territory had declared open rebellion against the United States government. Urged on by their powerful prophet, Territorial Governor Brigham Young, some four thousand armed Mormons had defied President James Buchanan's edict that they surrender claim to the "Valley of the Saints," replace Young with an official selected by Buchanan, and allow pioneers and gold seekers to traverse their land unmolested. Young had also declared his intention to wreak violence on any government troops sent to Utah to force a confrontation.[32]

A two-thousand-man expeditionary force had duly been sent to test Young's determination. Shortly after Hunt's arrival at Fort Leavenworth, the Mormons had retaliated as promised. They destroyed the expedition's supply train, burned off grazing land so that the army's horses would starve, and forced the soldiers to seek refuge in a partially demolished fort 120 miles northeast of the Valley of the Saints. The troops were forced to huddle among the garrison's ruins through a bitter prairie winter, their continued survival in doubt.

Apprised of this development, the government massed more troops at Fort Leavenworth to form a relief expedition a couple thousand strong. As commander of one of only two artillery units able to accompany a column on the march, Hunt signed on under Brigadier General William S. Harney.[33]

So much organizational work was required that the relief force was not ready to start westward until late in May 1858. The first week in June, however, saw it well on its way to Utah via the Oregon Trail and South Pass. The journey was long, dusty, and enervating. Hunt kept a journal during the trip, in which he penned frequent criticism of Harney's mode of march, the tiring effect of which "is shown in the necks & shoulders. The horses are a great deal fagged and men are beginning mostly to fall off in condition." But the weary procession continued, nighttime alone given over to sustained rest, the column averaging twenty miles per day. Infrequently the tedium was shattered, as on one afternoon when a herd of bison ventured too near the column, falling prey to expert marksmen. The troops enjoyed fresh meat that evening.[34]

All hardships went for naught: the majority of the relief force never completed the trip. Short of South Pass, Harney learned that the original expedition had survived the winter, returning to the valley to find the Mormons' pugnaciousness gone and Brigham Young in a conciliatory mood. On 12 June, while Hunt and his comrades lay over at Fort Kearny, Nebraska Territory, to catch their breath, the troops in Utah were "invited" into Mormon territory, ending the rebellion. The relief force did not receive the news until early in July. On the eleventh—minus a few units that continued on to Utah under Harney—the expeditionary force turned homeward. By 3 August its men were back at Leavenworth.[35]

Thus Hunt and his allies had spent more than two months of fruitless wandering in the Great American Desert. He could not recall ever having accomplished so little on any past occasion after devoting so much effort and time.

At least he was not given long to brood over it. On 1 September, orders sent him cross-country again—back to Washington City for the second half of his tactics board work. He spent the next eighteen months in the capital, whipping into publishable shape the reams of notes Barry, French, and he had compiled during their first session, as well as between then and the present.

Apart from such activity, this period was made notable for Hunt by frequent invitations to dine at the I Street home of a distant relative and long-term benefactor: Colonel Henry Knox Craig. As head of the Ordnance Bureau, the colonel had ingratiated himself with the younger officer by his integrity and sense of fairness, revealed in his reversal of such self-serving policies of his predecessor as had enraged Hunt and his comrades in the artillery. He and Hunt had also been drawn close because the colonel's youngest son, Lieutenant Presley O. Craig of the Second Artillery, had recently been one of Hunt's pupils.[36]

In time, Hunt virtually became a member of the Craig family. Much in the manner of his socializing among the De Russys at Fort Monroe, he had an amorous motive in spending so much time on I Street. It centered around the colonel's dark-haired, dark-eyed daughter: twenty-two-year-old Mary Bethune Craig. Again, as nine years before, the thirty-nine-year-old widower soon found himself pressing a suit for a pretty girl's hand.

This second courtship, however, was unique in that, as his distant cousin,[37] Mary had known him in a formal social relationship since childhood. During that time Hunt had never envisioned her as his future wife; soon he could think of her in no other role—all of which indicated that the emotional wounds inflicted by Emily's death were now protected by tough scar tissue; he could start life anew.

In June of '59, Hunt's courtship of Mary Craig, well in progress but far from conclusion, was almost cut short. The new secretary of war, John B. Floyd, had concocted a plan by which the mounted artillery would again be dispatched to isolated frontier forts as instructional units. For Hunt and Company M, Floyd had in mind Fort Randall, in the wilds of the Dakota Territory.

Foreseeing a repetition of the hardships that had crippled his command six years before, Hunt would not stand for it. He sent an angry letter to Commanding General Scott, informing him that he would tender his resignation before seeing Company M committed to a post known to lack adequate artillery-maintenance facilities and where equine diseases such as hoof rot were prevalent.

To his surprise, Old Fuss and Feathers, of whom he had entertained such a low opinion in past years, supported his stance. In a letter to Floyd, the general announced his total agreement with Hunt's view.[38] As a result, the war secretary finally shelved the project, though with great reluctance.

So, at last, Brevet Major Hunt had been able to impress his will on those monolithic administrators who had manipulated him so often in the past. He could remain in Washington to finish his tactical revision—and to complete his campaign to win the hand and heart of Mary Craig.

* * *

By the time the tactics panel resolved the last of its business, Hunt was engaged. But before he could secure a furlough during which to marry, he had to complete another tour of garrison duty. This assignment, which carried him farther from Washington than had his past several postings, closed out an epoch in his life and career.

His orders sent him to another locale he well remembered from decades before. This was Fort Brown, a well-furnished garrison on the left bank of the Rio Grande at the southernmost tip of Texas, near which he had idled away the weeks prior to his participation in the Mexican War. This time he went west to reach the fort via a route that led through Virginia,

Mary Craig Hunt, c. 1862 (COURTESY, CMDR. J. CONWAY HUNT, WASHINGTON, D.C.)

where he kissed his children goodbye and promised them a quick return in company with their new mother. By late March 1860, after several days on the seas and on the road, he was in lower Texas, where he rejoined his company after its transit from Fort Leavenworth.[39]

The region around Fort Brown, in contrast to its appearance late in 1846, looked peaceful—but deceptively so, for new war clouds dotted the horizon, this time to the north of the Rio Grande. The sectional antagonisms, whose formative manifestations Hunt had observed in Charleston harbor and on the Kansas frontier, had grown huge and frightening, and crisis weather was in the air. A pending presidential election would determine whether the storm would pass over, or would deluge the nation with a torrent of fratricidal violence.

To the end, Hunt hoped that the storm would not break. He remained receptive to the Southern ethos, and believed that the sobriety and restraint of its people would help resolve the crisis peacefully. That spring he had the opportunity to spend some days in nearby Thibodaux, Lafourche Parish, Louisiana, on a sugar plantation owned by his friend Braxton Bragg. He expressed to Bragg his fervent hope that bloodshed and open warfare would not be necessary to settle the political differences of the sections. His host shared that hope; sharing too a faith in an eleventh-hour national compromise to avert disaster.

Hope and faith were blasted during the 6 November election. Though long motivated by a desire to shun political involvement—considering politics an unfit realm for any warrior—Hunt followed a natural inclination by casting his ballot for the Democratic compromise candidate: John C. Breckinridge of Kentucky. But the Democratic party had been irreparably split by Breckinridge's candidacy in opposition to the organization nominee: Senator Stephen Douglas of Illinois. As a result, the Republican hopeful, another Illinois legislator, named Lincoln—whom the Deep South had labelled an abolitionist candidate—won less than thirty-five percent of the popular vote, but was elected the nation's sixteenth president.

By now, even a professed political innocent such as Hunt could hear the clang of doom. Abraham Lincoln's assumption of the presidency, which the South would never recognize, would bring forth the deluge.

Unable to influence events of such scope and aroused passion, Hunt sought a separate peace. On 13 December he secured his long-awaited furlough, bade farewell to Platt and Thompson and those others in M Company from whose presence he had detached himself so often, and returned to Washington. Exactly two weeks after leaving Texas, he stood beside Mary Craig before the altar at St. John's Episcopal Church on M Street N.W. And shortly thereafter—only a few days after South Carolina proclaimed her withdrawal from the Union—Hunt and his bride embarked on their honeymoon.[40]

5
Although Blood
May Flow Like Water

Hunt's second wedding trip was even briefer than his first. Because he and Mary spent their honeymoon in the capital, he reported his whereabouts to the War Office. Though available for duty at any time, he was surprised when, late on 2 January 1861, he was summoned to the office of the acting secretary of war, Joseph Holt, who had succeeded to that position only five days before, following the resignation of native Virginian, Floyd.[1]

Holt wished to know if his visitor was interested in a special assignment. Hunt could hardly have refused, and so the secretary pro tem elaborated: Hunt was needed at Harpers Ferry, Virginia, to defend the government armory and arsenal there. As true of many of the states below the Mason-Dixon Line, Virginia was edging toward secession, its officials considering seizing whatever government ordnance and matériel remained on their soil.

Holt then read him an alarming letter, which the civilian superintendent at Harpers Ferry, Alfred M. Barbour, had recently sent one of the officers in the Ordnance Bureau:

> I have reason to apprehend that some assault will be made upon the United States Armory. . . . My reasons I do not feel at liberty to disclose. They may or they may not be well founded. . . . But the armory might be taken and destroyed . . . unless the Government itself sees to the protection of its property by placing reliable regularly drilled forces to sustain me.[2]

The few government workers at the ungarrisoned armory would provide no deterrence should officials in Richmond decide to commandeer its fifteen thousand stands of arms; and in event of open rebellion, those arms would constitute a significant advantage to any enemy of the federal government. Holt added that there was little likelihood that Barbour, a Virginia-bred unionist of moderate stripe, would have overstated the danger.[3]

75

Holt had been enjoined by his superior—outgoing President Buchanan—to avoid stirring local unrest by making a great show of strength in garrisoning the armory. A small force had to be sent; yet one sufficient to hold the government stores for the present and, if necessary, to destroy them so they would be of no use to any rebels. A couple dozen soldiers could be rounded up and dispatched in a few days' time. As an officer intimately familiar with ordnance matters as well as artillery concerns, one of known prudence and political moderation, Hunt was Holt's first choice to lead those troops. It is also probable that Colonel Craig, who had directed Barbour's letter to Holt's attention, had recommended his son-in-law for the task, even at the risk of shortening his daughter's honeymoon.

Hunt must have been flattered by the assignment, especially as it indicated Holt's confidence in his loyalty, despite his avowed esteem for things Southern. But Holt knew the measure of his man; knew that no threat or entreaty could enlist Hunt in any campaign against his government, his flag, and his army.

That same day Hunt packed his belongings and eased himself apart from his bride of one week. From the Craig home he hastened to the Baltimore & Ohio depot, entraining for western Virginia.

The next morning he was at Harpers Ferry, scene of John Brown's unsuccessful antislavery raid of 1859. Alighting from one of the cars, he went directly to the armory, which fronted the Shenandoah River on its north shore, for a hurried conference with Superintendent Barbour.[4]

He was relieved to learn that no move had been made against the ordnance depot, though local rumor still had one in the making. Taking a careful survey of the armory's gunshops, machine shops, and warehouses, Hunt quickly discerned that such a wide extent of property could never be held by a few dozen soldiers, no matter how experienced and determined, should armed posses try to seize it. He then returned to his temporary lodgings in the vacant commanding-officer's quarters between Fillmore and South Cliff Streets, not far from the armory,[5] and wired Secretary Holt his findings. He received no immediate reply.

Four days after his arrival, sixty mounted cannoneers of the Second Artillery, direct from training camp at Carlisle Barracks, Pennsylvania, arrived on the scene, under command of thirty-one-year-old First Lieutenant Roger Jones, son and namesake of a former adjutant general of the Army.[6] The mismatch of artillerymen and their Mounted Riflemen commander suggested the haste with which the force had been collected. Hunt was pleased by the caliber of the troops, though still believing that such a force was incapable of making a strong show of force in a crisis.

Crisis was already a tangible fact in various parts of the South. On the day that Hunt reached Virginia, a secession convention had opened in Florida; and Georgia state troops had seized the United States garrison at Fort Pulaski, at the mouth of the strategic Savannah River. A day later,

Alabama militia took the government arsenal at Mount Vernon; and, on the fifth, two forts in Mobile Bay were occupied by state troops. During the next two days, a federal arsenal in Florida fell to state militiamen; a garrison at St. Augustine was taken over by the state; and members of Mississippi and Alabama secession conventions began deliberating.

Overt acts heralding war proliferated. On 9 January, while Hunt was positioning his men along various sectors of the armory grounds, Mississippi joined South Carolina in secession, followed the next two days by Florida and Alabama. No longer was it a matter of a single state defying the federal government. And on the ninth, full-scale war nearly erupted in Charleston harbor when a relief ship, dispatched from Washington, was fired upon by shore batteries. Thus ended the *Star of the West's* attempt to resupply Fort Sumter, where eighty-four artillerymen under Hunt's old tutor, Major Robert Anderson, seemed faced with starvation.

By 14 January, when Hunt again wrote the War Department for further instructions, he was acutely aware he might at any time be attacked by hostile troops able to legitimatize their violence as an act of war. But Secretary Holt's reply did nothing to ease his mind: Hunt was reminded that his command was not available "for purposes of defense against any powerful organized force. It is desirable to avoid all needless irritation of the public mind." He was cautioned against making "military display" in guarding the resources in his care, but must guard them nonetheless, and as tenaciously as humanly possible under the circumstances.[7]

By the last week in the month, despite the tension pervading western Virginia, Hunt's attention was drawn to events in far-off quarters. Not only did he worry about the young bride he had left behind, but he began to fear for the safety of his children.

A week after Hunt's remarriage, Colonel De Russy and his family had been transferred from Fort Monroe to a garrison in California. Rather than subject eight-year-old Emily and six-year-old Henry, Jr. to so long and arduous a trip, their grandparents had placed them in the care of their uncle, Major William A. Nichols, who had married Hunt's sister-in-law, Clara De Russy. The Hunt children had gone to live with the Nichols family in San Antonio, Texas, where the major served as adjutant general to Brevet Major General David E. Twiggs, the elderly Mexican War hero who headed the Department of Texas.[8] There, it was assumed, the children would be close to their father and stepmother, as soon as Hunt and his bride returned to Fort Brown following their wedding trip. Of course all had changed with Hunt's unexpected assignment in Virginia; now he had no idea when or if he could reach Texas.

And so his greatest worry concerned the secession fever now sweeping Texas. On 28 January—by which time Georgia and Louisiana had joined South Carolina, Mississippi, Florida, and Alabama in open rebellion—a secession council met in Austin. Four days later, the assembly voted to carry the state out of the Union. And on 23 February the state's electorate ratified this decision by a vote of almost thirty-five thousand to eleven thousand. By then, Hunt's children and their foster family were marooned in the midst of enemy territory.

San Antonio fell to the secessionists even before a popular referendum was called. On 18 February, General Twiggs—later to accept a major generalcy in the Confederate ranks—surrendered all the troops and military installations in his department, plus government property worth $1.2 million, to Texas Rangers and other state authorities—an act for which Secretary Holt would dismiss him from the United States Army on 1 March.[9]

Later Hunt learned that although the Nichols family had been part of the surrendered personnel and their dependents, none of its members had been harmed. In April, Twiggs permitted all soldiers and their families to be sent from the state under parole. Of course, they had to leave all military supplies behind.

Later, too, Hunt discovered that his brother-in-law had proved himself resourceful and courageous under pressure. A week before his commander's act of treachery, Major Nichols had smuggled a message noting Twiggs's intentions to Hunt's old crony, William French, then commanding Fort Duncan at Eagle Pass, Texas. Forewarned, French was able to flee overland to the Gulf of Mexico with his garrison troops, trundling valuable cannon behind them. From there the soldiers and cannon were shipped to safety in Key West, Florida.[10]

Equally fortunate was the garrison at Fort Brown, including Hunt's own company. Also given advance warning of Twiggs's actions, the troops snatched other heavy ordnance from the clutches of secessionists: these included the 12-pounder Napoleons, which Hunt had received at Fort Leavenworth in September of 1857. However, Company M and their garrison mates had been unable to salvage more than a handful of horses; therefore, they had still again been reduced to the status of foot artillery, their light cannon notwithstanding.

His mind was still burdened by the unresolved question of his children's fate when Hunt was called away from his job at Harpers Ferry and sent elsewhere. On 2 April, by which time he and Lieutenant Jones had worked out plans for destroying the armory to prevent its seizure, Hunt and fifteen of Jones's men were ordered to New York City, leaving the lieutenant and forty-odd others behind (a few of Jones's troops had recently been relieved of duty at Hunt's urging, for suspected secessionist leanings).[11]

Hunt left Harpers Ferry only two weeks before violence erupted. On the seventeenth, the state would adopt a secession ordinance, ratified by popular vote six weeks later; and, in the early evening of 18 April, Governor John Letcher would dispatch a couple thousand militiamen to take over the government property Hunt had guarded for three months. Acting according to their plan, Lieutenant Jones would ignite piles of straw and gunpowder distributed throughout the armory and arsenal buildings, transforming almost all fifteen thousand weapons into warped metal and charred wood. Afterward, Jones and his remaining men would escape over the Potomac River to safety, short steps ahead of pursuers.[12]

When he departed from western Virginia, Hunt had no inkling that all this would come to pass so soon; yet he sensed it would occur eventually. By now, secession and rebellion were more than topics of heated debate. On 4 February, representatives of the seceded states had assembled in Montgomery, Alabama, forming a confederation, adopting a constitution, making plans for appropriating war funds, and establishing their political hierarchy. For their president, the delegates had chosen Hunt's old nemesis: ex-War Secretary Jefferson Davis, more recently a United States senator from Mississippi. On 18 February Davis had been sworn into office. Only two weeks later, in Washington, a fellow-Kentucky native, Abraham Lincoln, had taken the oath of president of the United States.

Both Davis and Lincoln were strong-willed and determined in spirit; either could inaugurate war. But Lincoln would prove himself more given to speed and decisiveness than would Davis. A week after Hunt left Virginia for New York, the man in the White House would dispatch a new relief expedition to Charleston harbor. The act would provoke local rebels to open fire on Fort Sumter on Friday morning, 12 April: this in turn would prompt one Northern newspaperman to proclaim: "The ball has been opened at last!"[13]

* * *

After escaping from Fort Brown, Hunt's company M had been ordered to Fort Hamilton, in the Narrows, New York harbor. There, scene of his 1843–44 service tour, Hunt rejoined it on the morning of 3 April 1861. After greeting his old subalterns, he listened as Platt and Thompson provided full details of their near capture by Twiggs and the Texas Rangers, and their successful efforts to salvage their guns.[14]

All remained at Fort Hamilton for three days, during which Hunt wrote Mary and made repeated attempts to learn of his children's status in Texas. Ultimately, Emily and Henry would join him in New York, where they would remain in the Nichols fold for the duration of the war; Hunt's brother-in-law would spend much of his wartime service as adjutant general of the Department of the East, headquartered in the city, serving with the brevet rank of brigadier general of volunteers.[15]

Hunt had little time to wonder about what lay in store for his prodigal company. Its next mission had been mapped out even before his recall from Virginia.

During the last week in March the new president and his cabinet had met to consider resupplying not only Fort Sumter but other Southern garrisons not yet seized by rebels. One of those garrisons guarded what was considered the finest harbor on the Gulf of Mexico: Fort Pickens on the northwestern tip of Santa Rosa Island in Florida's Pensacola Bay. There, eighty-two members of Company G, First Artillery, under First Lieutenant Adam J. Slemmer, were sorely in need of reinforcements, as well as provisions.[16]

Following the *Star of the West* incident at Charleston, President Buchanan had declared a truce over Pickens and the four other army and navy installations in Pensacola. Nevertheless, on 6 February the transport *Brooklyn* had brought another company of troops to bolster Slemmer's garrison force. By late March, Buchanan's successor was convinced that the fort was in need of many more supports, now that Slemmer was under the guns of secessionists who had taken over all other garrisons in the harbor. Truce or no truce, Lincoln was determined that such supports would be sent.[17]

On Easter Sunday, 31 March, Lincoln and Secretary (of State) William Seward had directed army logisticians and administrators to draft plans whereby Lieutenant Slemmer might be reinforced and reprovisioned. Company M of the Second at Fort Hamilton, these officers discovered, was available in New York—the site from which the relief expedition would sail. Hence, recent orders had brought Brevet Major Hunt north from Harpers Ferry to lead it.[18]

On the evening of 6 April, in the midst of an unusual early spring snowstorm, the relief ship *Atlantic* steamed out of New York Harbor, carrying two companies of artillerymen, two of infantrymen, one of engineers —358 troops all told—and six months' worth of garrison provisions.[19] The entire detachment was under command of Hunt's regimental superior: Brevet Colonel Harvey Brown, an elderly West Pointer (class of 1818) in temporary command of the Second Artillery. Not until far at sea did Brown open the sealed orders given him by the War Department. Immediately afterward he informed Hunt and the rest of the expeditionary force, heretofore ignorant of the crucial details, about the precise nature of their mission and its ultimate destination. He also relayed the authority given him by his orders, by virtue of which he would, upon arrival at Fort Pickens, take command of all Federal troops in Florida.[20]

Hunt had mixed emotions over the assignment. Though glad to be on duty with his company once again, he could look ahead only to service as seacoast artillery. A colleague aboard the *Atlantic,* one who had helped plan this mission to Florida, noted his mood. Quartermaster Captain M.C. Meigs later wired Secretary Seward that Hunt was "somewhat depressed at going into the field without his horses . . . [his] company of well-trained artillerists finds itself, after eight years of practice in that highest and most efficient arm, the light artillery, going into active service as footmen." He conveyed Hunt's plea that efforts be made to remount the company in Florida, and he put in a special request (never heeded) that Hunt's unit be supplied with ninety of the strongest, best-trained battery horses available.

At the last, Meigs appended a statement of his high regard for the major, whom he had known since West Point days: "Such an officer should be encouraged, promoted, translated to that sphere to which his peculiar training and skill will be most useful to his country."[21] But the army would play deaf to these words also.

As well as by the lack of horses, Hunt was discomfited by the long voyage: he was anything but a sea dog. The trip proved especially rough when the *Atlantic* encountered a storm off Cape Hatteras, forcing her to lay to the wind a full twenty-four hours. As ever, Hunt persevered; he had no other choice.

The voyage, however, was made more bearable by the presence of old friends and friends-to-be. Among the latter were such shipboard mates as Lieutenant John C. Tidball, successor to Duncan and Hunt in charge of Company A of the Second Artillery; future cavalry general, Alfred Gibbs; future quartermaster chief, Rufus Ingalls; future infantry commanders, Godfrey Weitzel and George Hartstuff; and artillery Lieutenant Alexander Cummings McWhorter Pennington, who would later replace Hunt in command of light Company M. Other, more familiar faces would appear at Hunt's side after he reached Pensacola, including William Barry, whose dismounted light company would reach Fort Pickens in a later reinforcement expedition.

Fortified by such companionship, Hunt was in tolerable spirits by 13 April, when *Atlantic* reached Key West harbor. Three days later he sighted Pensacola Bay, and shortly before midnight on 16–17 April Hunt's ship unloaded half its human cargo on Santa Rosa Island. The next morning, Hunt and the other passengers followed their footsteps across the long island to Fort Pickens, meeting no resistance from the Florida state troops manning the guns at the forts across the harbor. Nor did the cannon speak on the twentieth, when a second relief ship, *Illinois,* entered the harbor and deposited more reinforcements and provisions on Santa Rosa.[22] Her arrival placed thirty-two officers and 926 enlisted men on the premises, more than enough to relieve the pangs of inadequacy shared by Lieutenant Slemmer and his artillerymen.[23]

Soon after stepping ashore, Hunt and his comrades from the *Atlantic* were apprised of the grim news from Charleston. On the morning of the thirteenth, Major Anderson had run up a white flag, after withstanding thirty-four hours of pounding from more than seventy cannon and mortars under Brigadier General P.G.T. Beauregard of the Confederate provisional army. Himself unharmed, with only a few of his men injured in the barrage, Anderson led his paroled garrison northward, where a hero's welcome awaited them. Finally, and formally, war had begun.

At Fort Pickens, Hunt took up the duties that Colonel Brown designated as his, including the emplacement of Company M's cannon, which had accompanied the expedition, to supplement Slemmer's garrison artillery.

When all guns were in place, Hunt became convinced that no degree of truculence by rebels across the bay could force the evacuation of this fortress. Certainly any full-scale attack against Santa Rosa Island would prove foolhardy.[24]

He was in the midst of refamiliarizing himself with the duties of a seacoast artilleryman when on the twentieth he received a letter of warm regard, tinged by bitter regret, from an old friend within the enemy's lines. The man whose Louisiana hospitality he had enjoyed a year ago was now Brigadier General Braxton Bragg of the provisional army of the Confederate States of America, who was in command of the rebel troops across the harbor from Fort Pickens, his headquarters at Fort San Carlos de Barrancas.[25] The kind thoughtfulness behind Bragg's greeting must have touched Hunt, though Bragg's denunciation of the Federal Union's tyranny deeply disturbed him. Yet he fully reciprocated Bragg's stated regret over the unfortunate status their relationship had attained.

Hunt spent two days drafting a reply, in which he purged himself of the anguish he had stored up as result of having to take sides and arms against old friends such as Bragg:

> How strange it is! We have been united in our views of almost all subjects, public and private. We still have, I trust, a personal regard for each other, which will continue whatever course our sense of duty may dictate, yet in one short year after exchanging at your house assurances of friendship, here we are, face to face, with arms in our hands, with every prospect of a bloody collision. How strange!
>
> My views on the immediate occasion of our trouble you know, they are yours; they are those, too, of my family, all of whom have fought in the North the [political] battles of the South. . . . [But] I think the South has not been just to themselves, nor generous to their friends in the North, in breaking off from them at the first partial defeat, the loss of the executive; all the other branches of government being in their hands. It is not a case in which *I*, born under the flag, can feel justified in deserting it, however much my sympathies were with my Southern friends in the immediate question at issue, and however much it pains me to be arrayed against them. I regret deeply that the secession leaders should have pursued such a course that except by dishonoring their flag, degrading their government and humiliating themselves, their friends in the North could not force an amicable separation. I am not much surprised at it however.

Hunt's might have been a letter written by any one of thousands of soldiers or soldiers-to-be, addressed to old friends who had become new enemies—even to his determined ability to look away into the darkness and glimpse a distant light:

> Notwithstanding this and the results that may immediately follow, I firmly believe that the unity of our people will be eventually restored.

We may have to suffer much. We may separate with or without further conflict, but we will be re-united, if necessary under new institutions, strong enough to secure all our rights. We shall again be one of the great powers of the earth and the name of America[n] will supersede that of Northerner and Southerner.

We must each, as you say, act according to the dictate of our consciences. Although you think my course a wrong one you know that I never have felt and I do not feel now, hostile to the South, her institutions or her people, nor can I have toward them the feelings of an "alien enemy". I trust and I believe notwithstanding the dark prospects before us, and although blood may flow like water, that the time will yet come, if neither of us fall in the struggle, when we will meet again not merely as friends, which I am sure we will continue to be, but as fellow citizens of a great, prosperous, happy and united country. . . .

We will not probably have much opportunity for communicating with each other, but my dear Bragg, continue to believe me as ever,

Your true and sincere friend,

Henry J. Hunt[26]

6

Savior of the Left Flank

For a time in April it looked as if war would begin at Fort Pickens. By the last week in May it seemed that events in Pensacola Harbor had lost all significance.

Foiled by the Yankee garrison's inaccessibility, Braxton Bragg contented himself with subjecting Fort Pickens to desultory cannonades from across the bay. He would not commit himself to a costly attack on the fortress, no matter what the wishes were of President Davis—especially after its reinforcement by Colonel Brown. By late June subsequent expeditions had raised the garrison's strength to 2,088 officers and men, and thereafter the Confederacy entertained no serious thought of attempting to batter it into submission. Until the end of the war, Pickens would remain in Federal hands.[1]

Annoyed by the tedium of stalemate, Brevet Major Hunt spent some of the most listless days of his career in late April and early May. Like the majority of his fellow countrymen, North and South, his attention had turned to more-decisive activity in Virginia and elsewhere. Already some skirmishes and engagements had been waged in the Old Dominion—most of them rebel victories—and a full-size battle seemed to be taking form not far below Washington City. That summer might see the single decisive campaign of the conflict. Hunt dreaded the prospect of spending that season confined to Santa Rosa Island.

Therefore he was vastly relieved when on 31 May word came that he and other members of Colonel Brown's relief force were to be sent to the Federal capital. They would be replaced at Pickens by a recently organized regiment of New York volunteer infantry.[2] Since these orders would also transfer both Barry and Tidball north, as soon as the volunteers arrived, it seemed obvious that the War Department had at last awakened to a fact that should have been plain enough to see long ago. With decisive campaigning shaping up in Virginia, a great percentage of the army's light-artillery strength, crucial to field maneuvering, had been confined to a stationary existence eight hundred miles to the south.

On 27 June, Hunt at last bade farewell across the bay to Bragg. Next day, along with his artillery colleagues, he boarded the steamer *Illinois* for the voyage home.[3] The return trip was even longer than the storm-delayed journey to Florida ten weeks before. It enabled Hunt and friends to anticipate events to occur in the near future, and to exchange worries, hopes, and regrets. All realized they would soon be battling old army companions. In so musing, Hunt must have conjured up the faces of Robert Lee, Joseph Johnston, Benjamin Huger, Cadmus Wilcox, and others who had cast their lot with their home states, rather than with their national government. Captain Barry's list of friends-turned-enemies was probably even longer; his West Point class of 1838 alone comprised a half-dozen officers who had joined the provisional army of the South, including the Creole stalwart, Beauregard (who had moved north from Charleston Bay to take charge of those forces gathering less than thirty miles southwest of Washington), and William J. Hardee, Henry H. Sibley, Edward Johnson, and Carter Stevenson.

Not until 12 July did *Illinois* slip into her berth in New York Harbor. Disembarking, her passengers found that the Empire City was astir with the bustle and commotion of wartime. Volunteer troops seemed everywhere, particularly the colorful, baggy-trousered, fez-capped Zouave outfits, their attire copied from uniforms worn by the Algerian army. Already New York, as had so many large cities and small towns in all quarters of the North, had sent dozens of her citizens-in-arms to Washington to meet the threat posed by the rebel army in Virginia. New units were embarking for the capital every day.

Unable to take time for a critical view of these enthusiastic amateurs, Hunt and his companions reported to the local military authorities. The officials handed them messages recently received via heliograph from the War Department: General-in-Chief Scott had ordered their immediate departure for the capital. All concerned hurried back to the harbor, loading their guns and baggage onto quartermaster's barges for a seaborne trip south.[4] Then—after Hunt had stolen a few hours to hold a reunion with his children at the Nichols' home—all started for Washington City aboard railroad cars already packed to their ceilings with boisterous volunteers.

On the fourteenth, arriving at their destination, they made a quick escape from the citizen-soldiers. Immediately, Hunt repaired to the Craig residence, where he swept up the bride he had not seen in six and a half months. He stayed only long enough to determine that she had not forgotten who he was. Then he hustled to the War Department to confer with the officer selected to organize and lead the first Federal field command during the rebellion: Irvin McDowell, a portly, goateed former major on General Scott's staff, who recently had won promotion to brigadier general. Though McDowell treated him cordially, Hunt was somewhat disappointed to learn that his superior had already selected Major Barry to be his artillery chief,

General William F. Barry (COURTESY, LIBRARY OF CONGRESS)

proving, if nothing else, that fraternity between West Point classmates was a durable bond.[5] Since Barry had Hunt's high regard, as well as a year of seniority, Hunt did not begrudge him this appointment.

After chatting with McDowell and probably also with Winfield Scott, Hunt went to the capital's quartermaster depot, where his company had been directed to assemble. Upon arrival, he found that Lieutenants Platt and Thompson had drawn enough horses to return M Company to mounted-artillery status.

He also learned that his cannon had not yet arrived from New York; however, John Tidball's had. Now, at Barry's request, Hunt gave his animals to Tidball, that Duncan's old company might be the first to take the field.

Finally, on the afternoon of the seventeenth, the barge carrying Company M's quartet of brass 12-pounders put in a belated appearance—whereupon Hunt discovered that some of its matériel had been damaged in transit.[6] With McDowell's thirty-one-thousand-man army of volunteers and Regulars ready to break camp, Hunt lost precious days restoring his equipment to working order.

He needed extra time for another vital chore. Since its last days on the frontier, his unit had received several recruits—including the fifteen that Hunt had brought with him from Harpers Ferry. (An additional twenty under a Lieutenant Brisbane had been dispatched from Carlisle Barracks, and even now were moving to join Hunt. These, however, would not reach Washington for several days.)[7] Many of the new men were woefully ignorant of the complexities of mounted-artillery service; so Hunt marched them into temporary camp on Capitol Hill and spent several hours drilling.

While he did, he grew acutely conscious of a dilemma that called for quick remedy. The recent additions had raised his company to a size that required a full wartime complement of officers, including a third and fourth lieutenant. The third was currently en route from Carlisle Barracks, and the fourth happened to be too ill to join Company M in the field. Thus, at a most critical time, Hunt's officer strength had been halved.

On the evening of the eighteenth, anticipating receipt of marching orders on the morrow, Hunt dined with Mary and her family on I Street; and, after the meal, over cigars and brandy, he discussed his problem with his youngest brother-in-law. First Lieutenant Presley O. Craig, an experienced artillerist, would have been in the field with his own company but for a recent tumble from a skittish horse, which had put him on crutches. Listening sympathetically to Hunt's plight, he agreed that Company M's lack of subalterns might prove a crucial handicap.

After Hunt had kissed Mary goodnight and returned to Capitol Hill, young Craig mulled over the predicament, remaining awake into the small hours. Just before dawn, he hobbled to his sister's room, woke her, and announced he was leaving to join Hunt in camp.[8] Despite Mary's protests and those by their parents, Presley, with the assistance of his orderly, maneuvered himself aboard his horse and, crutches strapped to his saddle skirts, rode to Capitol Hill. He of course received a hearty greeting from his brother-in-law, who accepted the offer of his services forthwith.

As Hunt had foreseen, the morning of the nineteenth brought orders that assigned him and his company to McDowell's army, and directed him to report to field headquarters, now far to the south.[9] With Presley beside him, he mounted, and his cannoneers took up perches on the limbers and caissons. Soon carriage and wagon wheels were spinning and spurs were brushing horses' flanks, and the outfit was moving toward the Potomac for the twenty-eight-mile trip to McDowell's new command post.

Technically, marching into his first campaign of the war, Hunt was no longer in command of Company M. While in Florida he had received word of his promotion to the full grade of major and of his transfer to a new outfit: the Fifth United States Artillery. Though not yet recruited, the regiment had been authorized by special proclamation of President Lincoln and would be formalized by an act of Congress in a few weeks' time.[10]

Hunt was gratified by the outfit's birth and by his connection with it, especially because it was to be composed exclusively of mounted field companies—units to be known by a term heretofore used only upon occasion: "batteries." At long last the government had perceived a decided need for light artillery as an adjunct to both infantry and cavalry power. Now, as in 1846, however, it had taken the outbreak of war to make the army see this need.

*　　*　　*

The wide, dusty road—well rutted from the passage of wagons and worn by thousands of hoof and heel marks—led Hunt and company to Centreville, Virginia. They arrived at their place of duty late that same afternoon and at once reported to McDowell's headquarters.[11]

Already Company M had missed much fighting, although this sun-drenched, sweltering afternoon in northern Virginia seemed placid enough. The previous day, one of McDowell's five infantry divisions had moved astride a creek named Bull Run, just south of Centreville, probing the right flank of General Beauregard's army. Though backed by ten thousand fewer effectives than his old West Point mate, Beauregard had reacted boldly. From his headquarters below the creek and near a strategic railroad depot—Manassas Junction—the Creole sent forward troops who caught the Federals unprepared for the fracas they stirred up. The fighting cost the Yankees eighty-three casualties—the rebels, far fewer; and ended with McDowell's fellows in hasty retreat northward.[12] Thus, this violent reunion of the USMA class of 1838 had seen Beauregard decisively victorious.

On the nineteenth, McDowell was kneading the pain from his injured command, and launching more-cautious reconnaissances. When Hunt appeared, the army leader had Major Barry direct him into position in the very sector that had seen action the previous day—a Bull Run crossing site known as Blackburn's Ford, on the Federal left flank. There Hunt and his company reported to the division commander who had directed Federal participation in that engagement: Brigadier General Daniel Tyler. In turn, Tyler sent them to the chief of his fourth brigade, Colonel Israel B. Richardson, an elderly, mildmannered but rugged old Regular, under whose immediate authority Hunt and his men would henceforth operate.

In Richardson's bailiwick abutting the ford, Hunt next day found himself beside a section of Lieutenant John Edwards's Battery G of the First Artillery.[13] Farther north, between Bull Run and Centreville, he found other, more familiar artillery cohorts: John Tidball, whose A of the Second had reached the scene the previous day, and Lieutenant Oliver D. Greene, commanding Battery G of Hunt's old regiment, the Second. Both Tidball and Greene had been attached to separate brigades of Colonel Dixon S. Miles's Fifth Division, most of which was in reserve near Centreville. But, along with a battery of New York volunteers, they would find themselves up front with Hunt and Edwards when the fighting resumed—and under Hunt's overall command. By virtue of seniority, the newly minted major had been given control over all artillery elements on the Union left.

The twentieth remained pacific, as had the previous day, which was fortunate, for Hunt had to continue training his raw recruits. Drill extended into the early hours of the twenty-first, during which period Hunt also aided pioneers and construction engineers in creating felled-tree emplacements to protect all the guns in that sector.[14]

Early on Sunday the twenty-first, a blood-red sun rose to proclaim another day of sweltering heat. By now, Hunt and his soldiers had been instructed to anticipate a rebel attack. In fact, McDowell would welcome such. His scouting missions finally over, the Union commander planned to launch a heavy feint near Hunt's position with Richardson's brigade and that of Colonel Thomas A. Davies, inviting a rebel counterstroke. While his enemy concentrated attention on his left, McDowell would strike from the other end of his battle line, hoping to toss the Confederates southward in confusion and defeat.[15]

Already Hunt had been ordered to move Platt's section of two cannon forward in advance of the rest of the company, as close to Blackburn's Ford as possible. Earlier that day, Edwards's unit had also been moved, forming an extension of the flank farther eastward. Hunt's remaining section, under the immediate guidance of Lieutenant Thompson, assisted by Presley Craig, remained unlimbered to the right of the ford road. Thanks largely to the pioneer and engineer teams, Company M's position was secure against direct assault, although a deep ravine on its eastern flank left it vulnerable in that direction. Infantry aides had attempted to assure Hunt that the gorge was under scrutiny by a full brigade of foot troops not far to the north. But neither staff officers nor field commanders heeded Hunt's suggestion that part of this brigade be formed in column on the brink of the ravine, ensuring its protection.

Richardson and Davies set about in midmorning to conduct their feint, doing so almost exclusively with their cannon. Platt's guns at the brink of the ford shelled the opposite shore, scattering some enemy units gathered there. Thompson's and Edwards's sections farther to left and rear did much less in the way of tangible destruction; Richardson used them to shell woodlots across the creek thought to be rebel sanctuaries.[16] This operation succeeded only in wasting ammunition—to Hunt's dismay.

As Hunt might have expected, the feint achieved indifferent success. At about ten that morning, with ammunition running low and the sun climbing high, Hunt was ordered to move both of his sections farther left, where Davies's brigade, having recently moved forward, had concentrated.[17] There M Company joined Edwards's gunners, hard against the ravine, in shelling other wooded areas south of the stream, easing the minds of infantry commanders who envisioned hordes of rebels hiding amid the trees. Hunt noted pointedly that this tactic "produced little or no effect, as there was no definite object, except when the enemy's moving columns came from time to time within our range." It would seem that the cannonade was designed more as a morale builder for the infantry than as a tactically effective artillery effort.[18]

For most of that day Hunt fought sunstroke rather than rebels. Eight miles farther west, however, Irvin McDowell's main thrust was rolling forward: there the conflict would be won or lost. On the far left, Hunt, Platt, Thompson, Craig, and their comrades in the ranks waited patiently, warding off listlessness and listening to the noisy progress of the battle in which they would take no part.

Perhaps this was well, for had they been engaged on the Union right they would have been mired in a fiasco. There McDowell was being outgeneralled by both Beauregard and his recently arrived associate, Joe Johnston, Hunt's prewar friend.[19] By 4 P.M. the offensive-minded Federals had not only been repulsed but routed. Volunteer recruits fled pell-mell to the rear, all unit formation suddenly gone, as though evaporated by the summer heat. Soon a gigantic traffic snarl would result, composed of quartermaster trains, sutler's wagons, gun batteries, and the conveyances of civilian spectators from Washington who had come to enjoy an improbable picnic on the fringes of the battlefield.

While the panic on the right and toward the rear neared its apogee, Hunt's people finally saw action. About 4:30 P.M., Company M's commander noted a movement of troops on his left. Eventually he detected approximately five thousand infantrymen and cavalrymen moving eastward parallel to his front and a few hundred yards off. Making no attempt at concealment, the soldiers were following a path that would carry them into the ravine adjacent to Hunt's position, from which, if the enemy, they might enfilade much of the Union line.

A myriad of Federal foot troops had recently been rushed into the fighting from the left flank; at first, Hunt and his colleagues assumed that these, too, were comrades. But, as their numbers increased, Hunt, squinting through his field glasses, began to suspect otherwise. On a hunch, he and his first sergeant, Terence Rielly, mounted and rode to the ravine, where a few infantrymen from Davies's brigade had finally been stationed. These men also assumed the oncomers to be friend, not foe. The advancing troops carried no visible colors and, at such a distance, their uniforms looked blue. Perhaps some were members of a New York regiment thought to be in the vicinity.

Hunt watched them draw nearer, until within effective rifle range. Suddenly he saw the truth. Losing not a second more, he and Sergeant Rielly spurred their horses back to the guns that had been maneuvered to bear on the approaching infantry and horsemen. Meanwhile, men from Davies's command rushed up to the ravine. But before all dispositions could be made, the oncomers halted and opened fire with a long, deadly volley, ending all doubt as to their identity.

Within a minute Hunt was ready to reciprocate with shrapnel and canister, his gunners with lanyards in hand. But at that juncture the troops that Davies had sent to support the artillery's flanks decided, instead, to form column at Hunt's rear. Fearing they would fire at the Confederates directly through his company, "destroying men and horses and crippling the guns," Hunt took several minutes he could ill spare to return the soldiers to the flanks. Then, at last, he ordered Platt, Thompson, Lieutenant Edwards, and all other officers within range of his voice, to open fire.[20]

The guns poured forth what Hunt later termed "the most rapid, well-sustained, and destructive fire I have ever witnessed." Only seconds before, the rebels had broken into a charge toward the cannon; Hunt's volley tore those members of Brigadier General D.R. Jones's brigade into human fragments. Taking time only to reload and reposition the cannon—completely oblivious to Hunt's normally enforced dictum on conservation of ammunition —the artillerists laced the oncomers time and again, Company M's light 12-pounders and Edwards's 20-pounder Parrott rifles doing equally formidable damage.[21]

At such murderously close range, Jones's men had no chance. One of the attackers, a sixteen-year-old Mississippian, later recalled:

> We sprang out of the ravine, and went up the hill at a double-quick. The Federal battery and infantry opened fire on us as soon as we emerged from the ravine, killing and wounding a number of us as we climbed the hill. A shell struck the ground and burst near me and threw up some rocks; one knocked me down, but I wasn't much hurt, and I jumped up and went on . . . we were confronted by an unexpected difficulty which changed the result of our attack from a certain victory to a repulse.[22]

Within fifteen minutes, seventy-six of Jones's soldiers had become casualties. These were relatively few, considering the size of the attacking brigade. Still, the speed with which such destruction had been inflicted almost entirely by artillery told Jones that his effort already was a mangled failure.[23] With cans of leaden balls hurtling all around, his survivors emulated their opponents on the other end of the field by scrambling rearward in wild retreat. However, even after they had taken refuge in woods across Bull Run, Hunt kept up a hail of metal, lobbing solid shot among the trees to ensure that a second assault would not be attempted.

Not until later would he learn the full significance of Jones's repulse. With only slight assistance from Davies's infantrymen, his gunners had broken up a formidable rebel effort to cut around the left flank and strike McDowell in rear, thus halting, or at least further complicating, the panicky retreat toward Centreville. Such a tactic, if successful, might have meant the annihilation of the already beaten Union army. Still, Hunt could glory in the immediate knowledge that he had turned back, with little difficulty, three infantry regiments and one company of cavalry, supported by a few guns of their own—even though he himself had nearly been captured before ordering a single salvo.[24]

When he turned from the sight of his fleeing enemy, however, he lost all heart for rejoicing. Only one artillerist had gone down in the fighting: Presley Craig. Hunt rushed to where his brother-in-law had fallen, blood congealed on his youngish face from a bullet wound in the forehead. But Presley's eyes were tightly closed, and Hunt saw that they never would reopen.

* * *

Much against his will, Hunt and his command became part of McDowell's retreat. A short time after Jones's Confederates repaired to their woodlots, Colonel Davies instructed all the artillery in Hunt's sector to fall back on Centreville. Thus, Company M limbered up, Lieutenant Craig's body carried upon a lead horse. Slowly, Hunt led the unit north, as sunlight and heat faded.

But their battle was not over. Noting the withdrawal, the Confederates emerged from their woods and began to pepper them with minié balls at long range. Those at the tail end of the column began to panic, and up went the frantic cry: "To the trot!"

In no mood to brook the chaos such a rapid gait might occasion, Hunt rode to the rear and quelled the clamor. He ordered the march resumed, as before, at a walk, calming the nerves of all concerned. As he had foreseen, the enemy, too demoralized to follow, appeared content to remain below Bull Run.

Perhaps a mile from Centreville, Hunt's company came upon a knot of tangled traffic: ambulances, teamster wagons, and miscellaneous batteries clogging one another's path; and blue-coated men of all arms and ranks, Regulars and volunteers alike, milling about in confusion and high anxiety. Hunt raised his strident voice to its loudest, calling for order. It was finally restored when he explained with calm deliberation that his guns had quailed the rebels; they would mount no pursuit. Assured by the confidence he exuded, stragglers sorted themselves out, extricated their conveyances, and smoothly renewed the retreat. Early that night, all reached Centreville safely, where McDowell himself thanked Hunt for his coolheaded assistance.[25]

The next morning, Company M, at the very end of the retreat column, arrived outside Washington at Fort Albany. There Hunt found that fame had preceded him. At once he was summoned to the War Department, where old General Scott pronounced himself pleased that Hunt's conduct at Bull Run had been "noble, noble." He added, however, that he had fully expected as much of him.[26]

7

Enter Little Mac

Beyond the pervasive tragedy of defeat, there was much sadness in Hunt's return to the capital. It culminated in his trip to the Craig home with the remains of a beloved son and brother. Hunt may well have held himself at least partially responsible for Presley's death, which plunged his family into mourning. But the Craigs held no grievance and sought no recrimination. A military family of long tradition, they had steeled themselves in advance of such a tragedy. In fact, they would furnish Hunt with a replacement for his fallen aide: the next year, Presley's older brother, John, would join his staff as adjutant general.

Though he wished more time could be spent with his bereaved wife—especially since she was seven months pregnant—Hunt had to depart the Craig household soon after reentering it. With McDowell's bloody and disorganized army streaming homeward, having suffered 2,645 casualties at Bull Run against Beauregard's and Johnston's 1,981 losses, and with the Federal artillery especially battered, Hunt was urgently required at field headquarters.

He threw himself into his remedial work so thoroughly that by the morning of the twenty-third he had been hard at work ministering to artillery wants for almost twenty-four straight hours. On that day, in recognition of his talents as administrator as well as field leader, he was named commander of all artillery units south of the Potomac River; his official title: Chief of Artillery, Department of Northeastern Virginia.[1]

The job of piecing together so many shattered batteries taxed his energies to their limit. In addition to being held responsible for the repair and future maintenance of several units too crippled even to limp across the bridges into the capital, he found himself pressed to provide for the upkeep of almost twenty fortifications surrounding Washington below the river, garrisoned by a heterogeneous assortment of Regulars and volunteers. The former were too few to impart widespread efficiency to the work; many of the latter were too short of know-how to justify their claim to the title of artillerists. Still Hunt proceeded with vitality and precision, endeavoring to ascertain and supply the needs of all in his charge, as well as to work in concert with engineer Captain Barton S. Alexander in drawing up a system of regulations for the armament and staffing of as-yet-unfinished forts on the Potomac. These regulations were deemed so valuable that the army published them in three editions between 1861 and 1864 for wide dissemination within the War Department, particularly in the Corps of Engineers.[2]

At least one major event at this time lightened Hunt's burden—and raised his spirits: on 26 July the embodiment of military revival and restoration reached Washington in the guise of a dapper, squat, mustachioed, and vigorous officer with whom Hunt had enjoyed infrequent contact since their first meeting fifteen years before near Vera Cruz, Mexico—Major General George B. McClellan, who had come east from Ohio and western Virginia to rescue McDowell's army from the doldrums of defeat.[3]

Aware that he and McClellan shared many sentiments, political and ethical as well as military, Hunt gave hearty greetings to the hero of the campaign beyond the Alleghenies. "Little Mac" reciprocated his cordiality, and at once made known his desire to attach Hunt to his staff as soon as possible.

Hunt's emotional renewal at McClellan's arrival quickly proved justified. Almost from the moment he stepped down from the Baltimore and Ohio express, the young general was absorbed in transforming McDowell's bulky rabble—soon swollen by a flood of recruits into an army well over 120,000—into an effective and mobile fighting machine. He strove to instill in all an overwhelming spirit of self-reliance and self-confidence based on a thorough grasp of the basics and nuances of soldiering—something McDowell had failed to provide. Within weeks, thanks to his guiding genius, and despite what McClellan considered the fogeyism and intrigue of General Scott (who in November he would displace as general-in-chief of all the Federal forces), the army seemed transfigured. The raw recruits knew the joy of decent training, proper rations and equipage, regular pay, well-policed camps, and strict but fair discipline. They had begun to think of themselves as soldiers in the professional sense—as well as future victors in the field. Soon they would appear eager, not merely willing, to return to active campaigning—this time to throttle the Confederates who, by some unaccountable fluke, had whipped them at Bull Run.[4]

Such a wholesale revival had an immediate and inevitable impact on the Federal artillery. Within eight months Little Mac would accomplish a remarkable transformation of Hunt's arm, thereby winning the artillerist's undying esteem.

On the day McClellan took command of his so-named Army of the Potomac, only nine "imperfectly equipped" batteries were available in Washington and vicinity, with only one fit for service south of the Potomac and, thus, under Hunt's immediate supervision.[5] All told, the artillery

General George B. McClellan (COURTESY, LIBRARY OF CONGRESS)

encompassed thirty guns, 650 men, four hundred animals, and a wholly inadequate stock of projectiles, carriages, fuzes, and other matériel. But the return of field campaigning in the spring of 1862 would find the capital overflowing with ninety-two fully equipped batteries, 520 cannon, eleven thousand artillery horses, and 12,500 cannoneers.[6] These statistics not only testify to the tremendous economic power of the industrial North; they indicate the enormous organizational burden that McClellan successfully handled through the initial, formative months of civil war.

Not that he effected the transfiguration singlehandedly, however. Major Barry, whom Little Mac maintained in direct command of the artillery, carried much responsibility in pushing the project toward fruition. Fortunately, like his superior, Barry was a superb administrator (more talented in this capacity, in fact, than as a battle leader). And beneath Barry, of course, was Hunt, who combined equal abilities as administrator and front-line commander. Thus, in actuality, it was a triumvirate of officers who put well-laid plans into effect, for resurrecting the cannon units of the main Federal army in the East, which soon would become the best-trained, best-equipped, and best-officered artillery in American history.

The trio's program of renewal was set in motion late in July, when the first artillery rendezvous, Camp Barry, sprang into existence along the dusty road to Bladensburg, Maryland, a few miles east of the unfinished Capitol.[7] There its namesake and commander collected all batteries—Regular and volunteer, intact and disabled—that had reported before or shortly after Bull Run. At Camp Barry the rebuilding, refitting, and retraining proceeded under the guidance not only of Barry and Hunt but of dozens of other experienced Regulars—officers, noncoms, even enlisted men—from the few prewar light companies. Some of the volunteer recruits also received guidance from the Hunt-Barry-French revised tactics, which Congress reprinted in limited quantity and distributed among the untried units.[8]

An atmosphere of spit-and-polish gradually materialized, enhanced by McClellan's successful bid to bolster his ranks with at least half the Regular Army's now-mounted companies. Yet Regular discipline and deportment constituted the extent of the contributions made by most of the men of these units. Years of service as foot artillery or solely as seacoast and garrison cannoneers meant that most of them, like the pea-green volunteers, had to be tutored patiently in the rudiments as well as the fine points of mounted artillery service.

Organization began to assume definite shape at the end of July, when Barry, at McClellan's request, drew up a list of administrative principles that were to govern the army's artillery. These rules, some suggested by Hunt and all later adopted by army headquarters, instituted such reforms as uniformity of cannon caliber within each battery; the apportionment of at least two and a half and preferably three guns for every one thousand infantrymen; the designation of at least four and ideally six pieces as standard content for each battery; the distribution of these batteries by attachment to army divisions (i.e., to approximately twelve thousand troops) rather than to the smaller and more numerous brigades, as McDowell had seen fit to practice at Bull Run—to the detriment of centralized administration; and the grouping of three volunteer batteries and one Regular battery for attachment to each division. The last was a particularly inspired edict: its proportion was realistic, in view of the more numerous volunteer units that would henceforth become available to McClellan; and the ratio was also efficient, due to the nucleus of general experience that the Regulars would lend their volunteer neighbors in the field.[9]

Hunt's guiding influence was most evident in additional principles that called for the organization of an Artillery Reserve and a siege train. Both would remain his pet projects throughout the conflict.

As its name implied, the Artillery Reserve would be a separate auxiliary —initially of one hundred guns—for those artillery units attached to the main army. But its functions would not be limited to the replacement and reinforcement of front-line batteries. As Hunt himself later explained:

> In marches near the enemy it is often desirable to occupy positions with guns for special purposes: to command fords, to cover the throwing and taking up of bridges, and for many other purposes for which it would be inconvenient and unadvisable to withdraw their batteries from the troops. Hence the necessity for a reserve of artillery.

A siege train would serve for stationary operations when time permitted the emplacement of the heaviest and most cumbersome of those cannon able to be lugged into the field: 30-pounder Parrotts, 4.5-inch ordnance rifles, and 8-inch howitzers. Though constituting a drain on the army's maintenance facilities and a hindrance to troop mobility, Hunt considered a siege train "an almost indispensable part of the organization when operating in an enemy's country."[10]

Both of those special artillery commands called for chiefs of varied organizational and administrative skills. Such officers were not lacking. Barry tendered the command of the siege force to the former head of the quartermaster depot in Washington, more recently the colonel of the First Connecticut Heavy Artillery: Robert O. Tyler, a husky, cherubic-faced ex-Regular of thirty. He would serve in this capacity, with great efficiency, for the next two years.

The man chosen to head the Artillery Reserve would serve with even greater efficiency: Major Henry Hunt. When given command of this massive unit on 12 September, Hunt, in effect, was designated second-in-command of the cannon outfits in McClellan's army.[11]

Of course he was gratified to have received such a responsible post, a clear indication of the respect in which his superiors held him. In fact, he was doubly gratified, for the assignment placed him in immediate command of a single, cohesive force. Ironically, Major Barry would not exercise as much direct authority as his chief subordinate. Though nominally in overall charge of every battery in Washington, including those in Hunt's Reserve, Barry would not be allowed to practice tactical supervision in the field without special permission from McClellan. Distributed among and attached to the elements of the main army, most of his batteries would come under the effective jurisdiction of infantry and cavalry-division commanders.

For obvious reasons, neither Barry nor any other conscientious artillerist thought this the most desirable arrangement. Soon after McClellan announced his willingness to keep Barry at the same post as he had held at Bull Run, the artillery chief had prodded his commander for full tactical authority as well as administrative supervision over the arm. At McClellan's order, a board of officers had then convened to explore the implications of Barry's request, with particular reference to artillery command procedures in foreign armies. When the board found that such procedures varied widely, it offered no clear-cut recommendations of its own. Thus, McClellan decided the issue on the basis of his own judgment, eventually announcing in published orders: "The duties of the chief of artillery and cavalry are exclusively administrative, and these officers will be attached to the headquarters of the Army of the Potomac." Thereafter, both Barry and Brigadadier General George Stoneman, head of the cavalry in the Army of the Potomac, served as glorified staff officers when in the field.[12]

Simple logic seemed to justify Little Mac's decision. His batteries scattered throughout the army, Barry could not be expected to be everywhere at once, in contact with all of them and issuing orders to guide their every movement. But trouble would result from the sanctioned practice by which division commanders would control the cannon attached to their units. Since few of these generals were personally acquainted with the subtleties of artillery employment, disaster would accrue from some of the instructions they issued to the battery officers. Each division leader would have a single artillery chief (originally the commander of the Regular battery attached to the division), but the chief would rarely rank higher than captain, at least during the early stages of the war. Thus, the single and double-starred division commanders could and would overrule such officers with impunity, frequently substituting their own ill-conceived judgment for the wise advice of their cannon chiefs.[13]

This unhappy situation was linked with another more complex dilemma regarding rank. As in all other arms of the service, artillery, at least on paper, had its full share of field-rank officers: majors, lieutenant colonels, and colonels (though from earliest days it always seemed to have relatively fewer of this endangered species than did infantry or cavalry). Most of these field officers, however, had had no experience in the tactical employment of mounted artillery. They had served strictly as foot-artillery administrators,

while mere captains had commanded those companies—such as Hunt's—
which in prewar times had been privileged to become light artillery. Therefore, few if any of these officers of field grade could be expected to perform
properly in the line during the campaigning that lay ahead. For this reason
the War Office soon reduced all of them, like Barry, to staff duties.

Even Hunt, with his long-term concern over lack of artillery rank,
admitted the justification in this ruling. But trouble arose when the high
command would not alter its decree to conform to unforseen circumstances.
As the war progressed, all artillery officers, including most of those of field
grade, would become thoroughly conversant with the complexities of light
artillery useage. But the law discouraging their service as tactical commanders
would still stand.[14]

This was, of course, bad enough. Yet the War Department not only
discriminated against field-rank artillerists; it did not much care for artillery
generals, either.

This lack of appreciation had roots in past precedent: Even in Mexico
in 1846–48 the highest-ranking artilleryman had been a colonel. Now, in
the fall of 1861, Adjutant General Lorenzo Thomas stated the official reason
why this restriction should be moderated only slightly, despite the volunteer-
induced increase in the size of the Federal artillery. The basic artillery
administrative unit, the company (or battery), was, said Thomas, the
equivalent of an infantry company and a cavalry troop. Laws long in force
stipulated that only one general officer could be appointed per each forty
infantry companies or cavalry troops. Since General McClellan was then
projecting a field force of sixty batteries, the artillery *was* entitled to a
brigadier general—but one only.[15]

This ruling destroyed McClellan's wish to appoint Hunt, as well as
Barry, to a brigadier general of volunteers. Little Mac had to display some
fancy footwork to secure any advancement at all for him. The alternative
was to lose Hunt's expertise altogether, since as a lowly major he risked
being overruled by less-able volunteer officers already mustered into service
as lieutenant colonels and full colonels of artillery. In the end, McClellan
resorted to the use of a recently enacted law, which authorized the appointment of volunteer or Regular officers as "additional aides-de-camp." Thus,
on 28 September, Hunt won a colonelcy—the highest rank an aide could
then attain—but only by the ruse of being assigned to McClellan's headquarters as a staff officer.[16]

Though forced to accept a rank lower than Little Mac felt him entitled
to, Hunt was favorably disposed to the spanking-new colonel's uniform he
was issued. Though still a full-rank major in the Fifth U.S. Artillery, his
new rank in the volunteers would enable him to wield more power than
might have been bestowed upon him after another twenty years of service
in the Regulars.

Then, too, although he might revert to his majority at the close of the present hostilities, there was always the chance that recognition of his services in the field would win him a higher rank in the Regular service as well as in the volunteer ranks.

* * *

To complement the rugged handsomeness of his new attire, he followed a fashion trend by cultivating a full-size beard—a wide contrast to the clean-shaven look that had characterized him and most of his fellow officers in earlier decades. He had his likeness taken while wearing his colonel's uniform, standing erect and dignified, one hand thrust into his tunic in Napoleonic fashion—a somber backdrop casting his martial splendor in high relief. With beard combed, uniform as free of wrinkles as if ironed while he wore it, and with a spotless paper collar and white kid gloves, he looked, for one of the few times in his life, like a pugnacious fop. But this effect would die soon enough; a few weeks of service in Virginia would turn both uniform and beard into something less than any dandy would affect.

He wore his dress uniform on several civil occasions other than this. On 30 September, Conway Hunt was born into the family, tangible evidence of his father's commitment to a new life following an interval as a widower. And on the sixteenth of November the infant was christened by the same Episcopal rector who had performed Hunt's marriage to Mary Craig. At the ceremony the proud parents were joined by Hunt's brother-in-law from his first marriage, Captain Gustavus De Russy, the child's sponsor, as well as by a close friend of the family, Robert d'Orleans, the duc de Chartres. Like his uncle, the French Prince de Joinville, the duke was a military observer at McClellan's headquarters as well as, like Hunt, a commissioned officer on Little Mac's staff.[17]

Following the christening and a small reception at the Craig residence, the young French nobleman went directly to army headquarters, while Captain De Russy followed his West Point friend Hunt to Camp Duncan, a training rendezvous on a muddy plain just east of the Capitol and not far from Camp Barry. At the rendezvous Hunt had ensconced his Artillery Reserve; there De Russy belonged: he had recently been assigned to duty as one of his brother-in-law's subordinates.

Many other allies of long association served in Hunt's new command, including John Tidball, whose company was now serving as horse artillery; Henry C. Benson, who recently had succeeded Hunt in command of Company M of the Second; and William Hays, Hunt's fellow lieutenant in Duncan's company during and immediately after the Mexican campaign, now a captain with a battery of his own. Unlike Hunt, all of these officers had been assigned to duty according to their old rank in the Regulars.

Thus, the leader of McClellan's supporting artillery was privileged to have under him men with whose talents and skills he was familiar. Such

Colonel Henry J. Hunt, 1861 (COURTESY, LIBRARY OF CONGRESS)

officers would prove of invaluable assistance in solving a plethora of problems that threatened to hinder the training programs now in progress at Camp Duncan. However, it seemed beyond even their ability to rectify other troubles.

Some of those problems were inevitable. Even after two months of training, a great many of the volunteer officers and men, in late autumn, were far from expert in light-artillery tactics. The hopelessly incompetent had long ago been weeded out by officers' examining boards, though in some cases replacements almost as inept had risen to power through the unfortunately tolerated practice of battery personnel electing their own officers.[18] This popular-election concept more than faintly hinted at a military egalitarianism that, in itself, constituted a vexing problem. Years afterward an old-line artillerist recalled:

> The officers knew but little more of their profession than the men, sometimes not so much, and this added to the impossibility of destroying, at once, that perfect equality between officers and men, the existence of which in a regular force would make discipline out of the question.[19]

By no means was this the extent of Hunt's troubles as Reserve chief. He also had to find enough equipage for the volunteer batteries that had reported to Camp Duncan, fewer than ten percent of which having arrived in condition fit for field duty. Here the pressing need was a sufficient number of cannon of uniform caliber and design, a task made all but impossible by contractors and foundry managers who had brought a vast heterogeneity of cannon into the field. Inevitably, this had led to unwise purchasing by the War Department. For example, an order placed by outgoing Secretary (of War) Simon Cameron, only a few days after Bull Run, called for the purchase of three hundred iron cannon—two hundred of them rifled—rather than a sufficient supply of the brass smoothbore Napoleons, which Hunt and many of his most highly respected colleagues favored.[20]

Hunt's list of dilemmas went on. Since the high command treated him as a staff officer—in the formal sense at least—it had provided him no staff of his own to assist in handling the numerous organizational tasks that had devolved upon him. Then, too, as autumn progressed, illnesses, including an outbreak of typhoid fever, ravaged Camp Duncan, creating all manner of manpower problems.[21] Still another personnel shortage came when Hunt found some of his most experienced subordinates defecting to infantry and cavalry service, in which they enjoyed greater opportunities to win the high rank and authority every self-respecting officer craved.

Despite so many hindrances, Hunt's war-child experienced rapid growth. In mid-October he had had on hand eight fully equipped batteries of six cannon each. By the fourth week in December the number had climbed to thirteen. And in February of 1862 he was authorized to group this total into several brigades—an organizational system that would remain in use throughout the upcoming campaigning. However, during that service the number of batteries would continue to rise, eventually totalling twenty. Of these, eleven were Regular units, including a few from Hunt's own regiment, the Fifth Artillery. In some cases, pairs of understrength companies from older regiments were merged, forming a combined unit known by the name of both its components; for example, E/G of the First United States. Each consolidated battery, as all single units in wartime, maintained six cannon.

At General McClellan's urging, Hunt placed as the leaders in the first two of his brigades a pair of trusted acquaintances: William Hays and George W. Getty—the latter a Fifth Artillery cohort. Their appointment came about logically, since by this time both had benefited from the same law via which McClellan had elevated Hunt; as lieutenant colonels of volunteers, they were his ranking subordinates. Paradoxically, in view of artillery's serious shortage of field officers, two of Hunt's other brigade chiefs were also of field grade. Majors Albert Arndt and Edward R. Petherbridge were, however, citizen-soldiers from states operating under the soon-to-be-discontinued artillery regimental system. Only the duo's extraordinary proficiency had prompted Hunt to appoint volunteer officers as his leading lieutenants. Finally, an old veteran, Captain J. Howard Carlisle of the Second Artillery, headed up the Reserve's fifth brigade, its smallest with only three full batteries on its roster. Of all the brigades, only the first was not conventional light artillery to be attached to infantry commands. Hays's First Brigade—which included Tidball's battery—was composed entirely of horse artillery.[22]

During this first autumn and winter of the war, Hunt could not be indicted for indolence. In addition to nurturing the several batteries and brigades, he was compelled to spend time sitting on two artillery boards. The first of these, of which he was named president, was convened to test various models of field guns and their several types of projectiles. The second panel was organized to recommend improvements in seacoast garrison armaments to conform to the latest advances in naval firepower.[23]

Eventually both boards submitted valuable proposals for the benefit of McClellan and the War Office, though many closely paralleled reforms that had already been instituted or suggested by both Hunt and Barry. Other findings, however, indicate that the president of the Board to Test Field Artillery and Ammunition had been overruled at least once: such as the published statement citing the value to horse artillerymen of the 3-inch ordnance rifle—a cannon that Hunt later called "the feeblest in the world." Still other recommendations, such as equipping each field battery with eight light cannon, saw no wartime adoption.[24]

Not even board work rounded out Hunt's duty schedule during late 1861 and early '62. Upon occasion, he also inspected and evaluated certain ordnance matériel, which private contractors sought to sell (and sometimes foist upon) the government. Several of these duties carried him far afield; such as that which called him to New York City in January to pass judgment on an embryonic ironclad with the improbable name of the *Stevens Floating Battery*. Like a good many imaginative but impractical devices that came under Hunt's close scrutiny that season, Mr. Stevens's marvelous creation sank from sight of the War Department.[25]

* * *

With his time so fully occupied, it was fortunate that Hunt was not called on to haul his embryonic command out of camp for premature field use. McClellan, a most patient organizer (overly patient, according to time-conscious critics), allowed his 120,000 men to loll in fixed camp, wearing down the drill plains, until the tag end of the cold-weather season. Yet, several times during the winter-quarters period, false alarms of rebel attacks placed Hunt's people on standby. Most were the work of jittery picket officers who had never forgotten the vulnerability of the capital before and shortly after First Bull Run.[26] Despite the frenzied mobilizations that followed these warnings—which Hunt uncharitably termed "stampedes" —McClellan confidently predicted, even before winter arrived, that his force was strong enough to withstand "*any* attack—I care not in what numbers." Yet he would commence no offensive "until I have reasonable chances in my favor."[27]

Here lay his vexing flaw. McClellan rarely waxed confident about taking up active campaigning. He seemed so unwilling to commit his disciplined, well-drilled army to the field that, eventually, President Lincoln resorted to any means to prod him into action. It seemed to do no good; well into the new year of 1862, several months after his appointment to army command, several weeks after succeeding Scott as leader of all the armies of the Union, Little Mac still idled away the days in the sung confines of fortress Washington.

At length, in view of the intense activity apace in the western theater of the war, where a general was winning fame under the sobriquet "Unconditional Surrender" Grant, Lincoln could no longer brook McClellan's inertia. Late in February, via direct order, he compelled Little Mac to move south. The commanding general stalled for time by substituting a grand plan of strategy for the president's simple and direct notions of advancing against the enemy. Finally, after much revision to conform to fluctuating dispositions among the Confederates, McClellan worked out a plan for a general advance by sea to the tip of the Virginia peninsula. From Fort Monroe his army would hike up the eighty-mile-long isthmus, along the line of the York River, passing towns such as Yorktown and West Point, and through the rear door into Richmond.[28]

Lincoln, a talented amateur at strategy (far more talented, in truth, than many of the military commanders running his war), had reservations about McClellan's intent to strip the Washington defenses for the campaign, and especially about Little Mac's notion that he was to operate against the enemy's capital rather than the enemy's army. Lincoln put aside his worries only when deciding that the principal rebel army—Joe Johnston's understrength command, still in the Bull Run-Centreville area (P.G.T. Beauregard had been sent to Tennessee to oppose Grant)—would perforce fall back upon Richmond when McClellan headed that way. Reluctantly, but resignedly, the president gave his approval to McClellan's strategy and ordered him to carry it out forthwith. Just as reluctantly, the general whom the newspapers loved to call the Young Napoleon, complied.

On the tenth of March, the Army of the Potomac at last moved from its camps, its advance elements marching toward the wharves of Alexandria, Virginia: there, to board dozens of convoyed transports for the trip down the coast to Rebeldom. On that morning Colonel Henry Hunt kissed his wife and infant son goodbye, donned his ornamented forage cap, tugged on his white gloves, mounted his warhorse, and, trailed by a small group of subordinates and orderlies, trotted out the Bladensburg Road to his headquarters. There, soon afterward, while bugles blared and guidons rippled in the frosty breeze, he led forward a column of mounted cannoneers and a formidable array of one hundred ordnance pieces—all bound for the seat of war.

8

Murder on Malvern Hill,
Hell at Antietam

On 23 March the forward contingent of the Army of the Potomac disembarked at Fort Monroe; not until the first week in April, however, did it start moving. While comrades still rode the Potomac River and Chesapeake Bay, advance regiments began a ponderous crawl up the peninsula along the south bank of the York, bound for what they supposed was the gateway to final victory.

If superiority in numbers indicates a decisive advantage, this army had already won its war. When the last of his people landed, McClellan would have over one hundred thousand effectives on the peninsula; 3,600 wagons, seven hundred ambulances, three hundred cannon, 2,500 head of beef cattle, and more than 25,000 horses and pack mules; plus millions of rations, quartermaster's, and medical provisions. To match the elements of the largest amphibious expedition in American history, the Confederate States army could muster a bit more than half as many soldiers and much less in rations, forage, and matériel.[1]

His debarkation at Hampton Roads symbolized a homecoming for Colonel Hunt. The fort there had been the scene of some of his most memorable years in uniform, and in the nearby town of Hampton (much of which retreating rebels had lately put to the torch) rested the mortal remains of Emily De Russy Hunt.[2] And ahead sprawled Yorktown, where Hunt's grandfather had enjoyed the fraternity of Lafayette, Hamilton, and other stalwarts of the Continental army.

Hunt could share this filial association with another, not far away on the ancient road to Yorktown, who could fully appreciate it. Lewis Hunt, now a captain in the Fourth Infantry, was another member of McClellan's mighty phalanx. Early in February he had come east with his outfit, following garrison duty in California, Utah, and the Washington Territory. Now his regiment formed part of a brigade in the Union II Corps, under Brigadier

General Silas Casey, who had been Lewis's regimental commander in the Far Northwest and, two years ago, had become his father-in-law as well. Lewis, his young wife Abby, and their infant daughter had set up residence in Washington, not far from the Craig home.[3]

Hunt's Reserve must have attracted wide attention along the trail to Yorktown, especially from Lewis and his infantry comrades. Certainly these foot soldiers shuffling along in front and rear could hardly ignore its massive presence or the rich quality of its composition. By now the unit comprised eighteen batteries, most of six guns: thirty-four light 12-pounder cannon, thirty 3-inch rifles, ten 10-pounder Parrott rifles, twenty 20-pounder Parrotts, and six 32-pounder howitzers. Of these, four batteries' worth (twenty-four of the 3-inch guns) were horse artillery.[4] Each battery towed portable forges, blacksmith's wagons full of farrier's tools, rations, forage stock and miscellaneous baggage, and other wagons crammed full of administrative paraphernalia and special tools for the care and feeding of the big guns. Behind all these conveyances rumbled a one hundred-wagon train, holding thousands of rounds of ammunition. With the permission of McClellan's chief quartermaster, Colonel Rufus Ingalls, Hunt had draped black waterproof cloth over the tops of the ammo wagons to increase their visibility when events demanded their quick location.[5] This inspiration would prove highly valuable on more than one occasion.

Adding to Hunt's command Colonel Tyler's train of one hundred of the heaviest cannon available,[6] plus the field army's two hundred-gun supply of light artillery (almost all of them 12-pounder Napoleons, 10-pounder Parrotts, and 3-inch rifles), it becomes vividly clear that George McClellan intended to blast Richmond into rubble with the most mammoth display of ordnance in military history. It appears that he hoped this vast superiority in weaponry, as well as in manpower, would prompt Confederate officials to flee their capital even before the Federals began their siege. This would seem eminently in keeping with Little Mac's strategic philosophy: he was captivated by a desire to seize victory, not by outfighting his enemy, but by outmaneuvering him and wearing him down psychologically with, for example, his awesome military might.[7]

At first, he did outmaneuver the Confederates. His amphibious movement down the coast had mystified Joe Johnston, still in position near the Rappahannock. Long after McClellan's drive commenced, Johnston sat immobile far above Richmond; when finally he saw McClellan's intent, he frantically shifted south toward the peninsula, but too late to prevent his adversary from capturing Richmond should he keep moving. Fewer than fifteen thousand troops of all arms were in position to meet McClellan's advance, stationed in and about Yorktown along the line of the Warwick River, about seventeen miles northwest of Fort Monroe. These soldiers, under former artilleryman John Magruder, now a major general in the Confederacy, should have posed no great barrier to McClellan.[8]

General Lewis Cass Hunt (COURTESY, LIBRARY OF CONGRESS)

So everyone believed but McClellan himself. Hamstrung by a hesitancy to accept battle, a hesitancy that increased with each stride taken toward his opponents, he allowed his advance to grind to a halt outside Yorktown on 5 April. Fearing the city heavily defended, he sent Major General Erasmus D. Keyes's IV Corps on a long flank drive to strike Yorktown from the rear—a drive halted by the Warwick which, aided by adjacent defenses constructed by Magruder, prevented Keyes from making an assault.[9] McClellan increased his travail by failing to cooperate with the naval fleet that had convoyed his transports from Alexandria, and which, under proper guidance, might have shelled the garrison into surrender via the York River. Calling up Tyler's siege batteries and Hunt's Reserve, Little Mac made ready to invest Magruder's command. Following a 16 April failure by another of his subordinates, who had projected an assault against Yorktown from a new direction, McClellan finalized his siege plans.[10]

As a direct result, Hunt's already-burdensome workload considerably increased. He put cannoneers and horses to work helping move up the siege supplies from Fort Monroe; other artillerists were reduced to laborers and assisted in building a prodigious assortment of redans, redoubts, lunettes, revetments, and various other defilading works. Hunt himself, and many of his officers, doubled as engineers, crawling toward enemy lines through swirling clouds of dust, studying likely locations for new batteries, rebel bullets whizzing over their heads.[11] When not engaged in building heavy works, the Reserve gunners were ordered to construct smaller defenses, designed either to protect cannon or to block passage of enemy troops: gabions, cylindrical baskets of woven twigs filled with earth; fascines, bundles of closely bound wood; and *chevaux de frise,* lengths of timber with pointed stakes driven through them. The work continued for more than a fortnight, in weather alternately balmy and rainy, neither of which was conducive to strenuous labor. "No command," Hunt opined, "worked harder or was more usefully employed" than his.[12]

All of it was wasted. His preparations deemed nearly complete by early May, McClellan issued orders for his heavy cannon and 13-inch mortar batteries to open against Yorktown on the morning of the sixth. But on the night of the third, spoilsport Joe Johnston (who had superseded Magruder) began to pull the Confederates out of the city. By the time Little Mac got wind of this, most of his enemy were well on their way up the peninsula toward Richmond. Not only had Johnston and Magruder stalled almost 117,000 invaders for a full month; they had added a superb finishing touch to McClellan's frustration.[13]

Suitably furious, Little Mac ordered a swift pursuit. While he began uprooting the cannon he had planted in previous weeks, Hunt detached his horse artillery for use by General Stoneman; the speediest of cannon units were needed in the chase ahead. At the same time, Colonel Tyler handed rifles to his siege artillerists and sent them off in McClellan's main body to fight as infantry.

On the morning of 5 May the Federal advance struck the butt of Johnston's army, now retreating through the old Colonial capital, Williamsburg, some fifteen miles northwest of Yorktown. Here was waged the rejuvenated artillery's first field engagement. The clash occured in a downpour upon ground too muddy and hilly to admit effective cannon deployment by either side. Nonetheless, Hunt was much pleased to hear that Tidball's and the other flying batteries made maximum use of what few opportunities the fighting gave them—the Duncan tradition seemed alive and flourishing.[14]

After the battle on the fifth, inertia again captured McClellan's army. While his enemy retired to Richmond, the Federal commander felt he had to bring up the entire array of forces and supplies at his disposal, reorganizing administrative procedures, before resuming his movement up the isthmus. He proceeded to do all of this as languidly as possible.

For the next four weeks Hunt and his comrades participated in this waiting game, warding off heat prostration, brackish water, mosquitos, and the late-spring illnesses prevalent among the Virginia lowlands. Hunt idled away free hours by writing Mary and his in-laws, playing five-card draw, sharing bottles of whiskey with his colleagues in the ranks, and, from 8 to .11 May, heading up a special military commission meeting in Yorktown to revise administration along lines that Little Mac favored. While his subordinates thrashed out such details, McClellan assiduously inspected and reviewed his troops; and, as assiduously, carried on correspondence with influential Democratic politicians, bemoaning his lack of support and cooperation in Washington. Despite such lack, he also bombarded the capital with demands, then pleas, for tens of thousands of reinforcements.[15]

Writing politicians and War Department officials seems to have consumed the greater part of his time. He considered a prodigious number of supports absolutely essential; for, in his mind, Johnston outnumbered him by a nightmarish margin. Yet he never explained why, if this were so, Johnston had run away from him at Yorktown.

* * *

On 31 May fighting resumed and continued for two days. Significantly, when battle broke out, McClellan, for all his preparation, was not ready to handle it.

By the thirty-first, the army commander, whom so many critics termed a master strategist and logistician, had maneuvered his command into an awkward position astride the Chickahominy River, a deep stream that meandered down the middle of the peninsula southeast from Richmond. Only a few rickety bridges connected the two corps he had stationed on the south shore, while the rest of the army stayed north of the stream.

Not wishing to wait until McClellan's strident urgings brought him the overwhelming reinforcements he craved, the recently strengthened Confederates sallied forth from their defenses; and, on a rainy morning, they struck one of the corps below the river in what would become known as the Battle of Fair Oaks, or Seven Pines.

The forty-eight-hour struggle produced five thousand Federal casualties, including Lewis Cass Hunt, who only ten days before had won an appointment as colonel of a New York volunteer infantry regiment. Soon Lewis was heading rearward with a severe thigh wound that would require a prolonged healing period.[16] In the Confederate ranks, the most notable among the 6,130 losses suffered was the critical wounding of General Johnston. On 1 June, while Johnston began a lengthy recuperation in a Richmond hospital, General Robert E. Lee took the field as his replacement in command of the Army of Northern Virginia, a position he would not vacate in three subsequent years of conflict.

Though initially successful, the rebels left the Seven Pines-Fair Oaks battlefield reeling from blows dealt them by a hastily reinforced Federal line. But, aghast by the beating his own army had absorbed, McClellan took another long respite to refit and conjure up new strategy.

Not engaged at Seven Pines, Hunt's artillery had no damage to repair. Still its commander found a profitable way to spend his time during the battle lull. Concerned by what General Barry had told him of ammunition waste during the struggle below the Chickahominy, he took steps to ensure that his own people would not prove guilty of that crime. He demanded on 20 June in published orders:

> The firing will be *deliberate*—and the greatest care will be taken to secure accuracy. Under no circumstances will it be so rapid that the effect of each shot and shell can not be noted when the air is clear. . . . There is no excess of ammunition, what we have must be made the most of.[17]

Undoubtably the decree would secure desired results. Yet, ironically, during one of Hunt's first opportunities to put it to the trial, extraordinary circumstances would render it inoperable.

Not until the last days in June did battle action resume. This time it would continue for a full week, ever afterward known as the Seven Days' Battles. The first two of these—fought at Oak Grove, below the Chickahominy, and at Mechanicsville, above the river—occurred on the twenty-fifth and twenty-sixth; both rendered results generally favorable to the Federals, though few Reserve batteries participated in either.

On 27 June, reinforcements from the Shenandoah Valley under Stonewall Jackson enabled Lee to land a vicious blow against Brigadier General Fitz-John Porter's V Corps, five miles southeast of Mechanicsville, near a granary known as Gaines's Mill. Throughout the fighting, Hunt's Reserve, attached to Porter's command, stood in rear of the Union left flank amid a dense wood, ready to fire in volley following any rebel breakthrough. Breakthrough came early that evening, when several Confederate divisions coordinated an overwhelming assault that pushed the Federal corps toward the Chickahominy bridges. At a crucial moment, Hunt's batteries, particularly thirty-two cannon under Lieutenant Colonel Getty, slowed the rebel pursuit, blasting back infantrymen and crippling several opposing artillery units. A Confederate colonel later recalled that "the Federal artillery tore gaps in the ranks at every step."[18]

Despite Hunt's aid, General Porter had been defeated, and told McClellan so. Beset by panic, the army commander gave him permission to retire south of the stream.[19] Below the Chickahominy, in the meantime, McClellan himself was flinching from punches thrown by Magruder's Confederates, who had rushed forth from the Richmond lines. So obsessed was McClellan with the thought of defeat that he failed to detect Lee's hazardous gamble in hurling all but twenty-five thousand of his men against Porter. Magruder's troops, fulfilling Lee's orders to march and shoot and shout as though many times their number, were so thinly deployed that McClellan's soldiers could have batted them aside, thereby capturing the enemy's capital.

For the second time in two and a half months—this time on the brink of entering Richmond—Little Mac turned away. As soon as Porter and Hunt had scrambled across the bridges, he ordered the spans torched and all fords guarded to stymie enemy pursuit. With a reunited command he then pounded southeast in full retreat, heading for his new supply base at Harrison's Landing on the James River.[20]

So began the pitiful collapse of McClellan's dream of grand conquest without bloodshed and grief. On the road to Harrison's Landing more blood was spilled—in three engagements: Garnett's Farm on the twenty-seventh and twenty-eighth; Savage's Station on the twenty-ninth; and on the thirtieth at White Oak Swamp. Hunt saw service in the first, though at arm's length from the crucial fighting. But even from afar he could see that his comrades more than held their own on that field. In truth, all three engagements were defensive victories for McClellan; during that singularly violent week, only Gaines's Mill had been a thumping defeat. Yet McClellan hastened his exodus to the James.

By midday on 30 June the army was nearly at the river. Shortly after supervising his Reserve gunners at White Oak Swamp (during which several cannon were captured through ineffectual infantry support), Hunt was directed by McClellan's headquarters to group all available cannon into a vast rear guard atop a 150-foot-high eminence known as Malvern Hill, a half mile above the James and a dozen miles southeast of Richmond.[21]

During the latter part of that day Hunt made the crest of the hill an impregnable position, emplacing not only most of his Reserve guns but also those field batteries that General Barry sent up from the low ground to the north. By 4 P.M., though his dispositions were incomplete, Hunt had placed thirty-six cannon, well protected by earth works, with which to confront any Confederates who appeared.

At that very hour some Confederates did appear: a division of infantry under Major General Theophilus H. Holmes, slowly advanced along the River Road from Richmond, on the southwestern flank of the hill.[22] About an hour later, having run batteries of his own to the forefront of his line, Holmes sought to soften Hunt's defenses before his attack. Fitz-John Porter, designated by McClellan commander of the field, reported the upshot: "In return for this intrusion the concentrated rapid fire of the artillery was opened upon them, soon smashing one battery to pieces, silencing another, and driving back their infantry . . . in rapid retreat, much to the satisfaction of thousands of men watching the result." Thus ended the brief and inordinately one-sided "Battle of Turkey Island Bridge," or "Malvern Cliff."[23]

Once the more extensive fighting at White Oak Swamp had faded out, the balance of McClellan's army trooped to Malvern Hill. Most of the Federals took position on the northern and western edges of its crest and on various levels of its slopes, while hundreds more cannon were trundled up the more gradual inclines to join those batteries that had routed Holmes. General Porter cast about for the most-advantageous positions for these new guns, which included fourteen heavy pieces from Tyler's siege train— five 4.5-inch Rodman rifles, five 30-pounder Parrotts, two 8-inch howitzers, and two 10-pounder Whitworth rifles, the last-named a product of British foundries.[24] There were plenty of excellent vantage points from which the corps leader might choose, and Hunt helped him pare down the overabundance, as did Brigadier Generals Barry, John G. Barnard, the army's chief construction engineer, and Andrew A. Humphreys, chief topographical engineer.[25]

When by mid-afternoon of 1 July all dispositions were complete, one hundred-odd cannon had been emplaced almost hub to hub across the mile-wide summit of the hill, aiming north and northwest toward ground on which Robert Lee was grouping his pursuers. Much of the Artillery Reserve was not even on this line for simple lack of room. It stood in park on the western and southern edges, facing the direction from which Holmes had advanced the day before, grouped near General Porter's headquarters. Still other cannon commanded positions below the summit, as well as to its rear. To bolster all, Federal gunboats in the James had moved just behind the hill, ready to add salvos from their large-caliber guns to any cannonade Porter might unleash upon his foe.

Protected by all manner of defenses, the cannon were also well guarded by various infantry commands. Corps and divisions had been deployed as skirmishers and sharpshooters in a semicircle from southwest to northeast around the northern tip of the eminence and behind Hunt's guns. One infantry unit guarded the road that ran from the river up the back slope, and comrades with rifles and pistols commanded almost every other square foot of ground at the base of the hill. Malvern Hill was as secure a position as any defender could wish.

Even so, it had been a near thing. During the confused withdrawal from White Oak Swamp, the army's trains had become snarled. Wagons belonging to the various corps and division artillery units had become so inextricably mixed that only Hunt's easily accessible Reserve ammo column had saved the day. Now, as the afternoon of 1 July moved to a close, each gun atop Malvern Hill had its normal allotment of shells to fling at any rebel force so foolhardy as to try to take the position by storm.[26]

About half past five, Lee's men proved themselves foolhardy. The rebels emerged from woods on either side of the Quaker Road, leading to the northern base of the hill, and deployed in attack formations, artillery going into position to smooth the way for a full-scale assault. Hunt could barely credit his eyesight. Such a tactic was suicidal.

It is difficult to understand Lee's frame of mind at this juncture. Not long after the Confederate guns started in, fifty Federal cannon singled out the most accessible of them and blew them to pieces in front of the waiting rebel foot troops. This ought to have told Lee and his subordinate commanders that nothing could be gained by challenging such firepower with mortal flesh arranged in attack order.

Someone gave the signal anyway, and about a quarter to six the gray-clad lines started forward with a wild, ringing yell, rushing the north and northeastern corners of the slope. They attempted their incredible task, according to one observer, "with all the frenzy of maniacs."[27]

Long before they reached the high ground Hunt gave a signal of his own, and the one hundred-plus cannon on the forward crest let loose with a barrage so deep, so deafening, so absolute in its thunder that afterward few could say convincingly that they had heard it—they *felt* it, a palpable tumult. After the first crashing, rocking cannonade, came volley after volley of rifle fire from the sharpshooters near the cannon. Soon this violent world of sound and fury was shrouded by an almost impenetrable cloud of powder smoke that blanketed Malvern Hill along the width of its crest.

The rebels went down in droves, flying backward and to the sides, bowling over one another as shot, shrapnel, and shell laid them flat or picked them up and flung them. Bodies caromed against bodies, and men were torn and mangled beyond physical recognition. The shells also gouged out great hunks of earth, tossing them high and far, levelled trees, and uprooted underbrush—destroying everything in their path with a violent intensity never before seen by American soldiers. Audible amid the thunder was the fearsome shriek of shells lobbed by the gunboats behind the hill.

Somehow, a few bands of rebels managed to reach the base of the hill, where they hid among brush and behind trees, blasting away at gunners and marksmen on the heights above. During the apex of the barrage, Hunt rode from one end of the artillery line to the other, overseeing all fields of fire. During his errand a rebel minié ball killed his horse, slamming him to the ground. Rising, he mounted another animal and resumed his ride—only to be tossed earthward again when this horse also went down with bullet wounds. Dazed but unhurt, he saddled a third time and completed his rounds, sending up Reserve batteries, including three of horse artillery, as well as supplies and additional ammunition, replacing damaged units and shifting others into more-advantageous positions.[28]

The blast of combat rolled on with varying degrees of intensity for almost four hours. Their first attack shattered, Lee's men reformed for a second assault; then, incredibly, a third. All were repulsed in bloody confusion. The third withdrawal was helped along by a bayonet charge by a part of the II Corps, as well as by parting salvos from Hunt, whose 32-pounder howitzers laced the fleeing ranks with shrapnel to frightening effect.[29]

Even after darkness settled over the field, the guns continued their shelling, oblivious to the orders regarding ammunition conservation issued by Hunt only eleven days before. Complemented by occasional salvos from the James River fleet, they mutilated woodlots in which some survivors sought to hide.

Only with dawn could Hunt and his comrades assess the extent of the carnage. When the sun rose, Colonel William Averell, officer in charge of the army's rear guard that day, peered from the summit at a grisly scene: "Over five thousand dead and wounded men were on the ground, in every attitude of distress. A third of them were dead or dying, but enough were alive and moving to give to the field a singular crawling effect."

Major General D.H. Hill, whose division had participated in the doomed assault, later rendered a bitter appraisal:

"It was not war—it was murder."[30]

* * *

It was ironic that McClellan's campaign against Richmond, so dismal a strategic failure, should close on such a high note of tactical success as Malvern Hill provided. It was most fitting as well: though either victorious or able to hold its own in almost every major engagement in the campaign, the Army of the Potomac continued its retreat. On the evening of the first, General Porter wired McClellan, far to the rear, about the great victory won that day, and proposed a renewed drive against the enemy capital. But neither he nor Hunt could persuade Little Mac to reclaim the offensive;[31] the army was ordered farther southeastward to Harrison's Landing—there, to settle into fixed camp within the protective range of the formidable gunboats whose offensive capabilities Little Mac had never sought to apply to his campaign.[32] At Harrison's Landing, careful evaluation would reveal that McClellan had taken 20,880 casualties during his drive toward and then away from Richmond—but forty fewer than Lee and Johnston had suffered. In killed and wounded exclusively, in fact, Little Mac's opponents had lost 10,744 men more than he.

Such statistics as were available caused a revision in Hunt's attitude toward McClellan. From the earliest days of McClellan's tenure in command, the artillerist had applauded and supported his campaign to fashion a fully professionalized field army. To Little Mac's everlasting credit, this end had been attained. Now Hunt still admired him as an administrator and organizer; but, after Malvern Hill, he put aside the respect he had previously accorded McClellan as strategist and tactician.

The Army of the Potomac lolled at and near Harrison's Landing for six weeks following Malvern Hill, sorting out its options, discarding them one by one—content to allow Lee to replenish his lines around Richmond.[33] Hunt spent the time patching up the Reserve units damaged on the long road between Yorktown and the James. He also launched a concerted effort to sanitize his camps, protecting the fragile health of his gunners, and to curtail the waste of ammunition that had occured atop Malvern Hill. In this last, cold fact bore him out: one battery alone had expended 1,392 rounds of ammunition during that battle, and would have used more had any been immediately available.[34]

The unhappy season beside the James finally closed during the second week in August when a large portion of McClellan's army marched back down the peninsula to Fort Monroe. There, as well as at Hampton and Newport News, the soldiers took ship for Aquia Creek Landing, a supply depot off the Potomac, about one hundred miles up the coast. For many of these men, the ultimate destination was the vicinity of Falmouth, Virginia, where they would be absorbed into a newly formed Federal army—initially forty thousand strong—under a former commander in the West: Major General John Pope. McClellan's newly appointed successor as general-in-chief of all the Union's armies, Major General Henry W. Halleck (like Hunt, a graduate of the West Point Class of '39) had decreed that three full corps from the Army of the Potomac should bolster Pope's so-called Army of Virginia. Under the Westerner they would attempt what they had been unable to accomplish under Little Mac: the conquest of Richmond and its defenders.

When McClellan's advance units reached Aquia Creek, Colonel Hunt was there to greet them, having led his Artillery Reserve to the depot on 21 July. He had been placed in charge of grouping, staffing, and supplying batteries, afterward sending them to Falmouth, ten miles inland. There his immediate superior, now-Major General Porter, would forward them to Pope's headquarters.

The work gave Hunt more than the normal quota of headaches since McClellan's embarkation from Hampton Roads and vicinity was a classic study in logistical chaos. In many cases, battery personnel were shipped north in one transport, their guns and horses in others. Even so, Hunt was able to sort through the confusion and relay to Pope about twelve of McClellan's field batteries, including a few Reserve units.[35]

General Porter had promised him sufficient warning before Pope moved out against Lee. But the warning never came. When in the last week of August the infantry ordered to Pope was put in motion toward Groveton and Manassas Junction, Hunt was still at Aquia Creek, up to his elbows in tangled batteries and confused artillerymen. Thus he found himself unable to participate in the fighting under Pope.[36]

He always regretted this—yet it seemed a boon that he did not join the Army of Virginia. On the final day of the month—by which time Hunt had gone to Falmouth, thence to Alexandria, where most of his Reserve was stationed—word came that the old Bull Run battlefield was ablaze once again with combat. And a few days later he learned that Pope had outdone Irvin McDowell by suffering a defeat the proportions of which made the latter's July 1861 fiasco pale by comparison.

Hunt could take pardonable satisfaction from accompanying news that inept artillery employment had helped undo Pope. Lacking the guiding hand of a Hunt or a Barry (the latter had also been left behind), the Union batteries, many led by officers handpicked by Pope, had failed to provide the effective mass fire that had won the day at Malvern Hill. According to a Confederate artillerist, at Second Bull Run the Union batteries "frittered away their efforts as individuals."[37]

Up from the scene of Pope's drubbing at the hands of Lee and Jackson trickled a ragged column of ill-used troops. To Hunt it seemed that no power on earth could restore self-confidence to this gloomy rabble. But it was a situation tailored to the skills of George B. McClellan who, inept though he might be in the field, was one of the most inspired and inspiring organizers going. Flushed with victory, the rebels were heading northward, perhaps heading for Washington itself. If anyone could convince losers that they were capable of stemming that advance, it was the Young Napoleon.

McClellan took full advantage of his opening. Even before the soldiers reached the capital, he rode out to meet them. Reinstated to full field command as of 2 September, he had been handed a second gleaming opportunity to make the country as a whole accept his own exalted opinion of himself as a complete soldier.[38]

When Little Mac regained the reins, Hunt was commuting between his headquarters at Alexandria and the capital. He had made several visits to the War Department since coming up from Falmouth, concerned about the fate of his estranged units now under Pope. More recently, information gleaned at the War Office had brought new concern. General Porter had been relieved of command at Pope's insistence that he had displayed criminal unwillingness to cooperate with the Army of Virginia in the campaign just ended; on 5 September, Porter was put under the scrutiny of an official court of inquiry, leading Hunt to fear for his friend's career. More tragically still, Hunt had received word that his bosom companion,

Isaac Stevens, a major general of volunteers, had been slain at Chantilly, Virginia, two days after Second Bull Run. Hunt's grief was deepened by the knowledge that Stevens's battlefield acumen, his engineer's background notwithstanding, had bred prevalent speculation that he would soon be elevated to command the Army of the Potomac.[39]

After regaining his army, General McClellan encamped near Washington, then looked up Hunt, pulling him out of his cloud of gloom and bereavement. Little Mac stated an intention to appoint him artillery chief for the entire army. He explained that General Barry had elected to leave the field for a War Department desk job as inspector of all artillery units in the Federal ranks.

Hunt was suitably gratified by the offer, though leery of accepting it under any circumstances that might reflect uncharitably on Barry's having vacated the post. McClellan assured him that the outgoing commander was in favor of the change. Still Hunt held back. He informed McClellan that he desired a promise of power never granted Barry: the right to oversee field dispositions whenever he deemed such supervision vital. In addition, of course, he wished full control over administration, supply, maintenance, and instruction relating to the batteries in both the field army and the Reserve.

To his probable surprise, Little Mac assented. Though no written order ever formalized this authority, the near future would reveal McClellan's intent to fulfill his promise.[40] The gift of such a wide latitude of power renewed the high esteem Hunt had granted his commander prior to the peninsula campaign.

So it was that on 5 September Hunt was elevated to command all the cannon in the Army of the Potomac. Three days later he reported at the army's new field headquarters at Rockville, Maryland, twelve miles northwest of Washington. And exactly one week after that—the day following his forty-third birthday—Colonel Hunt became Brigadier General Hunt by appointment of General McClellan and subject to the consent of Congress.[41]

* * *

Difficult as had been past artillery refits, that which Hunt instituted in the formative stages of the Maryland campaign dwarfed all of them. The primary difficulty was that it had to be completed while the army was on the march, most of the work taking place during such brief respites as McClellan permitted en route to the field of the bloodiest single day's fighting of the war.[42]

First, Hunt was compelled to shuffle about subordinates, replacing injured or incapacitated officers, as well as Lieutenant Colonel Hays, who had succeeded him as head of the much-depleted Artillery Reserve. This chore was complicated by Hunt's unfamiliarity with many of the volunteer artillerists in the main army. Still, assisted by wise advisors, he made judicious assignments.

Of great help to him in this and other chores was the small but efficient crop of staff officers that McClellan allowed him to raise. Though in the future some of his aides would be taken from him via various economizing programs, most would remain at his side for the rest of the conflict: Captain John N. Craig, his adjutant general; Captain Edward P. Brownson and Lieutenants W.S. Worth, C.E. Bissell, and Carl Berlin, aides-de-camp; and Lieutenant Colonel Edward R. Warner and Major Alexander Doull, inspectors-general of artillery. No longer would Hunt have to take precious time from more-important duties to handle the most routine bookwork.[43]

Even with their help, Hunt fared poorly in resupplying units with battery horses, for these proved all but nonexistent on such short notice. Consequently, some of the batteries had to return to Washington to await animals at the depots there—effectively out of the campaign. At first it did not seem that he would be able to minister to ammunition wants with any degree of success, either, but in the end he managed to secure almost three hundred wagon loads of projectiles to feed famished ammo chests.[44]

His efforts did bear fruit; by midday on the fifteenth, by which point McClellan had located Lee's army just east of the lower Maryland village of Sharpsburg, Hunt could proclaim that the artillery was "very respectably provided." All told, he could bring fifty-five batteries into battle, an aggregate of 322 cannon—two-thirds of it on the front lines, the rest under Colonel Hays.[45]

That evening the commanding major general gave Hunt instructions to emplace long-range cannon on the east bank of Antietam Creek, across from Lee's positions along ridges outside Sharpsburg. Little Mac provided only a general idea of his intentions and offered some suggestions for the heaviest "pieces of position"—these to spearhead a general attack on the seventeenth.

The next dawn Hunt, accompanied by Colonel Hays, rode along the heights adjacent to the creek, scrutinizing the terrain and selecting the positions to be occupied by the 20- and 10-pounder Parrotts, 12-pounder Napoleons, ordnance rifles, and other guns heavy and light. Hunt's task was complicated by the fire of Lee's longest-range cannon, but he nevertheless completed his errand by early evening to McClellan's full satisfaction.[46]

At dawn on 17 September the infantry went forward as ordered—and accomplished little of lasting consequence. Hampered by an unconscionably vague battle plan, the foot soldiers launched a series of uncoordinated assaults against the rebel left flank; then against the enemy center; finally against the right. The Confederate artillery, permitted by lack of infantry pressure to shift about almost at will, frustrated every attempt to roll up Lee's lines, resisting furiously beside hard-fighting infantry comrades.[47]

From the heights overlooking the creek, Hunt's gunners did their utmost to neutralize the harm caused by McClellan's faulty tactics, rendering a particularly devastating fire to cover General Hooker's early-morning assault on the enemy left. With forty fewer cannon, Lee nevertheless returned a barrage as fierce as he received, prompting one of his subordinates in after years to refer to Antietam as "artillery hell."

Except for briefly held advantages, such as that attained by Tidball's horse artillery against the rebel center, most of the Federal gun units saw no opportunity to demonstrate their awesome capabilities. Despite Hunt's newly won authority, front-line commanders attained effective control of the batteries in the crucial battle sectors; and used them badly. Many guns were sent so far forward that it made capture a likelihood; others were placed on wooded or hilly terrain from which they could not operate properly; and corps and division commanders failed to detect and utilize key ground features, which would have provided positions for enfilading fire. Hunt galloped to and fro along the line, but could not be at every important area at every decisive moment. As a result, Antietam rivaled Second Bull Run in the Union artillery's inability to produce effective massed fire.[48]

The battle closed with nightfall, darkness hiding the 12,410 Federal and 13,724 Confederate casualties. On the next morning both armies held their ground: Lee's more battered soldiers with the deep Potomac River at their backs; and McClellan's army, despite its losses, still fresh, with an uncommitted reserve of twenty-four thousand infantrymen. But with characteristic timidity, McClellan elected not to renew the fighting; and when Lee stumbled off southward that evening, his invasion ended, Little Mac let him go, not receptive to a close pursuit. For the second time in three months, he elected not to follow up a campaign, which, if not triumphant in the strictest sense, was at least more than a crushing defeat.

Though given ample opportunity, Hunt would not criticize his commander. Other artillerymen, reflecting on how their work on the seventeenth had been wasted for want of a coherent battle plan, wailed and gnashed their teeth; Hunt waited patiently for the future to bring improvement. In the interim, as so often before, he quietly ministered to ailing batteries, replacing officers, men, and horses rendered *hors de combat,* and calling up still more ammunition.

McClellan doubtlessly appreciated his unwillingness to carp and complain and point an accusing finger, unlike so many of Hunt's colleagues. He rewarded his artillery chief with generous praise, which, by some maddening oversight, was not inserted in his official report, but which made up a conspicuous part of a revised republication of same. Included was McClellan's acknowledgment: "The service of this distinguished officer in reorganizing and refitting the batteries prior to . . .the battle of Antietam, and his gallant and skillful conduct on that field, merit the highest encomiums in my power to bestow."[49]

Except its effect on the rise of his career, Hunt cared little for such praise as this. So often had flowery tributes been paid to him in official reports that they now seemed a debased form of flattery. No doubt he would have appreciated much more the unusual but sincere compliment given him at this same time by his enemy:

On the day following the hell of Antietam, the crew of a Confederate battery saw a group of Federal officers riding near, surveying the rebel lines through field glasses. One was conspicuous for his pale horse.

The range was tempting. "Let's give them a shot!" cried one cannoneer.

But a comrade raised his hand: "No, that's the chief of artillery; whenever you see him on his white horse look out for a battery. He's a brave man and I won't fire at him."

He paused a moment and then added, like a good artillerist: "Wait until the battery comes and we'll fire at that!"[50]

* * *

After the end of the Maryland campaign, Hunt began to wonder if it were futile to wait for desired change. Precious little of it seemed to come his way.

Not that he did not try. He proposed to McClellan, for example, a plan to consolidate all artillery, heavy and light, into a single corps, as well as to unite ordnance and artillery personnel therein. Little Mac was not responsive.[51] Another innovation, originally suggested by Colonel Tyler, would have established a seagoing twin to the siege train of peninsula days by outfitting river barges with seventy of the heaviest ordnance: 4.5-inch siege guns, 8-inch howitzers, 30-pounder Parrotts, and 10-inch mortars. The added mobility that this idea would afford the army much appealed to Hunt, who relayed it hopefully to the high command. But this project also died when General Halleck refused to take any cannon from the Washington lines to stock the barge train.[52]

Even if McClellan had been wildly enthusiastic about such proposals, he could have brought little influence to bear on their behalf in Washington. The truth was that his days in command were quickly running out.

He had no one but himself to blame. Not until 1 November did he lead his army back into Virginia to confront Lee; and by then his dawdling during and after Antietam had been brought clearly into focus by his failure to vigorously oppose and pursue J.E.B. Stuart, whose rebel cavalrymen had ridden a full circle around the Army of the Potomac on 9–12 October.

A month afterward, President Lincoln took decisive action. On 7 November he relieved McClellan for good, replacing him with a subordinate who had shown some promise on earlier fields: Major General Ambrose E. Burnside. Little Mac was directed to entrain for his home in Trenton, New Jersey—there, to await further orders that would never come.[53]

On the eleventh, Hunt and a host of associates went down to the Orange & Alexandria Railroad depot at Warrenton Junction, Virginia to bid their old commander farewell. It was a sad time; for Hunt, a sadder time than for most. Despite all of McClellan's flaws, he retained the ability to convince others that the war was somehow bright and glorious—at least worthwhile. Beyond that, he had touched something vital in Hunt's soul, but in a way not even Hunt could have explained. All he knew was that McClellan possessed in abundance qualities he cherished: honor and integrity, verve and spunk, courage and courtliness.

The war effort would not diminish with McClellan's departure. The spirit he had imparted to the army would remain; and that spirit—not the man—was the vital element. And yet, despite such knowledge, Hunt must have felt older as well as sadder when that train pulled out of Warrenton, taking Little Mac away.

9

Winter of Discontent

Ambrose Burnside had a fundamental honesty that helped make him likeable. He proved this by telling Lincoln and the War Office, when offered McClellan's job, that he was unworthy to command the Army of the Potomac—a statement he had made on two past occasions. When the Washington officials this time insisted he take the reins, Burnside reluctantly acquiesed, then proceeded to demonstrate that his self-appraisal was highly valid.

Before embarking on the campaign that would destroy his military reputation as well as a large portion of his newly acquired command, Burnside made one decision that strengthened his claim to perceptivity in evaluating personnel: he replaced some of the high-ranking holdovers from McClellan's regime; but, much impressed with Hunt's acumen, made no move to seek a new artillery chief. For the duration of Burnside's reign, Hunt would continue to lead the army's 375 cannon.

For his part, Hunt was uncertain in his attitude toward his new commander. Though fifteen years before both men had been lieutenants in the Second Artillery (six years after which Burnside had resigned his commission to design and manufacture firearms in Rhode Island), they had not developed close ties. Hunt knew little of Burnside's war record beyond some small-scale but much-publicized victories gained in North Carolina when the war was young. In any case, he suspended judgment, allowing Burnside ample time to confirm or dispute his own belief that he was unequal to his new command.

In putting into practice his early administrative programs, Burnside both pleased and distressed his artillery chief. One of the first of these, which he imparted to Hunt at army headquarters during the second week in November, won the artillerist's full approval. Burnside assured Hunt that he could consider his verbal agreement with McClellan still in force: he was to have both administrative and tactical control over all the artillery— at least to such extent as he could properly exercise in the field.[1]

General Ambrose E. Burnside, staff and field officers, November 1862: Hunt seated at far left; General W.S. Hancock seated beside him; General Marsena Patrick standing at far left. (COURTESY, LIBRARY OF CONGRESS)

Perhaps Burnside's most visible administrative reform struck Hunt as ill-advised, since it promised an unwieldy field force: the organization of three so-called Grand Divisions under Major Generals Edwin V. Sumner, Joseph Hooker, and William B. Franklin, each consisting of two full infantry corps and either a division or a brigade of cavalry. Burnside further disappointed Hunt by leaving the system intact by which batteries were attached to the divisions. By now, Hunt had endorsed a plan formulated by one of his subordinates: Colonel Charles S. Wainwright of New York, chief of artillery for the I Corps. Wainwright's proposal would have attached guns only to the several corps, grouping them into single units within each corps until detached for service on the battle line. Impressed by the cohesion and simplicity offered by the plan, Hunt was disappointed when Burnside rejected it without comment.[2]

Another Burnside decision affecting the artillery met Hunt's disapproval. Though willing to give Hunt overall command of the cannon, Burnside toyed with the notion of draining all authority from Colonel Wainwright and the other corps artillery chiefs. Since the first days of the war, such officers had exercised only so much power as the corps generals had allotted them; some, because of their obvious skill, had nevertheless been enabled to make the final decisions on cannon deployment. Now Burnside proposed to end this arrangement, formally subordinating corps artillery chiefs to their generals. By persistent opposition, however, Hunt persuaded Burnside to table the matter for the present.[3]

Burnside alarmed his artillery leader yet again by a proposal that would abolish Hunt's war-child, the Artillery Reserve. In this he seemed influenced by infantry commanders who had sought to affix blame for the Antietam stalemate on the Reserve; supposedly several infantry generals had been unable to receive replacements from Colonel Hays at the height of the fighting on 17 September. But these officers deliberately ignored a patent truth: after the hard campaigning on the peninsula and at Second Bull Run, the Reserve batteries had been so decimated that Hays had been able to muster only some cumbersome and balky 20-pounder rifles at Antietam. And those light batteries attached to McClellan's uncommitted corps and to other commands not heavily engaged had been jealously husbanded, their division commanders unwilling to loan them to embattled comrades who had greater need of them.[4]

This last fact constituted a powerful argument against disbanding Hunt's pet command. Without a Reserve, Burnside would have to rely on his subordinates' cooperation in sharing cannon—a spirit that Antietam had proved nonexistent. Pressing home this point, Hunt at last won the Reserve a reprieve. When Burnside's army moved south toward Richmond via Fredericksburg late in November, Colonel Hays still led nine light batteries, plus the two heavy batteries of the First Connecticut—remnants of the siege train used on the peninsula—and a company of Massachusetts foot soldiers serving as artillery supports. In the campaigning that lay ahead, the Reserve would dramatically display its value to a degree unforeseen even by Hunt.

On 4 December, two weeks after the 122,000-man Federal army reached the Rappahannock River above Fredericksburg, Hunt published a new order that would have far-reaching influence on his men. On too many fields, gunners had violated his strictures against needless expenditure of ammunition. Because replenishing the coffers of field units was an increasingly heavy burden, Hunt came forth with an edict that not even the infantry commanders who often controlled the batteries could ignore. No longer would artillery headquarters tolerate the actions of battery officers who frittered away their supply of projectiles, powder, and fuzes in brief time on the battle lines. Henceforth, such officers would leave themselves vulnerable to the suspicion that they had deliberately wasted their ammunition so they might withdraw from the fight. Such an accusation would dishonor and humiliate every future offender.

In his proclamation Hunt reiterated a previously publicized dictum: that the 250-rounds-per-gun capacity of the average ammo chest was ample, not only for a general engagement, but also for the skirmishing that usually preceded and followed battle. Therefore, batteries would no longer be permitted to disengage due to lack of shells; their section commanders must send caissons to the rear for replenishing, while guns and gunners remained under fire. Backed now by a full-size staff, Hunt was confident that such a law could be enforced.[5]

He found, however, that he had to wait a while before able to implement the decree. Heretofore, Burnside had shown commendable celerity in moving his huge command into central Virginia—even to the extent of stealing a march on Lee. But when he sought to move over the Rappahannock and engage Lee's army on the road to Richmond, his advance bogged down. Pontoons for bridge-building, vital to a crossing, had been ordered up long ago, but now, when needed, were nowhere to be found. Not until 25 November did the bridge material arrive at Burnside's headquarters at Falmouth; by then, Lee's people had formed a six-mile-long line atop a commanding series of ridges below the river and southwest of Fredricksburg. No longer did the Federal army enjoy an opportunity to battle its enemy on favorable terrain.[6]

This, however, Burnside refused to acknowledge. His original strategy had been to tackle Lee in a no-holds-barred struggle in which the Federals might isolate the rebels from Richmond. Burnside would not abandon that strategy. As a field general he was prone to many of the same failings that had cancelled out George McClellan's native abilities; but in one fundamental respect he did differ from Little Mac: once he determined a course of action, fluctuating conditions could not compel him to desist, revamp, or temporize.

At the beginning of the second week in December, Burnside called together his ranking subordinates, Hunt included, and held a council of war at Falmouth. After proclaiming his determination still to ford the river and move against Lee, he permitted his generals to advance tactical suggestions. Ultimately most of his officers agreed with Hunt's analysis of the situation: that the proper place to cross the Rappahannock was above Hamilton's Crossing, about four miles southeast of Falmouth and Fredricksburg. In that sector, Hunt believed, fifty thousand infantry could lap around the right flank of the enemy, aided by terrain more favorable to such an advance than that occupied by Lee's main body.[7]

Burnside appeared receptive to the idea. Yet he insisted that most of the army had to move over the river directly across from Fredricksburg, then against the heights beyond, to confront Lee in a secondary attack. At length he designated Sumner's Grand Division, backed by Hooker's, as the components of this supporting strike against Lee's left-center; while General Franklin's troops crossed not far from Deep Run, about two and a half miles from Fredricksburg, fanning out toward Hamilton's Crossing against the rebel right.

To permit the several crossings, Burnside's engineers were to lay at least five pontoon bridges, replacing several spans recently demolished by the Confederates. Two would be built downstream for Franklin's men, with three others thrown up across from the city for Sumner and Hooker.[8]

At this point Burnside concentrated on the roles that the artillery would play, specifically those he had designed for Hays's command. The day before, reconnoitering the high ground above the river, he had mentioned to one of his subordinates that the Artillery Reserve "has as yet had no chance to show its value, and I am going to make the crossing here and below, under cover of the guns of the reserve." He repeated this to Hunt during the war council, but waited until 10 December—twenty-four hours before crossing his army—to give his artillery chief the vital details.[9]

At that time Hunt learned that Burnside wished the auxiliary cannon to go into position on Stafford Heights: a 150-foot-tall chain of bluffs above the river. Along a six-mile front, the Reserve guns were to cover both the bridge-laying and the river-crossing. But in order to accomplish both, Hays's artillery would have to (a) silence the Confederate cannon on the ridges below Fredricksburg; (b) command the town itself in which enemy troops lingered; (c) control the movements of any rebel troops deployed on the vast plain between city and heights beyond; (d) provide a concentrated barrage to cover the crossings; and (e) furnish especial protection to Franklin's Grand Division, which might fall prey to an enfilading fire from Confederates near Massaponax Church, on Lee's extreme right.[10]

Hunt immediately remonstrated that the eleven batteries of the Reserve were insufficient to handle so many chores. Finally Burnside agreed to request his division commanders to detach all of their Napoleon batteries to equal the number Hunt required.

The wail of protest with which his generals responded convinced Burnside of how foolish had been his notion to disband the Reserve in favor of selfless cooperation within the main army.[11] Now he was forced to order each division general to loan out all but one of his batteries, with the promise of their prompt return as soon as the river had been crossed. No doubt Hunt observed this outcome with a smile of satisfaction. In his report of the campaign he would remark on the division commanders' tendency to "lose sight of the general requirements of the service in executing the orders specially applying to themselves."[12]

For most of 10 December, Hunt and his staff worked feverishly against a fast-approaching deadline to coordinate the intricate movements accompanying the detachment and emplacement of the batteries. They did a remarkable job. By sundown, thirty cannon units on loan from the main army were moving smoothly into assigned positions a few miles in rear of the bluffs overlooking the stream. The night was bitterly cold, with a recent two-foot snowfall that hindered movement. Nevertheless, with trace chains muffled and battery equipment securely fastened to maintain as much silence as possible, straining horses lugged cannon through the twenty-five-degree chill into side-by-side emplacement atop Stafford Heights. By 2 A.M. on the eleventh, 147 pieces had been set in place, most facing Fredricksburg from the crest.[13]

Hunt had parcelled them out to four of his ablest lieutenants, each in immediate command of a quarter of the line. The right division, on the extreme northern flank, consisted of forty rifled guns of various caliber, under Lieutenant Colonel Hays. The right-center division comprised thirty-eight pieces—eighteen light rifles and twenty 12-pounder Napoleons—commanded by Colonel Charles H. Tompkins, First Rhode Island Artillery. Farther south, the left-center division was composed of the heaviest long-range pieces, twenty-seven huge rifles including seven 4.5-inch guns and eight 20-pounder Parrotts; fittingly, they were under the guidance of recently promoted Brigadier General Tyler.[14] Finally, the forty-two guns on the far left of the line—thirty-four 3-inch rifles and eight 20-pounder Parrotts—were headed by Hunt's brother-in-law, Captain De Russy. Scanning this formidable bank of cannon, an infantry aide noted that the riverside had become "one vast battery."[15]

With all props in place, the drama could proceed. About four hours shy of dawn on the eleventh, members of the Fifteenth and Fiftieth New York Engineers took up pontoons and tools at river's edge and began laying four of Burnside's bridges, including the trio of spans opposite and immediately below Fredricksburg. By the time the sun appeared—its rays veiled by a thick morning fog—the three bridges on the northern end of the line were only eight feet short of the rebel shore.

Then and there came trouble.[16] An unexpected barrage of rifle fire from buildings along Fredricksburg's waterfront sent an engineer officer toppling dead into the icy river, and wounded two other officers and several enlisted men. Surviving bridge builders retreated across the nearly completed spans in hot haste.

In retaliation, Hunt's guns let loose. Cannon in Colonel Tompkins's right-center group lobbed a few rounds into the nearest buildings, seeking to rid them of a brigade of Mississippi riflemen. A few days before General Lee had placed these soldiers in the city, which at his order had been evacuated by its citizens.

After a few minutes, the barrage was curtailed; but not before the impact of recoil had shattered stock trails on five of Tompkins's Napoleons. In his report Hunt noted pointedly: "They were defective, and, it is almost needless to say, contract work, the contractors being Wood Brothers, of New York."[17] Here was yet another example of shoddy goods spewed forth from profit-hungry, apatriotic businessmen, continually a bane of Hunt's existence.

When the Federal guns fell silent, the pontoniers trotted out upon their bridges to resume work. But again rifle fire from the waterfront drove them back. Tompkins's cannon had accomplished nothing.

A second time, at Hunt's command, Tompkins's batteries went to work, their targets still masked by the thickening fog. The Mississippians took refuge in cellars and trenches as solid shot and shell exploded overhead and around them, toppling walls and showering them with flying brickwork and splinters.

After several minutes, Tompkins ceased firing, and for a third time the engineers attempted to complete their work. But, for a third time, surviving rebel sharpshooters peppered them at close range with minié balls, prompting still another retreat.

This time Hunt directed not only Tompkins's guns but other pieces along Stafford Heights to lace the shoreline with shot and shell. The cannon responded by raking buildings and open ground till about 8 A.M. This time, when they ceased, mounds of rubble could be seen through gaps in the fog. Supposing that the cellars and alleyways had been cleared at last, the New Yorkers cautiously reappeared. Soon yet again a volley of small-arms' fire sent them scurrying to the rear: enough Mississippians had survived to prohibit them from completing their labors.

By now Burnside, as well as Hunt, was growing angry and frustrated. Files of infantrymen had long been awaiting an opportunity to cross on the pontoons; the army's timetable, already warped by unanticipated delay, had now been disarranged beyond remedy.

At length, someone suggested that the six batteries of Napoleons still with the field army be brought to the river, where their heavy powder charges might resolve the stalemate in the army's favor. Burnside approved and gave the necessary orders; by 9:15 these thirty-six gun howitzers had been placed under Colonel Tompkins's supervision below the heights. Soon afterward they started in, augmented by many of the guns in the right-center division 150 feet above them, flinging solid shot and explosive shell into the near buildings, the earth trembling under the impact of the barrage. However, some of the shells lobbed by the guns on the bluffs burst short, endangering cannoneers, infantrymen, and engineers below; afterward Hunt had to use shot exclusively. Again he damned military contractors, especially those who supplied faulty time fuzes.

About ten o'clock Hunt again called a halt. After a long hesitation the pontoniers went forward once more. No sooner had they reached the unfinished portion of the spans than they were driven back a fifth time by the hardy Mississippians.

This time the rebel sharpshooters were to be reinforced by a column of gray-clad infantry, which the Federal gunners spied coming down one of Fredricksburg's streets toward the waterfront. One of Tompkins's units, Battery G of the Fourth Artillery, burst into action, shattering the support column with an accurate fire from its four Napoleons and sending it flying back to Lee's main army. Yet not even these Regular cannoneers could locate and disperse the riflemen obstructing Burnside's efforts to cross in their front.

Yet again Colonel Tompkins gave the go-ahead. The pieces of his division pounded the waterfront for another half hour with shot alone, adding to the piles of rubble, but otherwise doing no damage of discernable consequence. When the guns quieted to cool, the Mississippians resumed firing.

By now Ambrose Burnside was at Hunt's side, frothing with rage. Both of the lowermost bridges, including the one begun late, were finished. So, to waste no more time, he ordered Hunt to open with all of his cannon and to keep firing until the entire city, not just its riverfront, was levelled.

Hunt was shocked by the directive and protested against it. Burnside remained adamant. Shrugging, Hunt called in General Tyler, Colonels Tompkins and Hays, and Captain De Russy, and ordered them to fire deliberately at picked targets and to continue shelling until ordered otherwise. He then ordered the cannonade resumed.

What followed was a barrage even more intense than that which had decimated Lee's ranks at Malvern Hill. Beginning at 12:30, all 183 cannon bearing on Fredricksburg—including the batteries of siege guns from the First Connecticut—opened with a deafening, mind-shattering blast. Over and over again the cannon spewed fire, raining shot and shell on the city and its luckless occupants.

Via field glasses, Hunt witnessed such a firestorm as had to have engulfed Sodom and Gomorrah. Through gaps in the combined fog and cannon smoke, he watched church steeples topple, warehouses and stores and private homes buckle and collapse amid an immense spray of debris, and trees uprooted and cast about. Bulky shapes of cinderblock and brick along the shoreline suddenly vanished, gone without warning and forever. Other buildings glowed with an eerie, fog-piercing flame, then cracked and dissolved in splinters and flying masonry. Now and then huge geysers shot skyward as projectiles fell short and cut the icy layer upon the Rappahannock. The total effect was ethereal, scarcely real.

After several minutes given to such demolition, Hunt could stand it no longer. He neither understood nor condoned total war; battering an enemy army was a justifiably necessary part of warfare, but not so the mass destruction of noncombatants' property. To appease his conscience, he ordered the cannonade to cease.[18]

Given Burnside's frame of mind, Hunt fully realized the effect such an act might have on his career. As it happened, Burnside was angered by Hunt's unauthorized decree—but simply countermanded it. Once again the Federal cannon cried out, and again Fredricksburg stood wrapped in flame and smoke.

Observers North and South would long recall this barrage. Wrote a Rhode Island artilleryman years later: "The roar of the cannon, the bursting of shells, the falling of walls and chimneys; added to the fire of the infantry on both sides, the smoke from the guns and burning houses, made a scene of the wildest confusion, terrific enough to appall the stoutest hearts." Added a correspondent for *Frank Leslie's Magazine*: "The effect was, of course, terrific, and regarded merely as a phenomenon, was among the most awfully grand conceivable." Still another Northern newspaperman noted that "the earth shook beneath the terrific explosions of the shells, which went howling over the river, crashing into the houses, battering down walls, splintering doors, ripping up floors. Sixty solid shot and shells a minute were thrown 'till 9,000 were fired."[19]

Watching from Marye's Heights, beyond the city, the Confederates stared open-mouthed at the demolition, fearing for their comrades in Fredricksburg. Recalled General James Longstreet:

> In the midst of the successive crashes could be heard the shouts and yells of those engaged in the struggle, while the smoke rose from the burning city and the flames leaped about, making a scene which can never be effaced from the memory.

But it was Longstreet's superior, General Lee himself, who rendered the most anguished comment: "Those people delight to destroy the weak and those who can make no defense. It just suits them!"[20]

Even Burnside's thirst for retaliation was eventually slaked. About 2:30 he ordered the firing ended. Gradually the cannonade degenerated into infrequent salvos, then died out.

Each army held its collective breath, watching the rubble-strewn city, a third of which had been levelled. Surveying the destruction, Hunt shook his head sadly: "There was no such necessity" to justify the "barbarous" cannonade, though by rank and position Ambrose Burnside had had every right to overrule him.[21]

Forward came the engineers with their pontoons and implements. For many minutes they strode cautiously to the end of the bridges, nearing the deathly quiet city. Across the stream the multitude of flotsam was clearly visible, fog having dissipated at last.

And then—impossibly—rifle fire again spattered from basement windows and rifle pits. After all the destruction they had caused, Hunt's 180-plus cannon had done no tangible good—a few hundred Mississippians still clung to life and good vantage points. Even now, almost twelve hours after work had begun, the bridges could not be finished.

This time Burnside sent for Hunt. At headquarters the artillery chief found his commander almost crazed by wrath. "The army is held by the throat by a few sharpshooters!" he roared, looking at Hunt as though measuring him for a scapegoat.[22]

When Hunt replied, the major general commanding grew calmer. Hunt allowed that the only alternative was to send about one thousand infantrymen, under artillery covering fire, to gouge the rebels out of their nests by street-by-street, house-to-house fighting.

How, without the bridges finished? Burnside demanded.

Hunt gestured toward the unused pontoons at river's edge: in effect, overgrown rowboats. Burnside saw the point. He replied that if Hunt could win the approval of Brigadier General Daniel P. Woodbury, commander of the volunteer Engineer Brigade, he would issue the necessary orders.

Hunt trooped down to see General Woodbury, discussed the idea with him, and won a supporter. The engineer commander accompanied him back to headquarters and gave his consent in Burnside's presence.

Unexpectedly, Burnside hedged, stating that he could not accept the responsibility for authorizing such a chancy mission. He intimated, however, that if Hunt could round up infantrymen willing to make the assault, he would give his approval.

Back down to the river went Hunt, still accompanied by Woodbury. There he collared the nearest infantry commander, Colonel Norman J. Hall, whose Third Brigade, Second Division, II Corps had been protecting the engineers from sniper fire. Once told the plan, Hall said he would attempt to implement it. But soon afterward his Grand Division commander, General Sumner got wind of the doings and enjoined Hall to stay put. Hall acquiesced.

Just as the project teetered on collapse, Lieutenant Colonel Henry Baxter, commander of Hall's old regiment, the Seventh Michigan, agreed to chance Sumner's wrath by leading the assault. Following his lead, officers of three other regiments, the Eighty-ninth New York and the Nineteenth and Twentieth Massachusetts, volunteered as supports. In the face of such selfless conduct, Colonel Hall announced his intent to command the entire force.[23]

After imparting suggestions for carrying out his plan, Hunt stalked back to army headquarters. Meanwhile, infantrymen and engineers arranged themselves about the pontoons, ready to make the crossing.

But Hunt found that even now, with a willing herd of attackers, Burnside could not nerve himself to order the plan put in motion. Thoroughly disgusted, the artillery chief determined to give the go-ahead entirely on his own. "If not successful," he told Burnside, "every one of them would be lost." But he assured himself as well as his commander that the plan "*would* succeed."[24]

And it did. Aided by a fire from infantry comrades plus some of Tompkins's cannon, six pontoons stocked with Hall's men, each piloted by a few hardy souls from the Fiftieth New York Engineers, cast off from shore. Farther downstream, one hundred men of the Eighty-ninth New York, guided by pilots from the Fifteenth Engineers, rode the icy water aboard four other pontoons. On the far shore Michiganders and New Yorkers, later augmented by the Massachusetts regiments, pried the Confederates from the rubble in close-quarters combat. At last, Hunt's cannon smashed the Mississippians, as their survivors carried out orders recalling them to Marye's Heights. By 4 P.M. the Federals' bridges could, at long last, be completed. "A simple stroke of genius," said a battle correspondent of Hunt's plan.

General Burnside thought so too. In his official report he claimed all credit for planning it and carrying it out.[25]

* * *

Following so great an expenditure of effort and emotion, the fording of the Rappahannock, ironically, led directly to overwhelming Union defeat.

By the morning of 13 December, with his army on the rebel side of the river, Burnside sent it against Lee's extended line. His advance was halted soon after getting under way. Through vaguely worded instructions, he managed to thoroughly confuse General Franklin on the Federal left, with the result that the grand division commander made a limited and feeble attack, stopping far short of worthwhile objectives. Franklin's movement was also harmed by strong rebel resistance, plus the lack of an effective supporting cannonade. Unbelievably, Burnside forgot to inform Hunt of the starting hour of Franklin's offensive, ensuring a decided lack of cooperation between infantry and artillery in that crucial sector. When he learned that Franklin had gone forward, Hunt sent his gunners into action. But by then they could only hold off rebel troops pursuing Franklin's men after their repulse near Hamilton's Crossing.[26]

Even more tragic was the fate that befell Sumner's and Hooker's Grand Divisions. Sent against Lee's main force, the attackers were slaughtered regiment by regiment, brigade after brigade, on the naked terrain between Fredricksburg and Marye's Heights.

The artillery support Burnside had counted on proved woefully inadequate for his needs. Hunt had attempted unsuccessfully to convince his superior that most of the guns remaining on Stafford Heights were much too far from the rebel positions to do suitable damage. The guns in the right-center group, for instance, had to propel their projectiles 1,100 yards to strike Lee's center; while any shells fired by those in the left-center had to fly a whopping 5,400 yards to reach the same point. As at Second Bull Run and Antietam, no converging fire was possible.[27]

Burnside's perverse stubbornness would not permit him to quit until defeat became debacle. Fourteen times he launched close-packed attacks against the fireswept heights; and fourteen times his ranks were blown apart and their fragments sent hurtling rearward in full rout. Not until 4 P.M. on that frigid day did the army commander consent to call off the attacks. And by then almost thirteen thousand Federals had been butchered.[28]

The only grain of satisfaction Burnside could sift from the disaster was the knowledge that Lee could not come down from his heights to mount a pursuit. Even at long range the batteries on the Union side of the river would annihilate close-grouped commands heading in their direction.

On the fifteenth, Burnside's bloody army withdrew into its old camp outside Falmouth, where its commander availed himself of the guilt-purging relief of *mea culpa*. When the government reacted in shocked surprise to the slaughter at Marye's Heights, Burnside relayed an offer to resign his post. But the War Department ordered him to stay on—at least for a time.

Late in the month Burnside made a couple of pathetic attempts to recoup lost honor by seeking new ways to turn Lee's flanks. For several days he and his men floundered about beside the Rappahannock via open-ended plans that carried them through bottomless seas of mud and led nowhere. Early in January 1863 the army leader was finally determined to again cross the river—this time at U.S. Mine Ford, around Lee's left flank and under cover of some of Captain De Russy's heavy cannon still standing on Stafford Heights. But before he could supply Hunt with enough additional cannon to cover the crossing, the high command got wind of this foggy-minded offensive and stopped it forthwith.[29]

Desperately Burnside took thought anew, and by the sixteenth was ready to throw his troops over the Rappahannock around the rebel left, this time at Banks's Ford, much closer to Lee's positions. This second plan might have worked: years later Hunt learned that only one Confederate brigade could have offered resistance in that sector.[30] Again he went to work emplacing guns for the projected crossing—184 of them before the weary job ended. But just as the troops made ready to move, rain began to fall. Several successive days of it made roads muddy beyond both belief and endurance. "Even small streams were impassable torrents," a rebel officer remarked. "No end to mud," was a typical comment from a diarist in Hunt's own command.[31]

Stymied for the final time, Ambrose Burnside relinquished all hope of a renewed offensive. On 23 January he again drew his muddy, miserable soldiers back into winter quarters at Falmouth. His frustration outside Fredericksburg—coupled with the recent failure of Grant's Vicksburg, Mississippi campaign and William S. Rosecrans's gory stalemate at Murfreesboro, Tennessee—meant that the winter of 1862–63 brought a new low to Northern civilian and military morale.

Fortunately, General Hunt did not have to endure the gloom as long as most of his comrades. At the start of February he won a long-overdue furlough, which enabled him to exchange Virginia mud for the warm comfort of the Craig household in Washington—there, to spend a post-Christmas vacation with his family, including its youngest addition, four-month-old Maria ("Dolly") Hunt. When he embarked for the North left behind a completely immobilized army. The mud had grown so deep that rumor had a cannon sinking to its wheel rims in the gumbo.

Crude lettered signs beyond the river indicated the enemy's glee: BURNSIDE STUCK IN THE MUD. The Federals were willing to agree. Their own signs proclaimed: MUD IS KING.[32]

10

Demotion and Disaster

"O I am sick, sick, sick!"

So wrote Hunt's friend, Brigadier General Marsena R. Patrick, Provost Marshal General of the Army of the Potomac, on 1 February 1863. But Patrick was not physically ill. He had just come from a conference at the headquarters of the man who six days before had replaced Ambrose Burnside at the head of the army: this was Patrick's reaction to meeting Major General Joseph Hooker and staff.[1]

In some respects Hunt echoed Patrick's response. Though often at odds with Burnside over military matters, Hunt had been able to maintain decent relations with him. Like McClellan's, Burnside's enforced departure had somewhat saddened the artillery commander. Hooker's succession to top command saddened him even more. He had come to bear a personal dislike against the Massachusetts-born commander, and realized that their working relationship would be an exclusively formal one.

Hunt's motives were various. Joe Hooker was known in many circles, especially among the conservative cliques of the officer corps, as a blowhard and braggart, without refinement of any kind, and with an eye always open to the main chance.[2] Certainly his reputation as an intriguer was by now well established. His criticism of McClellan's leadership on the peninsula had been so bitter and so shrill that even some of Hooker's political backers in the capital had expressed distaste. He then worked so hard to undermine Burnside's already shaky position in command that short days before his relief the latter had demanded of the War Office that either Hooker went or he himself would. Since Hooker enjoyed much more formidable support in Washington City, the outcome was a foregone conclusion.

What damned Hooker in Hunt's eyes was his undisguised determination to play his political connections for personal gain. But even he had to admit that Hooker seemed extraordinarily gifted in the game. Thanks to a number of influential Republicans—including no less a personage than Treasury Secretary Salmon P. Chase—"Fighting Joe," at age forty-eight, had realized his most lofty ambition. The fact that he had climbed to his new position

by trodding on the carcasses of so many colleagues did not seem to bother
him in the least.

Finally, certain unsavory elements of Hooker's lifestyle, including a
penchant for the bottle and the company of women of easy virtue, scandalized
General Hunt.[3]

Even so, Hooker's assumption of top command left Hunt with no
pleasant alternative but to cooperate with him. And during the first weeks
of Hooker's tenure Hunt began to wonder if this might not be so difficult
a task after all. As had Marsena Patrick, Hunt admitted that Fighting Joe
showed signs of changing, for much the better. The pomposity and conceit

General Joseph Hooker (COURTESY, LIBRARY OF CONGRESS)

he had exuded during his days in corps command seemed to have disappeared
—or been placed under wraps. All that was visible was a spirit of humility
and good will toward all the members of his army—officers and men alike.

Hooker's commendable intention to transform the Army of the Potomac
into the most powerful fighting force "on the planet" was backed by several
creditable administrative performances during his early regime at Falmouth:
First, he abolished Burnside's cumbersome Grand Division system, substituting seven infantry corps and one corps of cavalry for his ever-growing
135,000-man army.[4] In creating the first full-scale corps of horsemen under
George Stoneman and providing it good weaponry, Hooker increased cavalry's
potential and self-respect. He also upgraded the military medical service;
strengthened the effectiveness of his construction and topographical engineers;
and vowed not to repeat his predecessors' mistakes in handling artillery. In
fact he proclaimed that, as an old artillerist himself, he recognized the
crucial necessity of retaining Hunt in control of the arm. Now Hunt began
to wonder in earnest if he might have to alter his opinion of Joe Hooker;
so, too, did pleasantly surprised subordinates: in mid-February Colonel
Wainwright noted in his journal that "Hooker seems to be gaining the
confidence of his generals by degrees."

But late that month, about ten days after Hunt's return to Falmouth
from leave, his honeymoon with Fighting Joe came to an end. During the
discharge of the most-elementary duties of an artillery commander, Hunt
consistently found his authority usurped by Hooker's staff officers, most
frequently by his pompous and obnoxious chief of staff, Major General
Daniel Butterfield, whom Wainwright believed "most thoroughly hated by
all the officers . . . as a meddling, over-conceited fellow."[5] When he sought
out Hooker over the trouble, Hunt discovered that the army leader's thinking
had described a 180-degree arc. Rather than both tactical and administrative
head of the artillery, Hunt was now designated neither. Hooker explained
that henceforth the batteries in the main army would be considered integral
parts of the divisions with which they served; no longer would they be
considered merely "attached." Thus from now on all corps and division
commanders would have officially sanctioned control—complete control—
over all field batteries. This was enough to floor Hunt, but it was not the
worst. Hooker also removed the Artillery Reserve from Hunt's purview,
even in the purely administrative sense. In the future the Reserve, as the
rest of the army's artillery, would receive orders from Hooker via the office
of the adjutant general of the Army. In turn, all batteries would send daily
reports, not to Hunt, but to the adjutant general. The chief of artillery
would no longer be informed of the movements or use made of any cannon
unit unless he requested copies of headquarters orders for his personal
knowledge. In effect, Hunt had been demoted to the status of artillery
advisor to the general commanding the army.

Though used to heavy dosage, this was the bitterest medicine Hunt had ever taken. For days he alternately sank into gloom and stalked about his headquarters exhibiting his vocabulary of profanity. The situation left him emotionally barren, confused, and on the verge of resigning.

But even after his startling audience with Hooker, he could not be certain of his revised status. Several times in subsequent weeks he found himself ordered by members of Hooker's staff to carry out duties far outside the narrow confines Hooker had placed on his authority. The dilemma led him back to army headquarters, where Hooker further complicated, rather than clarified, Hunt's position.

In reply to Hunt's query about the exact extent of his power, Hooker thought a minute, as though he had never considered the matter. At last he replied that in time of need, such as during battle, Hunt should "be about," noting artillery employment and issuing orders, whenever necessary, in Hooker's name.

Hunt cocked his head, straining to catch the new drift of Hooker's thinking. He remarked that it now sounded as though Hooker expected him to exercise some command authority after all. But just how much?

The commanding general countered with a lengthy parable of his own service in the Mexican War, when serving as adjutant general to Gideon Pillow. He recounted his role at a critical juncture in the battle of Chapultepec when he had issued orders in the name of his general, then absent from an important part of the field, thus saving the day for the American cause. Under such circumstances, he told Hunt, the judicious use of a superior's authority was not only proper but vital.

Hunt remained unmollified. He stated his refusal to place himself in the dangerous position of issuing directives in another's behalf, given the court-martial that might follow should disaster result. Finally he suggested that he draw up a list of what he believed ought to be the duties of an artillery commander, permitting Hooker to pass judgment on them point by point. Hooker agreed. So Hunt went back to his own tent, scribbled away for some hours, and handed the finished product to Hooker's chief of staff.[6]

A day passed without response. On the next, General Butterfield returned Hunt's list with his own endorsement: the commanding general "does not deem it expedient to change the duties of Chief of Artillery from what they are defined to be by existing orders. . . ."[7]

Again Hunt's temper climbed to boiling point. Hooker had not modified his earlier stand after all—Hunt was still artillery chief only in name. He vent his wrath particularly on Butterfield, incensed about the condescending manner in which the aide had relayed Hooker's decision. This much seemed clear: influenced by his chief of staff, Joe Hooker had decided to write new rules, "existing orders" be damned!

Weeks afterward, still sizzling with anger, but apparently resigned to his fate, Hunt wrote the deposed Burnside, with whom he found himself able to exchange a few cordial letters. He told his former commander:

My position is a painful one in some respects. I have been deposed from my Comm. of the Art'y of the Army and notified that I am "a mere staff officer" that my duties are such as a major (in the words of Gen. Hooker) or a lieutenant (in the words of his chief of Staff)—can do just as well as I can. And the latter took special occasion—so I am informed—to explain this interesting fact to the President when he asked if Stoneman did not command the Cav. and Gen Hunt the artillery.

Considering the sensitivity of Hunt's pride, his determination not to resign in the face of such humiliation is remarkable. But he was still a man of durable integrity: "My principle in this war," he told Burnside,

has been to do my duty independently of personal interest wherever it may please the powers to place one, and I shall continue to act on this principle. . . . In the meantime I am furnishing the information and the brains for the management of the artillery so far as I am consulted or permitted to do—and will continue to do so in the interests of the cause.[8]

By his decision to remain in the volunteer ranks, he ensured himself of more grief and embarrassment than heretofore. However, once the initial sting of his demotion had faded, he returned to Hooker's headquarters with various plans for revamping and streeamlining artillery administration. If he could not exercise effective control over the batteries, at least he could suggest ways in which others might do so.

First he tried to sell Hooker on Colonel Wainwright's plan to group corps batteries into large but cohesive artillery brigades. Hooker rejected it. Next Hunt suggested a more equitable distribution of cannon throughout the main army (the I Corps possessed ten batteries, for example; the recently attached XI and XII Corps owned only five each). Hooker said no. Then Hunt pressed for numerous promotions; that sufficient rank be allotted artillery officers—for nearly ten thousand gunners and 412 cannon, Hunt had but five field-grade subordinates. Again the commanding general shook his head. After this, Hunt lacked the courage to resubmit earlier requests that he receive a major general's rank and salary, commensurate with his titular sphere of authority. He could have predicted Hooker's reply.[9]

Not only Fighting Joe, but also General-in-Chief Halleck, went out of his way to frustrate the artillery commander. To Halleck, Hunt later applied for authority to appoint field-rank subordinates by granting several battery chiefs the brevet promotions that General McClellan had recommended for them long ago. Hunt's West Point classmate would not consent. Nor would he approve an idea relayed to him by Hunt from General Tyler, by which many of the thousands of heavy artillerymen manning the Washington defenses would be used to fill the almost 3,500-man shortage in the field artillery of the Army of the Potomac. Halleck committed this plan to his wastebasket. He also turned down a third proposal that Hunt submitted— this calling for the establishment of an Artillery Bureau in the War Department to centralize administration of the arm and to inspect all cannon units in the Federal ranks; supply them with the best available ordnance matériel; and to work in artillery's behalf in governmental circles. Reportedly, Halleck exploded into laughter at the idea.[10] Yet, only a few months afterward, an almost identical twin, the Cavalry Bureau, came into existence with fruitful repercussions for the administration and supply of mounted troops.

His repeated failure to make headway with his superiors in Falmouth and Washington did little to ease Hunt's bleakness of spirit—a bleakness that deepened as the winter wore on and problems multiplied. Perhaps the most serious of these was the continuing exodus of artillery officers to high-ranking positions in other arms or in departmental command. Early in '63, for example, Lieutenant Colonel Hays became the brigadier general in charge of the Second Brigade, Third Division, II Corps; erstwhile Captain De Russy was named colonel of the Fourth New York Volunteer Artillery, a regiment not in the field; and General Tyler temporarily took a desk job, heading up military districts around the capital. Though loath to lose their services, Hunt could not begrudge them the fruits of their conspicuous abilities.

Nor could he—even in the face of adversity—cease attempting to disprove those critics who considered "military efficiency" a contradiction in terms. Despite loss of power and prestige, he could still implement some minor, but needed, reforms. Toward the close of winter, for example, Colonel Wainwright noted that Hunt

> has just made an improvement in reducing the number of heavy spare parts, felloes, spokes, and so forth, carried in the battery waggons [sic]. Only one spare wheel to a section is to be carried hereafter, which will also save some horseflesh. The horse batteries, too, are to have but one chest on their caisson bodies hereafter: an excellent change for the three-inch guns, the ammunition chests of which, when loaded, are very heavy.

In sum, Wainwright decided: "General Hunt is doing his best to have the artillery at least in good order when the campaign opens. Most of his instructions are excellent, and if we can only carry them out, the artillery will do more service than ever before."[11]

* * *

In the midst of his toil and frustration, Hunt was plucked from the field and deposited in Washington. This time he was on no furlough. When he reached the capital on the morning of 10 March he could spend only a few hours given entirely to family concerns. Next day duty carried him to conference rooms at the Capitol, where he appeared, by order, before the Joint Congressional Committee on the Conduct of the War.[12]

This was a bipartisan panel of three senators and four congressmen, which had been sitting irregularly since the winter of '61, seeking to evaluate the degree of expertise with which the Federal war effort was being prosecuted: so, at any rate, was the formal characterization of the committee. In reality, the senators and representatives were seeking to evaluate the political orientation of the conflict and, if need be, to change it. Despite its professions to bipartisanship, it constituted a powerful tool in the hands of the radical Republicans, such as its chairman, Senator Ben Wade of Ohio, who dominated and controlled it. Already its members had gone witch-hunting for high-ranking officers who either adhered too closely to the Democratic faith or showed a tendency to forget that civilian authority was running the war. The panel's list of victims included an acquaintance of Hunt: Brigadier General Charles P. Stone, one of McClellan's favorite subordinates in the early days of the conflict. Accused by the committee of engineering the minor Federal debacle at Balls Bluff in October 1861 through a treasonous allegiance to secession, Stone had been tossed into prison in New York harbor several months ago, largely through the committee's efforts. There he had languished 189 days, though no formal charges had been drawn up against him—an unmistakable symbol of what must happen to all soldiers who treated their civilian overlords—especially those in the GOP—too cavalierly.[13]

This time around, the committee had zeroed in on bigger game, though there might seem no need to pursue it. They were seeking to indict for criminal misguidance during the peninsula campaign and at Antietam a man whom Hunt still admired and desired to protect: George McClellan. The congressmen knew little of Hunt's political leanings, though general knowledge had given them the assumption that Hunt leaned toward Democratic principles. They did know they had to treat him carefully if they were to wring from him testimony that would blacken McClellan's reputation in retrospect.

Hunt was determined not to serve as a bludgeon in the committee's hand. When queried about operations on the peninsula, he declared his fervent belief that the failure of the army to flank and isolate Yorktown had been the early turning point of the campaign, and one perhaps beyond Little Mac's control. He also implied that President Lincoln's last-minute detachment of most of Irvin McDowell's corps from McClellan's field force had materially contributed to the run of bad fortune that had dogged the Army of the Potomac ever afterward. Such opinions pleased neither Ben Wade nor his Republican colleagues, and they worked harder to lead Hunt in other directions.

Hunt refused to be led; so went a typical exchange:

QUESTION: Is it, then, your opinion that we were not strong enough at any time before Richmond to have coped with their army there?

ANSWER: I cannot say that; we might have been successful, or might not have been, if we had attacked [Richmond]. But I should have thought it imprudent or improper to have attacked, where there was not a fair prospect, or a certainty of making the attack a sure thing. In that, however, I am merely giving my own judgment about the matter.

Through it all, he made clear that second-guessing Little Mac was not his style. Thoroughly frustrated, the inquisitors temporarily conceded defeat.

Later in the session, however, they switched their attack to the disaster at Fredricksburg. Here the radicals sought vindication for Ambrose Burnside, with whom they happened to be on close terms. They wished to foist crucial blame on conservatively oriented General Franklin, indicting him almost alone for the failure of the battle strategy on last 13 December. Though unwilling to play into the panel's hands, Hunt had to restate his well-known opinion that had Franklin gone ahead in proper manner, "50,000 men should have carried that position." Even here he was charitable: "However, I do not know enough of the ground and the position to be justified in giving an absolutely positive opinion upon the subject."[14]

After further hours of thrust and parry, the congressmen allowed Hunt to stand down. He was so relieved to escape such an unappetizing intrigue that in leaving the Capitol he did not linger even for a moment to speak to the next witness, General Hooker, who passed him in the corridor going the other way. By no means did Hunt wish to listen to his new commander's testimony; he already knew the vein in which it would run.

Hooker did not disappoint him. The first question put to him elicited a reply clearly characteristic of the man:

QUESTION: To what do you attribute the failure of the peninsula campaign?

ANSWER: I do not hesitate to say that it is to be attributed to the want of generalship on the part of our commander.[15]

* * *

Spring touched central Virginia late that year. In the midst of April the weather remained cool, capable of sending icy rain, frozen mud, and numbing winds to make camp life ever miserable.

It was the rain that almost halted the spring campaign for good, before fairly under way. On the thirteenth of the month, Joe Hooker sent his rejuvenated horsemen over the Rappahannock and Rapidan Rivers to strike Lee in the rear, while the main army butted head-on into the rebels still ensconced below Fredricksburg. When foul weather sent rivers over their banks and turned the roads almost as muddy as in January, the cavalry was stymied. Hooker had to curtail operations and devise new ones.[16]

Not until the twenty-seventh was he ready to put new strategy to the test. Now he determined to move from Falmouth with the V, XI, and XII

Corps, and cross the Rappahannock at Kelly's Ford, far to the north and west of Fredricksburg, in a long envelopment of Lee's left flank. This done, Hooker would come hurtling in on his enemy's rear. He expected attack to come as a complete surprise, for his I and VI Corps, under overall command of Major General John Sedgwick, were to hold Lee's attention by crossing the river below the city and moving against Lee's center on Marye's Heights as if in repetition of the 13 December assaults.

In some respects Hooker's envisioned turning-movement copied the strategy that McDowell had attempted to employ against Beauregard at the First Bull Run. There it had proved a flat failure because of McDowell's inability to shield it from the enemy's eyes. If the same fate befell Hooker, his dilemma would be even more woeful than McDowell's. Whereas the latter had maneuvered mainly on open ground suitable for the deployment of troops in mass, Hooker's envelopment would lead his three corps, as well as his potential reinforcements among the II and III Corps, through the Wilderness—a God-forsaken ten-mile square of treacherous real estate, featuring horrid tangles of second-growth pine and matted underbrush. There Lee might rush up to give battle on terrain that would neutralize his opponents' great numerical superiority.[17]

Hooker fully realized the gamble he was taking. He seemed bound and determined to prove that he possessed in abundance that which he had criticized McClellan for utterly lacking: boldness and vigor.

When Hooker broke camp at Falmouth on the morning of the twenty-seventh, he enjoyed a tremendous advantage over Lee in artillery strength, as well as in infantry power. By this date he had amassed seventy-seven field batteries, with another group of six light batteries within the Artillery Reserve.[18] Yet his cannon dispositions revealed the dearth of expertise that had resulted from Hunt's demotion.

The trio of corps making the critical envelopment through the Wilderness took only a fraction of their artillery: one battery per division. Those guns left behind would not move south of the Rappahannock until the corps had successfully negotiated a crossing at Kelly's Ford. Then the batteries would rejoin their commands—if they could locate them at such long distance—via Banks's Ford, an even more crucial crossing-site, about seventeen miles southeast of Kelly's. Worse, the artillerymen who accompanied the corps into the Wilderness had been allowed to fill only limber and caisson chests, carrying no extra ammunition, except that which was in the wagon trains of the main army, far to the rear of the march column.[19]

The rest of Hooker's artillery was widely dispersed on the Falmouth side of the Rappahannock to aid Sedgwick's holding action. Twenty-seven batteries, including all those in the Reserve, were posted downstream from Fredricksburg to cover the crossing of the I and VI Corps upon bridges wisely constructed far from the partially ruined but still-inhabitable city. These guns had been emplaced on high ground in three general locations, under the direct supervision of corps artillery chiefs Wainwright and Tompkins, as well as Lieutenant Colonel Warner, Hunt's inspector-general. Recently Hunt had assigned the latter to field duty, as also his other inspector-general, Major Doull: this seemed the only device by which he might secure additional field-grade officers for tactical service. Still other cannon had been emplaced at Falmouth and atop Stafford Heights to give additional support to Sedgwick's fellows. Most of these were under the immediate control of Captain William M. Graham—Hays's *ad interim* successor as head of the Reserve.[20]

Lately, despite demoting Hunt, Hooker had seen fit to give him some vital duties. It had been Hunt who made the artillery dispositions in Sedgwick's behalf—a chore that had consumed considerable time and effort. Now, as Hooker moved out from camp with the leading elements of his envelopment column, he provided more work for Hunt. Determined to keep Banks's Ford open as an avenue for reinforcements, Hooker dispatched him thither on the twenty-seventh to select the best positions for field works to protect it.

There, Hunt found rebels entrenched on the south shore; Hooker's concern for the safety of the crossing site had been valid. Hunt noted advantageous terrain features and, then, as per Hooker's order, gave the task of holding them with cannon to Major Doull, who would assume command at the ford. From the river, Hunt rode back to the scene of Sedgwick's operations; in the meantime, Doull reached back to Falmouth for two batteries from Captain Graham's command, including the siege pieces of the First Connecticut, which Hunt had outfitted with special carriages for field duty after Fredericksburg. The major reinforced these units with field batteries temporarily detached from those corps marching with Hooker. Soon he was pounding away at the rifle pits below the stream, keeping the Confederates from crossing, thereby threatening to separate Hooker's flanking column from its base of communications.[21]

After certifying that all was proceeding smoothly with his old chum near Fredericksburg, Hunt left Sedgwick's headquarters to rejoin Hooker. En route, he must have felt a strange and unpleasant sensation, realizing that the artillery units he still nominally commanded were stationed at unknown points all around him. Back at Hooker's side not far from the Wilderness, he was further displeased to find himself again an idler, waiting for his commander to give him another errand to run, however far-ranging or trivial its nature.

Even though ignorant of detailed dispositions, by 1 May, Hunt had a fair idea of Hooker's strategic progress thus far, which—despite weird command arrangements—seemed well advanced. The V, XI, and XII Corps had crossed the stream at Kelly's; had forded the meandering Rapidan; and had entered the Wilderness. As anticipated, the clotted forest had loomed as a hindrance to movement (artillery could have done precious little fighting in it) but still, by that May Day morning, Hooker's trio of corps

Battery covering Sedgwick's crossing at Fredricksburg, May 1863. (COURTESY, LIBRARY OF CONGRESS)

had reached a wide clearing by a crossroads—Chancellorsville—fronting the northern extension of the Wilderness, but still a far piece from emerging onto open ground in Lee's rear. Still, with no Confederates thus far in sight, Hooker and his soldiers appeared confident of keeping their coming attack a surprise until the last minute.

Since most of Stoneman's cavalry had finally trotted south to menace rebel communications, Hooker lacked precise knowledge of Lee's whereabouts. Even so, shortly before noon on the first, he ordered his corps to press eastward from Chancellorsville, sending couriers to tell Sedgwick to begin demonstrating above Fredricksburg, making a prodigious display of truculence for Lee's benefit.[22]

Not long after Hooker messaged Sedgwick, however, the Federals' luck began to dissipate. Neither Hooker nor Hunt would learn the reason until much later, but that afternoon, shortly after departing Chancellorsville, the Union advance ran hard aground against Lee's infantry. As rifle fire began to echo through the woods, Hooker rode forward in alarm. Flabbergasted, he found deep lines of rebels in his front. Where had they come from? How had they detected his advance?

His confidence badly frayed, Hooker was further discomfited when appealed to by the commander of his forward echelon, who had grown concerned about his shortage of artillery. Hoping that additional cannon in the forefront of his column would enable the advance to proceed, Hooker turned to Hunt and ordered him to supply the advance brigades.[23]

A strange quandary now confronted Hooker's "artillery advisor." He did not know how to obey, for he was ignorant of the whereabouts of the cannon he supposedly commanded. And even should he scare up some guns, he lacked the authority to compel them to go forward as reinforcements.

Fortunately he found an artillerist who appreciated his dilemma— Lieutenant Colonel Charles H. Morgan, head of the cannon brigade in the II Corps, which was being moved within supporting range of Hooker's advance troops. Morgan volunteered to send one of his own batteries forward; and, shortly afterward, another battery, recently arrived in the Wilderness, reported to Hunt, its commander willing to do as he directed. But no sooner had this second unit started eastward than the division commander effectively in charge of it under Hooker's artillery administration demanded its recall. Hunt had no choice but to comply.[24] Before he could scare up a replacement, an order filtered back from Hooker, pulling the whole army back to Chancellorsville—there, to dig in for a stand against the attacking enemy. Obviously the army was about to surrender the initiative.

When he rejoined army headquarters at the crossroads clearing, Hunt found his commander again apprehensive about Banks's Ford. By now Major Doull and his cannon had packed up, left there, and rejoined their individual commands for the balance of the battle. With his army girding for a desperate fight in the woods, Hooker feared the secessionists might use the abandoned ford to come crashing in on his left and rear: exactly the same tactic he had hoped to use against Lee. Of additional concern were reports that enemy infantry were massing at Port Royal Junction, some twenty-five miles from Banks's Ford, perhaps soon to cross there and then spring upon Hooker in an unguarded sector.[25]

Fighting down panic, Hooker ordered Hunt to move all available cannon from Falmouth to Banks's Ford. He then rushed off, leaving Hunt to grope his way through trees and brush to U.S. Ford along the Rappahannock where a Federal telegraph station connected the main army with the reserves at Falmouth. After a long ride, made circuitous by detours to avoid Federal wagon trains and stragglers, the artillerist reached the ford and wired a directive to General Butterfield, minding the store above Fredricksburg: send the twenty-odd cannon under Captain Graham to Banks's Ford; if Sedgwick had any batteries to spare, ship them there, too.

This chore completed, Hunt galloped off to Banks's; Hooker had ordered him to assume command there. On the way, fortunately, he encountered Doull's 4.5-inch rifles, only now vacating their positions along the stream, although the rest of the cannon had long since moved on. Once again Hunt pointed the big guns toward the south shore, even though the enemy rifle pits now looked empty. He then settled back to wait for Butterfield to send

up the rest of the needed hardware. In the meantime, he paid anxious heed
to the sound of the fighting among the trees to the southwest, as well as
to the racket above Fredricksburg where Sedgwick's infantry was now
crossing. At about 7 P.M. the tension at Banks's Ford began to abate: the
guns from Falmouth loomed into view from the rear. Afterward Hunt wired
Hooker that, given a small infantry force (soon on its way to the ford),
he and the cannon should be able to secure Banks's easily enough.[26]

He spent the shank of the four-day battle there at the river several miles
above the crucial fighting in the Wilderness. With twenty cannon and a
brace of infantrymen at his side, he felt fairly comfortable. In the meantime,
however, his comrades in Hooker's main body were soon floundering in
calamitous straits.

Hunt began to suspect as much on the afternoon of the third, when
newly returned Confederates south of the ford suddenly vanished, yet again
melting into the trees as abruptly as they had appeared. Later he learned
that, as he had suspected, these troops had gone to contribute their weight
to a concealed flank attack—an attack that had struck Hooker with irresistible
impact on the second, continuing well into the next day.

J.E.B. Stuart proved to be Hooker's greatest nemesis. With his opponents,
the Federal cavalrymen, far afield, Stuart had gone into the Wilderness
with his division of cavaliers and had detected the Federal turning movement
in plenty of time to get Lee's infantry and artillery into position to oppose
it. Then, on 1 May, one of Stuart's chief lieutenants had spied Hooker's
right flank lying exposed and vulnerable in the midst of the woods. Again
he notified his commander, and again Lee moved quickly to take fair
advantage. This time he sent Stonewall Jackson and twenty-six thousand
men to smash the unanchored flank, which Jackson proceeded to do with
great verve and power, crashing out of the timber late on the second,
overwhelming those luckless Federals in his way, stampeding most of
Hooker's XI Corps, and scaring Fighting Joe out of his wits. Paralyzed by
nervous exhaustion and a near miss from a rebel artillery shell, the Union
commander lost all sense of direction, all mental coherence—and the final
remnants of his nerve.[27]

By midday on 3 May, though he had gone down with a wound that
would prove mortal, Jackson had thoroughly defeated his opposition. In
wildest panic Hooker sent a plea that Sedgwick, still operating against those
Confederates Lee had left to hold Fredricksburg, come at once to his relief.

At this point, the battle began to work its way to Hunt's bailiwick.
Early on 4 May, after four bloody repulses, Sedgwick managed to accomplish
what Ambrose Burnside had failed to do the previous December: break
through rebel lines atop Marye's Heights. From there Sedgwick's own VI
Corps headed westward toward Hooker, moving on Banks's Ford from the
lower shore; in the meantime, the I Corps, including Colonel Wainwright's
artillery, crossed at U.S. Ford after a long, wide-angled march from Fred-

ricksburg, and moved close to Hooker's main body to lend assistance.

Sedgwick, however, did not come so close. Seeing his approach, Lee left part of his army to battle Hooker's command in the Wilderness, then turned about with twenty thousand other troops to confront the VI Corps. Near Salem Church and not far from Banks's Ford, Lee struck Sedgwick from three sides, forcing him back across the river for good. Though Hunt lent his friend all the support his guns at the ford could furnish, it was insufficient to prevent Lee from defeating Sedgwick as completely and as dramatically as he had bested Hooker during the two days previous.[28]

While Sedgwick was being outfought at Salem Church, Fighting Joe remained in hastily constructed works near Chancellorsville, frantically trying to bolster them in fear of another assault by Lee's main force. His frenzy was increased by an inability to locate crucially needed batteries. Too late he had come to see the damage done by stripping Hunt of his duties, as well as his authority.

When Colonel Wainwright, at the head of the I Corps, made his way to Hooker's field headquarters, he found mass confusion: "It seemed to me all the artillery of the army was running around loose. I had met half a dozen batteries going to the front, and as many more going to the rear, blocking the road to no purpose." But when he reported, he found that the commanding general seemed determined to remain calm before an inferior officer. In his diary the colonel recorded their strange conversation:

GENERAL HOOKER. "Well, Wainwright, how is the artillery getting on?"
SELF. "As badly as it well can. Batteries are being ordered in every direction, blocking up the roads; and no one seems to know where to go. Where is General Hunt?"
GENERAL HOOKER. "What is the matter?"
SELF. "As near as I can understand, every division commander wants his own batteries, and battery commanders will obey no one else's orders."
GENERAL HOOKER. "Well, we have no time to talk now. You take hold and make it right."
SELF. "Where is General Hunt?"
GENERAL HOOKER. "At Banks's Ford. You take his place."[29]

Until Hunt could be located, Wainwright did as commanded. With the assistance of every capable officer available, including Hunt's crony, General Patrick, the I Corps artillery chief did an admirable job, bringing order from pandemonium. He built a 110-gun battle line around Hooker's new positions, cleared fields of fire, sent decimated batteries to the rear, and replaced them with fresh ones—all the while alert for Hunt's return.[30]

The artillery commander at last reached headquarters late on the fourth. His first act was to compliment Wainwright on his excellent stop-gap measures. Then he went to work firming up the colonel's line, overseeing the restocking of ammo chests, and redeploying surplus cannon pending renewal of an offensive that Hooker had promised for the morrow.

But by sunrise on the fifth, Fighting Joe had forgotten his promise. All morning and afternoon he held his ground, and, about 7 P.M., ordered a complete withdrawal from the Wilderness. Hunt protested, insisting that the army should push on until clear of the trees—but eastward, toward Lee's lines, not northward in abject retreat. With a wave of his hand, Hooker closed the discussion, ordering Hunt to post enough guns to clear a lane of withdrawal across the Rapidan and Rappahannock.[31]

This latest directive seemed to indicate clearly that Hunt had been restored to full authority in command of the army's artillery. Unfortunately it had come much too late; and, when Hunt trudged slowly north in company with the rest of the army, he cursed Fighting Joe all the way back to Falmouth.

* * *

The postmortem appraisal of the Chancellorsville campaign provided some enlightening particulars. At the top of the list were the several sins of omission and commission of which Hooker had proved himself guilty in handling his artillery. Too many guns had been left behind at and near Falmouth when his turning movement began; those that had gone forward in that movement were insufficiently supplied with ammunition. Hooker had allowed division and corps commanders to attain too much power over the batteries, with the usual results. He had permitted many batteries to be shifted from the front lines to secondary battle sectors, where they saw little employment. Other guns had been moved too close to the enemy; fourteen had been captured by Lee and Jackson.[32] Hooker had compelled gunners to operate in the thickest reaches of the Wilderness, confronted by trees and brush too thick to facilitate mobility or permit adequate sighting. He had placed infantry and staff officers in charge of the reserve ammunition train, ignorant of the special qualities of their job, and had kept the train far to the rear of his army, where front-line batteries low on projectiles could not locate it. Above all, by reducing Hunt to mere advisory status, Hooker had destroyed the centralization of artillery control so crucial to the success of the entire army.[33]

Sobered by the results of his inept planning, Fighting Joe made amends in the aftermath of his disaster below the Rapidan. He not only reinstated Hunt, but adopted his proposals for grouping batteries into brigades attached to corps, not to divisions in the main army; for borrowing infantry and cavalry recruits to bring artillery-unit strength up to par; for bestowing upon artillery officers jurisdiction over ammo trains; for setting up a reserve supply of one thousand battery animals for the relief of dismounted units; and for aiding mobility by paring down the field command from 412 to 372 cannon.[34]

Thus, once again, it had taken a debacle to bring about the implementation of long-needed artillery reforms. It seemed a great pity these had not been put into practice just a few days earlier. Said one artillerist: "If what was thus done as a restorative had previously been done as a preventative, the probabilities are that Chancellorsville would have had another and a very different ending."[35]

Hunt felt the same way, and said so in harsher terms. By the time he completed his official report of the campaign, his commander had gone the way of Irvin McDowell, John Pope, George B. McClellan, and Ambrose Burnside. Nevertheless, Hunt took careful aim and let Fighting Joe have it squarely between the eyes:

I doubt if the history of modern armies can exhibit a parallel instance of such palpable crippling of a great arm of the service in the very presence of a powerful enemy, to overcome whom would require every energy of all arms under the most favorable circumstances. It is not, therefore, to be wondered at that confusion and mismanagement ensued, and it is creditable to the batteries themselves, and to the officers who commanded them, that they did so well.[36]

11

Stemming the Tide of Defeat

For more than five weeks after Chancellorsville, the Army of the Potomac marked time near Falmouth. Well before the close of that period it had become obvious that Hooker was a lame-duck commander, incapable of making amends for past blunders or maintaining the confidence of his troops.

After his remarkable success in the Wilderness, Hooker's opposite number in gray decided upon another invasion of the North; by mid-June, Lee was well on his way toward the Mason-Dixon Line. Slow to get word of his withdrawal from Fredricksburg, the Army of the Potomac finally began a brisk movement northward, paralleling the Confederates' route of march, keeping between them and the Federal capital.

Despite their long series of battlefield setbacks, the men in the Union ranks seemed enthusiastic about again meeting Lee's soldiers in combat, especially on Northern soil, whose terrain would prove unfamiliar to the Confederate commanders. In time Hunt came to realize that the common soldiers and their officers had not been beaten in the Wilderness; only Joe Hooker had been vanquished.

In truth, Hooker, harassed and nervous, having lost basic poise and self-assurance, seemed the only impediment to a successful curtailment of Lee's offensive. That impediment was removed on 28 June, with the Army of the Potomac in Maryland, its headquarters at Frederick City, and its opponents several miles to the north and west, already in Pennsylvania. On that summer Sunday came word that Lincoln had removed Hooker from command, replacing him with an erstwhile corps commander: Major General George Gordon Meade.[1]

Unlike McClellan's departure, Hooker's relief saw no outpouring of regret from the men in the ranks. The survivors of the deadly nightmare that was Chancellorsville had put all faith in this man; had trusted him to lead the greatest army on the planet to enduring victory. But Hooker had failed them badly—had let them down, plain and simple—and now, when he was forced to pay the cost of that failure, these soldiers had no use for him at all.

Battery unlimbered on south bank of Rappahannock, June 1863. (COURTESY, LIBRARY OF CONGRESS)

Neither did Hunt. On the other hand, he sensed that his relationship with crusty George Meade would prove to be no love feast. Meade was perhaps too closely akin to Hunt to become his fast friend. Both possessed great pride and were capable of towering rage when provoked (Meade was probably more wrathful; certainly his reputation for contentiousness was more widespread). Yet both were no-nonsense taskmasters with a well-developed sense of integrity and fairness, plus a strong desire to accomplish needed work energetically, efficiently, and with a minimum of ostentation. Like Hunt, Meade also drew a clear line between matters military and political, rarely mixing the two. Where the pair parted ways was in their risibility. Even in the roughest going and during times of greatest stress, Hunt rarely lost his sense of humor—when demoted by Hooker, he could still laugh and joke among friends and colleagues, often to such an extent that companions believed he had no care in the world. But a sense of humor was something that Meade never found.[2]

On balance, solid-stolid Meade seemed to Hunt a decided improvement over his predecessor—especially after Meade announced a desire to continue in effect the beneficial artillery programs that Hooker had approved after Chancellorsville. In large measure, however, Meade simply lacked the time to implement any sweeping administrative changes. By the twenty-eighth, it was plain that another large-scale battle was imminent—one that might determine the outcome of the war, especially since the enemy was ranging almost at will through the Keystone State, perhaps heading for Philadelphia, New York, or Washington. Under these circumstances, Meade had all he could handle in familiarizing himself with Hooker's most recent dispositions.

This also meant, of course, that other undesirable practices under the Hooker regime would remain in force indefinitely; including the army's bias against field-grade artillerists. A listing of the several brigade artillery chiefs brought this discrimination into perspective: Colonel Wainwright headed the cannon in the I Corps; Captain John G. Hazard, those of the II Corps; Captain George E. Randolph, III Corps; Captain Augustus P. Martin, V Corps; Colonel Tompkins, VI Corps; Major Thomas W. Osborn, XI Corps; and Lieutenant Edward D. Muhlenberg, XII Corps. In the revitalized Artillery Reserve (which at least had a brigadier general at the top, Robert Tyler having given up his departmental command to head it), the five brigade chiefs were Captain Dunbar R. Ransom, Lieutenant Colonel Freeman McGilvery, Captain Elijah D. Taft, Captain James F. Huntington, and Captain Robert H. Fitzhugh. The two brigades of horse artillery attached to the army's cavalry were commanded by a pair of captains: James M. Robertson and John Tidball. Thus only four of the fourteen brigade chiefs held field rank, one of them ranking even lower than the average battery commander; by rights, all should have been at least full colonels. Hunt found this intolerable; but, since Hooker had not approved battery redistribution to secure an equitable balance of artillery throughout the main army, any proposal to improve this command and rank arrangement was beyond effectiveness.[3]

At the outset of Meade's tenure in command, Hunt found a much-thornier problem in need of resolution. Though after Chancellorsville, Hooker had indicated a willingness to restore full authority to Hunt, no subsequent battle had put his intent to the test. Now Hunt lacked time to secure from Meade an updated account of his duties and privileges. For all he knew, Meade preferred that he return to his pre-Chancellorsville status as a mere artillery advisor at army headquarters. And the first assignment Hunt received from his new commander did not involve his customary doings and, thus, did nothing to clear up the issue. His orders required him to roam far afield of the main army on an emergency reconnaissance mission.

Acutely aware that Lee's soldiers were liable to strike him from the northward or westward at any time—aware, too, that thanks to Hooker's laxity, the Army of the Potomac was widely dispersed through upper Virginia and central and southern Maryland—Meade considered maintaining the defensive posture Hooker had assumed after Chancellorsville. As head of the V Corps, Meade recently had passed the western flank of Big Pipe Creek, which ran about ten miles below Frederick. Impressed by the excellent positions afforded by ridges and rolling hills beside the stream,

Meade had wondered if the entire course of the creek might not offer advantageous terrain.

On the evening of 30 June, with army headquarters at Taneytown, Maryland and advance cavalry units forging twelve miles northward into the Pennsylvania village of Gettysburg, Meade instructed Hunt to visit Pipe Creek in his stead. He was to file a full report on the creek's defensive capabilities, in event of a fallback south against Lee, to be handed to Meade as soon as possible.[4]

When Hunt rode off on his errand, accompanied only by his aide, Lieutenant Bissell, he may have wondered if he were now an all-purpose troubleshooter instead of an artillery chieftain. Dutifully, however, he followed Big Pipe Creek from its western terminus near the town of Middleburg, northward and eastward through Union Mills, to its eastern flank near Manchester, one of the rearward supply bases of Meade's army.[5]

Like his superior, Hunt grew much impressed by the wide, flat valley of the creek and the high and wooded hills on both of its banks. He also noted that from Westminster, a half-dozen miles below the stream, roads fanned out to cover every important point of terrain along that line. By morning of 1 July he had formed the opinion that the creek was valuable for its "offensive-defensive" nature, and had studied likely positions for cannon emplacement. Then, under the boiling sun, he and Bissell spurred their horses back to the army.[6]

When they reached Meade later that afternoon, a few miles north of Taneytown, they learned that their errand was unnecessary. Events during their absence had made it imperative that the army continue into Pennsylvania. Still, Hunt would always lament that so commanding a position as that watered by Pipe Creek had to be abandoned.[7]

Fighting in the little crossroads town of Gettysburg had been raging for several hours already. Brought on by a sparring match between Union cavalry and Confederate infantry, it had eventuated, with amazing swiftness, into full-scale battle. In consequence, the advance units of Meade's main army, his I and XI Corps, had been rushed to the scene to aid the cavalry in grappling with the much more numerous people in gray. At Gettysburg, by the time of Hunt's return to headquarters, Meade's most trusted lieutenant, Major General John F. Reynolds, lay dead, victim of a sharpshooter's bullet or stray shell. Upon Hunt's arrival, in fact, he found Meade in process of dispatching Winfield Hancock, the II Corps commander, to succeed Reynolds in overall charge of the Federal effort and to report as to Gettysburg's advantages as a battlefield. Though Hunt and Hancock were on delicate terms in consequence of the corps commander's outspoken criticism of Artillery Reserve inaccessibility at Antietam and Chancellorsville, Hunt admitted that the intelligent, energetic Hancock would serve well in the role Meade gave him.

Soon after Hancock and his staff had galloped off, Meade gave orders for a general movement toward Gettysburg. For his part, Hunt instructed General Tyler and the Reserve, also at army headquarters, to proceed north with the more-mobile batteries.

By 11 A.M. on 1 July, the whole of the Army of the Potomac was in transit, heading for armageddon.[8]

*　　*　　*

Moonlight was flooding the earth when Meade and his entourage clattered into Gettysburg just after midnight. The near distance pulsed with the dull thump of cannon fire, flashes of light shimmering on the horizon. The stench of death was all-pervasive; Hunt realized that the darkness covered acres of corpses in both blue and gray.[9]

They had missed a hellish day. Under the Pennsylvania sun, thousands of men on both sides had gone down in fields, on plowed earth, amid woodlands and along the ridges west and south of the village. But the fighting had produced no decisive outcome. Though Lee, quicker to reach Gettysburg with his main body, had driven his outnumbered opponents to the south of town, here they were still, hanging on in the dark, their lines strengthened by General Hancock, their fate still in the balance.

Lee's people, generally victorious all along the line on 1 July, had nevertheless been slowed at numerous points by some of the most desperate fighting the Army of the Potomac had ever generated. Hunt was proud to learn that the artillery of Wainwright and Osborn, plus the horse artillerymen attached to the army's First Cavalry Division (including Duncan's old Battery A, now led by Lieutenant John H. Calef), had plugged crucial gaps in the blue ranks throughout the day, time after time turning potentially decisive rebel drives into gory standoffs. Following the Federal withdrawal to the south of town, Colonel Wainwright had repeated his impressive performance at Chancellorsville by constructing a formidable line of guns to the north and east on Cemetery Hill, where General Hancock had established a rallying point for the embattled troops.

Casualties in the 1 July fighting included a high percentage of artillery-men. The I and XI Corps had suffered seventy-seven cannoneers and six of their officers killed or wounded; eighty horses had been killed as well. However, though several times left vulnerable to capture when infantry support melted away, the gunners had lost only one cannon.[10]

In the deceptively tranquil night, Meade, Hunt, and the rest of the headquarters personnel, including Meade's cavalry escort, cantered up the Taneytown Road, halting at its junction with the road from Emmitsburg, Maryland, hard by Gettysburg's Evergreen Cemetery. Near the cemetery gatehouse many of the riders dismounted amid the creak of saddle leather and the jingling of harnesses, while several dark blurs moved out from the thick darkness and stepped forth to greet them. Lantern light revealed the presence of a bevy of brass: General Hancock, plus the commanders of

General Winfield Scott Hancock (COURTESY, LIBRARY OF CONGRESS)

three corps now at or near Gettysburg—Major Generals Daniel E. Sickles, III Corps; Oliver Otis Howard, XI Corps; and Henry W. Slocum, XII Corps. By seniority, however, Howard now led the army's left wing; Hancock its center; and Slocum its right—each general taking charge of two or more corps.

The subordinate commanders gave Meade a capsulized description of the day's events and current dispositions. All favored fighting on the present ground; none wished to fall back upon Pipe Creek unless later circumstances forced the issue. By now, in fact, Meade had buried the Pipe Creek idea deep in his mind; other worries monopolized his immediate attention: the most critical being that only half his army was on the field or close enough to it to be relied upon in a crisis, while, apparently, General Lee had all or most of his men in hand, with whom, come dawn, he might control the battle.

Obviously artillery would be critical in consolidating the army's hold on the ridges that led south from Cemetery Hill. Meade therefore bade Hunt to inspect the lines as they now stood, determining whether the batteries occupied suitable positions and ensuring that sufficient personnel, equipment, and ammunition were available where they would render maximum service when fighting resumed.

Hunt was elated by the directive. It seemed to indicate that Meade intended to reinstate him to full authority as artillery chief.[11] With General Tyler by his side, plus Lieutenant Bissell and the few other members of his recently depleted staff, he trotted across the cemetery grounds to observe the full extent of the hill that bore its name.

In the congested darkness he had to pick his path carefully, aware that the enemy might send a minié ball in his direction without preamble. After some difficulty, he located Colonel Wainwright and Major Osborn. They recited tales of the day's carnage, with appended declarations of confidence in their ability to hold their new positions. Cheered by their high spirits, Hunt kneed his pale horse, Bill, back to the gatehouse at Evergreen where, soon afterward, he accompanied Meade, General Howard, and headquarters people on a ride down the four-mile-long battle line farther south along Cemetery Ridge. As they rode, Captain W.H. Paine of the construction engineers, who had been in the 1 July fighting, provided details about the geographical landmarks along the route and the various dispositions down the line. From his information, one of Meade's topographical engineers sketched a rough map of the area, tracings of which would be handed to all subordinate commanders. At the same time, Meade issued the redeployment of some of the troops as he thought best, sending aides to carry the orders to various sectors of the ridge.[12]

As they jogged along, Hunt and his subordinates scrutinized the battery positions, dismounting and conversing with several artillerists. Most of what they told Hunt pleased him as well as assured him that his men were ready for almost anything the opposition could throw at them by daylight. Toward morning, however, he began to encounter a spate of bad news. When Sickles's III Corps arrived in full force at Gettysburg, for example, his artillery chief, Captain Randolph, informed Hunt that in its haste to reach the scene of action the corps had lost contact with its artillery ammunition train, which now was somewhere—anywhere—on the road from Taneytown. Later Hunt learned that General Hancock had been almost as careless: the II Corps, which had arrived some hours in advance of Sickles's men, had lost half of its ammo trains. Still another corps, Sedgwick's VI, would also misplace its gun ammunition when it later arrived on the field.[13] Hunt had anticipated as much: when corps and divisions stripped for a forced march, the first commodity cut loose was extra shot and shell. Here was another commmentary on army commanders' insensitivity toward the value of their cannon units.

Having anticipated, Hunt was prepared for such a crisis. In the aftermath of Chancellorsville, when a penitent Hooker had given him almost *carte blanche* to carry out artillery reforms, Hunt had taken the opportunity to create a special ammunition train, which he attached to the Artillery Reserve, carrying an extra twenty rounds for every cannon in the army over and above the quota (250 rounds per gun) designated as the army's campaign supply. Its creation was a covert operation; not even the quartermasters who furnished Hunt with the necessary wagons, no questions asked, learned what he had been up to. Fearing infantry interference with his project, Hunt never told Hooker of its existence; nor was he of a mind to inform Meade about it unless compelled to by circumstances.

Now the special train would demonstrate its utility. He had strictly enjoined the Reserve officers to keep the train well within their column of march. Though not yet on the scene, as was true of half the Reserve, the extra ammunition wagons would appear soon after sunup, in plenty of time to furnish projectiles, powder, and fuzes for the fighting on 2 July.[14]

Meade's inspection tour did not end at the southern tip of the Federal line, which rested at a point where the ridgeline dipped before rising again to two eminences: Round Top and Little Round Top. From there the knot of horsemen turned eastward, then northward, trotting three and a half miles to another steep eminence, Culp's Hill, not far below Gettysburg. Here Meade studied the natural defenses thrown up by part of Slocum's recently arrived XII Corps, and here Hunt compared notes with his lowest-ranking brigade chief, Lieutenant Muhlenberg.

From Slocum's positions, the mounted party passed to the farthest extension of the right flank, where the Baltimore Pike crossed Rock Creek. The horsemen then pulled rein and swung back to the ridge, with Meade establishing army headquarters at a vacant white-washed farmhouse once owned by a widow named Leister, several hundred yards behind the main Federal line. As a nominal member of Meade's staff, Hunt would remain here when not detailed to front-line duty. In the farmhouse he now sought sleep, though fearing it would prove a much-interrupted attempt. In this he was entirely correct.

* * *

Shortly before dawn he was prodded awake for the final time by one of Meade's aides-de-camp. Regaining his feet, he watched darkness slowly leave the earth, trees, ridges, and the far-off bulk of South Mountain taking on definition against the sky. From the near distance came the same thump of cannon fire, the ground still undulating with the reverberations. Soon the slapping sounds of small-arms' fire added to the shelling as fighting began to resume all along the lines.

After rubbing sleep from his eyes with balled fists, Hunt reported to Meade for a new assignment: Daylight had shown General Slocum a wide gap between some of his troops atop Culp's Hill and the right flank of a I Corps division, to the west of the knoll. The gap was to be filled by a XII Corps unit not yet arrived, but with rebels fronting and threatening to flank him, Slocum wished it temporarily plugged by artillery. Hunt was to tend to it.

He went gladly. There was no doubt now: Meade had restored him to full power. Obviously the army commander had profited from the widely bruited results of Hooker's artillery mismanagement in the Wilderness.

Accompanied by Lieutenant Bissell and Major John Craig, Hunt rode to Culp's, where he had Muhlenberg shift enough guns into battery to give Slocum peace of mind. However, his trained eye told him that the ground on Slocum's left was far too broken, too heavily wooded, to permit extensive cannon deployment on the immediate battle front.[15] Still, his efforts would suffice. The first chore of his day completed, the artillery chief galloped back to headquarters, dodging the couriers, wagons, and stragglers that clogged the intervening roads.

At the Leister house, he found George Meade harrassed and fretful. The army leader had learned of Hancock's and Sickles's errant ammunition wagons; with this in mind, plus the knowledge that on the day before the I and XI Corps had expended a tremendous quantity of shot and shell, he feared that ammo shortages would prevent effective battle participation this day. Such fear, increased by the supposed numerical superiority of Lee's army, had influenced Meade to fall back on his Pipe Creek strategy. Already, Hunt learned, he had had Chief of Staff Butterfield (the single holdover at headquarters from the Hooker regime) draw up contingency directions for a general withdrawal from Gettysburg to the Middleburg-Manchester line. Meade was fully prepared to follow such a plan should rebel pressure necessitate it. Now he asked Hunt's opinion of the idea.

Meade was still ignorant of Hunt's special ammunition train, and even now the artillery chief said nothing about it. But he did assure Meade that, although no ammunition could be wasted, a sufficient supply was on hand (or would shortly be on hand) to enable the army to accept full-scale battle.

His listener seemed satisfied with this reply and said no more about withdrawing. Hunt assumed that this time Meade completely forgot the Pipe Creek plan. He had not the faintest notion that the matter would later develop into a boiling controversy.[16]

Hunt's assurance was dramatically timed. Shortly after he spoke to Meade, the remainder of the Artillery Reserve, including the special ammo train, rumbled into Gettysburg. It had been conducted from Taneytown by the chief of Tyler's First Volunteer Brigade, Lieutenant Colonel McGilvery, a crusty ex-sea captain from Maine, but a talented artillerist by acquired experience. The colonel rejoined General Tyler at a point on the Taneytown Road, about half a mile south of Meade's headquarters, where Tyler had transferred the other half of his Reserve a short time before.[17]

Still the Artillery Reserve was not intact. It lacked the two batteries of heavy siege guns that Hunt had equipped for field service. Too hastily the high command had deemed them unwieldy and inappropriate for active campaigning with the main army and had dispatched them to the rearmost supply depot at Westminster. They would languish in idleness for the shank of the campaign, much to the chagrin of Hunt and of their immediate commander, Captain F.A. Pratt of the First Connecticut, who would later lament: "That guns of this range and calibre would have made terrible havoc in the enemy's forming columns and lines, none can doubt."[18] But the powers-that-be had doubted, another example of the fossilized thinking toward artillery employment so rampant in Hunt's army.

The artillery commander spent the better part of that morning wearing a path among Culp's Hill, Cemetery Hill, and the Leister farmhouse. On Culp's Hill for the second time since dawn, he observed foot soldiers digging rifle pits and building works to stymie would-be attackers. Hunt found the men, without exception, "in capital spirits," which he attributed to a prevalent rumor (deliberately started by some officers) that George McClellan—still the most popular commander the Army of the Potomac had ever known—was again at the helm. Hunt deemed it none of his business to disabuse them of the notion.[19]

After reinspecting the cannon positions atop Culp's, he retraced his steps to headquarters. The assignment awaiting him there would prove much more than the routine chore it appeared at the outset. In fact, it was to involve him in a political-military controversy that would join hand in hand with the conflict over Meade's contingency plan of withdrawal.

Back at the farmhouse, he found Meade in animated conversation with General Dan Sickles, which abruptly ended upon his entrance. At once Meade directed him to accompany Sickles to the far left of the line, near the Round Tops, to inspect artillery emplacement possibilities along a new position Sickles wished his III Corps to occupy.[20]

Thus Hunt joined one of the army's most ambitious politician-generals in a three-mile jaunt southward. During the trip, Sickles explained that Meade had ordered the III Corps to take position on the immediate left of Hancock's command, part of which was holding the Federal center. He added that, though unable to convince Meade, this prolongation of Hancock's line offered few advantages, either offensive or defensive, to his soldiers; the land was too low and open to be held against enemy attack. However, a taller ridge line astride the Emmitsburg Road about three-quarters of a mile west of Cemetery Ridge, plus a second ridge at a right angle to the first on its southwest corner, offered commanding positions for his infantry and even better ones for his batteries.[21]

Earlier that day Hunt had noted the weakness of Sickles's present position; thus, he readily followed the New York-born corps commander over that three-quarters of a mile. He and his colleague reined to a halt beside an extensive peach orchard about six hundred yards from Seminary Ridge: a stretch of high ground—much of it occupied by rebels—that ran south from Gettysburg and paralleled the line astride Cemetery Ridge. In the beguilingly quiet angle formed by the two ridges that had captured Sickles's enthusiasm, one of his staff officers who knew the terrain well, Major Henry Tremain, detailed its advantages for Hunt's benefit.

Looking where Tremain pointed, Hunt was duly impressed by the height of the ridges and the depth of position they seemed to offer. He noted, conversely, that "it constituted a favorable position for the *enemy* to hold. This was one good reason for our taking possession of it."

But the case for occupying the salient was not so simple as that. Hunt realized that, should the III Corps move into it, the soldiers would break Meade's continuity of alignment, forming a convex angle toward the enemy and permitting rebels to enfilade the position from either or both flanks. This danger would be partially ameliorated, however, by the extraordinary height of both ridges, which ensured that "each would serve as a 'traverse' for the other, and reduce that evil to a minimum."[22]

Another disadvantage could not so easily be neutralized, and Hunt took pains to explain it to Sickles. The III Corps was not strong enough (with only two divisions instead of the three possessed by most corps) to hold the new line and also to connect with Hancock's flank to the north; already thinly deployed, the corps would be stretched twice as long should Sickles carry out his plan.[23]

The New Yorker replied that Hancock's people were sufficiently numerous to plug any gap; let them sidle south and west till they touched the right flank of the salient. Hunt was not sure if this would suffice. In any case, he warned Sickles, if Confederates were holding any of the woodlots on Seminary Ridge that fronted the salient, no movement, either by the II or III Corps, could be undertaken with assured safety.

The politician-general began to argue more volubly than before in behalf of his idea, and Hunt saw that he wanted an army headquarters stamp-of-approval affixed to it. Sickles argued that had he come personally to examine the peach-orchard line, Meade would have agreed to it. But Meade was inordinately concerned with his far right flank, and insufficiently worried about his left. Dan Sickles was not so sanguine: he had visions of rebels getting ready to pounce on the double ridges before blue-clad troops could. It developed that the corps commander was especially concerned that a cavalry division on his left flank had recently been pulled to the rear to be refitted, but not replaced. The horsemen had been supplying him with vital information about rebel dispositions; with mobile reconnaissance units now gone, Sickles felt naked and vulnerable. There was nothing else he could do but take the double ridges, thus protecting himself against all contingencies.[24]

Hunt sympathized, agreeing that the present III Corps line left a great deal to be desired. Still, he would not authorize tactical changes on his own; Meade himself should come to the scene and decide the issue. Upon returning to the Leister house, Hunt would urge this upon the army commander. In the interim, he advised Sickles, some infantry better be sent to check the forward woods for lurking rebels. To this the corps leader assented; as Hunt pounded off, some companies from Colonel Hiram Berdan's First United States Sharpshooters were sent forward. Before Hunt was out of earshot, he could hear the sounds of heavy skirmishing from Berdan's front: apparently rebels were indeed concealed on Seminary Ridge.

After continuing south to Little Round Top, where Sickles's left flank still rested, and which Hunt sized up as the key feature of terrain on that flank, he rode back to Meade. At headquarters he strongly suggested that the army commander visit Sickles's position as quickly as possible, describing the III Corps general's predicament. From the Leister house he quickly went to Cemetery Hill, where cannonading, recently begun, indicated an artillery duel in progress.

On the hill he learned that rebels north and east of the I and XI Corps had emplaced ten cannon in a wheatfield; at a range of 1,200 yards, they were showering Wainwright's and Osborn's gunners with a deadly hail of shot and shrapnel. At once, Hunt knew disappointment: had the army allowed him to retain the heavy siege pieces instead of dispatching them to Westminster, they would have made short work of this annoying barrage.

Without such long-range guns, it took the I and XI Corps batteries considerable time to stifle the opposition; finally, however, massed fire convinced the enemy to quit the field, dragging off their cannon by hand, leaving twenty-eight of their horses lying dead among the trampled wheat.[25]

Throughout the fighting, Hunt's mind kept wandering back to the left flank. As soon as Wainwright and Osborn had the situation under control, he determined to learn what had transpired at Dan Sickles's headquarters during his absence. Leaving his few staff aides on Cemetery Hill to run various errands, he galloped alone to the peach orchard and the Round Tops.

Arriving there shortly before 4 P.M., he found trouble brewing. The first officer he spotted, Captain Randolph, the III Corps artillery chief, flagged him down. Randolph wanted Hunt's advice. Sickles had recently ordered him to emplace all the corps cannon in and near the wheatfield. Some had already been posted; would the general care to approve their positions and select places for the rest?

Peering westward, Hunt saw the backs of dozens of blue-clad soldiers, moving ahead through the open fields toward the Emmitsburg Road. Quite obviously Sickles had decided to abide by his own judgment—with or without Meade's sanction. Though all seemed quiet among the fields ahead, Hunt recalled the rattle of musketry he had heard when leaving Sickles to return to Meade's command post; he grew worried.

Though uneasy about the situation, he nevertheless went forward beside Randolph, and with him thrashed out the most advantageous positions the III Corps batteries might hold. But with only five such units with which to work, Hunt knew that more would soon be needed. Straightaway he put in a call for two batteries from the Reserve.

In the midst of his dispositions, he spied, at a distance, Meade and Sickles once again engrossed in earnest dialogue. But their conversation seemed so placid that Hunt grew convinced—or almost so—that Meade had given Sickles's new line his full endorsement.[26]

Yet some of his uneasiness remained—and with good reason. Like him, Meade had arrived here only after Sickles's movement had gone forward; he had not given prior consent.

Dan Sickles had acted entirely on his own, precisely because Colonel Berdan's marksmen had found rebels in the woodlots, which Hunt had specifically pointed out to him. This had confirmed Sickles's suspicion that rebels were massing to occupy the high ground between Seminary and Cemetery Ridges before the III Corps could take it. Tension at high tide, the corps leader had given the fateful order, leading his two divisions toward the peach trees through the open fields lying ahead. Once on the desired ground, he had placed one division along the ridge that held the Emmitsburg Road, and the rest of his troops astride the shorter but no less steep ridge line that ran south from the angle of juncture.

The movement had created just the situation Hunt had feared. Sickles now held a wide-open salient, vulnerable from the right and left as well as from the rear, which warped Meade's line, left General Hancock's southern flank unanchored, and offered strategic Little Round Top to the enemy as a gift of war.[27]

But the deed had been done—at Meade's approval, as far as Hunt knew—and his job at this point was to help bolster the new line with guns. In this he received much help from the rear. Anticipating trouble in that sector, General Tyler had already sent up the first two batteries Hunt had ordered; now, on his own initiative, the Reserve commander dispatched McGilvery's First Volunteer Brigade to the scene; Hunt met it on the road and was extremely relieved by its presence.

He was extremely relieved because, only minutes before, sharp conflict had broken out between Sickles's divisions and a heretofore hidden column of rebel infantry beyond the Emmitsburg Road. An increase of rifle fire from the west indicated that the enemy line was constantly growing longer and deeper; and just as McGilvery brought his units up to the line, Hunt detected a bank of rebel cannon going into position to sweep Sickles's salient. Quite obviously the III Corps was in prodigious trouble.[28]

As quickly as possible Hunt whipped McGilvery's units into line among Captain Randolph's guns and along a lengthy front that extended all the way to the salient angle at the orchard. In went the batteries at full tilt, drivers lashing the lead-, swing-, and wheel-horses into frenzied speed: Captain John Bigelow's Ninth Massachusetts Battery of four 12-pounders; Captain Charles A. Phillips's Fifth Massachusetts, six 3-inch rifles; and the four Napoleons of Captain Patrick Hart's Fifteenth New York Independent Battery. On their heels came a pair of units personally directed by General Tyler: Captain James Thompson's Combined C and F of the First Pennsylvania Artillery (their commander Hunt's erstwhile lieutenant in Company M of the Second Regulars), six more 3-inchers; and Captain John W. Sterling's Second Connecticut, two howitzers and four James 3.67-inch rifles converted from smoothbores. Farther to the rear bounced five more Napoleon batteries: Lieutenant Evan Thomas's C of the Fourth United States; Lieutenant Gulian V. Weir's C, Fifth U.S.; Lieutenant John G. Turnbull's F/K, Third Artillery; Captain Nelson G. Ames's G of the First New York; and Lieutenant Edward B. Dow's Sixth Maine Battery. With the quintet of light 12-pounder units came Captain R. Bruce Ricketts's F/G, First Pennsylvania, hauling a half-dozen 3-inch ordnance rifles. Finally, two batteries came up unsolicited, filched from part of the main army by one of General Sickles's staff officers. Aware that their own corps had greater need of them than did Sickles, Hunt gave the impulsive aide a tongue-lashing; and, later, in his report of the battle, made pointed reference to this instance of an infantryman impersonating an artillerist.[29]

Some time after four o'clock, all these units had unlimbered across a half-mile line stretching from the shorter of Sickles's ridge lines on the south to the Codori farm house on the north. They had gone into battery not a minute too soon: before four-thirty, the rebel artillery that Hunt had spied moving into position to the west let loose with a converging fire against the people of the III Corps. Not long afterward, gray-clad foot troops debouched from the timber on Seminary Ridge and bounded forward, the rebel yell keening across the broad valley. Heading directly at Sickles's salient, the Confederates threatened to lap it on both sides, then push onward to all-important Little Round Top.

Not all the Federal batteries supporting the III Corps held commanding positions, but ones that did were a long time in opening against the attackers. Consequently Hunt vaulted into the saddle and rode to the anchor point of Sickles's left-flank ridge line: a complex of huge piled rock known ever afterward as the Devil's Den. On the summit of the steep eminence Captain Randolph had positioned one of his units—the Fourth New York Independent Light Artillery; its immediate commander, Captain James E. Smith, had dismantled his 10-pounder Parrotts so that tubes and carriages could be manhandled up the slopes. Now Hunt clambered to the crest to prod Smith into reaping the rewards of such strenuous labor.

From the top of Devil's Den, Hunt had a long, broad, and nearly unobstructed view of the proceedings below. At the top of the valley, rebels were moving on the run, their batteries paving the way with shot and shell. Already, in fact, the III Corps seemed to be wavering against the onslaught. As it developed, only at the time of Hunt's arrival had Captain Smith completed his dispositions; ready now to go to work, he threw his first rounds at the oncoming enemy—to good effect. Hunt admired Smith's accuracy, as well as the excellent positions he had taken up: four of his guns were at the western lip of the crest, the other two farther to the eastern edge. Even so, Hunt doubted that the captain could evade capture should Sickles's line fail to hold back the enemy, especially since none of Smith's cannon could be depressed sufficiently to strike any rebels who reached the base of the den. Still, even as the captain began to draw a heavy counterbattery fire, Hunt ordered him to hold his ground to the last; he would personally scour up some infantry support for the New Yorkers.[30]

But when he descended the eastern slope of the eminence, Hunt found this errand impossible to complete without delay. He found himself at least temporarily stymied, not by the enemy, but by beef on the hoof.

A herd of horned cattle had been driven into the narrow valley between the den and, farther east, Little Round Top; there it milled about in fright at the sound of rebel shells whizzing near. One of the projectiles had exploded in its midst, tearing one of the animals to pieces, wounding several others with shards of iron, and increasing the terror of the entire herd, which was now rumbling en masse from one side of the valley to another.

Hunt hesitated. If Smith and his men were to be aided, he had to cross that valley to reach his horse; he could not take time to circle the other side of the den. On the other hand, the cattle might trample him to jelly if he intruded.

In later years he would recall this ludicrous predicament with quiet mirth. At the time, of course, he was too much concerned for his health to see the humor of it. At last, his sense of mission won out. Taking a long breath, he strode gingerly through the milling herd. After an eternity or two he reached Bill and swung aboard, but not before he had been "badly demoralized."[31]

* * *

After all his travail, he found that infantry supports were already heading toward Devil's Den and other points of Sickles's new line. Thus Hunt returned to the battle front, occupied by the gunners of the III Corps and the Reserve, to observe one of his command's most harrowing afternoons.

Not even the hastily summoned infantry had thus far halted the rebel drive, to the particular disadvantage of Hunt's badly exposed gunners. With waves of gray rolling all around them, some of the batteries in the forefront of the line went under, sucked into a vortex of death and devastation. Yet, despite the opposition and the ninety-two-degree heat (several artillerists, including General Tyler, fainted from sunstroke), other batteries held on stubbornly, hurling single and double charges of short-range canister at their opponents, determined to seal up the holes in Meade's line created by Dan Sickles's impetuosity.[32]

As the fighting neared its apogee, Hunt joined Lieutenant Colonel McGilvery near Cemetery Ridge, building a bulkhead of defense to the rear of the salient with batteries drawn from the II and V Corps and the Reserve. At the same time, he ordered Captain Hazard, Hancock's chief artillerist, to have the rest of the II Corps batteries farther north throw shells at the Confederates opposing Sickles, as well as at rebels supporting Lee's attack at a distance.

Hunt's and McGilvery's rear line was to prove crucial, for not even piecemeal Federal infantry supports, or all the cannon now in Sickles's front, could indefinitely hold off the enemy. In the early evening came the break: one of the III Corps divisions, under Major General David B. Birney, at last gave way, and soon afterward the whole of the salient caved in, its men turning and fleeing toward Cemetery Ridge, rebels in hot pursuit.

Seeing the collapse of Sickles's line, Hunt feared disaster: "Birney's division once broken, it was difficult to stem the tide of defeat."[33] And yet, even now, he could be tremendously proud of his cannoneers. Wholly deserted by infantry support, some of the batteries farthest to the front clung desperately to their ground, giving away not one square foot of real estate.

One unit, Bigelow's Ninth Massachusetts, particularly distinguished itself. Ordered to hold its position for a full twenty minutes after Sickles's infantry broke and ran, the Bay Staters sacrificed themselves to win the all-important time its comrades needed to reform along Hunt's and McGilvery's line. Eventually, Bigelow was severely wounded, almost lost his cannon, did lose thirty-five of his officers and men, and sixty-five of his eighty-eight horses. All around him, other units held to the last, flinging shells into the faces of massed infantry, Hunt's strictures against ammo wastage once again for-gotten.[34] One battery, Captain A. Judson Clark's B of the First New Jersey, a III Corps outfit, expended 1,342 rounds through afternoon and early evening.

Thanks partially to the tenacity and self-sacrifice of these gunners, partially to the bulwark built by Hunt and McGilvery, and partially to the ever-increasing reinforcements rushed to Sickles's part of the line, the Confeder-ates never quite seized decisive victory. Though overrunning Devil's Den (Captain Smith losing his guns as Hunt had predicted), the peach orchard, and other key points, they failed to take the most important position. Quick action by Meade's engineer chief, Major General Gouverneur K. Warren, brought supports to Little Round Top just in time to beat back lines of Confederates scrambling up its slopes.[35] Blocked there, harrassed on their flanks as well, the rebels eventually turned and fled back to Seminary Ridge, leaving behind hundreds of Union casualties—including Dan Sickles himself, his right leg shattered by shell fragments. The tide of defeat had been stemmed after all.

As twilight came on, Hunt's gunners lay dead in windrows beside broken caissons, exploded limbers, and bloated horses. Their resting place was a vast potter's field, with General Hunt having narrowly missed several opportunities to join its population.

It had indeed been a near thing. Sundown found Hunt bone weary, sick of combat, weak and harassed almost to tears. But he had survived—survived to reach the pinnacle of his career on the morrow.[36]

12

High-Water Mark

Evening did not end battle's horrors. In the darkness, mangled soldiers on both sides moaned for help, for water, for someone to put them beyond suffering. Long-range skirmish fire continued in great volume. Amid the rubble of guns, carriages, carcasses, and corpses, Hunt, Tyler, and other artillery officers worked tirelessly to replace batteries no longer fit for service and to feed ammunition chests, as well as to direct burial teams in locating and interring comrades fallen near the enemy lines.[1]

Even in the shadows, combat flared up. From Culp's Hill portions of the XII Corps had been detached to close gaps still existing on the far left. Their departure eventually led to a rebel effort to seize Culp's. An infantry division assaulted the knoll, screaming and shooting and flailing about with sabers and gun butts. Somehow a single Federal brigade, later reinforced, managed to hold back the opposition.

Meanwhile, parts of two other gray-clad divisions assaulted gunners and infantrymen atop Cemetery Hill. They overran Captain Michael Wiedrich's XI Corps battery and that of Captain Ricketts from the Reserve; and for a time held the commanding eminence. Then new troops from Hancock's corps and elsewhere rushed up to reclaim lost ground, challenging the enemy on their own terms, fighting with wild abandon. Major Osborn's gunners returned to the fray, lashing out with handspikes, rammerstaffs, even fence rails. By 2 A.M., all rebels had retreated—those who had attacked Cemetery Hill decisively beaten; but some of the Culp's Hill attackers still clinging to abandoned XII Corps earthworks on the forward slopes. Repairing to the scene, Hunt formulated plans to drive them away for good come dawn.[2]

From there he travelled to the headquarters of the Reserve, where he and Tyler (now recovered from heat prostration) took inventory of the special ammunition train, doling out projectiles to needy battery officers. Midway through the work, both generals were invited to Meade's headquarters to participate in a war council soon to convene. Not willing to interrupt his labors at so critical a time, Hunt continued his computations for a full half-hour before he and Tyler trudged to the Leister home.

Already Hunt had an inkling of the purpose behind the council: a discussion of the desirability of retreating on 3 July as result of the tremendous personnel and matériel losses suffered this day. Hunt was fiercely opposed to withdrawal, preferring to fight it out along the once again intact line on Cemetery Ridge; he would say so in unmistakable terms if given the chance—so too would Tyler. But neither had the opportunity; they arrived just as the conference broke up. They learned that a vote to stay or withdraw had indeed been taken: by unanimous vote, the subordinate commanders had influenced Meade to remain in position at Gettysburg until after Lee made decisive movements late on the third. After that, they would allow circumstances to determine their course.[3]

Hunt was elated by the outcome. Even so, Meade told him that events might yet dictate retreat. Hunt relayed this intelligence to some of his subordinates, advising them to make mental plans for evacuating their positions in case of an emergency.[4] Afterward both he and Tyler grasped what sleep they could find amid the Reserve camp.

* * *

Though probably awake far earlier, assuredly Hunt was on his feet by 4:30 on the morning of 3 July. His first chore that muggy day was to oversee Muhlenberg's XII Corps cannon as, for fifteen minutes, they flung shells into the wooded areas down the flank of Culp's Hill, flushing out Confederates. Soon after starting in, the lieutenant's guns were joined by others; so that by 5:30, five batteries were raking the slopes mercilessly. The pounding did not cease until sometime after ten, following which the infantry of the XII Corps rushed forward, reestablishing their old lines.[5]

Hunt did not linger to see the mopping-up. By 8 A.M. he was again on the move, cantering down Cemetery Ridge for a dawn inspection of the II Corps line, whose artillery, Meade believed, would bear the brunt of any attacks Lee might launch that day.

Hunt's ride eventually brought him abreast of Battery A of the Fourth U.S., which had unlimbered beside a tall clump of trees just north of the Union center. He dismounted there to trade words with the battery commander—a rather girlish young lieutenant, Alonzo H. Cushing (USMA June '61). The callow subaltern gave Hunt a hurried tour of the ground beside his six 3-inch ordnance rifles, proclaiming his readiness to handle whatever the day would bring.

Midway into his inspection, Hunt and his guide, plus Cushing's bearded first sergeant, Frederick Fuger, had to race for shelter. Their presence had attracted a couple of shells from rebel guns a mile away on Seminary Ridge. Though the trio escaped unharmed, subsequent shells burst nearby, detonating three of Cushing's limbers in a series of violent explosions.

Hunt remounted and rode on; he had too much unfinished business to allow himself to be blown to smithereens just now. As he galloped back toward Culp's Hill, the officer and men of Battery A returned the enemy's fire, prompting onlooking infantrymen to burst out cheering. Battery A blasted again and again at frequent intervals until eleven o'clock. On both its flanks, other cannon squared off at rebel antagonists a mile away, though careful to conserve most of their rounds for use in the more decisive short-range fighting that would assuredly come later.[6]

After the diverting interlude at Cushing's position, the artillery commander returned to Culp's Hill where he watched the finishing touches put to the work of regaining the XII Corps trenches. And, after this, he went back to Cemetery Ridge: Meade now wished him to put his discerning eye to work all along the battle line, where new battery dispositions were being contemplated.

Returning to the ridge, Hunt's attention was directed, not to his own line, but to a spectacle along Seminary Ridge that would have stirred the blood of any artillerist:

Our whole front for two miles was covered by batteries already in line or going into position. They stretched—apparently in one unbroken mass—from opposite the town to the Peach Orchard, which bounded the view to the left, the ridges of which were planted thick with cannon. Never before had such a sight been witnessed on this continent, and rarely, if ever, abroad.

Still he had to ask himself: "What did it mean?"[7]

It meant that Meade had been farsighted in predicting an assault against the center of the line. Following unsuccessful drives on both of Meade's flanks—to counter which, Meade had drawn troops from his center, leaving it thinly held—General Lee was wheeling up every available cannon to prepare the way for an all-out thrust against the median sector of Cemetery Ridge.[8]

When Hunt perceived the truth, he also realized that such a cannonade as these guns would unleash might involve his own batteries in an ammunition-wasting return barrage. To prevent this, and to facilitate a more concentrated and effective fire when the proper moment arrived, he told every artillery officer he encountered to hold his fire for at least fifteen minutes after the rebels started in, then reply en masse. He also imparted several other verses of the gospel according to Hunt: enjoining his officers "not to fire at small bodies, nor to allow their fire to be drawn without promise of adequate results; to watch the enemy closely, and when he opened to concentrate the fire of their guns on one battery at a time until it was silenced; under all circumstances to fire deliberately, and to husband their ammunition as much as possible."[9]

Continuing down the line, he expressed satisfaction with the battery dispositions, and was particularly glad to see that Colonel McGilvery had done an excellent job of filling the breaches torn in the line the previous day with his thirty-nine Reserve cannon. To the rear, General Tyler was marshalling other able-bodied units in case they, too, would be required at the front. Nor were these remaining Reserve batteries the only reinforcements Hunt could draw on in a crisis; eight others under Colonel Tompkins remained fresh and available for action along the line of the as yet uncommitted VI Corps.[10]

On the far left he came upon one battery whose vantage point would enable it to enfilade any column attacking the Union center. Climbing to the rocky summit of Little Round Top, he sought out D of the Fifth Artillery, which had been lugged to the top the day before to support the III Corps salient. Its commander, Lieutenant Charles E. Hazlett, had been killed by a rebel sniper occupying Devil's Den; today it was led by Hazlett's associate, Lieutenant Benjamin F. Rittenhouse. Hunt spent several minutes discussing with Rittenhouse the possibilities afforded by his position, and had just finished cautioning him as to the fifteen minutes' delay in returning fire, when the rebel artillery across the valley let loose with a resounding crash. By the time Hunt had left the summit and renegotiated a path to his horse, the cannonade had grown even louder and deeper, its racket much the greatest he had ever heard.[11]

Riding back along the ridge, he felt the earth roll and pitch under the impact generated by 138 cannon. Shells roared over his head, bursting in widely divergent sectors behind the Union line. The infantrymen and gunners all along the ridge crouched behind whatever cover was available, praying to their individual gods to spare them from obliteration.

Most seemed destined to survive. The Confederates were letting loose with all they had, and, even when Hunt's people replied, they would still dominate the contest, for only seventy-seven Union cannon were in position to bear directly on Lee's artillery line.[12] But the rebel barrage had begun in ineffective, scattered style, and seemed determined to continue in that manner. One factor in this was defective fuzes, causing many shells to explode short of their targets; a more serious cause was simple human error: most of the cannon were firing too high, landing not athwart the Union-held ridge, but upon its back slope, finding victims among the rear-echelon citizenry of the Army of the Potomac: escort troops, stragglers, medical personnel, provost guards, cooks, sutlers, and train sentries. Eventually the shelling prompted Generals Meade and Tyler to evacuate their headquarters and relocate out of range of the cannonade.

Even so, enough projectiles found their way to the front line to fill the air with exploded limbers and caissons, as well as with splinters from nearby fences and boulders from the low stone wall that skirted the forward base of the ridge. Those shells that reached human targets sprayed bodies and parts of bodies in various directions, depositing them in grotesque heaps several feet from where they had taken flight.[13]

The Union gunners were highly impressed by the noise, if not the effect, of the barrage. Watching from Cemetery Hill, Colonel Wainwright compared its roar to "that from the falls of Niagara." Sergeant Fuger of Cushing's battery thought the cannonade "the most terrible the new world has ever seen, and the most prolonged . . . terribly grand and sublime." And, from his perch atop Little Round Top, Lieutenant Rittenhouse noted that the earth shook as if in fright, and he likened the noise to "one loud thunder clap."[14]

It could have been much worse. At one point Hunt noted that a hidden battery on Lee's extreme left had unleashed a remarkably destructive fire that enfiladed Muhlenberg's batteries across the way. But apparently the rebels did not perceive this great advantage for they ceased their shelling soon after the XII Corps guns replied. Lee's artillerists seemed determined to make the least of their awesome array of heavy ordnance.[15]

Taking a detached, professional interest in his enemy's strategy, Hunt grew annoyed and even disappointed that such a potentially devastating cannonade should go to waste. Since one of the rebel cannon commanders, Colonel A. Lindsay Long, had studied artillery tactics under him years before at Fort Washita, Hunt began to question his abilities as a tutor.[16]

* * *

Though a few of the more anxious battery commanders started in prematurely, most of Hunt's officers waited the full fifteen minutes before opening. When the Federal cannon spoke in reply, their gunners scrupulously followed Hunt's directive to fire slowly and deliberately, "making *target practice* out of it."[17]

If the rebel barrage had been a fearsome thing, the combined Confederate and Union cannonade was unearthly. Reportedly, it could be heard more than 150 miles away.

Hunt's counter-battery fire proved more effective than the initial Confederate effort. Blessed with better matériel and, in the final analysis, more skillful officers and men, the Federal units dismounted several of their opponents' batteries, rained shards of iron, tree branches, and fence rails upon the heads of Rebel infantrymen, and in general scared the daylights out of Lee's onlookers. One of these, soon to participate in a grand attack afoot, remarked: "After lying inactive under that deadly storm of hissing and exploding missiles, it seemed a relief to go forward to the desperate assault."[18]

Even with its superior efficiency, Hunt's barrage could achieve only so much, since the body of Lee's army lay in woods too far off to permit accuracy. Thus, when Lee's cannonade neared the end of its second hour, Hunt decided he could not afford to waste any more ammunition, lest he have none remaining when the infantry attack rolled forward.

He happened to be at the Cemetery Hill position held by Major Osborn's cannon when he made his decision. Immediately the XI Corps artillery chief seconded his motion: "Why not let them [the rebel infantry] out while we are all in good condition? I would cease firing at once, and the enemy could reach but one conclusion, that of our being driven from the hill." When Osborn added that his men would remain calm under an unanswered barrage, Hunt told the major to stop his shelling.[19]

As Osborn moved to comply, Hunt spurred Bill down the line still again—this time spreading the word to cease firing and to refit and prepare to receive a full-scale assault; at the same time, his aides rushed to order up batteries from the Reserve. Ironically, in the midst of his errand, Hunt was paged by one of Meade's staff, who relayed his commander's own suggestion that Hunt's guns fall silent so as to conserve ammunition.[20]

Gradually the guns on Cemetery Hill quieted; then others along the battle line followed suit. For several minutes more they endured a cannonade that forced their gunners to crouch beside infantry comrades, hugging the earth more tightly than they had hugged their mothers or sweethearts.

As the Federals cowered in fetal positions, Hunt hauled damaged batteries from the ridge, sending up Reserve units and guns from the VI and XI Corps not needed elsewhere. Soon a steady stream of batteries were coming up, much as on the day before. This time: Captain Robert Fitzhugh's K, First New York, the guns of the Eleventh New York Battery attached; Weir's C, Fifth U.S.; Lieutenant William Wheeler's Thirteenth New York; Lieutenant Augustin N. Parsons's A of the First New Jersey; Captain Andrew Cowan's First New York Independent Battery; and other Regular and volunteer outfits.[21] Astride the ridge, drivers pulled back on reins; gunners dropped to the ground, running guns into battery and digging into caisson and limber chests; and officers shouted a volley of orders, repeating commands given time and again on other fields from Virginia to Maryland.

So engrossed was Hunt in getting these cannon on the line and sending disabled units to the rear, he did not notice that one brace of guns supposedly under his overall authority continued to exchange shells with the enemy. This had come about in consequence of such a conflict of authority as had bedeviled him since the genesis of the war.

Originally, the guns of Hancock's II Corps had complied with Hunt's cease-fire. But the corps commander would not force his crouching infantry-men to endure an enemy shelling without the morale-building benefit of a return artillery fire. Thus, he had compelled Captain Hazard to resume his barrage.[22]

That done, Hancock sought to impress his authority on other units not directly within his purview. Riding south along the ridge, he came upon the now-silent guns recently sent up from the Reserve under Colonel McGilvery, and demanded that their officers disobey Hunt's orders, employing language that one battery commander termed "profane and Blasphemous such as a drunken Ruffian would use."[23] His tirade produced mixed results. Although apparently some Reserve units did his bidding, he received no cooperation from McGilvery himself. Looking Hancock squarely in the eye, the old seadog from Maine told him to go to hell.[24]

It was fortunate that McGilvery defied Hancock. Because Hazard had obeyed, the II Corps batteries would find themselves devoid of all ammunition except canister by the time Lee's infantry attacked. Thus, almost one-third of the cannon able to bear on crucial sections of the enemy's line would have to wait until their foe was within four hundred yards before being able to fire. Moreover, Hancock's order ensured that Hunt would be unable to subject the rebel infantry to the sort of cross fire that might well have crippled their assault beyond repair before their attack was fairly under way.[25]

In confirmation of Major Osborn's belief, Lee assumed that the diminution of the Federal barrage meant his guns had overwhelmed their opposition. At about 3:15 he permitted his infantry—the divisions of Generals George E. Pickett, James J. Pettigrew, and William D. Pender (the latter led by Isaac R. Trimble)—to move from Seminary Ridge and charge the Union center.

From the trees on the high ground a mile from Cemetery Ridge, some 12,500 officers and men grouped for the attack. In their front, the Confederate cannon finally fell silent, batteries trundling back among the trees. After closing ranks and aligning their three-column formation, the foot soldiers started forward.

Federal infantry and artillery stood in awe of their coming, though most managed to return attention to preparations to meet them. The cannoneers along Hancock's front were particularly busy, sighting their guns and stock-piling what ammunition remained, fully aware that the attackers were heading their way, perhaps guiding their march by the grove of trees in the center of the wall-bordered ridge. Slowly, as though defiant of the odds against them, the Confederates continued toward the Emmitsburg Road, their flags hanging limp in the breezeless heat, their rifles loaded and bayoneted and ready for instant use.

Astride his horse, Hunt was struck by the grand pageant before him—but he too had to ignore it. Ranging up and down the line, he imparted last-minute advice to his gunners, gesturing to them, shouting instructions in his already-high voice, lending encouragement in the face of imminent conflict. Most of his gunners heeded his word, and waited silently for the command to resume firing.

Tension climbed by the minute. One battery officer stared with mouth agape at the ever-lengthening column approaching him, its alignment almost perfectly maintained: "When I saw this mass of men, in three long lines, approaching our position," he later recalled, "and knowing that we had but one thin line of infantry to oppose them, I thought our chances for Kingdom Come or Libby Prison were very good." Then he changed his mind: "Never was there such a splendid target for light artillery."[26]

Halfway between the lines, the Confederates broke down fences bordering the Emmitsburg Road, surging onward at a brisker pace. They bounded across the valley, shouting now at the top of their voices, flags spotting the horizon, gun barrels catching and throwing sunlight.

Then Hunt gave the call. A second later, the nearest guns let go with their fiercest volley of the day, blasting case shot across the valley and blowing great holes in the gray lines. Those II Corps guns destitute of shot and most of their shell soon were tossing canister at the rebels, though still at a formidable distance. Some of them, such as Cushing's, sought closer positions by rolling down the gentle ridge to the west, their crews keeping pace with armfulls of projectiles. At a range of just under four hundred yards, Cushing and his allies flung their tin-coated cylinders, iron balls hurtling free with a ringing jolt and whipping through the air like miniature scythes. Dozens of Confederates fell beneath their impact, though others stepped in as replacements, plugging holes and enabling the charge to keep moving.

Just before their first line reached Cemetery Ridge, Hunt galloped to Colonel McGilvery's position south of the grove of trees to observe the Maine officer as he poured "the ugliest kind of oblique fire" into the gray lines. Staggered by this unexpected blast, as well as by a devastating flank fire from Lieutenant Rittenhouse's guns on Little Round Top, many rebels turned to their left, thereby squarely fronting the II Corps batteries—all of which were hurling canister in a mad whirl of action, guns being fed double and even triple charges of ammunition, then spewing them from their barrels at point-blank range. As the luckless attackers toppled onto the grassy plain before the stone wall, clouds of powder smoke quickly sheeted them from view.[27]

Another of Hunt's battery officers marvelled at the enemy's determined endurance. Though rank upon rank were shredded by canister: "Still they would close in, then again advancing. . . . Sometimes a part would run back, then face about, and seeing their colors, would run toward them and reform and advance again. To me it was the grandest sight I had ever seen."

By superhuman effort the gray wave reached the stone wall in advance of the massed cannon. A few hundred men broke in amid Cushing's battery, bayonetting and shooting cannoneers and sending the young lieutenant reeling with mortal wounds of the groin and face. On Cushing's left, Andrew Cowan's First New York Battery was furiously engaged, its equally young commander spraying double canister at the inhuman range of ten yards into the faces of Rebels hurtling the wall and reaching toward his cannon. When the smoke cleared, Cowan saw only corpses.[28]

Riding up from McGilvery's position, Hunt himself witnessed the effect of Cowan's blast. The only officer on the ridge still in the saddle, the artillery chief reined to a halt beside the clump of trees, emptying his pistol at the nearest attackers and wildly shouting, "See 'em! See 'em!"

Suddenly Bill jerked against the impact of five minié balls, lurched to one side, staggered backward, then collapsed, dragging his rider to earth. Pinned beneath the animal, Hunt thrashed about in an attempt to extricate himself before the rebels swarmed over him. Finally, some of Cowan's gunners managed to pry him free.[29]

Wobbling onto his feet, the artillery chief stared into the forefront of Pickett's attack. Of that moment he later recalled: ". . . the display of Secesh Battle flags was splendid and *scary*." He also recollected the next object of his attention. A Federal infantryman standing beside one of Cowan's guns was pitched high into the air by an exploding battery wagon, "as if you were to take a *doll* by the foot and whirl it so as to make it turn heels-over-head." The soldier spun around two or three times in flight before his body landed a dozen feet to the rear.[30]

Turning to follow the grisly sight, Hunt saw files of Union troops coming up on the run, and for the first time realized that infantry support was all around in strength. He stood still, dazed by his fall and the mad panorama around him, as the reinforcements reached the stone wall and grappled with those rebels who had flooded around the cannon. As if time were completely warped, it seemed to him that in a matter of seconds the wall no longer blossomed with gray uniforms. Blue now predominated: the survivors of the attack were staggering off into the plain, limping, crawling, falling down, bobbing up, falling again—thousands of beaten men making their way back to the other flank of the mile-wide valley.

Hunt peered out across that plain, temporarily free of cannon smoke, watching the infantry scramble after the retreating rebels, and noted that the ground lay strewn with ragged bodies—a rich crop of death in full bloom.[31]

The gray wave that had washed over the wall and had seeped around his cannon had receded, flowing back over the grass toward its source beyond the Emmitsburg Road. The grand attack had come and gone, but Hunt, preparing to remount on a horse rounded up by his orderly, scarcely comprehended that the high-water mark of the Confederacy—as well as the high tide of his own career—was already history.[32]

13

Seasons of Repose

Gettysburg took a staggering toll of both armies, victor as well as vanquished. The disorganization into which the Army of the Potomac had been thrown during those three days of battle, particularly during Pickett's massive assault against its center, was the ruling factor in Meade's decision not to close 3 July with a counterattack or to strike his opponents a blow on the day following. On Independence Day, Lee's people began a slow retreat southward from lower Pennsylvania, another invasion at finale; again Meade resisted the impulse to harass and pursue with vigor.

All of which perhaps should have pleased General Hunt. At first glance his batteries seemed in no condition to mount a close pursuit of the troops they had repulsed on the third. All told, the Federal artillery had suffered 737 casualties at Gettysburg—including 670 officers and men killed or wounded—almost ten percent of the number engaged. Additionally, 881 battery horses had been killed or maimed, and an aggregate of 32,781 rounds of ammunition had been expended. An average of more than one hundred rounds had poured from every Federal gun during the fighting, exclusive of those used by the horse artillerymen of Captains Tidball and Robertson in combat against J.E.B. Stuart's horsemen three miles east of the main battlefield on 3 July.[1] Such statistics would seem to indicate that Hunt's command required the most extensive of refits before being able to depart Gettysburg.

But Hunt did not agree. The figures were misleading: most of those batteries dispatched to the rear on 1 and 2 July were already repaired and fit to resume active campaigning; and relatively few had been disabled by Pickett's assault on the third. Furthermore, ammunition remained plentiful, contrary to Meade's earlier fears: the staggering expenditure from start to finish of the battle amounted to but a third of the supply available; more than sixty-five thousand projectiles were still on hand.[2] For these and other reasons, Hunt was disappointed by Meade's unwillingness to launch a counter-stroke following Pickett's repulse. Late on the third, he tried to convince his

178

superior that the enemy was much more demoralized than the Army of the Potomac, which still had several fresh divisions and whose men were in high spirits following their obvious victory. The stakes were such that a fight to the finish should be brought on at Gettysburg: "We must risk to win," was Hunt's philosophy.[3] When on 4 July Meade still hesitated, Hunt's hope for final, complete triumph died.

Instead of leading his batteries against the enemy, the artillery commander spent the eighty-seventh birthday of his country burying the dead, sending the wounded rearward, and arguing with Meade over the fifteen-minute return-fire delay on the previous afternoon. In this, Meade merely relayed irresponsible complaints from some infantry commanders ignorant of the true state of affairs on Cemetery Ridge at the height of battle on the third.[4]

Hunt also took time to notify his wife of his safety. He wrote Mary: "I have never been in so much and so long continued peril as on yesterday and the day before, but, thanks be to God; I have escaped as by a miracle, when it appeared as if there could be no escape."[5] He was not alone in this belief. Writing in his journal, Colonel Wainwright calculated the odds against sustained survival during two days of almost constant exposure to enemy fire along the main battle line, and concluded: "It is a wonder that General Hunt has escaped."[6]

Not long after annoying Hunt by his 3–4 July timidity, Meade again incurred his displeasure for the same reason. On the fifth, the Army of the Potomac followed its enemy from Gettysburg, but found no opportunity to bring its collective weight to bear against Lee's veterans until after the eleventh. On that day the Federals found Lee backed against the raging Potomac at Williamsport and Falling Waters, Maryland. There, Hunt urged an attack before the heavily outnumbered rebels could scamper across to safety via pontoon bridges. A small force—mostly cavalry—could cross at a nearby ford, Hunt explained, and on the southern shore seal off the rebels' retreat route. On the opposite bank, in the meantime, the artillery could shell the entrapped Confederates into fragments.[7]

Meade did not abide by such advice. He did determine, however, on an infantry assault, and on the morning of the twentieth was ready to send forward a "reconnaissance in force." At the last minute, unfortunately, scouts reported that the rebels had occupied formidable positions on high ground along the river and were too well entrenched to be attacked successfully. When Meade's subordinate commanders declared their unwillingness to go forward under such circumstances, the movement was cancelled. The upshot was that on 13–14 July the rebels made good their escape, crossing upon and then dismantling their bridges.

Not only Hunt was depressed by Lee's flight. General-in-Chief Halleck promptly sent a series of acidic telegrams that Hunt found "perfectly consistent with a determination on the part of the War Department to discredit under all circumstances the Army of the Potomac and any commander identified with it."[8] Meade took personal affront from Halleck's tone and immediately proffered his resignation. The general-in-chief refused to accept it; nor would War Secretary Edwin McMasters Stanton.

A few days afterward, ironically, Hunt himself threatened to resign. It came about in consequence of a feud, not with the War Office, but with Meade.

Unsettled by the harsh criticism coming his way from the ranks as well as from Washington, Meade took the leash off his temper, feeding his military family on daily helpings of verbal abuse. He doled out a particularly venomous serving on 20 July—the day after the army had begun to cross the Potomac into Virginia. Near the river he sought out Hunt and called him to account for what the artillerist later called "some mismanagement in the marching of the heavy ammunition trains of the reserve artillery and the general [artillery] park." Meade remained unsatisfied by Hunt's reply— that under the Hooker regime he had exercised no direct control over the Reserve, and, since the arrangement had never officially been altered, he felt he lacked the power to undo such mischief as Meade had called to his attention.[9]

Apparently the army leader castigated him nonetheless. Such reproof, coupled with the censure Hunt had received on 4 July, and Meade's continued unwillingness to clearly define Hunt's position in command, led the artillery chief on the twenty-sixth to forward an intention to resign or to seek transfer to another theater of combat. He insisted: "Under existing orders and practices the position is not one that I can hold with any advantage to the service, and, consistently with self-respect."[10]

Meade ought to have proceeded tactfully, displaying not the stick but the carrot, for if Hunt were serious, Meade stood on the verge of losing his most able specialist. But instead of mollifying his chief artillerist, he further antagonized him: he would regret Hunt's departure, he replied, but should Hunt feel compelled to resign, Meade would see him quickly mustered out of the volunteer service, so that his brigadier's commission might be conferred upon his successor.

It is probable that, in threatening to resign, Hunt merely wished to call attention to his lack of proper rank and anomalous position in the chain of command, which loud grumbling might somehow rectify. Now, instead, Meade was proposing his muster-out. Enraged by such treatment, in the face of devoted service to the army, Hunt refused to back down. Finally, Meade's diplomatic new chief of staff, Major General Andrew Humphreys (who had replaced the ill-regarded Butterfield, wounded on 3 July), negotiated an amicable settlement of the dispute.[11] Meade made some form of apology for using harsh words, and Hunt, pride and integrity restored, agreed to withdraw his resignation. Though not on the best possible terms with his superior, and still with a single star on his shoulders, he would stay on.

*　　*　　*

Soon after the resignation crisis passed, Meade decided that Hunt had legitimate grounds for complaint on at least one score. On 21 August, he sought to remove those grounds by promulgating a formal decree, defining for the first time since the McClellan era the sphere of authority of the army's chief artillerist.

The order declared Hunt's power to be both executive and administrative —though "executive" was not clarified. Nevertheless, the order definitively stated that Hunt was empowered to supervise and inspect every battery in the army, and in battle to employ them "under the instructions of the major-general commanding." Likewise stressed was Hunt's subordination to the commanders of the various corps to which the field batteries were attached, unless special orders from Meade declared otherwise.

Whatever its flaws, the order was thorough-going and fairly precise, and, thus, filled a long-standing need.[12] However, it brought mixed reaction. Colonel Wainwright thought it "a kind of halfway thing as regards his [Hunt's] powers," for while it made all artillery answerable to him regarding supply, efficiency, and discipline, it gave him "no control over those supplies, or any power to regulate leaves of absence, or do anything else much."[13] Yet the man most affected by the decree voiced a different opinion. Eight months later he told a Congressional committee that the order

> amounted to giving me the command of the whole of the artillery, as in other armies. . . . I believe all, or nearly all, the powers of a corps commander have been conferred upon me under special orders, so that now I occupy a position much like that of the commander of the cavalry, and it is, to all intents and purposes, the same that was given me at first [that is, by Little Mac in September '62].[14]

Here, however, Hunt was magnifying his powers, since "special orders" were not required to give General Alfred Pleasonton, the new commander of cavalry, direct tactical control over the army's mounted units. As in pre-Hooker times, Hunt retained direct control only over the Artillery Reserve and over miscellaneous batteries that were not attached to the main army. He had full authority only in matters of equipment, supply, and instruction of personnel. Still, this constituted the extent of power any Federal artillery chief, in any army and any theater of combat, could hope to attain.[15] Realizing that fact, Hunt seemed content with his lot.

But by no means did the 21 August proclamation relieve all pains. It made no provision to remedy the distressing lack of high rank available to artillerists. If he truly believed that the order accorded him power equivalent to those exercised by Alfred Pleasonton—*Major* General Pleasonton—he must have grown even more disappointed and perplexed than before about his inferior rank.

He was likewise displeased by the continuing scarcity of field-rank officers under him. He restated the problem in late September, when completing his lengthy report of the Gettysburg campaign. Noting that during that period the corps artillery of the army had been led by two colonels, one major, three captains, and a lieutenant, he remarked:

> In none of our corps ought the artillery commander to have been of less rank than a colonel, and in all there should have been a proper proportion of field officers, with the necessary staffs. . . . Not only does the service suffer, necessarily, from the great deficiency of officers of rank, but a policy which closes the door of promotion to battery officers, and places them and the arm itself under a ban, and degrades them in comparison with other arms of service, induces discontent.[16]

Other, more minor concerns annoyed him throughout the remainder of that summer. One that he continually mentioned in headquarters memoranda related to the recently instituted practice whereby gaps in artillery units were filled by detached cavalry and infantry recruits temporarily assigned to duty and often recalled to their original commands soon after mastering the essentials of cannon tactics. To be sure, something had to be done to round up new artillerymen; after the carnage in southern Pennsylvania, 2,841 were required to bring the Regular and volunteer batteries to full strength. But the deficiencies would remain on the ledger for a long time to come.[17]

Even so, by making efforts to bring his command up to par, and by advocating so many other reforms, Hunt was fulfilling the role of the dedicated, faithful, and vigorous artillery chief. The pity was that his was a lone voice in the bureaucratic wilderness. It failed to carry as far as Washington, and at army headquarters, where it penetrated, it was constantly ignored.

*   *   *

Through August and September, Meade's and Lee's armies jockeyed for position in central Virginia, each seeking the clear initiative, neither finding it. During the stalemate, national attention turned toward other theaters of action. News had already come of Grant's brilliant success at Vicksburg; the Mississippi River citadel had surrendered the day after Pickett charged, with twenty-nine thousand prisoners and a strategic stretch of the Father of Waters falling into Union hands. Late in September, however, word came that Rosecrans's Army of the Cumberland, the largest Union field force in the West, had been whipped by rebels under Hunt's old comrade, Braxton Bragg, at Chickamauga, Georgia, on the nineteenth and twentieth of the month. Rosecrans and his men had retreated to Chattanooga, Tennessee, besieged by Bragg's Army of Tennessee.

Shortly thereafter, Hunt and his colleagues in Virginia learned that local reinforcements would be sent to Rosecrans. On 25 September, the XI and XII Corps, both led by recently returned Joe Hooker, left the Army of the Potomac and rode the rails westward. In October and November they would assist other supports fresh from Vicksburg under Grant in raising the siege of Chattanooga and chasing Bragg from the state. Coming so soon after his masterful victory along the Mississippi, Chattanooga's rescue would raise Ulysses S. Grant to a level of national prominence attained not even by George McClellan in his earliest, most promising days in the field.

The loss to Meade of twenty thousand troops led Lee to seek a confrontation above the Rappahannock River early in October. So began the first of a pair of campaigns waged that autumn.

The first culminated in battle near Bristow Station, on the Orange & Alexandria Railroad, not ten miles from the Bull Run-Centreville battlefields. There, on 14 October, Lee repeated, on a smaller scale, the sort of ill-advised assault that had brought him grief at Malvern Hill and Gettysburg. One of his three corps lost 1,900 casualties to the massed rifle fire of Meade's rear guard, the II Corps, now under General Warren (Hancock had been invalided home after a Gettysburg wounding), dug in behind a steep embankment along the right-of-way.[18]

Hunt saw limited service in the one-sided engagement since most of the artillery remained in Meade's forward echelons while fighting raged in the rear. But he did see some participation in the second of the season's campaigns—though prevented from engaging in large-scale action through last-minute alterations in strategy.

On 7 November, Meade reacted to War Office pressure by commencing an aggressive movement toward his much-outnumbered enemy, now back on the Rappahannock line. This time Lee fell back, and, during the next two and a half weeks, maneuvering took the place of the slugging-match Meade had sought to instigate. Finally, on the twenty-sixth, the Federals crossed the Rapidan and drove toward their enemy's right flank, backing Lee up against a nondescript little stream known as Mine Run. After fumbling away some opportunities to land a killing punch, Meade designated dawn on the thirtieth for a general assault against both rebel flanks, aided by a feint against the center. Hunt and his righthand assistant, General Tyler, did their part by positioning dozens of light cannon on the Federal right and center; and, as soon as sun touched horizon that morning, they let loose with a preassault barrage.[19]

The assault, however, never took place. Daylight revealed to General Warren, who carried responsibility for launching the flank drives, that during the previous night Lee had built impregnable works, stocking them with an overwhelming assortment of cannon. Without notifying Meade, Warren called off the attacks, ending the final active operations of the year.

For Hunt, the abortive battle on the thirtieth had a modicum of significance. To assuage Meade's worry that, because the V Corps had lost part of its ammo train, the Mine Run barrage would prove too weak, Hunt at last told him of the existence of his special ammunition reserve. Curiously, Meade was not angry that Hunt had concealed its presence from him;

remarking that it sounded like a good idea, the army leader authorized its continued use.[20]

Following the standoff at Mine Run, both armies crawled into winter quarters, Lee's troops below the Rappahannock and Meade's above, in the Brandy Station-Stevensburg-Culpeper vicinity. The camp of the Army of the Potomac was hardly the abode of good cheer, even during the Christmas holidays—not with so many bitter failures and lost opportunities immediately behind it. Assuredly Hunt had spent happier seasons.

(From left), Generals Gouverneur K. Warren, William H. French, George Gordon Meade, Hunt, Andrew A. Humphreys, and John Sedgwick, c. November 1863. (COURTESY, LIBRARY OF CONGRESS)

The greater part of the winter, as several of recent memory, he spent hard at work, firming up batteries damaged in battle, training recruits, reassigning personnel—and safeguarding the health of his animals. Alarmed by a decreasing availability of able-bodied horses, he urged his officers to take stringent measures to prevent winter diseases from ravaging their stables. When forage stock ran low, he condoned unauthorized means of replenishing the feed bags. To one artillerist, complaining about a brother officer who foraged off private property, Hunt replied with a grin: "I suppose Captain

Barnes knows what the orders are; but by God, I like to see a man take care of his horses!"[21]

As ever, Hunt enjoyed some diversions in camp. One was a constant influx of visitors, including numerous British and French observers whom General Meade posted to artillery headquarters. The practice long predated Meade's rise to command and had been continued because guests uniformly praised Hunt's conviviality and old-style hospitality, which seemed never to diminish, no matter how long he was imposed upon. It was shameful, however, that no one at army headquarters thought to reimburse him for the two thousand dollars he spent yearly to lodge his visitors in the style to which most of them had grown accustomed.[22]

That winter, Hunt also sought relief from the drudgery of rosters, requisitions, and reports, by directing his attention toward the national political scene. At first this provided little pleasure. Recent gubernatorial and Congressional elections had seen expansive Republican gains in states, including Pennsylvania, Iowa, and Indiana. In Ohio, however, the defeat of a Democratic aspirant to the governor's chair pleased Hunt considerably, for the loser was the anti-Unionist Clement L. Vallandigham. The one creature Hunt detested more than a fanatical abolitionist was a peace-at-any-price "copperhead," who sought to dilute the patriotic spirit of the Democratic Party. He wrote his father-in-law, Colonel Craig, of the Ohio contest: "I cannot say that I regret the success of the 'Union' ticket = The opposition suffered itself to include the 'peace men'—it touched pitch and became defiled." In fact, Hunt's major complaint against Abraham Lincoln's party directly concerned a willingness to fight and win in the field. Speaking of the G.O.P. he opined:

> Unless the war is vigorously prosecuted and with more ability than has characterized past operations it will be swept out of all branches of the government. That is my opinion, and unless radical changes are made in certain quarters this war will *not* be prosecuted with more ability.[23]

Should Lincoln and his band be swept out, who would replace them? Who had sufficient executive ability and moral fortitude to rule the land and win the conflict at the same time? For Hunt the answer was elementary: George B. McClellan.

As the personification of the staunchly Unionist, conservative Democrat, one of unquestioned integrity and high breeding, Little Mac already was being groomed to oppose the Illinois Republican as the Democratic presidential candidate in 1864. Hunt could not have been more pleased. His overriding belief was that McClellan was capable of ending the conflict without immersing it a bloodbath of revolutionary proportions—a bloodbath that would make future reconciliation between North and South impossible.

A number of associates echoed such sentiments—and by doing so, nearly ended their own careers this winter.

In the main camp near Culpeper, Hunt and some of his more conservative comrades, including John Newton, William French, George Sykes, and John Sedgwick (commanders, respectively, of the I, III, V, and VI Corps), proposed to make their support of McClellan highly visible. Lately, in his new role of civilian political aspirant, McClellan had delivered a New York speech that included words of fraternity and praise for his old subordinates still in the ranks. Now these men decided to "join in returning the good will." A testimonial was proposed, Sedgwick alone pledging a twenty-thousand-dollar contribution from the officers in his command. Hunt and the others agreed to take up a collection in their own outfits.

Several days after the fund drive began, General Meade went up to the capital for a conference at the White House. During the proceedings, Lincoln and War Secretary Stanton mentioned the McClellan testimonial, which had received much publicity in Eastern newspapers. Neither official was pleased by it. Meade, a political atheist, replied that he saw no harm in the idea—purely from personal friendship, he too had pledged a donation for McClellan. But because pro-Administration organs had labelled the testimonial politically oriented and thus unethical, the president and his war secretary demanded that Meade quash the drive. Finally, and reluctantly, the army commander complied.

Of course the generals who had fathered the idea were incensed when political pressure killed it—particularly when rumor had Meade stopping it only after Stanton drew up a list of pro-McClellan generals to be cashiered for insubordination. Not surprisingly, the rumor placed Hunt's name at the top of the page. His like-minded subordinate, Colonel Wainwright, later commented: "Had the order come out it would have been a glorious role of honour, on which not a few would have been proud to see their names inscribed."[24]

Afterward Hunt sat out the cold weather in silence, exclusively minding his own affairs. He had decided that his own name did not look well when gracing heated editorials in Republican prints or vindictive War Office memoranda.

Fortunately, he was soon able to quit that scene of stasis and discontent. On 14 January, he secured leave to visit his married sister and her family. It ended, however, as a convalescent furlough: early in February he developed a severe case of catarrh, with accompanying pharyngitis. Thus, his belated attempt to celebrate Christmas at the home of Mrs. Julia Hunt Tompkins, her husband, and their several children on Spruce Street, Philadelphia, provided something less than unadulterated pleasure.[25]

But up north, at least, he had the proper setting in which to push from mind the memory of the cramped confinement in winter camp. On the other hand, while he roamed far from Virginia, a pervasive reminder of his influence remained behind. The very day he entrained for Philadelphia, he had issued General Orders #2 for the year—a synthesis of his most cherished precepts, for "the government of all concerned." Like its author, the order was thorough, concise, and no-nonsense. It treated fourteen diverse topics under the general headings of administrative and tactical control of artillery, ranging from considerations governing selection of battery positions to the evils of that hoary bugaboo, excess expenditure of ammunition. Throughout it abounded in cogent aphorisms:

> Concentration of fire, rather than its distribution, is of importance. . . . Too much elevation should be avoided, since the fire is more effective in proportion as the projectiles pass more closely to the ground. . . . Distances must be accurately judged, the projectiles carefully prepared, the fire slow and deliberate, and its effect well-noted. . . . Even on perfectly open ground the flanks of a battery must be protected from assaults. . . . It must be laid down as a rule that artillery should not fire over our own troops. . . . Against an enemy's battery the fire should be concentrated on a single piece until that is disabled, and should then be turned upon another. . . . It is too much the habit to open fire on wagons or single horsemen, or small parties, and sometimes, as in almost all cases of shelling woods, on a mere suspicion that an enemy may be in a certain locality. . . .[26]

The compilation went on for several pages, remarkable for both scope and clarity.

In the long haul, such maxims would constitute Hunt's most enduring monument to his never-flagging effort to acquaint artillerists—officers and men alike—with the rules of right order that passed for standard in the Army of the Potomac.

14

The End Begins

When Hunt returned to the army in late February, he found snow and sunshine still wrestling for dominance in middle Virginia. He realized, however, that the resumption of active campaigning was only as distant as springtime; and springtime was only as distant as the third week of March. Thus, in the remaining four weeks he made full use of his last respite from field duty, working harder than ever before to outfit his command for marching and fighting.

Early the next month the man under whom Hunt's cannoneers would march and fight paid his first visit to the Brandy Station vicinity, to meet George Meade, who was now his upper-echelon subordinate. Hunt had foreseen the stranger's advent: while in the capital recuperating from his severe cold, he had learned that Ulysses Grant was to receive the recently revived rank of lieutenant general in command of all the armies of the Union, and that he would make his field headquarters with Meade's army.

Grant's first stay was brief, but on 24 March the victor of Forts Henry and Donelson, Vicksburg, and Chattanooga returned to the Army of the Potomac—this time for the formal introductions. In honor of the occasion, Hunt and his people turned out to pass in review, wearing their finest uniforms and their best parade-ground demeanor.

His reception was impressive, but, in return, Grant failed to impress. Many artillerists, as well as infantrymen, were surprised and disappointed by the lieutenant general's appearance. Most of them would probably have endorsed Charles Wainwright's impression: Grant was "stumpy, unmilitary, slouchy, and Western-looking; very ordinary in fact."[1]

The army was impressed by Grant's reputation, at least. Willing to please, the soldiers gave their new general-in-chief a rousing shout of welcome.

Such a show was beneath the dignity of a brigadier like Hunt, but when Grant reached him, the artillerist returned a snappy salute and pumped his outstretched hand in a spirited greeting. He added a few words, including a question: did the lieutenant general happen to recall the last time, but one, they had met—in Mexico?

Grant looked perplexed, so Hunt efreshed his memory of their encounter outside Mexico City in September '47, when Lieutenant Grant of the Fourth Infantry had bewailed his inevitable relegation to obscurity.

Grant chuckled. Yes, now he recalled that occasion; recalled it vividly.

His companion beamed. "Well, sir!" he said. "I am glad to find you with some chance yet left for military distinction!"[2]

* * *

The two found it simple to work in tandem, at least at the outset—which could not be said about Grant's more delicate and friction-prone command relationship with Meade. Hunt and Grant had much in common, which fostered a spirit of cooperation. Neither was fastidious about externals, especially in the mode of field attire; neither was genuinely comfortable in political circles; neither craved military pomp or gaudy display. Both were fundamentally conservative in many aspects of outlook and endeavor; both were Western-born and of humble enough origin (at least in regard to their immediate families); and both displayed an unusual combination of decorous formality and casualness, neither having lost the common touch. Both were energetic and determined, dedicated to the preservation of their integrity and inclined to speak candidly, no matter what icons might shatter at the pitch of their voice. Both were capable of instilling both respect and affection in men under their command. Circumstances relating to rank and position would conspire to keep them apart—physically and sometimes philosophically—during much of the campaigning that lay ahead. In later years, conflicts over military policy would widen the rift in their friendship. However, shared qualities, plus family ties (for several years Grant had been a close friend and army bunkmate of Hunt's brother)[3] would enable them to pursue a smooth professional association during the remainder of this war.

From the first, Grant gradually strengthened this relationship. Hunt was particularly pleased by the commanding general's willingness to meet head-on the thorniest of administrative and organizational problems. Under Grant's supervision, for example, a huge army reorganization begun by Meade received crucial impetus. The most visible reform was the consolidation of the six infantry corps into three: the II, under Hancock (temporarily returned from convalescence at home); the V, under Warren; and the VI, under Sedgwick. A fourth command, the IX Corps, headed by the Fredericksburg culprit, Ambrose Burnside, was attached to (and later would become an organic part of) Meade's army. Counting all four units, plus a reinvigorated cavalry corps led by Major General Philip H. Sheridan, the Army of the Potomac numbered more than 120,000. All would remain under the tactical guidance of Meade, while Grant, accompanying the army in the field, would chart grand strategy for it and the rest of the Union armies.[4]

Relative to artillery administration, Grant's edicts generally pleased Hunt. Like Meade and his predecessors, Grant proved highly reluctant to delegate increased authority to the army's ranking artillerist. Nor would he implement some innovations Hunt endorsed, including a plan devised by Charles Wainwright that would have established a single, full-scale corps of cannon units with a large complement of field-rank officers to govern it—an arrangement somewhat similar to the command system of the British Army. For lack of resources, Grant also vetoed a Hunt proposal to transport artillery ammo on mobile caissons rather than in slow-moving wagons.[5] Nevertheless, the new commander made more field-grade subordinates available to Hunt than ever before, and worked diligently to supply him with the finest horses, ammunition, and equipment. These and other pressing artillery needs won Grant's early and constant attention, to the arm's great benefit and Hunt's gratification.

In the final days of March, with snow gone and sun in full strength, Hunt announced the recently revised artillery rosters for the campaign under Grant. To head the cannon brigades of the three integral corps, he had appointed Colonels Tidball, Wainwright, and Tompkins. At the outset, each led eight batteries of forty-eight guns, but, later, Tidball received an extra six-gun battery. There was wide variance in the personnel totals: 1441 officers and men serving under Tidball, 1514 under Wainwright, and 1225 under Tompkins. Each brigade chief could draw upon between nine hundred and one thousand well-trained battery horses, and each was assisted in various ways by a battalion of foot artillerists.

The Artillery Reserve now comprised three brigades, which in turn consisted of foot artillery, siege guns, and the heavier field cannon of the army—all under Colonel Henry S. Burton, a West Point graduate of Hunt's class of '39, as well as, ironically, his superior by virtue of his Regular Army status as commander of the Fifth Artillery. He had succeeded General Tyler, who would soon accept command of a combination infantry-foot artillery brigade in the II Corps. All told, Burton had immediate control of twelve batteries and sixty-two pieces.

Finally, the artillery attached to Sheridan's cavalry consisted of two brigades, under Captains Robertson and Ransom; initially the first was the only horse-artillery brigade in the field, Ransom's command being attached to Burton's Reserve. The two captains managed an aggregate of a dozen batteries, sixty-two cannon.

Including later additions brought in by Burnside's corps, Hunt in 1864 would have effective control of no fewer than 346 cannon. After three years of steady conflict, all batteries had to be considered veteran outfits from which the utmost effectiveness in campaign and battle could be expected.

Apart from the quality of the men, the guns themselves were topflight.

Grant's coming had coincided with a campaign to alter the ratio of Napoleons-to-rifles in the Army of the Potomac—a ratio that, since the early days of the war, had meant rifle dominance by a wide margin. By March of 1864, rifled cannon still outnumbered the smoothbore gun-howitzers that Hunt preferred, but only by a slim margin: 154 rifles against 120 Napoleons in the organic components of the army. The dominant breed of grooved cannon, however, was the 3-inch ordnance rifle, which Hunt had once termed "the feeblest piece" ever purchased by the government. By now, at least, he was burdened with only a handful of another type of cannon he detested because of its fragility; the 20-pounder Parrot. And even these few remnants he managed to ship back to Washington in later weeks, no doubt raising the morale of he who had gone on record with the comment: "If anything could justify desertion by a cannoneer it would be an assignment to a Parrott battery!"[6]

With capable guns, ample supplies, talented subordinates, experienced enlisted men, and a commanding general who seemed to appreciate artillery's unique qualities, Hunt believed that, when the long roll was sounded at camp-breaking time, he would lead south the finest artillery command, bar none, in American history. Few critics, contemporary or of later vintage, would dispute him.

* * *

Before he could put his faith on trial, he faced an unappealing prelude. On the third of April he again rode the cars to Washington City—this time in company with Meade and other high-ranking commanders—to reappear before Ben Wade's Committee on the Conduct of the War. In the capital, as he had anticipated, he was permitted only a brief reunion with his family before being whisked up to Capitol Hill and escorted into a committee room, where the legislative watchdogs were now delving into the maneuvering—on and behind the battle lines—at Chancellorsville and Gettysburg.

Chancellorsville presented the inquisitors a hefty problem, since their favorite son, Hooker, seemed patently to blame for the disaster in the Wilderness. Ben Wade and his cohorts nevertheless tried to rehabilitate him. The substance and tenor of their inquiries told Hunt their several aims: they were seeking to indict a cabal of Hooker's subordinates for conspiring to subvert and thwart him, as well as for engineering a series of tactical blunders that lost the battle. Apropos to Gettysburg, the Congressmen were obviously maneuvering George Meade toward the chopping block. In particular, they sought to prove that Meade had grasped victory in lower Pennsylvania through no fault of his own—primarily because of the strategic plan his predecessor had bequeathed to him—and that, even so, Meade had tossed away an extraordinary opportunity to crush Lee's survivors following Pickett's repulse.[7]

The charges against Meade had recently assumed a sinister aspect. Early in March a *New York Herald* correspondent signing himself "Historicus," and obviously privy to the machinations of the Federal hierarchy during the Gettysburg campaign, had accused Meade in newsprint of drafting an order to abandon the field on 2 July 1863—an order he had been prevented from implementing only by the boldness and commendable impulsiveness of General Dan Sickles. Rather than menacing the Federal line, the III Corps' advance that afternoon, in an attempt to grab stronger positions, had exposed a crucial gap in the *enemy's* flank. Sickles's gain, said Historicus, was not exploited, but still his daring and initiative had committed the army to a battle, so that it could not turn tail and flee. As if this were not food enough for controversy, Historicus struck a second time, repeating his assertions in an issue of the *Herald* appearing the day after Hunt and Meade had reached Washington.

Though the correspondent's identity was never to be revealed, Hunt and most of his associates in the ranks did not doubt that Dan Sickles himself was the man behind the pen. The one-legged corps commander, a Republican stalwart, had been the initial witness during this current round of committee testimony, and, as Hunt might have expected, had played fast and loose with fact. He had stated, for example, that on 2 July, Hunt had "approved of in general terms" the forward thrust off Cemetery Ridge, hinting that this was tantamount to officially sanctioned authority to go ahead. And he had flagrantly perjured himself by asserting that when he moved westward from the Union line "my left had succeeded in getting into position on [Little] Round Top." The interrogators knew full well that he meant Devil's Den—a much more vulnerable position, three-quarters of a mile closer than Cemetery Ridge to Lee's veterans.[8]

Once in the witness chair, General Hunt counterattacked with a formidable weapon: truth. He steadfastly denied Historicus's statements and Dan Sickles's vindicatory fantasies, maintaining that Meade no longer thought about retreating, once he was assured that ample artillery ammunition would enable the army to stay and fight. In any case, Meade's orders regarding withdrawal constituted contingency planning in the strict sense of the term; in no truthful way could they be construed as the result of a foregone conclusion to retreat.[9]

Continuing, Hunt carefully refuted other erroneous parts of Sickles's testimony whenever the panel gave him an opening. Though by no means Meade's bosom friend, neither would Hunt see him pilloried by vindictive inquisitors who twisted fact for political gain.

Nor would he see Hooker reinstated to public esteem. Hunt missed few opportunities to berate his old commander for his unconscionable meddling in the affairs of the artillery, particularly at Chancellorsville. For some reason, the panel even allowed him to deliver a lengthy and scathing indictment of the artillery policies of Hooker's predecessors; Hunt supposed that the Congressmen hoped he would defame McClellan by branding him the instigator of all artillery's woes (something Hunt did not choose to do). Yet in giving him a forum to depict his long-term sufferings, the joint committee did Hunt one great favor.

In the end, he emerged from the committee room once again the victor. Thus Meade could write his wife that the artillerist had not played along with the committee, though: "They went to work & in the most petty fogging way by a cross examination" tried to use him to further their designs.[10] In the end, Meade would be supported by President Lincoln and would remain at the tactical head of the great Federal army in the East, no matter what the desires were of Ben Wade and his colleagues.

Back at the Craig household after his ordeal, Hunt found time to write some old friends before boarding a down train. One of his correspondents was George McClellan, still at home in Trenton. For his old commander Hunt depicted the venomous atmosphere not only atop Capitol Hill but within the War Department, which he had also visited this day. There, Hunt confided, certain officers professing fraternity and benevolence, had reached his ear with soft-spoken suggestions that his continued support for, and identification with, Little Mac was a hindrance "to my preferential advancement." Those men had urged him to finally rid himself of the McClellan albatross by accepting the goodwill held out to him by the Administration. Hunt added that he lacked a vocabular sufficiently filthy to properly characterize such "friends."[11]

All of which was most disheartening. It seemed bad enough that Hunt had to expose himself at the front to murderous men in gray. It was unbearable when he also had to guard his rear and flanks against those in his own camp who professed comradeship, all the while stealing up with concealed weapons.

* * *

Less than a month after returning to Virginia, Hunt found the long-awaited campaign—last of the war in the East—about to get under sail. On 4 May, the Army of the Potomac filed from its cabins and tents above the Rapidan and swung south toward the same woods in which Joe Hooker had lost his nerve and his reputation exactly one year ago.

While Meade's soldiers took the road, four other general movements, all under Grant's remote supervision, made ready to commence their march. From Chattanooga trekked Major General William T. Sherman and ninety-eight thousand veterans divided among three armies, heading toward a Georgia showdown with the principal rebel army in that theater. From Louisiana, Major General Nathaniel P. Banks would soon move against Mobile, Alabama, the last Confederate port on the Gulf Coast; that is, if he could pry himself away from one of his typically hopeless sideshow campaigns, now apace in his bailiwick. Back east, in the meantime, Major

General Franz Sigel was leading six thousand Federals to cut communication lines amid the Confederacy's breadbasket, the Shenandoah Valley. And on the Virginia peninsula Major General Benjamin F. Butler and his Army of the James, almost forty thousand strong, was shuffling toward Richmond, hopeful of investing it from the south while Grant swung down upon it from above, driving Lee's men before him. For the first time since the shooting had started, all the principal Federal forces were cooperating via simultaneous movements toward a common goal: the annihilation of the military and industrial structure of the Confederacy.[12]

The main road led to ultimate triumph, though its byways would prove rocky beyond endurance for Banks, Sigel, and Butler, each of whom would fail miserably in his assigned task. Even Meade's people had a twisted, arduous road to negotiate. It proved so almost from the first hour of the march, primarily because of the trees through which it wound.

As it had a year ago, the Wilderness stirred a primordial dread in those who entered it; one of Hunt's soldiers called it "a region of gloom and the shadow of death."[13] The man was proved correct on both counts on the fifth, when the clotted tangle of second-growth flora, spidery creeks, and steep ravines became the unlikely battleground for Grant's initial contact with the foe. For, like Hooker before him, he found it impossible to clear the trees before Lee, divining his coming, rushed up wild-eyed for a fight. That fight was predictably bloody and just as predictably inconclusive. Both sides fought blindly, firing at unseen targets and grappling without plan or intention in a world of vines and undergrowth so lush that not even small units could maintain simple cohesion.

For the most part, Hunt and his men sat it out, unable to maneuver guns while surrounded by so many natural barriers. Cannon piled up on the fringes of the fighting, and were sent to the rear so as not to clog the few precious woodland roads. Colonel Burton and the whole of his Reserve were ordered back out of the forest, and Hunt did not see them again until after the two-day struggle had died out. By the finale, artillery's plight had not appreciably altered. "We could do nothing," complained one cannoneer, "because no horses could have pulled a gun through the brush in which the infantry were fighting."[14]

Added to Hunt's woe was a series of incredible performances by various infantry commanders. On 6 May, a V Corps division leader, Brigadier General Charles Griffin, tried to compel Colonel Wainwright to place three or four batteries on a ridge near some hastily dug but well-defended Confederate trenches amid a narrow clearing between the main lines of the armies. Wainwright was incredulous that a former artilleryman could issue such an order. He pointed out that the enemy was so near, their guns could enfilade the new position as well as the ranks of Federal infantry behind the guns, which would be exposed once the batteries were moved up. Griffin then called up Hunt, demanding that a "competent" officer overrule the colonel. Only after Hunt denounced Griffin's scheme as "pure absurdity"—an opinion seconded by another infantry general—was the idea squelched.[15]

The infantry soon found a new way to bedevil Hunt. Though Burton's command had been shoved rearward, its foot artillery brigade, under a smooth-faced, curly-locked young colonel named J. Howard Kitching, was not permitted to accompany it. Infantry generals got their gloves on it and sent the brigade moving first in one direction, then another, exhausting its men to no apparent end. During the second day of the combat in the Wilderness, the brigade was sent marching, entrenching, marching again, supporting foot troops, and marching some more; after which it was permitted to go to the rear for some little rest, only to be recalled the next morning, sent rearward again late on 8 May, and ordered back to the front for another purposeless day on the ninth. When Hunt learned of its plight, he blasted Generals Warren and Hancock, into whose clutches Kitching's men had fallen.[16] Both officers bristled, with the result that Hunt's relations with Warren turned bad, and his relations with Hancock, already bad, worsened.

Even before the foot artillerymen suffered such abuse, Grant admitted stalemate in the Wilderness. Unlike so many of those who had gone before him, however, he refused to retreat northward. Sliding around Lee, he sent his sore but intact army ten miles southeastward, passing out of the woods and into the sunlight. On a path that ultimately led to Petersburg and Richmond, the Army of the Potomac neared its next immediate objective: the strategically located village of Spotsylvania Court House.

At Spotsylvania, 8–21 May, the Federals and their enemy suffered far more casualties than either had lost in the Wilderness, because now, on somewhat more open ground, the antagonists could see each other all too well. As the rebels held the more favorable positions and were permitted to remain on the defensive, the Federals seemed to feel compelled to attack them outside the town. It proved a fatal compulsion.

At Spotsylvania, Hunt's gunners contributed to the fighting much more effectively and extensively than the week before. But maneuverable cannon, even in mass, could not staunch the blood spilled by infantrymen mowed down while charging impregnable breastworks along all sectors of the rebel line. Even when close-range combat ceased and distant skirmishing took over, the Federals suffered the more. On 9 May the Confederate sharpshooters also maimed Hunt emotionally. That morning his cherished friend John Sedgwick fell dead with a sniper's bullet below his left eye.[17]

Other unhappy incidents would make Spotsylvania perversely memorable for him. On the tenth, one of Hancock's generals ordered a Rhode Island battery beyond the Federal line, exposing it so temptingly that the rebels scrambled from their works and seized it. Later that same day another II Corps brigadier placed one of Colonel Tidball's Napoleon units directly in front of its sister batteries in an effort to mask the latter from rebels along Lee's left flank—but succeeding only in blocking the rear units' fields of fire.

The general then ordered the battery farthest to the rear to commence firing at such a long range that the unit in the forefront was nearly chopped to pieces. Only by hastily abandoning their positions did its gunners escape.[18]

Yet again that day, Hunt vented his wrath at Gouverneur Warren, this time when the V Corps commander decided to ignore advice given him by his artillery chief, Wainwright. Such discourtesy irked Hunt as well as the New York colonel, but Warren's patent inability to direct his guns properly was an even greater sin. On the evening of 10 May, Hunt added a bitter entry to his campaign journal: ". . . in the management of the Art. Genl. Warren has managed the worst, then Genl. Hancock."[19]

From first to last, the fighting around Spotsylvania was a heavy drain on Hunt's physical resources as well as his patience. During the attacks Meade launched on 12 May alone, batteries supporting them expended nearly half the available supply of 12-pounder ammunition.[20] With increasing frequency Hunt found it necessary to order up surplus artillery supplies from Belle Plain Landing—a supply depot on a Potomac River estuary about forty miles below Washington. Toward the end of May, Belle Plain began to run dry, and rush orders were sent to the capital for more of everything in the line of ordnance equipment.

Then Hunt received perhaps the most painful blow of the war. Ever since breaking camp above the Rapidan, Grant had doubted the desirability of lugging south so many cannon, sensing that their utility would continually decrease as the army moved through the wooded areas that gave access to Richmond. By the sixteenth of May he had made a significant decision, now firmly convinced: "This arm was in such abundance that the fourth of it could not be used to advantage in such a country."[21] It was on that day that he broke the news to Hunt: he was ordering the Artillery Reserve disbanded, its units to be sent to the Washington defenses.

The artillery leader was stunned. When he regained his composure, he implored Grant to reconsider, stressing the terrible jolt such an order would deal artillery's morale, and citing the accomplishments the Reserve had accumulated during its two-and-a-half-year existence. When Grant remained unmoved, Hunt offered an alternative solution, whereby only the single remaining 20-pounder Parrott battery in the Reserve would be sent to the capital; each battery in the field army would be reduced from six to four guns; and the remaining Reserve units would be distributed through the II, V, and VI Corps. This would increase each corps artillery brigade to at least twelve batteries, but of fewer cannon, caissons, and other paraphernalia that would hinder mobility; most significantly, it would keep the Reserve units intact while lopping ninety-four pieces from the rosters. In the end Grant approved Hunt's idea, agreeing to send the discarded guns to Belle Plain in event of future need in siege operations.[22]

Yet, even the knowledge that he had sustained the cannoneer strength of his command failed to repay Hunt for the anguish of seeing his Reserve formally dissolved. Certainly it did not stifle the wails of protest from displaced Reserve officers such as Colonel Burton, who was compelled to accept the less-prestigious post of inspector of artillery at army headquarters. Hunt found new employment for one other luckless brigade chief, by delegating Lieutenant Colonel McGilvery authority to preside over the special ammunition train (and also an attached unit of foot artillerymen who would guard it). Grant had permitted Hunt's train to remain in operation indefinitely, seeing in it the sort of value that he could no longer perceive in the Artillery Reserve.

Eventually Hunt would realize that he had made the best of a bad business—especially since ultimately the Reserve would regenerate itself, returning to field service under Grant, though via unofficial status. Still, even had he been privileged to know this, it is doubtful that he would have rejoiced at the time, so seriously did the formal death of his war-child depress him.

Soon after Grant had called him aside with the unhappy news, Hunt had scrawled a grim epitaph in his journal: "So goes an organization which it has taken nearly three years to bring to its present condition of efficiency."[23]

15
Siege

The third week in May 1864 brought undistilled gloom to the Federal armies
in the field. By the twentieth, the major fighting at Spotsylvania had ceased,
with Grant still a vast distance from Richmond, but with thirty-three thousand
fewer able-bodied men than when he had crossed the Rapidan. That day, too,
Ben Butler's army, having failed in its campaign to lay hands on Richmond
or Petersburg—the rail center twenty-two miles below the Confederate capital
—had begun retreating to its jumping-off point, Bermuda Hundred. Hemmed
in on three sides by the nearby James and Appomattox Rivers, and on the
fourth by outnumbered but formidably entrenched Confederates, Butler
was "bottled up" and effectively out of the war. As for the rest of Grant's
strategy, General Banks had never commenced his assigned errand in Alabama,
and Franz Sigel's troops had been overwhelmed at New Market, Virginia,
on the fifteenth, by a far-undersize rebel army, with Sigel now in rapid flight
northward. Finally, far to the west, Uncle Billy Sherman was resting after a
two-day clash at Resaca, Georgia, against Confederates under Bragg's successor,
Joe Johnston. Thus far, Sherman had garnered precious little in the manner
of tactical or strategic success.

Hunt was more disgusted by this revolting series of failures than most of
his comrades. His disgust was motivated by specific aggravations in his own
sector, including, of course, the obliteration of the Reserve and the lack of
opportunities for artillery to see decisive campaign participation. Like the
Wilderness, Spotsylvania had provided the Federal guns with few dramatic
means of making their presence felt in critical circumstances. The prognosis
for artillery in the immediate future was not encouraging, either.

On 21 May the Army of the Potomac again skirted Lee's right, sidling
southeastward in another attempt to reach Richmond via a wide envelopment.
But, as before, Lee matched his opponents' swiftness. The next day the armies
faced each other in what appeared another stalemate—this time along the
North Anna River. After a sharp but inconclusive engagement there, Grant
concluded his side-stepping, crossing the Pamunkey River on the twenty-

eighth and driving toward a sweltering, landlocked hamlet with the wholly incongruous name of Cold Harbor. Since leaving Spotsylvania almost a week ago, neither Hunt nor his gunners had been provided a chance to earn their employ.[1]

During the first days in June they at last saw action—though not of the sort they relished. On the first, the armies collided near Cold Harbor, less than ten miles north and east of Richmond. Next day, when his main army came up, Grant projected a sweeping attack, but through staff mismanagement, torpor bred of merciless heat, and the ineffectuality of several subordinates, the strike had to be postponed twenty-four hours. This at least gave Hunt time to mass his batteries for the assault.

But when it was launched, at 4:30 on the morning of the third, not all the cannon in the North could have ensured its success. In a sequence of frontal charges against well-entrenched rebels, Grant lost some seven thousand men within less than sixty minutes, making Cold Harbor one of the most devastating chapters in American combat history.

Hunt was sickened by the butchery, which fell heaviest upon the XVIII Corps of Major General William Farrar Smith, recently detached from Ben Butler's army. At the height of the action, despite his sympathy for Smith's plight, Hunt enmeshed himself in a fierce argument with the man, who happened to be one of the prickliest commanders in the Union ranks. The shouting contest ended with Hunt threatening to withhold further ammunition if Smith continued to permit his artillerymen to throw away their supply by battering positions obviously impossible to breach.[2] Hunt was probably right in saying such a cannonade would be wasted: when the fighting at Cold Harbor closed, more than twelve thousand Federals lay dead or wounded in the grassy meadows; only 1,500 Confederates had been rendered casualties.

Reacting to the criticism of those who, like Hunt, considered Cold Harbor an exercise in mass murder, Grant by 7 June concluded that he had been pursuing improper strategy. Reassessing his goals, he decided that Petersburg, not Richmond, should be his primary objective. Via the former, twenty-two miles below Richmond, the rebel capital clasped hands with the interior of the Deep South, drawing most of the rations and much of the matériel that sustained it.

Thus, Grant sidled southeastward around Lee's right one final time. By feinting one way, then another, he left his opponent ignorant of his true intentions. On 12 June the Army of the Potomac crossed the Chickahominy River, due east of Richmond, and continued southward. By the next afternoon the troops were at the James River, and by the morning of the fifteenth most of the 105,000 Federals under Grant and Meade had been ferried south of the James, with wagons and cannon rolling across a 104-pontoon, 2,200-foot-long bridge—the work of Brigadier General Henry W. Benham and his men of the Engineer Brigade.

Four days passed before Lee realized that Grant was in the vicinity. On the fifteenth, long before the Army of Northern Virginia could arrive, the Federals were in position to capture the city that provided the key to Richmond. Smith's corps, ferried up the Appomattox and James Rivers in advance of the rest of Grant's command, was first to come within sight of Petersburg that day, and it had support within easy distance, for Hancock's II Corps was coming down quickly from the north. Poised on the threshhold of glory—perhaps immortality—Smith hesitated, failing to move forward after taking the city's outer defenses, manned by most of the 3,000 troops available to protect Petersburg. Stymied by vague orders, unknown terrain, and irresolution in a crisis, Smith gave the local commander, Pierre Beauregard, enough time to draw south thousands of supports who recently had battered Butler's army into withdrawal. In fact, Smith dawdled so long (a performance copied by other corps generals in Meade's employ) that finally General Lee learned Grant's location and came down to challenge him, making the Petersburg lines strong almost to the point of impregnability.

At first Grant did not see the truth. He had Hunt emplace a powerful array of guns east of Petersburg, particularly on the far right of that part of the Federal line held by Burnside's IX Corps. Then, on the eighteenth and nineteenth—before Lee could come up in full strength—he had Meade toss infantrymen against the city in a series of energetic but futile assaults. It seemed like Cold Harbor all over again; finally Grant crumpled up that strategy and threw it away.

His single alternative was to lay siege to the city. Grant adopted it.[3]

* * *

By 19 June the work of firming up siege lines had already begun. On that afternoon Hunt commenced a campaign of armament emplacement destined to continue for almost six weeks, through the hottest regions of Virginia, and while Union morale seemed at an all-time low.

On the first day, Hunt laid the groundwork for his long, busy summer. With Colonel Wainwright, he toured the lines that Grant's soldiers had established days before, and that were now being strengthened and expanded. Frequently the pair had to move forward on hands and knees, crawling the length of rifle pits and redoubt trenches to avoid the bullets that rebel pickets inconveniently provided. Minié balls, Wainwright noted, "whizzed about our ears at the rate of at least thirty a minute. I do not remember ever being more scared."[4] Hunt may have felt likewise, although, having ignored personal safety on so many past occasions, it may have seemed to him a trifle late in the game to grow self-protective.

Having pinpointed preliminary locations, Hunt next day sent for the heavy guns. He had plenty from which to draw. A new siege train had been born—of even greater size and variety than its 1861–62 edition. With Butler's army expected to invest Richmond from the south while Grant came down from above, siege ordnance had been recognized as vital to the

Battery outside Petersburg, June 1864 (COURTESY, LIBRARY OF CONGRESS)

fate of the 1864 campaign. In mid-April, at Meade's request, Hunt had drawn up a memorandum for outfitting a train able to be floated to the Richmond vicinity via barges or two hundred-ton-capacity schooners, the transport to be furnished by General Benham. Hunt had specified that the train should consist of, at minimum, forty siege cannon (either 4.5-inch ordnance guns or 30-pounder Parrotts), ten 10-inch mortars, twenty 8-inch mortars, and twenty Coehorns (lightweight and long-range forty-five-degree-angle mortars, each able to be lugged about on its wooden base by a pair of husky soldiers). He further stipulated that each cannon in the train, except those held in reserve, should be accompanied by at least one thousand rounds of ammunition; each large mortar by six hundred rounds, and each Coehorn by two hundred.[5] To supervise the entire array both during its formative stage at Washington and in the field, Hunt suggested General Tyler's replacement as head of the First Connecticut "Heavies": Colonel Henry L. Abbot. Though a prewar engineer, the colonel was an able artillerist through acquired experience, and possessed the sort of mechanical aptitude that would stand him in excellent stead in such a position.

Abbot had fully repaid Hunt's confidence. By working long and industriously he had met all but a few minor specifications by the 10 May deadline, shipping his schooner-borne train down the Atlantic Coast, then up the Virginia peninsula to Butler's supply depot at City Point, at the confluence of the James and Appomattox Rivers. Unfortunately, Abbot found less than a week of significant duty ahead of him; by 17 May, Butler was in inglorious flight to Bermuda Hundred, where Abbot also wound up, sitting out the remainder of that month and most of June as well—a siege artillerist nowhere near enough to his objective to lay effective siege.

By Hunt's order, he finally returned to work. In the third week in June, Abbot began to fragment his train, sending piece after piece to Petersburg via the Appomattox, while storing those guns not yet needed up front, at Broadway Landing, on the south bank of the river and directly across from Grant's headquarters (the lieutenant general had commandeered Butler's former quarters at City Point; he would keep them for the rest of the war). There, Abbott was in a handy spot to supply Hunt with as much firepower as he could handle at the front.[6]

No sooner had Abbot's big guns appeared outside Petersburg than they were defiled by the insensitive touch of infantry commanders. Enchanted by a vision of a Petersburg reduced to rubble at their hands, corps and division generals ordered the siege batteries, as soon as emplaced, to start firing—and neglected to stop them.

Grant required no warning from Hunt to see the danger here. For that reason, the situation redounded to Hunt's benefit. Chiefly to curtail such waste of ammunition, Grant on the twenty-seventh decreed that Hunt would henceforth possess authority over all siege operations south of the Appomattox—which encompassed all forces around Petersburg, excluding only the single corps remaining at Bermuda Hundred under Butler.[7]

Hunt, of course, was very pleased. At once he used his new power to bring Colonel Abbot to the front, where he could personally direct the location and emplacement of the siege units. At the same time, he furnished new work for the deposed Colonel Burton, by installing him as artillery chief of Smith's corps.

But Hunt's pleasure had a brief life, thanks largely to the lack of administrative cooperation he received from General Meade. To his disgruntlement, for instance, Meade failed to support his attempt to bring General Warren to account for various artillery crimes. Still in progress was the V Corps leader's campaign to ignore his artillery chief by flouting his wishes and disregarding his recommendations. Not only had Warren transferred batteries without notifying Wainwright, he had formed his own corps artillery reserve, in opposition to the artillerist's objections. When Hunt complained to Meade, the latter's reply was disheartening: such exercise of authority, tactful or not, was rightfully Warren's.

More than anything else, this made Hunt see that he did not exercise as much clout over corps and division commanders as he thought Grant's edict had given him. Probably he realized that Grant deferred, whenever possible, to Meade's wishes, especially in matters wholly pertaining to Meade's army. In any case, Hunt did not refer the dispute to the lieutenant general. Thenceforward, he exercised control over only Abbot's siege batteries, not the artillery still attached to the several corps.

Soon afterward, Hunt again clashed with Warren. This fight began when engineers engaged in constructing siege works in the V Corps area complained that Warren deliberately made their labors more difficult than did the sun and dust and Rebel pickets. By keeping up an almost constant barrage against Petersburg, despite Hunt's antipathy to the practice, Warren ensured that rebel cannoneers would retaliate by continually blasting his positions, thus menacing the engineers' safety. Colonel Wainwright agreed that Warren's shelling habits made the situation unhealthy for all concerned, including the Federal gunners themselves. But, as before, Wainwright's superior would not listen to him.[8]

At length Hunt visited Warren's command post and personally stated the particulars of the situation, but received no cooperation. By now, Gouverneur Warren's personality had been damaged by the strain of constant campaigning under the most trying conditions, and his temper was uglier than ever before. General Marsena Patrick had noted some months before: "Warren has been so puffed & elated & swelled up, that his arrogance & insolence are intolerable—". Recently Colonel Wainwright had rendered a more humane judgment: " . . . these awful fits of passion are a disease with Warren, and a species of insanity, over which he has no control."[9]

His own temper now afire, Hunt left Warren, went to his own quarters, and slashed out a letter to Meade, detailing Warren's violations of military custom. Though prefacing his remarks with a stated unwillingness to deprive a corps commander of delegated authority, he called Meade's attention to

the mode in which this transfer of duties has been effected, as one not merely wanting in courtesy to the chief of artillery of the corps, but as calculated to destroy on the part of his subordinaates the respect due to his position and to impair his just authority.[10]

Hunt's pen proved more effective than his tongue. This time, despite a loud protest from Warren, Meade compelled him to return to Wainwright the authority that had been given him by practice and precedent. Predictably, however, aroused passions led to other run-ins between Hunt and Warren, most involving relatively trivial concerns, including requests for V Corps artillery transfers granted by Hunt against Warren's wishes.

As June wound down and July pushed forward, Hunt had ugly confrontations with a number of other infantry generals, including several with Warren's subordinate, Charles Griffin, with whom he had been on poor terms since Griffin's ill-advised artillery deployment scheme of 6 May. It was inevitable that short-fused tempers would explode into personal conflict; the weather and the general military situation provided the proper setting. Remarked General John Gibbon: "This period of the operation of the army was a very trying one. The heat was intense, water was scarce and bad and the dust intolerable."[11]

Gibbon spoke plain truth, his words endorsed by all involved in the siege. As the temperature climbed and resistance to its discomfort lowered, Federal morale began to crumble. Therefore, Hunt, Grant, Meade, and all others concerned with the army's spiritual well-being, were grateful when, late in June, a project materialized that would help distract the men's attention from missed opportunities and oppressive campaign conditions— if only temporarily.

Though having decided on a siege, Grant would not restrict himself to unimaginative prosecution of such strategy. Already, despite a bleak outlook, he had set in motion some infantry diversions and one large-scale cavalry raid designed to isolate Petersburg from the rest of the Confederacy. None had succeeded, but still Grant remained receptive to resourceful ideas.

One such was presented to him by Lieutenant Colonel Henry Pleasants—a prewar mining engineer, now commanding the Forty-eighth Pennsylvania Infantry in Burnside's IX Corps. Pleasants had visions of an immense underground shaft extending beneath an enemy salient just four hundred yards west of Burnside's position. At the end of the shaft, he believed, enough blasting powder might be detonated to blow Robert E. Lee's boys, literally, sky-high. Furthermore, Pleasants had just the men for the job: a goodly percentage of his regiment were coal-crackers from the anthracite fields of upper Schuylkill County. These miners were rugged as well as skilled; and, like their comrades in the trenches, they had plenty of free time for digging.[12]

Though he did not officially sanction the mine project for some three weeks, Grant was immediately responsive to its possibilities. Therefore, on 25 June, Colonel Pleasants put his miners to work with whatever tools were available. Though General Meade was instructed to furnish other implements, they never materialized—probably because Meade, like most of his engineer advisors, thought the idea hare-brained. For one thing, the engineers maintained, no tunnel such as Pleasants envisioned could escape detection: air holes necessary for ventilation would immediatelyy be spotted by the rebels. With the crucial element of surprise lost, the project would prove a fizzle.

Pleasants did not see it that way, nor did his miners. Grimly determined, they continued their labors. From the outset they made remarkable progress, solving the ventilation-duct problem by constructing a chimney at the entrance to the tunnel, and running pipes from it the length of the shaft; when the chimney was heated by a small fire at its base, the heat caused air to rise through its stack, simultaneously sucking in fresh air.

This obstacle cleared, the major part of the digging could be handled. Because he was refused timber to shore up the tunnel, Pleasants drew lumber from a nearby, abandoned sawmill at which he put some of his surplus personnel to work; having been refused mining picks, the colonel refashioned those ordinary picks on hand; refused wheelbarrows with which to cart away displaced earth, he improvised from hardtack boxes. Through the remainder of the month and well into July his men burrowed beneath their comrades' feet, drawing ever closer to a heavily occupied hillside within the rebel lines. Once this hill had been cleared of the enemy, Burnside's men could easily take the one beyond, which commanded the interior of Petersburg.[13]

By the end of June, General Meade began to pay some attention to the project, noting that both Grant and Burnside seemed enthusiastic about its success. Grant had good basis for optimism: during his investment of Vicksburg, a shorter mine shaft had succeeded in blowing out a section of the rebel works, though an attempt to exploit the breakthrough failed. He could only hope that Colonel Pleasants's project would see a more worthwhile outcome.

In consequence of Meade's growing interest, Hunt entered the project on 29 June. That day Meade ordered him to requisition five tons—twelve thousand pounds—of black powder and one thousand yards of fuze. Hunt was also instructed to order Colonel Abbot to send up more heavy guns to protect Burnside's sector in event the undertaking proved exploitable.[14] At this point the artillery chief personally sought out Pleasants, and came away from the conference highly impressed by the colonel's know-how and determination. Less than a week later, Hunt and Major James C. Duane, Meade's chief engineer, were instructed to make a lengthy reconnaissance to determine if any offensive operations were feasible at any point along the Federal front. Hunt decided to pay especial attention to the sector held by Burnside's corps.

On 8 July, following a two-day tour of the lines, Hunt and Duane returned a detailed report. Their findings indicated that a successful offensive might be conducted against the salient facing Burnside, but only if enough heavy cannon could be brought to bear on rebel flanking batteries north of the IX Corps' position and "upon the salient and batteries in front of the Fifth and Eighteenth Corps." Other conclusions influenced Grant and Meade to inform the army on the ninth that siege operations against Petersburg (with the exception of the offensive planned against the salient) would consist of "regular approaches."[15] This meant a yard-by-yard campaign whereby the trench lines would be extended ever nearer to the enemy with the ultimate aim of making the rebel positions untenable. Later, Hunt claimed that his report had its roots in traditional operations—"extracted bodily from Genl McClellan's instructions for the siege of Yorktown."[16]

Immediately after he and Duane filed their report, he had Abbot send up, not only additional cannon, but ten more 10-inch mortars, plus six 8-inchers—all for use in the V and IX Corps sectors east and southeast of the city. More Coehorns were also sent up (Hunt had a highly favorable opinion of the weapon), until virtually all Union-flanked reaches of the Confederate lines were susceptible to vertical fire.

While Hunt and Abbot worked long hours supervising the ordnance buildup, Major Duane and his engineers surveyed and constructed complex works, especially timber-and-wire-meshed abatis, to protect the siege weapons. Their labors were safer now, thanks to Hunt's campaign to curb General Warren's penchant for continuous shelling.

But Hunt's own work was dangerous to his health. Constant exposure to the baking heat eventually laid him low: for a week in mid-July he lay incapacitated from sunstroke and overexertion. In his absence, Colonel Abbot and other subordinates carried on capably, lining work after work with 30-pounder Parrotts, 4.5-inch rifles, heavy and light mortars, and various other instruments of death.[17]

The most awe-inspiring member of this array of hardware symbolized the mammoth industrial strength of the North, on which the Army of the Potomac could draw. This was a huge seacoast mortar, *Dictator,* which had been the prize pet of Ben Butler's ordnance cache at Bermuda Hundred, and which was now positioned in rear of Smith's corps, on the extreme right flank. The weapon weighed seventeen thousand pounds and the diameter of its bore measured thirteen inches. When fed a charge of twenty pounds of powder, it could heave a 218-pound projectile the incredible distance of 3,600 yards—more than two miles—enabling Grant and Meade to send an unholy terror through those unfortunates subject to its fire.

Thirteen-inch mortar Dictator *outside Petersburg, c. July 1864. Hunt stands third from right, in foreground; Colonel Henry L. Abbot on his right; Hunt's staff on rear portion of platform.* (COURTESY, LIBRARY OF CONGRESS)

Dictator even frightened its own crew by the effects of its strength. At Butler's suggestion, the iron monster had been mounted on an eight-wheeled flatcar plated with iron and strengthened by steel rods and wooden beams. The car rode curved track on the Petersburg & City Point Railroad, permitting easy alterations in its plane of fire. Fortunately, the track was lengthy, for the recoil produced by *Dictator's* dischage sent the mortar sliding two feet across its platform and its car careening twelve feet down the track. Now and then, not even the track helped prevent trouble. When fired at an angle too oblique from the railroad, as on 13 July, *Dictator* had a disconcerting proclivity to crush the iron-plated car with its recoil.[18]

But toward the tail end of July, even the iron behemoth lost the ability to dominate the army's attention. By the twenty-seventh, Colonel Pleasants's mine was complete, and just about everyone in blue knew it. Not only had the colonel and his four hundred miners dug a 511-foot-long main shaft, stretching far into the hill occupied by the rebel salient, but they had added a thirty-eight-foot-long wing gallery to the right and left of the shaft. Nothing of its kind had precedent in this war—or in any American war, for that matter.[19]

By now, too, the enemy had heard enough noise underground to suspect something ominous; a deserter entering the Union lines on 17 July had informed Hunt that his ex-comrades were frantically countermining in an attempt to locate it. Even so, Hunt did not fret: at twenty feet, Pleasants's tunnel was so deep that no enemy could locate it unless provided with months of working time and an incredibly large labor force. Finally the rebels gave up their efforts and apparently convinced themselves that no mine existed.[20]

* * *

By the twenty-ninth the tunnel was armed and awaiting usage. Four tons of blasting powder, in 320 kegs, had been stored in eight underground magazines, and a multispliced fuze ran most of the length of the main shaft. Hunt, long since recovered from his debility, had done well on his part: some eighty-one siege guns and mortars, plus eighty field cannon, had been trundled into position. Armed and fully manned, each weapon, from the smallest Coehorn to the seventeen thousand-pound mortar on its flatcar, prepared to subject the enemy lines to the most concentrated barrage ever unleashed.[21]

Irrespective of the strenuous physical labor involved, the project had been a great ordeal for Hunt. Though General Warren had been prevented from making further trouble, other infantry commanders had hindered the buildup. Foremost of these was the general for whose immediate benefit most of the cannon had been emplaced. Due to Ambrose Burnside's foolish stubbornness, a thick grove of trees had been allowed to remain in front of a crucial sector in the IX Corps' front, blocking the field of fire of a fourteen-gun siege battery Hunt had painstakingly erected. His labors would count for nothing; Burnside would refuse to send men to level the timber, afraid that the rebels, hearing the noise, would suspect something akin to the attack that the IX Corps planned to launch in the wake of the mine's detonation on 30 July.[22]

By sunup on the appointed day, Hunt had issued detailed instructions governing the duties of all artillerymen in Burnside's front and on his flanks, listing targets in order of priority and suggesting the best methods of achieving maximum effect in laying down a supporting barrage for the IX Corps assault. Later that day, Lieutenant Colonel Theodore Lyman of Meade's staff noted: "General Hunt had been everywhere and arranged his artillery like clockwork; each chief of piece knew his distances and his directions to an inch."[23]

But elsewhere the assault had not been planned quite so well. Long before the sun rose that morning—with the rest of the army holding its breath—Burnside's regiments were huddling in mass behind their forward works, awaiting the explosion—set to occur at 3:30 A.M.—which would signal their charge. But the lead troops were not well versed in the assault plan.

Burnside's single division of black soldiers had originally been chosen to spearhead the assault; accordingly they had been well rehearsed for the job. But at the eleventh hour Grant had decided to substitute a white division for the main attack column, fearing charges of racial insensitivity should the assault fail. The trouble was that the white unit knew next to nothing of what to expect when it went forward; its officers were as ignorant of any timetable or attack plan as the enlisted men. But now the well-trained blacks would bring up the rear as an all-purpose reserve.[24]

By 3:30, as Hunt and his subordinates watched intently from the rear, all seemed quiet. Even as one of Colonel Pleasants's men lit the fuze, the rebel lines lay wrapped in darkness and near-complete silence. Along the crest of the salient pickets paced to and fro, blissfully ignorant of impending doom—some of their comrades stirred just enough to provide a light skirmish fire. Hunt alternately glanced at his pocket watch, then through his field glasses at the salient, murkily visible in the first streaks of dawn.

But H-Hour came and went without incident. About forty-five minutes later, two of Pleasants's hardier volunteers entered the main gallery, found a break in the fuze, respliced it, relit the fuze—then raced for daylight.

At 4:44 the earth, for several hundred feet around the salient, began to tremble, and a rolling wave of sound started to break. A Union infantryman stood enthralled: " . . . there came . . . a terrible rumbling, that lengthened into a muffled roar, and as we looked toward the rebel line, we saw a great, black cloud of smoke and dust rise high in the air. Great blocks of clay were flying upward, and some thought they could see men and cannon." In a more distant sector, Colonel Wainwright had a less commanding view: "Very quickly the whole of our front was covered with a dense cloud of white smoke so that all objects were obscured from my view save . . . the rise of a great black ball, with a fiery tail, rolling over and over high up into the air until it was lost in the smoke." His characterization of the racket was detached and thoughtful: "The roar was not greater if equal to that at Gettysburg, but there was more variety of notes in it."[25]

When the huge geyser of dirt and rock had settled, the Federals gaped at a smoking crater almost two hundred feet long, fifty feet wide, and twenty-five feet deep. Buried in mounds of excavated earth, and lying at the pit of the gorge, were nearly three hundred dead or wounded rebels, plus many shattered batteries, some of which had been heaved high into the air before hurtling back to earth.[26]

Though awed by the blast, then by a silence so deep it stung the ears, Hunt's gunners jumped to their pieces and let loose with another overwhelming roar. Along a six-mile line, the field batteries, plus the 4.5-inch guns, the 10-inch mortars, the 30-pounders, and all other siege pieces, sent a huge converging fire at positions adjacent to the leveled salient. "It was a great gun conflict," wrote one overly descriptive rebel, "with thundering, booming, flashing, blazing, smoking, shrieking, thudding, crashing, majestic terrors of war." Under such a pounding, all those guns that might have bore directly on Burnside's attackers were silenced within ten minutes.[27]

Thus an apparently ridiculous scheme concocted by a soldier who seemed to consider himself still a civilian engineer, had succeeded beyond the bounds of prudent expectation. But though a yawning pit now led into Petersburg, perhaps to Richmond, General Burnside proved wholly unequal to his opportunity. Several minutes after Hunt's gunners had beaten down their opposition, the men of the IX Corps at last sought to go forward—and found themselves entangled in their abatis. It developed that Burnside had made no provisions for guiding his men beyond their own line; he had ignored Hunt's repeated advice to provide his advance column with axes to use in cutting their way out. Now Hunt watched incredulously as the foot soldiers took precious time to wriggle free, then, their ranks broken, to forge ahead with only a four-man frontage.[28] Still, at least they went: Burnside did not; neither did the general in command of the leading division. At this hour, the latter was cowering in a bomb-proof far to the rear, guzzling whiskey commandeered from one of his surgeons.

Once past their own barriers, the attackers made another fatal error, by piling into the deep crater—from which they could not easily escape—instead of skirting it. Given time to reorganize, surviving Confederates came up with loaded rifles, while their officers rounded up more cannon. Soon the enemy was tossing minié balls and shells into the tangled blue ranks that coated the sides and floor of the crater—targets they could hardly miss. The fourteen Federal cannon that bore on this crucial sector, and which might have prevented the slaughter, could not fire, the timber in their front still intact.

Like the advance unit, the second of Burnside's white divisions, then the third, was guided into the crater—indicating execrable leadership as well as faulty planning—and, there, they too lay trapped. Newly arrived rebels swelled the gray masses lining the rim of the gorge and the ridges behind it, gunning down the helpless Federals with cool deliberation. It was not long before survivors—including those from the black division, which had been thrown in as a forlorn hope, only to be chopped to pieces by rifle fire— were scurrying back to the point of origin of the attack, leaving behind four thousand casualties. For several hours Hunt's artillerists kept pouring lead wherever their guns could reach, eventually expending 3,833 rounds of ammunition to add to an aggregate figure of 18,061 rounds fired in front of Petersburg since 18 June. But by midmorning on the thirtieth, Grant and Meade had conceded failure at the crater.

The army was, at the least, vastly disgusted with this outcome, in the face of so great an amount of sweat, brainpower, and hope. Hunt was even more disgusted than the average soldier, for he had personally contributed a herculean portion of labor. He was also emotionally crushed. Burnside's debacle, plus Grant's resultant decision to shift fifty-two pieces of siege weaponry back to City Point and Broadway Landing, told Hunt that the war would go on—and on.[29] In the unrelenting heat and the pervasive dust, it seemed likely to go on forever.

16

The Soul of Our Artillery

For Hunt it was a hellish summer, followed by an equally unbearable autumn. After Burnside's fiasco (which led to his relief from command, this time for good), the Army of the Potomac locked into a grim, implacable, tedious siege. In August, Grant made a strong effort to break the stalemate, sending Warren's men on a wide arc south of Petersburg to chop up railroads; but, as the general-in-chief probably foresaw, the tactic failed. The vicious fight it occasioned cost 2,400 Federal casualties and prompted one of Hunt's gunners, involved in the fracas, to write his brother: "I hope in God, David, I shall never whitness [sic] such scenes again as I did that day." In the final analysis, it achieved much less than did the dozens of skirmishes, engagements, and small-unit confrontations that had gyrated back and forth both above and below the Appomattox River the rest of the year. Though also costly in casualties, these fights at least enabled the Federals slowly but surely to gain ground west and south of the besieged city.

As the tortuous siege continued, Hunt's patience wore threadbare on a daily basis. The upshot was renewed conflict with associates including Meade—which made him reconsider past decisions not to resign. Too often the feud between artillery's authority against that of corps and division commanders, seemingly raging since Genesis, had expanded into pitched battles between Hunt and Warren, Hunt and Hancock, Hunt and Smith.

Early in September he had a particularly bitter clash with Hancock, stirring up half-dormant animosities of years past. One afternoon Hancock requested the artillery chief to remove some unattached batteries from the II Corps' front, so that Hancock could replace them with "more dependable" units from his own corps. Since the corps general strongly implied that his units were dependable only because he, not Hunt, guided them, the latter took offense. He replied that he was agreeable to do anything Hancock proposed, "however absurd or unreasonable," adding, however, that Hancock knew full well that he had enough authority to effect the transfer without troubling Hunt about it. When the II Corps commander shot back a harsh reply, the feud spiraled still higher, eventually driving both antagonists to

211

Meade's headquarters with mutual complaints. Once again it was the tactful chief of staff, General Humphreys, who negotiated a cease-fire. But less than a week later the opponents were again at it—this time arguing over Hancock's power to detach foot artillerymen from Hunt's command without prior notice.[2]

In mid-September, Hunt also fought another corps commander, General David Birney, who now led the X Army Corps at Bermuda Hundred, under Butler. This confrontation would have a longer-range influence on Hunt's subsequent career than any other feud.

During a stretch of twenty-five hours, from 10 A.M. on 14 September until 11 o'clock the next morning, Birney maintained an incessant shelling of Petersburg from his lines above the Appomattox, using all seventy-six cannon and mortars in his sector. Not until 1,741 rounds had been hurled into the city, to no obvious advantage, did he admit what Hunt had been trying to teach him and his infantry-trained colleagues all along: that such indiscriminate shelling wasted resources and, moreover, forced the civilian citizens of Petersburg to suffer needlessly. Though technically the X Corps was out of his area of jurisdiction, Petersburg was very much Hunt's concern; thus he angrily informed Grant's headquarters: "The mortar shells can only reach the suburbs, and it is doubtful if any probable military advantage warrants the destruction of life and property of non-combatants, or even the expenditure of the ammunition."[3]

If nothing else, this demonstrated that Hunt had lost none of his compassion for those of his enemy not in uniform. The profession of humane sympathy made in his 1861 letter to Braxton Bragg was yet in effect: "I never have felt and I do not feel now, hostile to the South, her institutions or her people, nor can I have toward them the feelings of an 'alien enemy'." Since the day he had written this, in confirmation of fears stated in that same letter, blood had indeed flowed like water. But even now he thought of Confederates as countrymen—wrong-minded certainly, deluded and manipulated by political authority, but countrymen nevertheless. By the same token, Southern civilians he saw as pawns in a savage game.

Many of Hunt's colleagues neither agreed with him nor wished to understand his stated position. Such humane considerations were so alien to some that they considered him lukewarm on the issue of the war—even labelling him, at heart, a "Rebel sympathizer," with all the frightening characterizations that the term connoted. But not for several years would the full significance of such accusations become clear.

Certainly Hunt remained a staunch conservative and a devout McClellan man. Thus, he had been cheered by recent news of Little Mac's nomination as the Democratic standard-bearer in the upcoming presidential election. Still he saw McClellan as the last, best hope of earth—the only stalwart capable of saving America from future decades of the same sort of civil strife now strangling it.

Late that summer he corresponded at length with McClellan over the issues of the election, receiving replies that enabled him to inform his associates in uniform that if elected McClellan would work vigorously to bring the Confederacy to the peace table on honorable terms. If the Confederacy would not agree to such terms, McClellan asserted, he would have no recourse but to continue the war by rigorously enforcing conscription, placing in power the mightiest generals, and going to all lengths to win battlefield triumph—though via the honorable, traditional, and conservative brand of warfare that was his hallmark.[4]

Hunt's hope of a Democratic sweep at the polls come November propelled him through the remainder of the warm-weather season, during which he labored unstintingly to administer to his thirty-odd siege guns and 1,143 officers and men—inspecting investment lines countless times, helping engineers improve and expand the defensive works, and keeping all involved supplied with the ordnance, ammunition, fuzes, sandbags, and entrenching tools necessary to keep the siege going at proper pitch.

But even before autumn came, McClellan's chances suffered a series of heavy blows. On 1 September, Sherman captured the strategic citadel of Atlanta, "Gate City of the South," his rebel opponents having fled far and wide. And Phil Sheridan's victory at Winchester eighteen days later, plus his later Shenandoah Valley triumphs at Fisher's Hill and Cedar Creek, left the "Breadbasket of the Confederacy" securely in Union hands. In celebration of the victories, Hunt's guns filled the waning weeks of summer with commemorative salutes, while army bands thumped and tootled away in accompaniment. But Hunt himself was not carried into a joyous mood by the music. He knew that the Lincoln Administration reaped the full psychological benefits of these victories, and he sensed that, because of them, the Republican Party would maintain executive power for four years more. Still, he continued to hope right to the end.

The end came on 8 November, when Lincoln won an overwhelming mandate at the polls, riding to victory on the crest of a Republican tide that swept McClellan under, then cast him adrift—political flotsam.

* * *

The violent decisiveness of the Federal September victories was symptomatic of a new brand of warfare visiting Virginia and elsewhere in the occupied Confederacy—a symptom that Hunt greeted with dismay. With McClellan gone beyond hope of recall, politically as well as militarily, the last vestiges of the ethic of warfare which he typified disappeared.

Gone, too, were the conservative, gentlemanly warriors who had given the war for the Union its character in earlier years—relieved or cashiered like McClellan himself: Fitz-John Porter, William Franklin, and William French; or shot dead at the front: John Sedgwick and John Fulton Reynolds; or tossed into prison for adhering to articles of political faith: Charles Stone, whom Senator Wade had ambushed. Now those on center stage were the Shermans and the Sheridans, men who embraced and practiced total war—

war against not merely men in uniform but against the enemy's country and the whole spectrum of the enemy's population; they sought to uproot an entire society rather than to defeat an army. Thus, once in firm possession of the Shenandoah, Sheridan burned and stripped it, that it would not yield a final crust of bread to rebel commissaries. And once he took Atlanta, Sherman sacked it, then moved on to the Atlantic Coast, plundering and devastating, blazing a swath of desolation for thirty miles on either side of his route of march.

Such a style of warfare was hideously alien to General Hunt, still motivated as he was by old concepts such as honor, tolerance, and charity toward one's opposition, and still certain that such concepts could coexist with the inescapable violence and brutality that civil conflict bred. Yet fewer and fewer of those to whom he related such beliefs seemed willing to listen.

Chiefly for those reasons, the harsh autumn and the winter that followed, left him almost spiritually bankrupt. Even the growing realization that Petersburg and the Confederacy were doomed failed to elevate his spirits to levels they had maintained in 1861–62. Before the end came, there would be more suffering and more destruction, in battles named for various locales near Petersburg: the Boydton Road, Poplar Springs Church, Forts Harrison and Gilmer, the Weldon Railroad. For Hunt these would become harmless names cloaking tragedies beyond hope of redress. Ironically, then, the flame that had guided his steps through so many months of miserable defeat seemed on the verge of guttering out just when total victory was on the skyline.

And yet, even so, by no means was his life unadulterated gloom. The final winter of the war had its cheery aspects, and these Hunt played for all their worth. Despite having made so many enemies in the ranks, he still enjoyed the friendship of many colleagues; and with them he spent as much free time as possible, swapping tales of happier climes and times, exchanging shoptalk, sharing simple camaraderie. New guests kept coming his way, most of them foreign observers who so seldom failed to avail themselves of his vaunted hospitality. They came in such a steady stream that Meade's aide Colonel Lyman once remarked: "Really, General Hunt . . . ought to get board free from his many former guests for the rest of his life."[5]

Despite the somber outlook, despite the crumbling of his political hopes, Hunt could be heartily cheerful about such people. Shortly before winter finally gave way to spring, he and Colonel Wainwright, and no doubt a few of those visitors as well, spent part of an afternoon touring positions in the V Corps' sector, Wainwright noting:

> The General was in most excellent spirits, and amused me very much as well as filling me with wonder at his memory. I happened to refer to the *Rejected Addresses* [a collection of British literary parodies] soon after starting; when he took it up, quoting page after page; and then almost whole volumes of comic poetry, interspersed with stories. Still he

saw everything as we rode along and was just as much alive to the object of his visit to the lines as if he had been thinking and talking of nothing else. He is certainly one of the most wonderful men I have ever met.

Other outings provided pleasure. One weekend late in '64, Hunt and some of Grant's subordinates accompanied some staff aides on a trip to Norfolk, where they enjoyed what Wainwright called a "small spree." While most of his companions discharged official business, Hunt looked up prewar acquaintances and inspected several lots that he owned.[6]

Other times he had to content himself with visiting family and friends by mail. He maintained a steady correspondence, not only with Mary and the children, the Nichols, Craigs, and De Russys, but also with stalwart cohorts from better days: McClellan, Porter, French, Franklin, Samuel P. Heintzelman, and William Barry. It seemed significant that of these once prominent soldiers only Barry—now Sherman's chief of artillery—was still on active field duty in the volunteer ranks. Less frequently Hunt wrote his brother, now a brigadier general of volunteers who, after distinguished service in North Carolina, had returned to staff duty in Washington, where his old comrade Ulysses Grant was furnishing him inspection chores.[7]

Such friends and loved ones sustained Hunt, as did his inbred core of endurance. Thus, when the final weeks in March 1865 heralded the final, renewal of active campaigning, he was in tolerable spirits after all, no longer pursuing a gleaming goal as in '61, but resigned to the effort that had to be made if the long and bitter war were to attain some ultimate meaning.

* * *

By spring Hunt was at least encouraged by the obvious fitness of his command, which he now headed by virtue of his newly acquired brevet rank of major general of volunteers (the same rank in the Regular service would be accorded him in the near future).[8] Over the winter it had been pared down to easily manageable size: forty-two batteries and 202 cannon in the field army, in addition to the 188 heavy pieces in Abbot's siege train— the whole encompassing 7,952 officers and men. Hunt also exercised authority over a rejuvenated though non-official Reserve, under immediate command of Captain Ezekiel R. Mayo, his position soon to be reassumed by its former leader, General William Hays. Finally, Hunt had power over a maintenance command, the Artillery Park, whose direct commander was Captain Calvin Shaffer. To a man, the artillery was sleek, hardy, and well experienced. Only the battery horses were in questionable health; the winter had seen decreased supplies of forage.[9] But all other tools of the artillerist's trade—cannon, caissons, limbers, forges—were in plentiful supply and in the finest condition, capable of rendering maximum service as soon as forward movement was ordered.

By any indicator, the order was imminent. By spring the continually reinforced Army of the Potomac had forced its much-depleted enemy to occupy a line thirty-seven miles long, east, south, and southwest of Petersburg.

Somewhere along that line, all realized, Lee's thirty-five thousand effectives had to be stretched awfully thin. Even a moderately hefty push, if aimed at one of those weak sectors, would cause the Confederate line to cave inward, leaving not only Petersburg but also the rebel capital open to seizure.

Ironically, the enemy was the first to make a decisive push. At 4 A.M. on 25 March 1865, in a last-ditch attempt to break free of investment, Lee sent almost half his infantry, plus some mounted troops, to capture Fort Stedman, an unbastioned Federal redoubt on the far right flank. The great stealth of the attackers led to the quick capitulation of the fort, which had been manned by units from the Fourteenth New York Heavy Artillery, and which lay in the sector occupied by the IX Corps, now under Burnside's successor, Major General John G. Parke. After seizing the fort, some Confederates turned its cannon on Federals on the flanks, while other rebels rushed through this breach in the line, fanning out right and left to capture other key redoubts and redans believed in the vicinity.[10]

Not till 5:40 A.M., a full hour and forty minutes after the attack had begun, did Hunt get word of it—and he was the first ranking commander to hear. Rushing out of bed to army headquarters, uniform hurriedly thrown on, he discovered that, by ill-timed coincidence, both Meade and Grant were far to the rear on extramilitary business, thus unable to order up crucially needed supports. With no alternative, Hunt bustled about, giving orders on his own, rushing cannoneers to thinly held works near the breach, to save them from Fort Stedman's fate. He also hustled word of the attack to General Parke, as well as to other corps and division leaders. For several hectic minutes, until one of these commanders reached the scene, Hunt was virtually commanding the Army of the Potomac.

When finally alerted to the danger, the corps leaders took prompt remedial measures, ensuring that Lee's success would be only temporary. By 8 A.M. Parke had thrown a fresh division at the captors of Stedman, shoving them back to their own quarters after a brief struggle in which some of Hunt's 30-pounder Parrotts and eight-inch mortars lent the IX Corps crucial assistance. Parke's men retook the fort, the fighting degenerated into light skirmishing, and Lee's last offensive was a memory. For his promptitude in rushing up reinforcements, liberally committing what foot artillerymen and surplus gunners were in his direct command, Hunt was singled out for glowing praise to be circulated throughout the army in a formal order. But when the order was found to cast unfair aspersions on the leaders of those IX Corps units routed by Lee's surprise assault, it was suppressed. Thus Hunt, passed over for formal recognition several times in the past, was passed over again.[11]

The easy repulse of the attack against Fort Stedman seemed to proclaim the general debility of the forces holding Petersburg. Therefore, the Army of the Potomac wasted little time making final preparations for its own climactic offensive. By the last day in March, almost all was ready. Sheridan and the cavalry had left the valley and had rejoined the army. Butler's old Army of the James, now under Major General Edward O.C. Ord, yet another of Hunt's West Point classmates as well as a distant relative, was prepared to attack Richmond. The II, V, VI, and IX Corps had been equipped and briefed for the last engagements of the war in the East. Abbot's heavy pieces had been returned from Broadway Landing to pave the way for the grand assault on Petersburg. And the field artillery had been stripped for hard marching, only six batteries allotted to each of the maneuver elements in the coming campaign, the II and V Corps, of whom the hardest and fastest marching would be required.[12]

The campaign commenced on the afternoon of 31 March, by which time warm weather had stamped out the last vestiges of Virginia winter. Phil Sheridan and Meade's cavalry, plus the II and V Corps, and the horsemen in Ord's army, were sent toward the rebel rear, around Lee's right flank, as far as the key crossroads locale, Five Forks, eighteen miles southwest of Petersburg. There, Sheridan (whom Grant had set up as an independent army commander) struck and mangled the last line open to Petersburg—the Southside Railroad. There, too, the V Corps flanked and annihilated a Confederate rear guard of all arms under overall leadership of the Gettysburg hero, George Pickett. However, the attack came so sluggishly and so late on 1 April that it impelled the fiery Sheridan to relieve Gouverneur Warren from command of his corps. This outcome, especially in the face of an overwhelming Federal victory, saddened many of Warren's brother officers, but lowered Hunt's spirits not one notch.[13]

Early on that All Fool's Day, with Lee earnestly contemplating an evacuation of Petersburg, Colonel Abbot's big guns hurled the first of 5,560 rounds of shot and shell the doomed city was fated to absorb during the next several hours.[14] The bombardment did not cease until well after 4:40 A.M., by which time the designated attacking force, Major General Horatio G. Wright's VI Corps, was well on its way to smite Petersburg's eastern flank. As many had anticipated, the flank crumbled apart at first contact; and, as other elements of Meade's army moved up to capitalize on Wright's success, Lee began pulling out of the city, his men streaming west, then north across the Appomattox. Lee's final, fragile hope was to reach Amelia Court House, forty miles west of the Appomattox fords, thence move to Lynchburg and, if possible, to the Carolinas, where he might somehow establish a junction with Johnston's remnants, there confronting Sherman.

Flushed with triumph, the Federals clambered after the evacuees. Sheridan, with the V Corps and the cavalry, raced to cut across their path, while the II and VI Corps bayed at their heels. Meanwhile, much of Ord's army flooded into Richmond, also abandoned by its defenders, and in which fires of destruction were soon raging, consuming a great many homes and stores. One building that was razed was the Bank of Richmond, whose demolished assets included some $3,500 deposited there before the war by Henry Hunt. Finally, while all other commands moved west and north, the IX Corps, supported by Abbot's siege gunners, took possession of the abandoned trench lines and field works outside Petersburg.[15]

Hunt might have remained behind with Abbot, or have idled in a soon-quiet sector in the Federal camps, savoring the fruits of victory. Instead, he accompanied his field cannoneers on their last march, during which the Army of Northern Virginia and the Army of the Potomac crossed arms in a series of bloody skirmishes: at Sutherland's Station, Gravelly Ford, and Scott's Cross Roads, on the second; at Namozine Church on the third; at Amelia Springs on the fifth; at Sayler's Creek on the sixth; and at Farmville on the seventh. Before the last was joined, Lee's hope of reaching rail depots from which he might ship his troops to North Carolina had vanished: Sheridan's horsemen and infantrymen had interposed between him and his objectives.

On 7 April, when Hunt established artillery headquarters at Rice Station, on the Southside line,[16] Grant sent his entrapped enemy an invitation to lay down arms and thus save "any further effusion of blood." As Hunt observed in his diary, Lee misinterpreted the offer and asked Grant for an interview to clarify its terms—he hoped, in truth, to negotiate a peace that stopped short of total, abject surrender. When Grant refused to treat and began to close in for the killing, the situation teetered precariously between continued bloodshed and armistice.

On the eighth, Lee's army trekked a few miles farther west, challenging Sheridan and leading Grant and Meade through nameless hamlets along the road to Lynchburg. At last Lee halted, his men exhausted and half-starved, thus weakened beyond continued endurance. That evening, near the village of Appomattox Court House, about seventy miles northwest of Petersburg, Sheridan added the finishing touches to Lee's encirclement, and the Confederate leader was forced to talk surrender. Next day, after the principals on either side met at the home of one Wilmer McLean, Hunt appended a prosaic diary entry, headed April 9, 1865:

"Lee accepted the terms of General Grant and surrendered."

* * *

Hunt did not participate in the frolic that ran through the Army of the Potomac after Lee's capitulation. In keeping with the traditional tone of that Palm Sunday, he remained quietly thoughtful, sending home word of his relief at the coming of peace, and of his concern for the well-being of the defeated.

The next day found him confiscating and disposing much of the heavy ordnance abandoned by the Confederates in the final campaign. To discharge these responsibilities he had to enter the ranks of the sullen, dejected men in gray who now lay encamped on broad plains east of the courthouse village, their adversaries clustered all around them. Hunt employed the opportunity, not only to talk business with his opposite number in gray, Brigadier General William N. Pendleton, Lee's chief of artillery, but to seek out a host of prewar friends from whom he had been estranged those past four years. Foremost of these was Lee, by whose command tent Hunt lingered. The reunion was cordial, though strained by Lee's somberness, the result of emotions in tumult. Characterizing him as "'worn, but quiet, calm, and courteous, as his habit is," Hunt sensed that the meeting was an ordeal for Lee, and took early leave of him.

He found widely varying spirits among other old-army colleagues. Lee's righthand subordinate, James Longstreet, with whom Hunt had campaigned in Mexico and later at Fort Leavenworth, he found "in very good spirits." So, too, appeared Major General Cadmus Wilcox, another Mexican War cohort, recently a division leader under Lee. In contrast to the demeanor of this pair, Hunt discovered A. L. Long, his cannoneer pupil from Fort Washita days, "much broken." He may have been speaking of Long's physical health, which was declining, but he probably was referring to his emotional well-being as well. Still, Hunt spent the better part of an hour attempting to cheer him, and succeeded when reminiscing about the artillery duel on the third day at Gettysburg, in which student had opposed teacher. When Hunt recalled the scattered ineffectuality of the cannonade preceding Pickett's assault, Colonel Long brightened considerably. With a grin he remarked that he had spent that afternoon wondering what Hunt's reaction to his poor performance might be. Their conversation also touched on the retreat of Lee's army from Pennsylvania, Long informing Hunt that, contrary to the latter's convictions on 14 July 1863, had Meade attacked Lee's positions near Williamsport, Maryland, the Army of the Potomac would "have been thumped" without question. In response, Hunt expressed relief that so few people seemed to take him seriously in his military opinions—at least in this case.

When time came for Hunt to return to his own camp, he took a lingering survey of his enemy's ranks and decided that "the rebel troops looked well, the men in good condition."[17] Credit for this, however, may well be owing to Grant who, upon learning that Lee's famished men had outmarched their commissary wagons, had sent thousands of rations to their camp.

Hunt had little time for observing the formal surrender ceremonies at Appomattox on the afternoon of the eleventh, during which the Federals, drawn up in column, gave their adversaries a salute of honor as the rebels stacked arms amid a broad field between the lines. Soon afterward he was rounding up other trophies: eighteen cannon and two hundred rifles that the rebels had abandoned near the town of Farmville, west of the courthouse village. There, and later that same day, at Burkeville, almost fifty miles west of Petersburg, he also took up a mound of paperwork that had accumulated during Lee's doomed retreat.

He was shuffling papers late on the fifteenth, when came word that Abraham Lincoln had been shot in Washington the evening before. Next day brought confirmation of rumors that the president had died. Though far from a Lincoln partisan, Hunt was as sobered by this intelligence as by word of Lee's surrender. Others reacted more demonstratively; he noted that "great excitement and comm[otion]" swept the camps not of the artillery alone but of the rest of Meade's army as well. At noon on the nineteenth, in accord with a directive from Secretary Stanton, Hunt ordered the firing of twenty-one minute-guns in memory of the army's commander-in-chief, whose funeral was held that day. By then Hunt had also draped his headquarters with black bunting.[18]

Later in the day he turned his command over to John Tidball (now in charge of the IX Corps artillery), took the train to City Point, and from there left Virginia for the last time in the uniform of a volunteer officer. An army transport carried him up the James River to Chesapeake Bay, thence, via the bay, to Washington City. Official business called him there: he had to appear as a witness for a former subordinate being tried by courtmartial in the capital.[19]

He relished the trip as a personal homecoming, as well. At the Washington depot he took Mary in his arms, then hoisted up four-year-old Conway and three-year-old Dolly. Soon afterward he was reunited with Emily and Henry, Jr., and his in-laws, the Nichols. When time enabled, he related for all the scenes of adventure and adversity he had lived before coming home from the wars.

The court-martial before which he appeared did not adjourn until 31 May;[20] thus he remained on detached duty at home long after the Army of the Potomac marched up from Virginia in full panoply. By now the conflict was truly ended, rebel armies elsewhere in the country, including Joe Johnston's, having capitulated, thus restoring America to its former status as a nation intact.

For some time the government had been planning a grand pageant to honor its soldiers' service through four hellish years of conflict. That planning culminated on 23 and 24 May in a grand review in Washington, featuring most of the forces eligible for speedy return from the seat of the late war. During those two days, 120,000 men in blue, equipped as if for active campaigning—but with rifles polished to a silver gloss, uniforms scrubbed and pressed for show, horses expertly groomed, and marching formations assiduously maintained—trooped down Pennsylvania Avenue to the thump of drums and the blare of bugles and the deafening cheers of a multitude of civilian spectators. The onlookers included a bevy of high officials, including Lincoln's successor, President Andrew Johnson, ensconced in spacious reviewing stands.[21]

The twenty-third was devoted to the Army of the Potomac, Sherman's command to take its place the next morning. Thus, Hunt participated in a pageant favored by clear blue skies and warm, invigorating weather. Riding a black charger beside his superior, General Meade, at the head of the procession, he saluted smartly as he passed the beribboned platform near the White House, from which hung a huge national standard. Behind him rode Major General Wesley Merritt, with what had once been Sheridan's cavalry, horsemen in turn followed by rank upon rank of the infantry, amid whose lines rumbled the polished brass cannon and whitewashed carriages of the image-conscious field artillery.

Originally Hunt had been told that he might head a full corps composed of all the army's light batteries, which would have made a magnificent spectacle. But when corps leaders protested, claiming the right to retain the batteries attached to their commands, the magnificent spectacle went by the board. Still, the altered marching order had one benefit for Hunt: at the end of his ride, he was able to repair to one of the auxiliary reviewing platforms to observe the rest of the procession. There, beside Mary, one of her sisters, Major John Craig, and a coterie of other relatives, including Colonel and Mrs. Henry Craig, he watched his own men troop, trundle, and canter past. Upon the platform he received and returned dozens of salutes from subordinates who had followed him over many a violent parcel of real estate between Bull Run and Appomattox.

Honors continued coming his way even after the parade ended. A long line of officers joined him by the viewing stand, saluting again—most of them for the final time—and then shaking his hand, while expressing pleasure at having served under him. Those gestures, coupled with President Johnson's repeated assertions that his cannoneers had made much the best spectacle of all participants, must have warmed Hunt's heart and caused his spirits to soar. Quite possibly it was his proudest and happiest hour in uniform.

Looking on with approval, Colonel Wainwright thought such honors wholly deserved: "It is no more than is due to General Hunt, who has been the soul of our artillery, and has made it what it is, by far the best arm in the service."[22]

17

Black Marks
at the War Department

Hunt's detached service ended on 5 June, when he was again provided with specific employment. According to his brevet rank of major general of volunteers, he was placed in charge of all Regular batteries in the vicinity of the capital; his title: Commander of the Artillery Division, Department of Washington. Upon the Bladensburg Road site of Camp Barry, he established a new rendezvous and, there, collected all artillery units for miles around. These he fastidiously inspected, remedying their deficiencies; he also devised a course of general instruction for all recently commissioned officers and noncoms.[1]

The work was routine to the core, terribly unimaginative and unexciting. But closeness to home and family kept him content, until a new assignment sent him from the capital. General Orders #130, issued 28 July, gave him command of the newly created Frontier District, headquartered at Fort Smith, Arkansas.[2]

The assignment was an outgrowth of a governmental policy of Southern reconstruction, whose structure had been built during the past few months by Congress, the War Department, and the White House (although the three agencies often seemed to be working at cross-purposes).

Late in May, President Johnson had announced a policy of amnesty for most Southerners who had joined the rebellion, excluding several classes of wealthy, influential, and politically and militarily prominent ex-Confederates. As yet, however, the president had revealed no plan whereby the seceded states could qualify for readmission to the Union, thus renewing their Constitutional rights and privileges. Other Washington officials deemed several prequisites to be vital, including a sweeping social alteration of the conquered South, as well as its economic regrowth and political reorientation. Thus had been established a system whereby Regular troops, as well as some volunteer units not yet eligible for muster-out, would be stationed throughout the seceded states to implement and enforce programs to these ends.

In most of the South, a similar program had been in force for some years, dating from the time Federal troops had secured enemy territory. But these provisional reconstruction programs could not hope to reach all the goals desired until the coming of countrywide peace. Hence the act of 28 July, which gave Hunt new employment, was a sweeping reorganization of the wartime occupation administration, in which some departments had been replaced or reassigned to new executives, while other, brand-new occupation districts were established and staffed.[3]

Understandably, Hunt had misgivings about the desirability of military reconstruction. Democratic spokesmen had already termed the presidential plan a means by which radical Republicans could wreak vengeance upon the vanquished South. To be sure, some of the implications of the concept were disturbing. It appeared that Washington did not wish merely to return the Confederacy to a firm economic and political footing, but to restructure civilization below the Mason-Dixon Line. As such, it seemed that the North was still fighting a war long after Appomattox had caused the shooting to cease.

In particular, Hunt acknowledged hesitancy to serve as a governmental tool for safeguarding the new status of blacks in the South. He was far from alone in his opinions. His colleague, William Sherman, for instance, agreed whole-heartedly: "No matter what Change we may desire in the feelings and thoughts of the people [of the] South, we cannot accomplish it by force. Nor can we afford to maintain an army large enough to hold them in subjugation."[4]

In the end, of course, Hunt bowed to the demand of higher authority. He, Mary, Conway, and Dolly left Washington early in September, and on the twelfth arrived in Arkansas. At Fort Smith nine days later, he relieved the erstwhile departmental commander, Brigadier General Cyrus Bussey, who had been a desk general in Arkansas since '63.[5]

Hunt's command encompassed authority over black and white soldiers, infantrymen and artillerists; his jurisdiction covered the western fifth of Arkansas as well as the whole of an adjacent tract in later years known as Oklahoma, but in 1865 called the Indian Territory—a government-maintained reserve for the "Five Civilized Tribes": the Cherokees, Creeks, Chocktaws, Chickasaws, and Seminoles. The District of the Frontier was one of five such areas of military geography within the larger Department of Arkansas and the Indian Territory, commanded by Major General J. J. Reynolds. Even though but twenty percent of Reynolds's bailiwick, Hunt's own sphere of authority was vast and teeming, his charges not only the Five Tribes but also smaller-size communities of Osages, Arapahos, Cheyennes, and Kiowas, not to mention thousands of white settlers and almost as large a group of freed blacks.

Soon after taking the reins at Fort Smith, Hunt found himself thrust

into an unenviably difficult position, made still more difficult by those same
political machinations that had dismayed and disgusted him throughout
his career.

One political controversy affected the future of the several Indian tribes
who claimed the territory as home. A week before Hunt relieved General
Bussey, several of the local tribes had signed a treaty of allegiance to the
United States government; others participated in a similar ceremony on
the day Hunt took over. Such was deemed necessary because the Five
Civilized Tribes had sided with the South during the rebellion (more in
an effort to safeguard property and possessions, including a considerable
number of slaves, than because of any heartfelt fealty to the Confederacy).
But apparently a formal treaty was insufficient to satisfy the Federal government. Soon Hunt was apprised of rumors that the White House also was
seeking vengeance in the form of confiscation of some tribal lands. For this
reason, Hunt entered upon his duties at Fort Smith with the nagging fear
that he might be forced to serve in another unappetizing capacity: as an
instrument of reprisal in the hands of politicos whose integrity he believed
nonexistent.

He expressed this fear in a letter he sent to General Sherman, his
direct superior as commander of the Department of the West: "I think
that there is a strong effort to be made to throw open the Territory to
white settlement. If so, goodby Mr. Indian!"[6]

His words, seemingly flippant, underscored a genuine concern for the
well-being of his charges—and in the long run would become prophetic.
Fortunately for his peace of mind, however, they would materialize as fact
only after he had left his post in Arkansas. At a not-too-distant date, Washington would force the Five Tribes to surrender a large percentage of the
western part of the territory as a resettlement area for tribes booted off
other lands recently opened to white settlement and commercial exploitation.
Not until 1889, however, would extensive tracts in the territory be thrown
open to settlement by whites.

In various ways, Hunt ran hard aground when trying to steer clear of
politics at his new post. Perhaps it was inevitable that political problems
would dictate his ultimate relief from Fort Smith after only six months
of service. And yet, during that half-year, he accomplished a great deal. His
record as head of the Frontier District would engender much satisfaction
and pride, especially when examined in retrospect.

One of his most vital tasks was the suppression of guerrillas and bush-
whackers who, long after Appomattox, terrorized both Indians and blacks,
both native Southerners and transplanted Yankees. Though in the end
achieving mixed results in running elusive criminals to earth, Hunt strengthened the spirit of law and order by continual displays of military might,
though in a way suggestive of local police power, thus bringing citizens
peace of mind. He was unstinting in efforts to track down lawbreakers with

the troops at his disposal; he offered substantial rewards for fugitives, which brought prompt results; he energetically assisted local magistrates and sheriffs; and he rendered swift, impartial justice before the bar.[7]

Much of his time was also absorbed by the necessity of fending off local carpetbaggers and radicals, including Brigadier General John B. Sanborn, Andrew Johnson's representative to the Civilized Tribes. A radical anti-slaveryite, Sanborn was also much concerned with the plight of local freedmen and thought of himself as an all-purpose humanitarian in uniform. Hunt thought him a nuisance and an irritant who continually buffeted Fort Smith with rumors of atrocities supposedly perpetrated on blacks and trans-planted Northerners by local ex-rebels. To Hunt's particular displeasure, Sanborn kept demanding that martial law be proclaimed and enforced throughout both Arkansas and the territory to halt such crimes. He also opposed Hunt's intention to help reinstate local municipal government in Arkansas. Because fact-finding commissions empaneled by Hunt invalidated most of Sanborn's charges,[8] he gave Johnson's emissary little cooperation. The news spread to Washington, where powerful politicos began to doubt that Hunt was the proper man for his position.

Hunt was not deliberately courting political disaster by an apathetic or antagonistic attitude toward recently liberated slaves. As post commander he had led many black soldiers and had left no evidence of discriminating against them in favor of the white troops at Fort Smith. In fact, in January of '66, he wrote the commissioner of Indian Affairs, D. H. Cooley, about his concern for those blacks freed from a life of servitude and now residing in the territory, "turned adrift in midwinter before provisions can be made for them." Then, too, he vocally deplored the few confirmed incidents of whites violating blacks' civil rights, as well as those sporadic instances of blacks attacked and either killed or injured by some of the local tribesmen. Still, he took pains to explain that violence between Indians and whites and among Indian tribes was at least as prevalent on the frontier as the sort of racial troubles with which Sanborn was principally concerned.[9]

In truth, it was the Indian rather than the freed black who seemed most in need of government solicitude. In the same letter to Sherman in which he voiced fears of governmental vengeance against the Five Tribes, Hunt noted that most of those in his charge were mannerly and subdued because "hunger is an excellent tamer—and there is a plentiful lack of grub in these regions." Nowhere was this more true than among the tribes. In the Cherokee Nation alone, some 2,500 were destitute and verging on starvation by late 1865, as well as suffering from smallpox and other dis-eases that threatened to reach epidemic proportions.

To ease their suffering, Hunt demanded of Commissioner Cooley increased quantities of foodstuffs, medicines, and other vital health provisions. When the commissioner did not respond as he might have, Hunt sought and won departmental authorization to sell surplus corn, beef, salt, and other foods to the needy tribes and also to impoverished whites and blacks. At the same time, he stockpiled medical stores and sent his surgeons to inoculate those susceptible to the most threatening ills.[10]

Those and other aid programs established Hunt's popularity among the tribesmen. "I know," the Chief of the Chocktaw Nation later wrote him, "you are our friend." More-detailed testimonials reached Washington from white citizens' delegations: "Genl. Hunt," read one, "has done more than any other officer to effect the restoration of order in our country." In addition to his relief programs: "He has taken the most active and stringent measures to prevent outrages of all kinds and to secure peace and harmony."[11] By numerous such petitions, denizens of Hunt's bailiwick sought to secure his permanent assignment to command.

Hunt had a simple explanation for such popularity. In 1867, looking back, he wrote George McClellan: "As I succeeded some radical commanders, I got to be quite popular by simply not stealing myself nor allowing others to steal. I even went so far as to return stolen property and protected rebel property."[12]

This may also provide an explanation for his relief. Not only did he make himself seem unconcerned about the black, but he displayed an impolitic propensity to fraternize and cooperate with former Confederates. Some of his more noticeable crimes were his eagerness to assist Arkansas judges and process-servers—even when they sought to bring black criminals to justice; his willingness to provide military protection as readily to whites as to blacks and Indians; his proclivity for exploding such radical myths as that which had native Arkansasans systematically persecuting local Unionists; and his desire to loudly assure Federal officials that none of his provost marshals had been able to "discover a disposition [on the part of ex-Confederates] to revive any former animosities or any desire to renew feuds."[13]

Thus, despite his widespread popularity among whites and redmen, Hunt was returned to Washington for reassignment by the War Department under orders dated 24 March 1866. He deeply regretted the transfer. As in 1853, he had developed a sincere fondness for this stretch of country. Here on vast, open land, his family had enjoyed a contented existence, Mary very much at home in the post community, the children immensely enjoying life under the sun—riding, hunting, playing about the garrison, growing dark, chubby, and happy. Hunt was just as happy as they, writing Sherman shortly before his relief: "I like this country, prefer it to the East, would a heap rather have command of the Indian Territory as a permanency than any Eastern command."[14]

But the War Department cared not at all for his preferences.

* * *

The commanding general himself ensured that Hunt's wishes would be disregarded. For this, Grant incurred his animosity, joining a small legion of Hunt's enemies.

The same order that relieved Hunt from command of the Frontier District placed him at the head of a "Permanent Artillery Board." This panel had been created two months before as an agency

> to which questions pertaining to the artillery arm of service may be referred by the Secretary of War or the general-in-chief for discussion and recommendation. The board shall also have the power to make original recommendations to the general-in-chief in reference to the interests and efficiency of the artillery arm.[15]

At least to some extent, he must have been gratified by so prestigious an appointment, as well as by his opportunity to return to full-time work in artillery administration. Still, he was also chagrined, not only by the loss of his position at Fort Smith, but by a suspicion that Grant had placed him on the board to rob him of free time that he might otherwise have devoted to a controversial project. He may well have been correct: he found his time absorbed by so much paperwork that he was compelled to curtail well-publicized efforts to publish a detailed accusation of plagiarism against Emory Upton, currently compiling his tactics manual for adoption by the Army, under the auspices of his friend and mentor, Grant.[16]

Neither was Hunt cheered by his muster-out of the volunteers a few weeks after taking his board seat. The action lowered him to the full-rank status of lieutenant colonel, Fifth Artillery, to which he had been promoted in 1863. The tangible benefits of brevet rank having substantially diminished under laws adopted toward the end of the war,[17] his brevet major generalship in the Regulars and volunteers now seemed a barren honor. Though realizing that muster-out was an inevitable consequence of the conclusion of the volunteers' war, Hunt seems to have attributed its untimely occurrence to a lack of solicitude on Grant's part. For these and other reasons, the esteem and fraternity he had once espoused for the lieutenant general had died. By mid-1867, he would write McClellan that Grant "is neither a just man himself, nor a lover of justice."[18] Harsher commentaries would follow.

The Artillery Board, despite Hunt's diligent presidency, had a checkered existence. The only major reform it spawned was the reopening of the Artillery School of Instruction at Fort Monroe—a dead issue since September 1860. Hunt's efforts and those of his board associates John Gibbon and Albion P. Howe, a lengthy report filled with recommendations for the curriculum of such a school, published late in '67, influenced Sherman, Grant's successor as Commanding General of the Army, to sustain the institution during its problem-strewn formative period. Other board recommendations, many based on ideas Hunt had conceived while at Fort Smith, prompted Major General John McAllister Schofield, secretary of war for a brief period in 1868–69, to enlarge on the artillery school's success. At Hunt's urging, Schofield instituted a school at Fort Riley, Kansas, wholly devoted to light-battery instruction. Unfortunately, the latter soon afterward folded for what Schofield called "some inscrutable reason."[19]

Hunt's panel suffered the same fate. Though a going concern as long as Grant showed interest in it, the Permanent Artillery Board proved highly impermanent as soon as the commanding general departed the capital for a lengthy period. In December '66, after but eleven and a half months in session, it adjourned, never to be reconvened.[20]

Yet Hunt was left with little idle time. Almost immediately he was appointed to a seat on yet another board sitting in Washington—this to determine standards of caliber, type, and proportion of rifled cannon to be purchased by the government for use in the nation's permanent fortifications. Again, for lack of time, he was forced to shelve plans to disseminate allegations about the true author of Emory Upton's tactics. But by the time this latest board adjourned, without having produced any accomplishment of great moment, Hunt had been made to see the futility of waging a one-man campaign against a popular, ranking antagonist, who enjoyed the full support of the man who was, at one and the same time, the country's most popular soldier and a strong prospect as a presidential aspirant (Grant would reach the White House in March 1869 after a successful campaign as a Republican candidate).[21]

In February 1867, new orders sent Hunt from the capital to Castle Island, in Boston Harbor; there, to take command at Fort Independence. His stay was of short duration: two months in all. But during that interval two notable events affected his state of mind in profound ways. The first, a most joyous occasion, occurred that 28 March, when his daughter, Julia, was born in the infirmary at the masonry garrison.

The second—which began late in April, immediately prior to Hunt's transfer to command at Fort Sullivan, near Eastport, Maine—was a far less pleasant experience. That month he pressed charges against the erstwhile adjutant general of the Army, Lorenzo Thomas, in response to Thomas's recent accusation, contained in a published letter originally sent to the Senate and House military committees, that Hunt was the author of a certain memorial circulating through the War Department. The memorial indicted Thomas and several other former bureau chiefs for flagrantly unethical conduct, some of which allegedly dated back a quarter-century and more. The charges centered on profits supposedly garnered from the clandestine sale of extra army rations, which were illegally received by Thomas and the other administrators, all of whom were specifically identified in the circular. Undoubtably Thomas suspected Hunt as the man behind the charges, due to Hunt's bitter animosity toward him, which had been smoldering at various temperatures since Thomas's unpopular 1861 ruling defining artillery's inferior status regarding rank.

Hunt was not content to deny Thomas's accusation; his countercharges accused the former adjutant general of seeking to damage his reputation by published statements affecting Hunt's "honor and veracity." As he wrote Secretary (of War) Stanton, he considered Thomas's charge "the cowardly stab of an assassin in the dark."[22]

As had many past feuds in which Hunt had participated, this controversy soon reached proportions far in excess of its significance. Eventually, Grant took action to establish a reconciliation, but in so doing again managed to reap Hunt's anger. Though the commanding general termed Thomas's accusation "entirely unwarranted" and persuaded him to tender some sort of apology, Hunt remained unsatisfied, asserting that the former administrative chief was willing to admit to only so much "as was *proved* against him." Therefore, he demanded a formal court of inquiry to uphold his integrity and professional standing.

This, Grant absolutely refused to consider, ordering him to drop all such efforts. Only after defaming his superior with some bitterly unfair contentions,[23] including his opinion of how Grant had risen to his station as commanding general, did Hunt allow the controversy to blow over. One of the mildest of Hunt's criticisms of Grant as general-in-chief was his stated belief: "If I am not mistaken the price *paid* for the office was some 100,000 lives—there or thereabouts."[24]

When Hunt penned those remarks, he was also influenced by his recent assignment to command such a poorly maintained, single-company garrison as Fort Sullivan. Not surprisingly, he attributed this treatment to political feuds, past and present. Reflecting on his own plight and those equally undesirable duty assignments recently given other members of the old conservative clique—such as Barry, Duane, French, and Brevet Brigadier General Nelson B. Sweitzer, another of McClellan's old aides—he wrote McClellan that "we all still have the black mark opposite our names at the War Dept.!!"

It would appear that the single pleasurable circumstance attendant to Hunt's service at Fort Sullivan (which lasted until February 1869), was the satisfaction of having by his side, for the first time, not only those children by his second marriage, but Emily and Henry, Jr. as well. But even this fortunate situation had its grim aspect: his firstborn daughter and son had been forced to leave their foster-parents' home because Brevet Brigadier General Nichols had fallen gravely ill; he would die, at fifty-one, early in 1869. Nor was Emily in good health. A sickly child from birth, unlike her robust young brother, her physical welfare often alarmed her father. This had been one factor behind her residence with the Nichols in New York City, where she might have benefitted from the best in medical facilities. Almost inseparably attached to her, Henry, Jr. had had to live in New York as well. Now, however, she had to share the rough, uncertain, and rather rigid confinement of garrison life.[25]

And yet, from Fort Sullivan, Hunt could inform his father-in-law, Colonel Craig, that his three grandchildren "are getting to be as black as Indians rolling, jumping, running & swinging all the time." In a later letter he told Craig that the baby Julia "has taken to walking within the past two days, and is of course the wonder of the house." The month following, he elaborated: "Dolly is picking up flesh. And Julia is as fat, as jolly and as impudent as she can be." As he also remarked that Harry and Conway were both attending school at the garrison, and doing well in their studies, though Conway was by far the more astute pupil.[26]

When not watching his children romp about the post and not tackling antagonists in the War Department, Hunt tended to a myriad of administrative duties—overseeing company drill, target practice, and inspections. In extraduty hours he continued to promote artillery reforms by contributing technical articles to such periodicals as the *Army and Navy Journal* (submitting controversial administrative suggestions under the pseudonym "Z").[27] He even found time to accept active membership in the prestigious Society of the Cincinnati and to deliver speeches and papers—primarily on American military history—before organizations including the Massachusetts Commandery of the Military Order of the Loyal Legion of the United States, the Military Historical Society of Massachusetts, the Society of the Army of the Potomac, and the Aztec Club of 1847.[28]

Additionally, as always, he carried on a prolific correspondence with a great many friends and acquaintances, including many of those with black marks on their War Department ledgers. His personal missives, as also his articles and papers, were uniformly well received. "His letters were such as men do not destroy," commented one recipient, "but file away where they can be got at again because of the information they contain." This man added: "As a writer it is questionable if he had his equal in the army."[29]

Following Hunt's transfer from Fort Sullivan early in '69, however, his official duties again increased to such extent that his correspondence and membership activities diminished. This was made inevitable by the frequency of his transfers alone. From Fort Sullivan he went to Fort Jefferson, off Florida's Gulf Coast. After serving only eight weeks at that garrison on Garden Key, he was shuttled back to New England, where he assumed command of his old post home, Fort Adams. This time he returned to Brenton Point as colonel in command of the Fifth Artillery, by virtue of his promotion to fill the post left vacant by the recent death of his wartime subordinate, Colonel Henry Burton.[30]

He was permitted eleven months at Fort Adams before another transfer came his way. In April 1870 he and his family found themselves at Malone, in upstate New York, where he helped quell Canadian border disturbances much akin to those he had observed thirty years before as a very young junior second lieutenant. At Malone he spent seven weeks, commanding a half-dozen batteries of his regiment, which had been dispatched there to collect, disarm, and disperse bands of Irish-American militants, including many Union veterans, who had concocted a scheme to seize Canada from the British. By the third week in May this latest crisis of international diplomacy had been defuzed, due primarily to the efficiency and tact of General Meade, who was in overall command on the border as head of the Division of the Atlantic.[31] At this point, Hunt and most of his troops returned to Fort Adams.

The hectic series of duty transfers did not cease. He was permitted two more months on Narragansett Bay—barely enough time to send his eldest son, now sixteen, to the Naval Academy at Annapolis.[32] Despite his own background, the midshipman's father soon came to form a highly favorable view of Harry Hunt's school, particularly impressed by its happy balance between fostered discipline and the encouragement of individuality.

Soon thereafter, Hunt was again thrust into the fire of Southern reconstruction, for the first time in four and a half years, via a temporary appointment as head of the newly established District of North Carolina. Unrest in that state, much of it centering around Ku Klux Klan terrorism, demanded the installation of a prudent yet forceful commander, qualifications that General Meade, asked to recommend a candidate, had found in Hunt.[33]

The colonel of the Fifth Artillery proved his old Civil War commander a shrewd judge of character. Hunt set up headquarters at Raleigh late in July 1870, assuming command of a constabulatory force eventually to comprise five companies of artillerists and one of foot soldiers. Yet, he resorted to using these forces only in routine provost work. Violence, reportedly to erupt during a well-publicized trial of local Klan terrorists, never materialized.

Hunt's widespread reputation as a man of fairness, moderation, and compassion toward most ex-Confederates stood him in good stead throughout his two-month tenure in Raleigh, as did his obvious determination to maintain municipal order. By late September, the Klansmen's trial had adjourned without incident; soon afterward, Hunt was sent north with the troops in his regiment, rejoining his family at Fort Adams.[34] Once again he had served effectively as a departmental executive, maintaining his good name as a soldier and a human being, as well as emerging from a delicate situation in civil affairs with popularity among those over whom he ruled.

* * *

During the last three and a half years, Hunt had served at seven different posts. The frenzied pace continued. After ten months at Brenton Point following his return from the South—during which time his third son, Presley, was born—he and his family went back to Washington. Beginning in July of 1871 he spent ten months' work on yet another board, this called by Secretary (of War) William W. Belknap, to update the regulations that had guided the nation's armed forces, with only minimal revisions, since 1861.

Like earlier board work, this was something of a prestige post, awarded in recognition of Hunt's undisputed claim to artillery's principal spokesman and defender. Recognizing the high responsibility given him, he labored as long and as hard as on past panels, taking special pains, as Belknap had anticipated, to challenge past practices regarding the proper role for light artillery, proposing new administrative standards, and once again advocating the appointment of an artillery chief to coordinate all duties of the arm.[35]

Unhappily, in the end, he and his several collaborators saw their efforts come under critical attack from many quarters. Such criticism—much of it levelled by brother officers opposed to the extreme reforms advocated by the panel—influenced Congress to declare itself "far from satisfied that they [the revisions] are just the thing in all respects required for the government of the Army." The legislators printed the board's recommendations for official study, but at length decided that the revisions themselves had to be revised in order to prove acceptable.

Of course, Hunt was angered by such ex post facto alterations, especially since those the lawmakers had in mind would lower the degree of authority he had sought to provide future artillery commanders. The controversy that attended their additions and changes embroiled Hunt in a renewal of hostilities with a long-time antagonist in uniform, Winfield Hancock, soon to succeed Meade as head of the Division of the Atlantic and thus become Hunt's departmental superior.

In published correspondence with the House Military Committee, Hancock in January 1872 condemned the proposed revisions as "mischievous and subversive of discipline," especially those regarding artillery rank and status. Predictably, he praised the 1861–65 arrangement in the Army of the Potomac, whereby corps commanders were given jurisdiction over artillery deployment directly affecting their units. He noted one regrettable exception to the rule: during the battle of Gettysburg the army's artillery chief had meddled with the command system, with potentially disastrous results. In referring to what he termed the irresponsible cessation of Federal counter-battery fire preceding Pickett's charge on 3 July 1863, Hancock left no doubt as to the specific target of his ire.[36]

Hunt responded by sending the military committee a blazing letter of protest. Through some means, Hancock secured access to it and after reading it filed a counterprotest with General Sherman, sending him copies of all correspondence involved in the controversy. The commanding general then worsened the situation by working Hancock's letter into the Congressional Record, while pigeon-holing Hunt's.

When Hunt saw this obvious example of preferential treatment for General Hancock, he fairly exploded. This time he wrote Sherman condemning "the grave charges and imputations" lodged against him by the former II Corps commander, and also implying that Sherman was unfairly abetting the feud in Hancock's behalf. He added that Hancock's original letter to the military committee was

a casual review of a published Congressional document . . . [which] reflected with great severity—even to the imputation of base acts for base purposes—either upon the Secretary of War, or upon the Board of officials who prepared these [revised] regulations, or on both![37]

Though he demanded that Hancock officially be reprimanded for his unprofessional discourtesy to a colleague, Sherman gave him no comfort, finally resolved to end this latest row as quickly and as quietly as possible. But Hunt would neither be hurried nor silenced: as late as 1880 he was entreating the commanding general to publish a document he had composed in rebuttal to Hancock's long-dead criticisms.

Though the episode indicates the perverse stubbornness of which Hunt was capable when his pride was gored, it closed on a rather pathetic note that rang with sad truth. Shortly before conceding defeat late in 1880, Hunt insisted to Sherman that Hancock's accusations "involve my good name— literally the only thing I have—after forty years service—to leave to my children."[38]

18

No Better Soldier

For Hunt the 1870s had begun badly enough. The decade had commenced shortly after an antagonist's rise to the presidency and soon had encompassed the aggravations of revising army regulations.

It also witnessed his mounting concern over the dwindling of personal finances. In his early fifties, he began to think more ruefully than ever about those worldly riches that had eluded him as result of low rank and prestige. His fiscal health continued to deteriorate. In '73 a nationwide business depression wrought havoc on his investments, seriously devaluing the few stocks he owned. The slump also ravaged the funds of his recently widowed mother-in-law, Mrs. Craig, forcing her to give up her comfortable residence on I Street and, for a time, to move in with the Hunts at Fort Adams, to which they had returned when the regulations-revision board had dissolved. So badly injured were Mrs. Craig's finances that upon her death in 1888, a nine-hundred-dollar yearly inheritance, promised Hunt's wife in event of her widowhood, would be found exhausted.[1] These occurrences, plus the added financial burden caused by the elderly woman's residence within the family, contributed materially to Hunt's fear of the future—a fear that increased as mandatory retirement age crept closer to him.

Ill fortune would not desist. Added to all these reverses was the grief occasioned by the death of Hunt's firstborn. In the spring of 1873, twenty-year-old Emily died at Fort Adams after her latest bout with poor health.[2] Only by the stoutest spirit was her father able to bear her loss. But he not only recovered; he made a tangible commitment to regeneration by siring a fourth son, John Elliott Hunt, and a fourth daughter, Jane ("Jennie") Hunt, born in January 1874 and June 1875 respectively.

* * *

As always, the army kept him moving. Through the latter half of 1873 and during most of the following year, court-martial duties took him up and down the East Coast, then as far westward as Fort Sanders, Wyoming. En route he probably took the opportunity to visit his brother, now lieutenant colonel of the Fourteenth Infantry, stationed in the Dakota Territory.[3] He returned to Fort Adams to reassume post command in September of '74, and remained there until late in '75.

Then a transfer sent him and his family southward—this time to Charleston. On 4 December 1875 Colonel Hunt assumed command of the recently relocated headquarters of the Fifth Artillery, most of whose elements were now distributed throughout South Carolina, Georgia, and Florida.[4]

Technically Hunt, his command, and the thousands of other troops recently shifted south by Secretary Belknap, were no longer required to oversee reconstruction in the old Confederacy. In June 1868 South Carolina had returned to the Union, the army losing its jurisdiction there as of that date.[5] And, yet, the service Hunt would perform in Charleston would seem much akin to his Reconstruction service in Arkansas and North Carolina.

Like many other Southern states supposedly reoriented to peace and prosperity, South Carolina lately had experienced a great deal of social and political turmoil, especially in regard to race relations. The first six months of Hunt's term of rule, however, were consistently placid, largely because local whites responded to his fair-minded regime. During that period he won a score of new friends among the ranks of old enemies—these included ex-Confederates still serving in a quasi-military capacity, such as those who officered the local Rifle Clubs. Thereby Hunt again involved himself in political peril.

The Rifle Clubs, formed in the summer of '69, were also known as Red Shirts, or Regulators. They purported to be social organizations, with the mere trappings of the military. But Congress and the War Department viewed them as extralegal bodies whose primary purpose was to overawe freed blacks by constant display of military might—a not too subtle reminder of what might result should blacks take their recently won freedom too seriously. Hunt did not hold with this characterization, believing the clubs to be composed of law-abiding citizens, including many estimable gentlemen of high birth and refined taste. This vocal belief soon won him the opposition of the state's Republican governor, Daniel E. Chamberlain, and Chamberlain's man in Charleston, Mayor George I. Cunningham. In turn Hunt voiced a high regard for neither official, considering them carpetbagger minions of the radicals in Congress.

In July of 1876, at which time Hunt's regiment was in summer camp at a hamlet named, appropriately enough, Summerville—about twenty-two miles from Charleston—the peaceful state of affairs under his regime was abruptly shattered by several statewide outbreaks of racial violence. During the first week of the month, a race riot swept the village of Hamberg, Aiken County, in the southwestern corner of the state. Several weeks later, bloodshed again erupted there, during the court trial of some of the white instigators of the July riot.[6] In September, a much larger disturbance rocked Ellenton, also in Aiken County, lasting five days and ending with fifty blacks and several whites dead. Highly alarmed, Governor Chamberlain secured from Washington authority to disband all the Rifle Clubs, whom he considered the primary agitators.[7]

Despite the governor's action, racial unrest threatened other sections of South Carolina, including Charleston. Several times during that autumn, Hunt perceived himself straddling a huge powder keg. The unrest noticeably intensified with the coming of the November gubernatorial election; for the first time since Appomattox, an ex-Confederate hero—General Wade Hampton—stood a strong chance to capture the state house.

Determined that their party would stave off this challenge, high-ranking Republicans spread propaganda among blacks in the state, whose vote would prove crucial in the election: a victory for Hampton would mean an officially sanctioned reign of terror directed against all freedmen. Hunt thought this nonsense, considering Hampton a fair-minded moderate popular in many camps of the electorate, noting that more than a few black Democrats had pledged him their support at the polls.[8] Thus, he characterized both Chamberlain and Cunningham as adding to the crisis fever by inciting the blacks with terror tactics. When his view became known, both officials suggested that he tend strictly to military matters.

The results of this campaign of fear came vividly to hand on 8 November—the day following the election. At that time the final tallies were still incomplete, though early returns indicated a small but increasing lead for Hampton. This sufficed to push many black Charlestonians toward panic. Too, they began to congregate on city streets, exhorted by black spokesmen to vent their emotions not only on Hampton's supporters but also against the carpetbaggers who had exploited and manipulated freedmen since the end of the war. Soon the crowds turned hostile to any symbols of repressive white rule—whether police officers, militiamen, or Regular troops. Isolated violence struck portions of the city, ending with one white killed and another wounded.[9]

By afternoon, the situation had so worsened that all of Charleston seemed hovering on race war. For this reason, Hunt decided to disobey recent orders that would have returned to Summerville all four companies of foot artillerymen that he had brought to the city to assist the local marshal, Robert M. Wallace, in keeping the peace on Election Day. Though half this force had already entrained for Summerville, he had the other pair of companies—perhaps sixty men—turn about; then he marched them from the rail depot to City Hall, through streets now teeming with agitated citizens, black and white.

His arrival at the hall was well timed. Immediately he was importuned by the chief of police, Captain Henry W. Hendricks, for aid. Hendricks explained that at this hour of pregnant crisis, Mayor Cunningham and his minions had seen fit to retire to parts unknown, leaving the chief entirely responsible for crowd control. However, Hendricks's men were far out-numbered by the throngs of blacks now blocking several of the busiest avenues, many of them armed, several drunk, all capable of violence. Hunt agreed to lend the chief what support his soldiers could provide.

Almost at once he was given ample opportunity to test that support.

Potentially the most dangerous crowd had congregated not far away—at the intersection of Broad and Meeting Streets—one onlooker placing its size at several thousand. After Captain Hendricks's men fell in at his flanks, Hunt led his companies up the street, rifles at shoulder-arms, going into battle for the first time since the shooting had stopped in Virginia.

When he reached the congested corner, he ordered the mob to disperse, his voice pitched even higher than usual. But neither his demand nor a declaration that no black citizen had just cause for alarm, achieved desired results. In fact, his words were greeted by bricks and paving stones flying from the crowd. Then some of the bystanders began to close in on the soldiers and policemen.[10]

Despite the danger, Hunt determined to maintain an unwavering posture. He directed his troops to remain rigidly in column, their rifles still shouldered. Captain Hendricks issued similar orders to his policemen. As though angered by the troops' seemingly nonchalant attitude, the crowd threw more and heavier stones, causing a white spectator to marvel that Hunt's men could remain "like statues, with their faces bleeding, while they awaited orders under a perfect shower of missiles."[11]

Just before the tension snapped and full-scale violence exploded, Hunt noticed that the crowd had begun to draw back, to melt away at the fringes, its attention obviously drawn to a more compelling sight. Not for several moments, however, did he realize that coming down the block were several dozen armed men from the Rifle Clubs, marching directly toward the mob with the same martial tread and disciplined bearing as Hunt's own troops had exhibited. Glimpsing hope of salvation, Hunt pushed his way to the side of one of the club leaders—one-legged ex-Confederate general, James Selden Connor (a future attorney general of South Carolina); and, acting purely from necessity, he invited the general's men to fall in behind his own troops and Hendricks's officers. Connor, a close friend of Hunt since the arrival of the Fifth in the Charleston vicinity, replied he would be happy to do so.

Reportedly, Connor's men raised a shout of triumph at this recognition of their status as law enforcers. But Hunt would not permit them to exercise as much police authority as his critics would later maintain; keeping the clubsmen well in hand, but utilizing their powerful presence to the maximum degree, he assisted Captain Hendricks in sweeping the remnants of the mob from the intersection. Within ten minutes the street was clear. Back to City Hall paraded some of Hunt's artillerymen while others, under his executive officer, fanned out to calm other isolated pockets of unrest throughout the city. All such efforts were eminently successful; rioting had been averted for good.[12]

The next day, Mayor Cunningham materialized at his office and sent for Hunt, who had remained in the city to certify its pacification. Agitated by returns that continued to indicate an erosion of Republican power at the polls, Cunningham gave Hunt a verbal lashing for his conduct the previous day, especially for sanctioning vigilante power such as the clubsmen wielded. The mayor was further incensed when his visitor suggested he advise blacks to remain off the streets until all returns were in and the crisis weather had passed over. When Cunningham hotly replied that black citizens had as much right to walk freely about the city as whites, Hunt agreed in principle but added:

> My object, Mr. Mayor, is not to discuss principles and rights, but to provide for the peace of the city. I know that the whites will not provoke a disturbance. But your party has been industriously teaching the blacks all the summer that if Hampton is elected they will be remanded to slavery, and every telegram that comes makes it more certain he is elected. You who have done the mischief can alone undo it, and your advice [for the blacks] to go home will be better than my order to that effect.

This little speech demonstrated two things: that Hunt's attitude about racial inequality held firm; and that, after thirty-seven years in uniform, he was still, at base, a political innocent. In many ways he was an astute judge of the contemporary political scene, but never had he learned to elude the pitfalls of the political-military coalescence. He had suffered for this ignorance a great many times; now he would suffer again. A few minutes after Hunt turned and left City Hall, again to enforce law and order without Cunningham's cooperation, one of the mayor's functionaries observed quietly that Hunt's tenure in local command would soon be over.[13]

Cunningham immediately acted to make it so. Without Hunt's knowledge, the mayor influenced Governor Chamberlain to wire Hunt's direct superior, Brevet Major General Thomas H. Ruger, commanding the Department of the South, about Hunt's postelection activities. The highly colored account stressed the colonel's willingness to side with ex-rebel groups, which President Grant himself had condemned as unlawful. Thanks to Ruger's close connections with Commanding General Sherman, the sensationalistic news was soon sweeping Washington.

A full six months would pass before a plethora of election irregularities were investigated and resolved and the 7 November election decided in Wade Hampton's favor. Refusing to concede defeat, even in the face of hard statistics, Dan Chamberlain vowed to bar Hampton from the Governor's Mansion. But he could do this only as long as Federal troops backed him. On the seventh, ballots cast across the nation had elevated to the White House as Grant's successor Republican Rutherford B. Hayes, former governor of Ohio. As part payment for Southern support, Hayes in April '77 would remove from the South all troops other than permanent garrisons, thereby ending military reconstruction. Bereft of armed support, Chamberlain would surrender gubernatorial power to a triumphant Hampton and his supporters.

In sharp contrast, the election's effects on the future of Colonel Hunt came much more quickly. On 12 December, Sherman personally ordered him to turn over his command in Charleston and report forthwith to the capital.[14]

Hunt travelled north with wife and children. It was well that they accompanied him, for he would be forced to stay in Washington for the next five weeks. This stemmed from the pronounced displeasure of the new war secretary, J. D. Cameron, who treated Hunt to another helping of the sort of criticism he had received in Mayor Cunningham's office. When given the opportunity to defend his course and to refute the fabrications of his detractors, however, Hunt managed to cool the secretary's temper. Under the circumstances, Cameron could hardly have faulted him from doing his utmost to protect the physical safety of his command.

Still, Hunt had embarrassed the War Department by siding with ex-Confederates against freedmen, and as punishment he was forced to spend the holiday season brooding over his inactivity. He also grew worried when informed that influential Republicans were howling for his ouster from command. Conceivably such pressure would bring his military career to conclusion—seven years prematurely.

There is reason to believe that Sherman, nursing a grudge against Hunt, was largely responsible for his enforced layover at Washington. A few months before, Hunt again had tried the patience of the commanding general —this time by raining verbal blows at Sherman's faithful Adjutant General, E. D. Townsend, whom Hunt alleged to have given orders affecting the Fifth Artillery "of his own volition" but in Sherman's name. This time it was Hunt who nearly received a court-martial for libelling a brother officer—at least for accusing him of wrongdoing without adequate evidence. Not until Sherman expended a great amount of haggling and cajolery was he able to secure an amicable settlement of the dispute without an embarrassing trial, despite Townsend's wishes.[15]

Still Hunt was not permitted to return to South Carolina, though no longer at odds with Townsend or Sherman. He was released from inactive duty in late January 1877; then only through official embarrassment over a newspaper story. On the twelfth of the month, a highly influential print, the *New York Sun*, printed in full Hunt's own report of the postelection crisis in Charleston, concluding that

the election in that State was exceptionally quiet and peaceable, and that whatever attempts at intimidation were made came from Republican Negroes, who, in several instances, assembled in armed bodies for the purpose of preventing colored Democrats from voting for Hampton.

The paper gave Hunt much favorable publicity by divulging choice information to the detriment of some of his foes, including a note that Mayor Cunningham had recently been indicted for civil fraud by a federal grand jury.[16]

At first the story seemed to worsen Hunt's plight. Enraged that a popular paper had gained a copy of a confidential report, Cameron instituted an investigation into the case. Eventually it was determined that a Democratic member of a Congressional committee, recently returned to the capital after a trip to South Carolina to investigate the election riots, had smuggled a copy of the report to the *Sun*.[17]

After 12 January, because of his unidentified ally in power, Hunt found himself less frequently reviled on Capitol Hill for his resistance to mobocracy in the South. By the end of the month he and his family were back in Charleston, where he resumed his old command.

* * *

The remainder of his term in South Carolina passed as had its first six months—without incident. He, Mary, and the children made so comfortable a home there that when Hunt was transferred to Georgia in April of 1879, they were nearly as reluctant to leave as they had been to depart Arkansas thirteen years before.

They left with profuse expressions of regret from the local populace, especially from Charleston's militia groups. The officers of the Washington Light Infantry, toward whose members Hunt had been cordial since his 1852 tour at Fort Moultrie, presented him a particularly heartfelt tribute of affectionate esteem:

> This command has from its earliest record, preserved the pleasantest relations with the officers of the Army and with none has this intercourse been more agreeable than with yourself and with the officers of the "5th". . . . Now that you have left us, we desire to give expression to our sincere regret at our separation and in testimony of our feeling to[ward] you, the Company has by a unanimous vote enrolled your name as an Honorary Member.

In a written response, Hunt noted his pleasure at the long association, and restated his gratitude for the help "of the young men constituting the Military organizations of Charleston" in maintaining order in the city during difficult times.[18] For many years thereafter, generations of Hunts would be assured of a cordial welcome and gracious hospitality from Charlestonians.

Hunt's latest orders sent him to McPherson Barracks, in Atlanta, where he served a two-year term as garrison commander. The period was notable for little more than the poor health with which he now suffered, but which had roots in the childhood illnesses he had contracted on the frontier. Specific ills included migraine headaches, which he had endured for at least three decades,[19] and the nascent symptoms of gout and rheumatism, to became acute in the near future.

Happily, the interests and endeavors of his children claimed much more of his attention than his maladies. Conway, now eighteen, had gone to New York State and had become a promising student at Troy Polytechnic Institute. He would become a railroad engineer, then a civil engineering executive of handsome ability, eventually to design some of the most enduring landmarks in Washington, D.C. Already young Presley was showing an interest in biology and science that would ultimately propel him into a career as a physician.[20] And Hunt's oldest son was roaming the oceans in a heroic role.

Though among the lowest-ranking graduates of the Naval Academy class of '75, Lt. (j.g.) "Harry" Hunt had compensated for his lackluster scholastic record by a noteworthy career as an Arctic seaman and rescuer of seafaring explorers. Early in 1880 he would solidify his reputation by signing aboard a hazardous mission to free members of the *Jeannette* expedition, caught fast by ice floes in the Polar Sea. Though Harry's relief ship, the *Rodgers,*

Lieutenant Henry J. Hunt, Jr., USN, c. 1875 (COURTESY, CMDR. J. CONWAY HUNT)

would meet much the same fate as the vessel she set out to rescue, Lieutenant Hunt and some mates would persevere until eventually locating some survivors of the *Jeannette,* arriving back in the States to a hero's welcome.[21] Four years later, however, Harry would travel aboard another Arctic rescue ship—against his young bride's wishes—and would return home under much more tragic circumstances.

General Hunt's prosaic stint at McPherson Barracks ended in December 1880, and the next month he was assigned his final—and most prestigious—departmental post as head of the newly expanded Department of the South. The position, which encompassed authority over military personnel in Tennessee, Kentucky, North and South Carolina, Georgia, Florida, Alabama, and Mississippi,[22] had been tendered him by virtue of seniority—he, the ranking brevet major general.

In January of '81, two weeks after the realignment of his realm, Hunt and family moved into their final garrison home—at Newport Barracks in Louisville, Kentucky, just across the Ohio River from Cincinnati. From there he coordinated administrative programs for such diverse posts as Fort Gaines and Mount Vernon Barracks, Alabama; Florida's Forts Barrancas and Brooke and St. Francis Barracks; and, in Georgia, Oglethorpe and McPherson Barracks, and Forts Pulaski and Macon. For a time, installations in Arkansas and Louisiana were placed under him as well, but even their later removal did not relieve him of a prodigious amount of paperwork and a vast extent of acreage to oversee via frequent personal inspections.[23]

Despite such a heavy schedule, he somehow found time to continue authoring articles on military and historical themes, as well as keeping in contact with friends by letter and, whenever possible, by visit. He worked hardest to keep in touch with old cronies from the ranks, many now in the political arena, such as George B. McClellan, just completing a term as governor of New Jersey, and Fitz-John Porter, soon to become police commissioner of New York and that city's commissioner of Public Works.[24]

Porter received a great deal of Hunt's attention, and much of his correspondence. Ever since running afoul of John Pope almost twenty years ago, Porter had been suffering under the stigma of a court-martial dismissal from the service—an act Hunt joined him in considering a gross miscarriage of justice. Finally, a three-officer panel of inquiry had been convened in April of 1878 to reexamine the evidence by which Porter had been convicted; the panel had concluded that the general had been cashiered groundlessly and that the court-martial should be annulled and Porter restored to duty. Republican President Hayes, however, had not seen fit to carry out the recommendations, leaving the matter in the lap of Congress.

Hunt was almost as dispirited over this outcome as was Porter himself—especially so because neither Hayes's successor, James A. Garfield, nor Chester A. Arthur, who succeeded to the White House upon Garfield's assassination, possessed enough fortitude to grant Hunt's friend tardy justice.

Hunt had especial reason to fume at Arthur's lack of moral courage, for at the same time as Porter tried to win passage of a bill to set aside his court-martial ruling, Hunt strove equally in vain, to persuade the president to promote him to fill the full-rank major-generalcy recently vacated upon the retirement of Irvin McDowell. By virtue of his seniority—only one other artillerist in the ranks had longer service than he, but lacked Hunt's brevet major general's rank—he considered himself entirely deserving of the honor.[25] Ex-governor McClellan and other prominent officals supported his efforts with a flood of endorsements aimed at the War Department, but despite Hunt's impending retirement, Arthur stubbornly barred his way to advancement.

For this reason and various others, Hunt found it difficult to comport himself cordially toward the president, in whose immediate presence he found himself when attending the Washington wedding of his eldest son, home from the seas, in late June of 1883. Arthur was present as a family friend of Harry Hunt's bride, Henrietta "Blossom" Drum, daughter of Adjutant General Richard C. Drum. But Blossom and her groom, whom she had met in her native California when Harry served there years before on shore duty, made such an engaging and handsome couple that the groom's father exuded good will to all, the president included.[26]

Returning to Newport Barracks with Mary and the rest of the family, Hunt thereafter spent the last months of his active career disposing of desk work. In addition to paper-shuffling and inspection duties, he grappled with many unusually vexing problems, including widespread complaints of poor army rations, increasing desertions from posts in the Deep South, yellow fever outbreaks at the Georgia and Florida garrisons, and Ohio River floods that inundated his own office at Louisville.[27]

He served devotedly to the last. In the second week in September he submitted his final reports to his departmental superior, General Hancock, and on the fourteenth, one day shy of his sixty-fourth birthday, gave his command and his desk to his successor, Colonel John Hamilton.

He was compensated for the desk. That afternoon his staff officers, subordinates, and several of the enlisted men in the Fifth Artillery, presented him with a new desk as a token of their esteem. With years of correspondence and creative writing yet ahead of him, he would put the gift to good use.

Yet he was probably more thankful, as well as deeply touched, by a speech one of his officers delivered on this occasion, speaking on behalf of all assembled. The speech related their pleasure that retirement day found their commander in "the enjoyment of good health, and possessed of strength that is given to few men of much younger years."

The balance of the address centered upon the sincere regret that his departure occasioned among the whole regiment. Still:

A service of nearly forty-nine years entitles you to rest. . . . The fact that it has not been rewarded with the recognition it deserved, is in no way hurtful to you and it is not the least of our hopes that tardy justice will yet be done you.

In conclusion, Hunt's subordinates opined: "History may treat of greater soldiers, but the historian will search in vain for a better one than Brevet Major General Henry J. Hunt."[28]

19

Final Battles

As his subordinates had so feelingly observed, Hunt's career entitled him to honorable and comfortable retirement. But such would not be granted him. Financial need, a chronic concern, would not permit him a life of ease.

By determined frugality he had managed to save enough cash to rent a spacious three-story rowhouse in the 2000 block of G Street N.W., in Washington.[1] If nothing else, its location was excellent—a short jaunt from the War Department, into which he might dart to seek out old friends, many of whom still staffed the various administrative bureaus. But with passing time the house on G Street drew ever more heavily on his resources, whittling away at his colonel's pension. The financial situation was of course worsened by the necessity of providing for two sons and three daughters still living at home.

Several family friends were well aware of his unfortunate situation, and were indignant over the apathetic attitude by which the army had allowed it to come about. By all manner of precedent, and by simple justice, the War Department ought to have retired Hunt as a brigadier or major general, the rank which he truly deserved by virtue of a long and glittering career, especially in 1862–65.

At length, the most influential of his friends decided to seek action. Three months after the colonel of the Fifth Artillery entered civil life, a few allies in Congress lobbied for a retirement bill that would grant him the status and pension due a major general. The legislation was formally introduced in the House of Representatives on 10 December 1883 by General William Rosecrans of California, chairman of the House Military Committee.[2]

The bill related in shameful detail the log of injustices Hunt had borne year after year—especially the nearly fifty thousand dollars in salary, benefits, and emoluments he had forfeited because the army considered him so indispensable to the artillery that he could not follow the easy road to advancement offered by transfer to another service arm. Also stressed were the size of his commands and the vastness of his duties and responsibilities

244

during and after the war. The measure then listed a long series of precedents, naming colleagues such as Samuel Heintzelman, E.O.C. Ord, James B. Ricketts, and Samuel W. Crawford who, though colonels in the Regular Army, had been permitted to retire with the prestige and pay of their brevet rank as brigadier or two-star general. Such a privilege had been granted each by special acts of Congress, or joint resolutions thereof, and in recognition of distinguished services, particularly during the Civil War. Hunt's bill contended that none of those officers had rendered service more honorable or more beneficial to the nation than he.[3]

The grimmest cynic might have foretold the outcome: unlike Heintzelman, Ord, and the other fortunate retirees, Hunt was accorded the treatment due a much less privileged individual.

Congressional debate over the bill was prolonged and sometimes quite bitter, especially in the lower house. As Hunt may have anticipated, his imprudence in political matters while in uniform worked to his great detriment, though to an unforeseeable degree. A number of Republicans, including black congressman, Robert Smalls of South Carolina, and white congressman, William McKenna of Illinois, repeated on the House floor allegations of Hunt's bigotry when serving in the postwar South. Later a steady flow of those carpetbaggers who had infested Charleston in the mid-1870s trooped up Capitol Hill to revive old lies, including one that had Hunt sending his soldiers, disguised as civilians, from poll to poll on Election Day '76 to cram ballot boxes in behalf of Wade Hampton.[4] Other biased witnesses attempted to prove that Hunt's patriotism was a sham: some publicized his reluctance to bombard Petersburg in 1864–65 for fear of injuring rebel friends. Though farfetched, such tales helped break up Republican support for the bill and induced a few Democrats, such as Representative William Springer of Illinois, to line up with the bill's opposition. Soon it was obvious that this First Session of the Forty-eighth Congress would not pass Hunt's relief measure, no matter how hard his friends pushed it. Thus the seeds planted by his political naivety and tactless candor had at last produced a bumper crop of grief.[5]

Passing time eventually worked to the benefit of the bill, but not quite strongly enough. The Second Session of the 1883–85 Congress finally passed the measure, but only after a second round of bitter oratory; not until 3 March 1885 did it clear both houses of Congress and receive formal submission to President Arthur.[6]

The next day Arthur left the White House for good, his successor, Grover Cleveland, moving in. The Hunt bill remained on the outgoing president's desk, lifeless and dead, killed by a pocket veto.

Arthur had refused to sign it into law for the same primary reason behind his refusal to sign the measure that would have returned Fitz-John Porter to the army rolls: he felt that, by its wording, such a bill usurped the appointive power of the executive, forcing him to create a single, specified "office," or "position," to be filled by a single, specified "candidate."

A few days after departing office, Arthur was hailed by a War Department colonel, a friend of the Hunt family, who asked him to reexplain his reasoning. Afterward the officer informed Hunt that the president expressed regret at his inability "consistently, to make the bill a law," then added that since he had killed Porter's bill on similar grounds "I should have been laughed at" when signing Hunt's.[7]

Few disappointments Hunt had absorbed when in uniform were as painful as this when in mufti. Later attempts were made to revive the bill, but all failed to bring results. This was not so with General Porter, whose supporters convinced Democrat Cleveland to sign the relief bill restoring him to the army retired list, on 1 July 1886. In a characteristic gesture, Hunt offered his old superior prompt and hearty congratulations, declaring Porter much more deserving than he himself of belated vindication.[8]

* * *

The defeat of his own bill marked an onslaught of a long series of personal and family sorrows, these striking throughout Hunt's retirement. Most were caused by the merciless advance of death.

As the 1880s drew to a close, many of his oldest and most cherished friends passed on, including McClellan, Barry, French, Hunt's brother-in-law and aide John Craig, and Fitz-John Porter, too. Their passing, due to illness or the weight of years, left Hunt bereft in the most acute degree.

In 1885 and '86, death paid a lengthy visit to his own family, not departing until it had taken an agonizing toll. Though long estranged from his brother by personal matters as well as physical distance, Hunt knew genuine bereavement when in September '86 he received word that Lewis, lately the colonel commanding the Fourteenth Infantry, had succumbed at Fort Union, New Mexico Territory, to the residual effects of the illnesses that had pursued him since youth. The melancholy intelligence followed by barely three months news that Lewis's wife Abby had died at her family home in Ann Arbor, Michigan, to which she had returned to attempt to recover from chronic ills. Hunt made long journeys to see both brother and sister-in-law committed to the earth, and voluntarily added to his financial burdens by adopting the deceased couple's youngest child, eighteen-year-old Henry Jackson Hunt III.[9] Like Hunt's own youngest boy, John, Henry would carry the family tradition into his generation by serving as a commissioned officer in the Regular service.

But the tragedy that affected Hunt most immediately had run its course long before Lewis and Abby died. In the latter part of 1884 Lieutenant Harry Hunt had returned from the North Pole after helping rescue a weather-observation expedition under A.W. Greely. But he had come back with health shattered. During the voyage home he had dived into frigid waters to rescue a deckhand who had fallen overboard. By failing to change into warm clothing immediately after the rescue, Harry had come down with a severe throat infection, which developed into pneumonia, and finally

Henry J. Hunt, c. 1885 (COURTESY, LIBRARY OF CONGRESS)

into a deadly tubercular condition. Late that year, doctors had removed part of one lung. Though he survived the operation, Harry's prognosis seemed grim, his survival chancy. His illness not only profoundly affected his father and step-mother but also his pregnant young wife and their yearold son.[10]

Hunt's concern for his son's health, dwindling at a distressing rate, forced him to shelve ongoing plans for resurrecting his pension bill and to curtail several in-progress writing projects. He had Harry, Blossom, and their son move in with them on G Street, and in a desperate hope of finding a cure for what some doctors frankly termed a hopeless case, he went through his meager store of personal funds to cover new medical and surgical bills. Early in 1885, however, these funds began to run out.

By that February, Hunt's fiscal outlook was hopeless. When nearing the point at which he had to give up his home, he applied for the post of governor at the Washington Soldiers' Home—a haven for retired, eldery, and/or disabled Regular Army enlisted men. The post would provide no salary but it would furnish a strenuous workload. Hunt wanted it because it offered living quarters free of rent and maintenance costs.

For once, good fortune favored him. On 25 April, less than three months after submitting his application, he won appointment to succeed Brevet Major General Samuel D. Sturgis, himself retiring as governor.[11] A couple of weeks afterward the two Hunt families—including a bedfast Harry—moved into their new residence.

Hunt was immediately pleased by the surroundings. Soon he was writing a St. Louis friend, Judge Thomas Gantt, who had served with him on McClellan's staff in 1861–62, that the home provided "a beautiful spot and the change will be good for my children, for our house in town has been one hospital for the last two months." Some weeks later he added that the home's five hundred-acre grounds were "beautiful . . . Much enjoyed by the children and by *us* as well." Already, he noted, his rent-free existence had proved a godsend.[12]

Yet doctor bills kept coming. In addition to medicines, attending physicians, and nursing care, Hunt helped finance a series of trips that Harry made to Colorado in company of wife and father-in-law in vain attempts to regain his health. Later that year—soon after the birth of his second son—Harry fell into rapid decline, until by February of '86 he was so weak and so short of breath that he could barely speak. Once robust, able to tower over his father—at the academy a championship boxer and all-around athlete—Harry now appeared stooped, gaunt, and wizened far beyond his years.[13]

Late that month he sought a sad confrontation with his father, candidly acknowledging that his death had to be only weeks off and stating his firm intention to accept no more money from his father's pocket. Hearing his son speak in so fragile a voice, Hunt nearly broke down in tears. Finally he admitted to Harry that outside assistance from wealthy friends, including Judge Gantt, had all but been forced upon him in his son's behalf.

For a time the younger man said nothing. Then he placed his arms around his father's neck and said, "At last what you have been doing for others is coming back to you!"[14]

With springtime, Harry approached the end. His father took a brief leave of absence to accompany him to old friends' homes in South Carolina, in a final attempt to seek restoration of health in a mild climate—but the trip proved barren of benefit. Upon his return to the Soldiers' Home, Harry lay on his deathbed. On 5 May, he called his father, stepmother, wife, children, in-laws, and other loved ones to his bedside, speaking individually to each for as long as his voice and strength endured. To General Drum he stated his own epitaph: "I'd like to be thought of as if I were away on a long cruise where no one need worry. I don't want to be mourned as if I were lost."[15]

A few days later Hunt saw his son laid to rest in the little cemetery at the Soldiers' Home. The funeral was a simple ceremony, though attended not only by relatives and friends but by high officials—such as Navy Secretary William C. Whitney and Secretary (of War) William Endicott. When earth was tossed over Harry's coffin, Hunt saw broken his last flesh-and-blood link with his first marriage.

Some days afterward, he wrote Judge Gantt: "He was a noble lad of whom any father might feel proud."[16]

* * *

Somehow, even in the midst of multiple tragedies, Hunt found the energy and the will to labor conscientiously as head of the Soldiers' Home. With the invaluable aid of Major Benjamin Rittenhouse, a former artillery subordinate and now the home's secretary-treasurer-quartermaster-commissary all in one, he was able to exercise tight fiscal control and yet provide, not only for the comfort and care of his charges, but for their recreation and entertainment as well. The inmates of the home quickly warmed to his rule, endorsing the view that he was "a strict disciplinarian," but "most approachable" in a human and humane manner.[17]

His labors were many and arduous. The home was overcrowded, with an average yearly increment of two hundred residents, and it threatened to remain so for a long time to come. By late 1886, its population had swollen to more than one thousand, hundreds more than its resources could properly accommodate. At the same time, its expenditures far exceeded the appropriations it received from Congress. As Hunt wrote Commanding General Philip Sheridan, who also served as the head of the home's board of governors: "We are burning the candle at both ends. Our members and expenses are largely increasing and our capital rapidly diminishing." In the end, however, Hunt's persuasiveness led Congress to settle the institution's outstanding debts.[18]

Even with financial woes cured, Hunt had more than enough problems with which to contend—problems that would have taxed the energy and ingenuity of many a younger administrator. He still had to cope, for example, with overcrowding (eventually he was able to add an annex to handle the overflow); he had to arrange all manner of medical care for the aged and infirm; and he had to provide religious services and funeral rites for the residents.

Acutely aware of that monotony which too often was the predominant feature of inmates' lives, he bolstered recreational facilities, adding many volumes to the home's library, arranging lectures, concerts, and exhibitions, and securing funds to outfit the musically talented members—including several old buglers and ex-drummer boys—as a full-fledged band, which soon was giving concerts of its own thrice weekly.

One form of recreation he sought to ban was nevertheless provided by local grog shops, which helped separate many of the residents from their scanty pensions. Thus, Hunt helped institute a fervid campaign to promote temperance, and went far beyond his responsibilities in providing medical care—and the water cure—for dipsomaniacs. Though reminded by his superiors that he need not cater to the plight of habitual drunkards, Hunt considered treatment "a matter of humanity," and never refused inmates' requests for it.[19]

When not engaged in administrative concerns, the governor of the home remained an active member of various veterans' and historical societies, speaking occasionally before the local Loyal Legion commandery, and attending dinners and other functions given by organizations such as the Aztec Club and the Old Guard of New York City, of which he was an honorary member. By 1886 he was also senior vice-president of the Society of the Army of the Potomac, the year before having presided over its annual convention held in Baltimore. Every summer, he managed to hoard enough time to accompany old cronies to Gettysburg, Chancellorsville, and other fields of past glory.[20]

Some of his lectures formed the basis for articles that appeared occasionally in learned periodicals. Perhaps his best-known contribution to military administrative history is a lengthy piece—"Our Experience in Artillery Administration"—published posthumously in the widely read *Journal of the Military Service Institution of the United States*. The article, which stands as an expert overview of the administration of his own branch of service before, after, and especially during the Civil War, originated as a paper delivered before the Military Historical Society of Massachusetts.

But his most prominent contribution to literature related to his participation in the campaign that had lifted him to the apogee of his career. The three articles that eventuated from his interest in re-creating the Gettysburg campaign had their genesis in November 1885. In that month he was contacted by the editors of the *Century Magazine*—a New York-based monthly with a high reputation among popular-consumption periodicals. Its associate editors, Robert Underwood Johnson and Clarence Clough Buel, were engaged in compiling a wealth of first-person narratives relating to

Hunt (standing at far right) and other veterans at Chancellorsville Battle-field, c. 1887 (COURTESY, CMDR. J. CONWAY HUNT)

the Civil War, hoping to exploit an ongoing national revival of interest in the great struggle of two and a half decades before.

Though flattered by their interest in him as a writer, Hunt at first begged off, suggesting other, more qualified writers, though he admitted that "you have tempted me sorely."[21] But Johnson and Buel persisted, and the result was a long period of research by Hunt among records and the recollections of his colleagues, followed by the publication of three articles in the *Century* for November and December 1886, and January 1887. The work soon was recognized as clearly written, cogent yet thorough-going, and scrupulously impartial (save perhaps in Hunt's pardonable attempt to redress historical neglect of Federal artillery's role in the great campaign).

Critically acclaimed from the day of its appearance, this series was to enjoy enduring fame. Modern-day historians have termed Hunt's articles "both comprehensive and fair," and "among the best available records of the battle," adding that their author was "highly observant, with a fine eye for the detail of terrain, thoughtful, and generous." It is perhaps significant that many of these comments have come from the pen of Southern-born historians of latent Confederate sympathies.[22]

Hunt's work was made available to a large reading audience when later reprinted as the cornerstone of the Century Company's four-volume compilation: *Battles and Leaders of the Civil War*. Hunt was so encouraged by its favorable critical response that he projected other works on Civil War history. By the spring of '87 he was ready to begin work on a monograph dealing with McClellan's tenure at the head of the Army of the Potomac—a work intended to rehabilitate his old commander's reputation. But he never progressed far on the manuscript; nor on another he began a year later—a study of the political controversy that engulfed Little Mac as result of the fiasco at Balls Bluff in October 1861.[23]

Neither saw completion because financial remuneration would have been small; he spent most of his free time—unsuccessfully—seeking new ways to increase his store of worldly goods. He was painfully aware that should Mary survive him, as his children surely would, he could leave few funds to secure her economic future.

A second reason why Hunt's writing projects died stillborn was the increasing severity of his physical infirmities, which made desk work an ordeal. Several of these had been with him a good many years, including gout and rheumatism. But by now these had become so severe that his legs and ankles were grossly swollen, at times preventing him from walking

Mrs. and Gen. Hunt with family at Washington Soldiers's Home, c. 1888. Children (from left): Jane, Julia, Presley, Maria, John, and Conway. (COURTESY, CMDR. J. CONWAY HUNT)

about. His headaches were still bothersome, and by this point he had grown all but totally deaf.

Despite his pains he was highly reluctant to take refuge in narcotics, writing one friend: "I detest drugs—I was over drugged in my younger days, and look upon them all as poison." But in time the pain so increased that to maintain stamina he took temporary relief in large doses of carbonate of lithium. When, as increasingly proved the case, even this did not suffice, he could do nothing but stoically endure his discomforts. "Have suffered a great deal this month—Gout & rheumatism," he wrote a South Carolina acquaintance in April of 1888, "and have been unable to do much [for] myself."[24]

With decelerating strength he passed the rest of that year, observing his sixty-ninth birthday on 14 September with wife, children and a host of veterans clustered about. On this day he was happy and serene, pain or not.

It was his final birthday. Early the next year his health all but completely shattered, and he was hospitalized at the home with a severe case of pneumonia. The new illness placed such added strain on his endurance that he soon realized he was dying. At an early hour on 11 February, he called an old acquaintance to his bed and to him supposedly addressed a last plea:

"Ask my friends and country to save my wife and children from starving. I have tried in vain—could only serve my country."

So, at any rate, reported the *New York Times,* which had a penchant for putting pithy sayings into the mouths of dying notables. But even if the *Times* took artistic license here, it cannot be denied that it fashioned appropriate words. It could have offered no more fitting epitaph for the man.

At 10:30 on that Monday morning, the eleventh—for the first and only time—the General's heart failed him.[25]

* * *

The War Department outdid itself at his funeral, held on the fourteenth at the Soldiers' Home. With as much pomp as seemed consistent with Hunt's request that the ceremony be simple and devoid of music, it committed him to the earth and to history. Among the honorary pallbearers were several of the surviving heroes of his war, including John Schofield, current commanding general of the Army, and former Generals William Rosecrans, George Getty, Confederate commander Joe Johnston, and Senators Joseph R. Hawley and C.F. Manderson. Yet an honor guard of a half-dozen orderly sergeants, as per his dying request, bore Hunt's bier to its final resting place in the home cemetery, beside that of Lieutenant Henry J. Hunt, Jr., U.S.N. To the last, the common touch predominated.[26]

Solemn rites concluded, the nation commenced a frantic campaign to honor a soldier so often passed over for honor during his lifetime. In marked contrast to action taken to pass a bill to reward him, in retirement, for his services, a bill to provide his widow a monthly pension of one hundred dollars (later trimmed in half) was rushed through Congress by Senators Hawley and Manderson and their colleagues in the House.[27]

Soon the army emulated Congress in an attempt to salve its conscience by promulgating a series of panegyrics praising Hunt the soldier. The rhetoric adhered to predictable lines. Secretary (of War) Endicott struck the keynote in ringing tones: "It is needless to recite his deeds; the Army of to-day knows them well; the Army of the future will find them in history."[28]

But such tributes flowed too freely and were built of too many pious bromides to admit of sincerity. Moreover, they conspicuously omitted mention of past wrongs, injustices, and neglect heaped upon the man whose deeds it was useless to recite. Much better spoke the *Army and Navy Journal*:

> He was a man of decided opinions, which he was accustomed to present with vigor, but his spirit was generous even toward an opponent, and his heart was one of the truest and warmest, and he will long be remembered with affection by those who were brought into intimate association with him.

Nor did the *Journal* fear to acknowledge the central tragedy of Hunt's career:

> Had his services and his abilities received their proper recognition he would not have died as a colonel upon the retired list.[29]

Notes

ABBREVIATIONS USED IN NOTES

A&NJ • *Army and Navy Journal* (New York, 1863–   )

ACPF • Appointments, Commissions, and Promotions File, Record Group 94, National Archives

B&L • *Battles and Leaders of the Civil War* (4 vols. New York, 1887–88)

Cen-C • *Century* Collection, New York Public Library

HJH • Henry Jackson Hunt

HP • Hunt Papers

HR • *House Report*

HSP • Historical Society of Pennsylvania

JCCW • *Joint Committee on the Conduct of the War* (8 vols. Washington, D.C. 1863–68)

JMSIUS • *Journal of the Military Service Institution of the United States* (61 vols. Governors Island, N.Y., 1880–1917)

l, ll • leaf, leaves

LC • Library of Congress

M-, R- • Microcopy, Roll

McCP • George B. McClellan Papers

MOLLUS • Military Order of the Loyal Legion of the United States

NA • National Archives

NJHS • New Jersey Historical Society

OR • *War of the Rebellion: A Compilation of the Official Records of the Union and Confederate Armies* (128 vols. Washington, D.C., 1880–1901)

OR-N • *Official Records of the Union and Confederate Navies in the War of the Rebellion* (30 vols. Washington, D.C., 1894–1922)

RG-, E- • Record Group, Entry

SHSP • *Southern Historical Society Papers* (52 vols. Richmond, 1876–1959)

USMA-L • United States Military Academy Library

INTRODUCTION

1. HJH, "Our Experience in Artillery Administration," *JMSIUS*, XII (1891), p. 201.

2. *HR 122*, Jan. 30, 1884 (48th Cong., 1st Sess.), p. 2.

CHAPTER 1

1. Peter Young and Richard Holmes, *The English Civil War: A History of the Three Civil Wars, 1642–1651* (London: Ian Allen, 1974), pp. 191–92; J.L. Weisse, *Records and Traditions of the Families of Hunt and Weisse* (New York, 1866), p. 30.

2. Edmund Soper Hunt, *Weymouth Ways and Weymouth People: Reminiscences* (Boston, 1907), p. 288. According to a leading chronicler of the Hunt family, the first Hunt progenitor in America was one Enoch, who settled in Weymouth in 1638 after leaving his native home, "Titenden, Parish of Lee, England": see T.B. Wyman, comp., *Genealogy of the Name and Family of Hunt* (Boston, 1863), pp. 252 and 271. However, Weisse, *Records and Traditions,* pp. 31–32, explains that "Enoch" was the assumed name of an older, unidentified man who accompanied Sir William Hunt from England to Massachusetts in 1645, posing as the latter's father, while William adopted the alias of "Ephraim Hunt."

3. George Frederick Robinson, "John Hunt, (Gentleman)," *Bay State Historical League Bulletin,* XX (1935), pp. 2–4.

4. Weisse, *Records and Traditions,* p. 45; Francis B. Heitman, *Historical Register of Officers of the Continental Army During the War of the Revolution, April, 1775, to December, 1783* (Washington, D.C., 1914), pp. 309–10.

5. HJH to Alexander S. Webb, July 4, 1881, Webb Papers, Yale University Library; Henry P. Johnston, *The Yorktown Campaign and the Surrender of Cornwallis, 1781* (New York, 1881), pp. 145–46.

6. William E. Birkhimer, *Historical Sketch of the Organization, Administration, Matériel and Tactics of the Artillery, United States Army* (Washington, D.C., 1884), pp. 349–50.

7. James Ripley Jacobs, *The Beginning of the U.S. Army, 1783–1812* (Princeton, N.J.: Princeton University Press, 1947), pp. 172–76; "Memoirs of General John Elliott Hunt, 1798–1877," TS. in Toledo-Lucas County Public Library, 1 1. *Note:* all references to the geographical details of particular garrisons, unless otherwise specified, are drawn from Francis P. Prucha, *A Guide to the Military Posts of the United States, 1789–1895* (Madison: State Historical Society of Wisconsin, 1964). In this source, forts are listed alphabetically.

8. Robert W. Frazer, *Forts of the West* (Norman: University of Oklahoma Press, 1965), pp. 68–69.

9. Elliott Coues, *History of the Expedition under the Command of Lewis and Clark* (3 vols. New York, 1893), III, p. 1212n; Richard Dillon, *Meriwether Lewis: A Biography* (New York: Coward–McCann, 1965), pp. 258–59.

10. Francis P. Prucha, *The Sword of the Republic: The United States Army on the Frontier, 1783–1846* (New York: Macmillan Co., 1969), p. 100; "Memoirs of John Elliott Hunt," ll 1–2.

11. Wyman, comp., *Name and Family of Hunt,* pp. 291 and 387.

12. *A&NJ,* Sept. 18, 1886.

13. HJH to Col. Henry Knox Craig, Sept. 10, 1874, HP-LC.

14. George Walton, *Sentinel of the Plains: Fort Leavenworth and the American West* (Englewood Cliffs, N.J.: Prentice-Hall, Inc., 1973), p. 13.

15. Elvid Hunt and Walter E. Lorence, *History of Fort Leavenworth, 1827–1937* (Fort Leavenworth, Kans.: Command & General Staff School Press, 1937), pp. 13–14.

16. *A&NJ,* Sept. 18, 1886.

17. Hunt and Lorence, *Fort Leavenworth,* pp. 284–85; Frazer, *Forts of the West,* p. 56.

18. James M. Bugbee, ed., *Memorials of the Massachusetts Society of the Cincinnati* (Boston, 1890), p. 271; copy of commission given Lt. Col. Henry J. Hunt, Michigan Territorial Militia, Aug. 10, 1818, courtesy of Cmdr. J. Conway Hunt; *Eunice {Hunt} Tripler: Some Notes of Her Personal Recollections* (New York, 1910), pp. 16 and 19.

19. Russell F. Weigley, *History of the United States Army* (New York: Macmillan Co., 1967), p. 566; HR 220, Feb. 23, 1843 (27th Cong., 3rd Sess.), pp. 2–3.

20. "Memoirs of John Elliott Hunt," 1 1.

21. HJH to Thomas T. Gantt, May 16, 1885, HP-LC.

22. All references to Hunt's academy grades and class rank are drawn from letter to author from Kenneth W. Rapp, Assistant Archivist, USMA Archives, June 26, 1974.

23. Stephen E. Ambrose, *Duty, Honor, Country: A History of West Point* (Baltimore: Johns Hopkins University Press, 1966), pp. 106–8, 116.

24. HJH to Lt. James Duncan, Mar. 11, 1844, Duncan Papers, USMA-L.

25. *Washington Star,* Feb. 11, 1889.

26. All references to command assignments of Hunt's West Point colleagues are drawn from George W. Cullum, *Biographical Register of the Officers and Graduates of*

the U.S. Military Academy (2 vols. New York, 1868). In this source former cadets are listed in order of scholastic rank within their graduating class. The 1891 updated edition of this work has been consulted for information pertaining to the careers of Hunt's junior associates.

27. Morris Schaff, *The Battle of the Wilderness* (Boston, 1910), p. 45.

28. Weigley, *History of the United States Army,* pp. 150–51; Ambrose, *Duty, Honor, Country,* pp. 93, 108, 110.

29. W.A. Swanberg, *First Blood: The Story of Fort Sumter* (New York: Charles Scribner's Sons, 1957), p. 37.

30. Roswell Park, *A Sketch of the History and Topography of West Point* (Philadelphia, 1840), p. 95. For information about improvements in artillery drill at the academy, c. 1838, see "Report of the Committee on Military Instruction," *Senate Documents 338,* Doc. 1—June 18, 1838 (25th Cong., 3rd Sess.), p. 256.

31. Park, *Sketch of West Point,* p. 105; Ambrose, *Duty, Honor, Country,* p. 90.

32. Hunt accumulated his demerits as follows:

Fourth Class Year:	72
Third Class Year:	98
Second Class Year:	180
First Class Year:	159

509 demerits!

The source for this information, as for all reference to Hunt's delinquency record, is letter to the author from Kenneth Rapp, July 16, 1974.

33. Park, *Sketch of West Point,* p. 105.

34. Grady McWhiney, *Braxton Bragg and Confederate Defeat: Volume I, Field Command* (New York: Columbia University Press, 1969), p. 7.

35. Copy of academy diploma awarded Hunt, June 21, 1839, courtesy of Cmdr. J. Conway Hunt.

CHAPTER 2

1. William E. Birkhimer, *Historical Sketch of Artillery* (Washington, D.C., 1884), pp. 189n, 189–90.

2. HJH, "Artillery Administration," *JMSIUS,* XII (1891), p. 206.

3. At this time, "light artillery" exclusively referred to horse artillery, whose gunners served in concert with dragoons (and later with cavalry and mounted infantry). See Birkhimer, *Historical Sketch of Artillery,* pp. 54n–55n.

4. Fairfax Downey, *Sound of the Guns: The Story of the American Artillery* (New York: David McKay Co., Inc., 1956), p. 64.

5. HJH, "Artillery Administration," p. 207. The differences between guns and howitzers are several: the latter have a more arching trajectory, a shorter barrel, are lighter-weight, were originally designed to fire only shells—projectiles with a bursting charge inside a hollow or shot-filled casing—and had a chamber at the bottom of the barrel to concentrate the smaller powder charge deemed necessary to fire the more fragile shells. It follows that a gun, as a howitzer, is a *particular* artillery piece, though in common useage (as in the title of this book) it may denote artillery in general. "Pounder" designations refer to the weight of the solid projectile standard for a particular cannon. Cannon were also classified by proper name—the name, for instance, of a foundry owner or of the inventor of a special casting process, etc.—as in Rodman, Blakely, and Parrott guns. Still another means of cannon classification was predicated upon the size of the diameter of the bore expressed in inches; for example, the 3-inch ordnance gun or the 4.5-inch heavy rifle. Finally, differences between smoothbore cannon and the rifle, whose grooved barrel imparted a spin to discharged projectiles, thereby increasing accuracy, are obvious.

The mid-nineteenth-century artilleryman had five principal types of projectiles to fire, most fixed by straps to a wooden base, or "sabot," and also its powder charge; these were: solid shot, shell, shrapnel (a shell filled with musket balls that scattered through the air upon discharge), canister (a tin-cased shell filled with smaller and more numerous iron balls packed in sawdust, which also scattered when fired), and, until shortly before the Civil War, grapeshot. The last-named, which from 1861 to 1865 was used only in coastal and garrison artillery, consisted of nine huge iron balls arranged in three tiers around a steel pin and fixed between iron plates; it looked something like a bunch of grapes, hence its name. By 1861 field artillerists had discarded it in favor of the somewhat similar but more reliable and more deadly canister and shrapnel.

6. J. Fred Rippey, *Joel R. Poinsett, Versatile American* (Durham, N.C.: Duke University Press, 1935), pp. 172–74.

7. Downey, *Sound of the Guns,* pp. 86–87; William L. Haskin, comp., *The History of the First Regiment of Artillery* (Portland, Me., 1879), p. 72.

8. Headquarters, 2nd Artillery, Returns for Aug., 1839, M–727, R–10, NA. All references to the dates of Hunt's garrison postings, 1839–83, are drawn from his detailed service record in *HR 212,* Feb. 3, 1886 (49th Cong., 1st Sess.), pp. 3–4.

9. Post Returns, Detroit Barracks, Aug.–Oct., 1839, M–617, R–312, NA; W.A. Simpson, "The Second Regiment of Artillery," in T.F. Rodenbough and William L. Haskin, eds., *The Army of the United States* (New York, 1896), p. 316. All references to the postings and promotions of Hunt's colleagues—such as this note about his company commander's absence on detached duty—are drawn from F.B. Heitman, *Historical Register of the United States Army* (Washington, D.C., 1890). In this work officers are listed alphabetically.

10. Post Returns, Buffalo Barracks, Oct., 1839–Sept., 1840, M–617, R–157, NA. All references to the identity of commanders at the various posts at which Hunt served, and to the composition of their garrisons, are drawn from the *Official Army Register* (Washington, D.C., 1840–83). In this source, garrisons are listed alphabetically.

11. J.M.S. Careless, *Canada: A Story of Challenge* (Cambridge: Cambridge University Press, 1953), pp. 180–81; Donald Creighton, *A History of Canada: Dominion of the North* (Boston: Little, Brown, 1958), pp. 241–45.

12. Haskin, comp., *First Regiment of Artillery,* p. 71.

13. Emory Upton, *The Military Policy of the United States* (Washington, D.C., 1904), p. 184; Edward S. Wallace, *General William Jenkins Worth, Monterey's Forgotten Hero* (Dallas: Southern Methodist University Press, 1953), pp. 38–40.

14. Simpson, "Second Regiment of Artillery," p. 316; "Sketch of Some of the Important Military Services of the Late. Col. Duncan," *The Democratic Review,* I (1852), pp. 193–94.

15. William S. Rosecrans to Chester A. Arthur, Mar. 27, 1882, HJH ACPF; William H. Powell, *The Fifth Army Corps* (New York, 1896), p. 57.

16. Morris Schaff, *Battle of the Wilderness* (Boston, 1910), p. 45.

17. James M. Bugbee, ed., *Massachusetts Society of the Cincinnati* (Boston, 1890), p. 282.

18. Simpson, "Second Regiment of Artillery," p. 316.

19. George W. Cullum, *Historical Sketch of the Fortification Defenses of Narragansett Bay* (Washington, D.C., 1884), pp. 20–21, 29–30.

20. Hazard Stevens, *The Life of Isaac Ingalls Stevens* (2 vols. Boston, 1900), I, p. 77.

21. Bugbee, ed., *Massachusetts Society of the Cincinnati,* pp. 271–72.

22. Returns, Headquarters, 2nd Artillery, 1841–42, M–727, R–11, NA.

23. HJH to "Colonel," Nov. 19, 1842, HP-LC.

24. HJH to Commissary Gen. George Gibson, Nov. 19, 1842; Gibson to Capt. Allen Lowd, Dec. 5, 1842; both, HP-LC.

25. A.L. Long, *Memoirs of Robert E. Lee* (New York, 1887), p. 66.

26. Douglas Southall Freeman, *R.E. Lee: A Biography* (4 vols. New York: Charles Scribner's Sons, 1934–35), I, p. 193.

27. Haskin, comp., *First Regiment of Artillery,* p. 67; Upton, *Military Policy of the United States,* pp. 190 and 193.

28. Frank B. Woodford, *Lewis Cass, the Last Jeffersonian* (New York: Octagon Books, 1973), pp. 231–38; HJH to "Citizen Delegato," Mar. 17, 1844, Duncan Papers, USMA-L.

29. William Nisbet Chambers, *Old Bullion Benton, Senator from the New West* (Boston: Little, Brown, 1956), pp. 296–99.

30. *HR 220,* Feb. 23, 1843 (27th Cong., 3rd Sess.), pp. 1–6; Birkhimer, *Historical Sketch of Artillery,* p. 60.

31. HJH to Lt. James Duncan, Mar. 11, 1844, Duncan Papers, USMA-L.

32. Post Returns, Fort Adams, Oct., 1845–June, 1846, M–617, R–3, NA.

CHAPTER 3

1. Robert Selph Henry, *The Story of the Mexican War* (New York: Frederick Ungar, 1961), pp. 32–42.

2. John Edward Weems, *To Conquer a Peace: The War Between the United States and Mexico* (Garden City, N.Y.: Doubleday & Co., Inc., 1974), pp. 95–96, 103, 112–13; N.C. Brooks, *A Complete History of the Mexican War: Its Causes, Conduct, and Consequences* (Philadelphia, 1849), pp. 105–7.

3. All references to dates of Hunt's promotions and commissions are drawn from *A Statement of Services of Bvt. Major General Henry J. Hunt, Colonel (Ret.): Compiled from Authentic Sources by an Artillery Officer* (Washington, D.C., n.d.), pp. 4–5.

4. George Winston Smith and Charles Judah, eds., *Chronicles of the Gringos: The U. S. Army in the Mexican War, 1846–48* (Albuquerque, N.M.: University of New Mexico Press, 1968), pp. 275, 283–84, 322–25; Holman Hamilton, *Zachary Taylor, Soldier of the Republic* (2 vols. Indianapolis: Bobbs-Merrill Co., 1941), I, pp. 166–67.

5. David Lavender, *Climax at Buena Vista: The American Campaigns in Northeastern Mexico, 1846–47* (Philadelphia: J. B. Lippincott Co., 1966), pp. 71–72; Weems, *To Conquer a Peace*, pp. 132–35.

6. HJH, "Artillery Administration," *JMSIUS*, XII (1891), p. 209; William L. Haskin, comp., *First Regiment of Artillery* (Portland, Me., 1879), pp. 80–83.

7. HJH to Mjr. W.W. Bliss, Aug. 24, 1846; Bliss to HJH, Aug. 28, 1846; both, HP-LC.

8. Hazard Stevens, *Isaac Ingalls Stevens* (2 vols. Boston, 1900), I, p. 106.

9. HJH to Thomas Gantt, May 8, 1888, HP-LC.

10. Bvt. Col. Benjamin Huger to HJH (quoting an earlier letter from HJH), Mar. 24, 1852; HJH to Sen. Solon Borland, Jan. 1, 1852; both, HP-LC.

11. William E. Birkhimer, *Historical Sketch of Artillery* (Washington, D.C., 1884), p. 205; Fairfax Downey, *Sound of the Guns* (New York: David McKay Co., Inc., 1956), p. 86.

12. Birkhimer, *Historical Sketch of Artillery*, pp. 51 and 63.

13. Winfield Scott, *Memoirs of Lieut.-General Scott, Ll. D.* (2 vols. New York, 1864), II, pp. 397–405.

14. Edward S. Wallace, *William Jenkins Worth* (Dallas: Southern Methodist University Press, 1953), pp. 116–17; HJH, "Artillery Administration," p. 212.

15. Wallace, *William Jenkins Worth*, pp. 120–21.

16. Smith and Judah, eds., *Chronicles of the Gringos*, pp. 325–27.

17. A.L. Long, *Memoirs of Robert E. Lee* (New York, 1887), pp. 68–70.

18. Lavender, *Climax at Buena Vista*, p. 226; HJH, "Artillery Administration," p. 208.

19. Haskin, comp., *First Regiment of Artillery*, pp. 94–95; Justin H. Smith, *The War with Mexico* (2 vols. New York, 1919), II, pp. 50–60.

20. "Z" [HJH], "Anecdotes of McClellan's Bravery," *Century Illustrated Monthly Magazine*, XXXI (1886), p. 515.

21. Dwight L. Clarke, *Stephen Watts Kearny, Soldier of the West* (Norman: University of Oklahoma Press, 1961), pp. 128–45; Henry, *Story of the Mexican War*, pp. 107–20, 225–37.

22. *Messages of the President of the United States . . . on the Subject of the Mexican War* (Washington, D.C., 1848), pp. 994–95.

23. "Z," "Anecdotes of McClellan's Bravery," pp. 515–16; Wallace, *William Jenkins Worth*, pp. 133–34.

24. HJH to Bvt. Mjr. Isaac I. Stevens, Nov. 14, 1850, Stevens Papers, University of Washington Library.

25. *Message from the President of the United States, to the Two Houses of Congress, at the Commencement of the First Session of the Thirtieth Congress* (Washington, D.C., 1847), pp. 316–17.

26. Ibid., Appendix, p. 43; Lt. Col. Joseph E. Johnston to HJH, Sept. 3, 1858, HP-LC.

27. Edward D. Mansfield, *The Mexican War* (New York, 1848), pp. 283–84.

28. Ibid., pp. 286–88; *Message from the President to the Thirtieth Congress*, p. 448.

29. HJH to Thomas Gantt, May 17, 1886, HP-LC.

30. Raphael Semmes, *Service Afloat and Ashore During the Mexican War*

(Cincinnati, 1851), pp. 456–57; J.F.H. Claiborne, *Life and Correspondence of John A. Quitman* (2 vols. New York, 1860), I, pp. 357–63.

31. *Message from the President to the Thirtieth Congress*, Appendix, pp. 228–29. However, see also T. Harry Williams, ed., *With Beauregard in Mexico: The Mexican War Reminiscences of P.G.T. Beauregard* (Baton Rouge: Louisiana State University Press, 1956), p. 99.

32. *Message from the President to the Thirtieth Congress*, Appendix, pp. 171–72.

33. Semmes, *Service Afloat and Ashore*, pp. 458–60

34. *Message from the President to the Thirtieth Congress*, Appendix, p. 172.

35. Smith, *The War with Mexico*, II, pp. 161–62; *Complete History of the Late Mexican War. . . . By an Eye-Witness* (New York, 1850), pp. 97–98.

36. HJH to Capt. H.L. Scott, Jan. 6, 1848; Gen. Winfield Scott to HJH, Jan. 7, 1848; Lt. James Duncan to Capt. A.F. McReynolds, Oct. 30, 1847; all, HP-LC.

37. George R. Agassiz, ed., *Meade's Headquarters, 1863–1865: Letters of Colonel Theodore Lyman from the Wilderness to Appomattox* (Boston, 1922), p. 313; Lloyd Lewis, *Captain Sam Grant* (Boston: Little, Brown, 1950), pp. 260–61.

38. Long, *Memoirs of Robert E. Lee*, p. 70; Douglas Southall Freeman, *R.E. Lee* (4 vols. New York: Charles Scribner's Sons, 1934–35), I, p. 288.

39. Smith and Judah, eds., *Chronicles of the Gringos*, pp. 437–41; Scott, *Memoirs*, II, pp. 583–84.

CHAPTER 4

1. William E. Birkhimer, *Historical Sketch of Artillery* (Washington, D.C., 1884), p. 65; William L. Haskin, comp., *First Regiment of Artillery* (Portland, Me., 1879), p. 122.

2. "Sketch of Services of Col. Duncan," *Democratic Review*, I (1852), p. 202; Grady McWhiney, *Braxton Bragg, Volume I* (New York: Columbia University Press, 1969), p. 120.

3. Emily's mother was Harriet Elizabeth De Russy (d. 1834), second wife of a three-time widower, Lieutenant Colonel De Russy.

4. Information courtesy of Cmdr. J. Conway Hunt.

5. HJH, "Artillery Administration," *JMSIUS*, XII (1891), p. 213; HJH to Inspector Gen. G.W. McCall, Mar. 31, 1851, HP-LC.

6. Hazard Stevens, *Isaac Ingalls Stevens* (2 vols. Boston, 1900), I, p. 259. For examples of papers drawn up by Hunt, see HJH to Bvt. Mjr. Stevens, Apr. 6, 14, 1851, HP-LC.

7. HJH to Sen. James Shields, June 16, 1852, HP-LC; HJH to Bvt. Mjr. Stevens, Aug. 21, 1852, Stevens Papers.

8. HJH to Sen. Salmon P. Chase, Apr. 5, 1852, HP-LC; McWhiney, *Braxton Bragg, Volume I*, pp. 131–32. The full text of Shields's bill is in Birkhimer, *Historical Sketch of Artillery*, pp. 376–77.

9. HJH, "Artillery Administration," p. 213. Hunt's reforms did not meet with universal acceptance, even among artillery cohorts. Wrote his friend, John Sedgwick: "Mr. Shields['s] military reforms are likely to prove abortive—finding favor with few, and advocates in none": Sedgwick to anon., May 24, 1852, Gratz Collection, HSP.

10. W. A. Simpson, "Second Regiment of Artillery," in T.F. Rodenbough and William L. Haskin, eds., *Army of the United States* (New York, 1896), p. 318.

11. Ernest M. Lander and Robert K. Ackerman, eds., *Perspectives in South Carolina History: The First 300 Years* (Columbia: University of South Carolina Press, 1973), pp. 135–36.

12. Harold S. Schultz, *Nationalism and Sectionalism in South Carolina, 1852–1860* (Durham, N.C.: Duke University Press, 1950), pp. 27 and 41.

13. Post Returns, Fort Washita, 1853, M–617, R–1387, NA; Birkhimer, *Historical Sketch of Artillery*, pp. 66–67.

14. Edwin Bearss and Arrell M. Gibson, *Fort Smith: Little Gibraltar on the Arkansas* (Norman: University of Oklahoma Press, 1969), p. 218.

15. McWhiney, *Braxton Bragg, Volume I*, p. 137. The quote is Bragg's.

16. A.L. Long, *Memoirs of Robert E. Lee* (New York, 1887), pp. 17 and 75; *A&NJ*, May 8, 1886.

17. McWhiney, *Braxton Bragg, Volume I*, p. 139.

18. HJH to George B. McClellan, Dec. 13, 1867, McCP-LC.

19. A good exposition of the Uptonian model in tactical drill can be found in Russell F. Weigley, *History of the United States Army* (New York: Macmillan Co., 1967), pp. 275–76.

20. HJH to George B. McClellan, Dec. 13, 1867, McCP-LC.

21. HJH to J. B. Lippincott Co., May 24, 1875, HP-LC.

22. Birkhimer, *Historical Sketch of Artillery*, pp. 66–67; HJH, "Artillery Administration," p. 213..

23. Report of Board to Revise Artillery Tactics, Jan. 15, 1858, M–567, R–600, F–10, 1859, NA.

24. Francis Lord, *They Fought for the Union* (Harrisburg, Pa.: Stackpole Books, 1960), pp. 42–43; Fairfax Downey, *Sound of the Guns* (New York: David McKay Co., Inc., 1956), p. 88.

25. Birkhimer, *Historical Sketch of Artillery*, pp. 307–8, 323–24.

26. Hunt's Barry's, and French's text appeared in a second edition in 1863. If any defect can be attributed to it, it is a tendency to generalize about certain tactical details that called for specifics—doubtless a direct result of its rigorous cogency and brevity. This shortcoming was overcome in later, longer works, notably in John Gibbon's highly detailed *Artillerist's Manual* (New York, 1860).

27. David Fitzgerald, *In Memoriam: Gen. Henry J. Hunt, 1819–1889* (Washington, D.C., 1889), p. 3.

28. Information from gravestone in St. John's Cemetery, Hampton, Virginia. Courtesy of Cmdr. J. Conway Hunt.

29. Post Returns, Fort Leavenworth, Oct., 1857–Aug., 1858, M–617, R–611, NA; Elvid Hunt and Walter E. Lorence, *Fort Leavenworth* (Fort Leavenworth, Kans.: Command & General Staff School Press, 1937), pp. 231 and 284.

30. Edward J. Nichols, *Toward Gettysburg: A Biography of General John F. Reynolds* (University Park: Pennsylvania State University Press, 1958), pp. 57 and 65; Hunt and Lorence, *Fort Leavenworth*, p. 231.

31. The text of the order by which Company M was remounted is in Birkhimer, *Historical Sketch of Artillery*, p. 367. For data on the gun/howitzer, see Downey, *Sound of the Guns*, p. 120, and Stanley L. Falk, "How the Napoleon Came to America," *Civil War History*, X (June, 1964), pp. 149–54.

32. Allan Nevins, *The Emergence of Lincoln* (2 vols. New York: Charles Scribner's Sons, 1950), I, pp. 314–17; II, pp. 478–80; Charles P. Roland, *Albert Sidney Johnston, Soldier of Three Republics* (Austin: University of Texas Press, 1964), pp. 186–88.

33. Ray B. West, Jr., *Kingdom of the Saints: The Story of Brigham Young and the Mormons* (New York: Viking Press, 1957), pp. 258–60.

34. HJH, Journal of the Utah Expedition, May 28–Aug. 11, 1858, entries for May 28, June 21, July 4, 1858, HP-LC.

35. George Walton, *Sentinel of the Plains* (Englewood Cliffs, N.J.: Prentice-Hall, Inc., 1973), p. 86.

36. For background on Henry Knox Craig, see Robert V. Bruce, *Lincoln and the Tools of War* (Indianapolis: Bobbs-Merrill Co., 1956), p. 27.

37. The involved familial relationship between Hunt and his second wife goes like this: Mary Craig Hunt's grandmother was the second wife of Hunt's great-uncle, William Hunt (Colonel Thomas Hunt's older brother). Information from Hunt family genealogical charts, drawn especially for the author by Cmdr. J. Conway Hunt. For other family history details pertaining to the Craigs, see *The New-England Historical & Genealogical Register*, XLII (1888), p. 422.

38. HJH to Gen. Winfield Scott, July 9, 1859; Scott to Sec. John B. Floyd, July 13, 1859; both, HP-LC.

39. Post Returns, Fort Brown, Mar.–Dec., 1860, M–617, R–151, NA.

40. Copy of Family Register, Hunt family bible, courtesy of Cmdr. J. Conway Hunt. Though married in an Episcopalian rite, Mary Craig Hunt had been born and raised a Roman Catholic. On his deathbed in 1889, Hunt himself apparently converted to Catholicism.

CHAPTER 5

1. HJH, "Report of Service, 1861–63," copy in his ACPF.
2. John D. Imboden, "Jackson at Harper's Ferry in 1861," *B&L*, I, p. 125n.
3. Boyd B. Stutler, *West Virginia in the Civil War* (Charleston, W. Va.: Education Foundation, Inc., 1966), p. 16; Donald B. Webster, Jr., "The Last Days of Harpers Ferry Armory," *Civil War History*, V (March, 1959), p. 37.
4. Manly Wade Wellman, *Harpers Ferry: Prize of War* (Charlotte, N.C.: McNally, Inc., 1960), p. 5; Webster, "Last Days of Harpers Ferry Armory," p. 32.
5. See map in *B&L*, I, p. 115.
6. Post Returns, Harpers Ferry, Jan.–Apr., 1861, M–617, R–455, NA.
7. *OR*, Series I, Volume 51, part 1, pp. 310–11; copy of Adj. Gen. Samuel Cooper to HJH, Jan. 16, 1861, courtesy of Cmdr. J. Conway Hunt.
8. HJH to R.U. Johnson, Apr. 14, 1887, *Cen*-C. Mjr. Nichols had married Emily De Russy's older sister, Clara, in 1850.
9. Caroline Baldwin Darrow, "Recollections of the Twiggs- Surrender," *B&L*, I, pp. 35–39; *Philadelphia Inquirer*, Feb. 26, Mar. 1, 4, Apr. 1, 1861.
10. E.D. Townsend, *Anecdotes of the Civil War in the United States* (New York, 1884), pp. 48–50; William L. Haskin, comp., *First Regiment of Artillery* (Portland, Me., 1879), pp. 136–39.
11. Post Returns, Harpers Ferry, Feb. 1, 1861, M–617, R–455, NA; Wellman, *Harpers Ferry*, p. 19.
12. Frank Moore, ed., *The Rebellion Record: A Diary of American Events* (12 vols. New York, 1861–68), I, p. 30; Stutler, *West Virginia in the Civil War*, p. 17.
13. *Philadelphia Inquirer*, Apr. 13, 1861.
14. HJH, "Report of Service, 1861–63"; *OR*, I, 1, pp. 369–70.
15. Mark M. Boatner, III, *The Civil War Dictionary* (New York: David McKay Co., Inc., 1959), p. 597.
16. Post Returns, Fort Pickens, Mar. 1, 1861, M–617, R–913, NA; J.H. Gilman, "With Slemmer in Pensacola Harbor," *B&L*, I, pp. 26–27.
17. John E. Johns, *Florida During the Civil War* (Gainesville: University of Florida Press, 1963), p. 26.
18. E.D. Keyes, *Fifty Years' Observation of Men and Events, Civil and Military* (New York, 1884), pp. 385–86.
19. John C. Tidball, "Memoirs," MS. in LC, ll 153–54.
20. *OR-N*, Series I, Volume 4, p. 107.
21. *OR*, I, 1, pp. 369–70.
22. HJH, "The Second Expedition [to Reinforce Fort Pickens]," *JMSIUS*, XLV (1909), pp. 273, 274n, 275n; Post Returns, Fort Pickens, Apr., 1861, M–617, R–913, NA.
23. Russell F. Weigley, *Quartermaster General of the Union Army: A Biography of M.C. Meigs* (New York: Columbia University Press, 1959), pp. 149–53.
24. HJH, "The Second Expedition," p. 274; *OR-N*, I, 4, p. 142.
25. Grady McWhiney, *Braxton Bragg, Volume I* (New York: Columbia University Press, 1969), p. 171; Johns, *Florida During the Civil War*, p. 45.
26. HJH to Bragg, Apr. 23, 1861, TS. in U.S. Military History Research Collection, Army War College.

CHAPTER 6

1. John E. Johns, *Florida During the Civil War* (Gainesville: University of Florida Press, 1963), p. 47.
2. HJH, "The Second Expedition," *JMSIUS*, XLV (1909), p. 274; *OR*, I, 1, p. 427.
3. Ibid., I, 52, pt. 1, p. 184.
4. HJH, "Report of Service, 1861–63," copy in his ACPF; *New York Times*, July 13, 1861.
5. *JCCW* (1863-Volume II), p. 143.
6. HJH, "Report of Service, 1861–63."
7. HJH, *Report of Light Battery M, Second Artillery, U.S.A., Under Command of Major Henry J. Hunt: Battle of Bull Run, July 21st, 1861* (Washington, D.C.,

1861), p. 4. This is a republication of Hunt's official report (*OR*, I, 2, pp. 377–81).

8. *New York Times*, Feb. 17, 1889.

9. HJH, "Report of Service, 1861–63."

10. James C. Bush, "The Fifth Regiment of Artillery," in T.F. Rodenbough and William L. Haskin, eds., *The Army of the United States* (New York, 1896), p. 376; William E. Birkhimer, *Historical Sketch of Artillery* (Washington, D.C., 1884), pp. 52–53, 69.

11. HJH, *Report of Light Battery M*, p. 1.

12. R.M. Johnston, *Bull Run: Its Strategy and Tactics* (Boston, 1913), pp. 130–35.

13. Thomas M. Vincent, "The Battle of Bull Run, July 21, 1861," *District of Columbia MOLLUS: War Paper 58* (1905), p. 21; *OR*, I, 2, pp. 374 and 381.

14. Joseph Mills Hanson, *Bull Run Remembers* (Manassas, Va.: National Capitol Publishers, 1957), pp. 21–22; *A&NJ*, Feb. 16, 1889.

15. Johnston, *Bull Run*, pp. 144–46; R.H. Beatie, Jr., *Road to Manassas: The Growth of Union Command in the Eastern Theatre* (New York: Cooper Square Publishers, 1961), pp. 135–41.

16. HJH, *Report of Light Battery M*, pp. 1–2.

17. Beatie, *Road to Manassas*, p. 179.

18. HJH, *Report of Light Battery M*, p. 1.

19. Johnston, *Bull Run*, pp. 224–35.

20. HJH, *Report of Light Battery M*, p. 2.

21. William Miller Owen, *In Camp and Battle with the Washington Artillery of New Orleans* (Boston, 1885), p. 42; L. Van Loan Naisawald, "Bull Run: The Artillery and the Infantry," *Civil War History*, III (June, 1957), pp. 174–75.

22. George Alphonso Gibbs, "With a Mississippi Private in a Little Known Part of the Battle of First Bull Run," *Civil War Times Illustrated*, IV (April, 1965), p. 45.

23. Hanson, *Bull Run Remembers*, p. 174. For a clear expression of the enemy's attitude toward Hunt's combativeness, see Mjr. G. Campbell Brown to HJH, Jan. 27, 1885, HP-LC.

24. Vincent, "Battle of Bull Run," p. 23.

25. HJH, *Report of Light Battery M*, p. 3.

26. David Fitzgerald, *In Memoriam* (Washington, D.C., 1889), p. 5. For more official praise extended to Hunt at Bull Run, see *OR*, I, 2, p. 431.

CHAPTER 7

1. HJH, "Artillery Administration," *JMSIUS*, XII (1891), p. 216.

2. *OR*, I, 51, pt. 1, p. 423; Special Orders 42, July 23, 1861, Records of Headquarters, Department of Northeastern Virginia, RG–393, E–3684, NA.

3. Warren Hassler, Jr., *General George B. McClellan: Shield of the Union* (Baton Rouge: Louisiana State University Press, 1957), p. 20.

4. Ibid., pp. 23–34.

5. George B. McClellan, *McClellan's Own Story* (New York, 1887), pp. 114–16.

6. J.G. Barnard and W.F. Barry, *Report of the Engineer and Artillery Operations of the Army of the Potomac, from Its Organization to the Close of the Peninsula Campaign* (New York, 1863), p. 105; *The Atlantic Monthly*, XIII (1864), p. 387.

7. John C. Tidball, "Memoirs," MS. in LC, 1 113.

8. L. Van Loan Naisawald, *Grape and Canister: The Story of the Field Artillery of the Army of the Potomac, 1861–1865* (New York: Oxford University Press, 1960), p. 40.

9. Barnard and Barry, *Report of Engineer and Artillery Operations*, p. 106; George B. McClellan, *Report on the Organization and Campaigns of the Army of the Potomac* (New York, 1864), pp. 12–13.

10. *OR*, I, 46, pt. 2, pp. 83–84.

11. W.F. Barry to HJH, Sept. 12, 1861, HP-LC.

12. William E. Birkhimer, *Historical Sketch of Artillery* (Washington, D.C., 1884), p. 213.

13. HJH, "Artillery Administration," pp. 217–18.

14. Birkhimer, *Historical Sketch of Artillery*, p. 213; *OR*, I, 46, pt. 2, p. 85. Long after the war, Hunt reviewed the War Department's bias against ranking artillerists:

"This *doubled* my labors and responsibilities, it took from me all hope of making the artillery service what it should be, it condemned me to hopeless hard labor, without prospect of reward either in rank or reputation." Still he served. HJH to Thomas Gantt, Apr. 17, 1888, HP-LC.

15. The situation was further complicated when in 1862 General-in-Chief Halleck decreed that (in Hunt's words) "a battery was equal to a regiment of infantry, that it was commanded by a captain, therefore could not need field officers.": HJH, "Artillery Administration," pp. 217–18.

16. *McClellan's Own Story*, p. 114.

17. Family Register, Hunt family bible, courtesy of Cmdr. J. Conway Hunt.

18. Naisawald, *Grape and Canister*, p. 40.

19. John Gibbon, *Personal Recollections of the Civil War* (New York: G. P. Putnam's Sons, 1928), p. 15.

20. Allan Nevins, ed., *A Diary of Battle: The Personal Journals of Colonel Charles S. Wainwright, 1861–1865* (New York: Harcourt, Brace & World, 1962), p. ix.

21. *OR*, I, 5, p. 92.

22. Ibid., pp. 15 and 19; I, 51, pt. 1, p. 528; "The Opposing Forces in the Seven Days' Battles," *B&L*, II, p. 315.

23. *OR*, III, 1, p. 676; David Fitzgerald, *In Memoriam* (Washington, D.C., 1889), p. 6.

24. Birkhimer, *Historical Sketch of Artillery*, pp. 296–97, 297n; HJH to George B. McClellan, Dec. 16, 1861, HP-LC.

25. HJH to Headquarters, Army of the Potomac, Jan. 13, 1862, Ibid. For more on the Stevens Battery, see *Senate Executive Document 34*, Mar. 24, 1862 (37th Cong., 2nd Sess.), p. 1; *New York Sun*, Apr. 26, 1904; and William C. Davis, *Duel Between the First Ironclads* (Garden City, N.Y.: Doubleday & Co., Inc., 1975), p. 5.

26. W.F. Barry to HJH, Oct. 12, 13, 1861, Hunt Papers, New-York Historical Society. See also marginal comments added by Hunt three months after the fact.

27. George B. McClellan to anon., Nov. 8, 1861, McCP-LC.

28. Hassler, *General George B. McClellan*, pp. 70–71.

CHAPTER 8

1. Joseph P. Cullen, *The Peninsula Campaign, 1862: McClellan & Lee Struggle for Richmond* (Harrisburg, Pa.: Stackpole Books, 1973), p. 15.

2. *OR*, I, 4, p. 571.

3. James M. Bugbee, ed., *Massachusetts Society of the Cincinnati* (Boston, 1890), p. 275.

4. HJH, "Report of Service, 1861–63," in his ACPF; *OR*, I, 5, p. 19.

5. HJH to Gen. Rufus Ingalls, Sept. 30, 1863, Records of Headquarters, Chief of Artillery, Army of the Potomac, RG–393, E–4005, NA.

6. E.B. Bennett, comp., *First Connecticut Heavy Artillery: Historical Sketch* (East Berlin, Conn., 1890), p. 17.

7. Bruce Catton, *Terrible Swift Sword* (Garden City, N.Y.: Doubleday & Co., Inc., 1963), pp. 294–95.

8. Ibid., pp. 270–72; Cullen, *Peninsula Campaign*, p. 42.

9. E.D. Keyes, *Fifty Years' Observation* (New York, 1884), p. 442.

10. Ibid., p. 446; Warren Hassler, Jr., *General George B. McClellan* (Baton Rouge: Louisiana State University Press, 1957), pp. 88–90.

11. "Z" [HJH], "Anecdotes of McClellan's Bravery," *Century Illustrated Monthly Magazine*, XXXI (1886), p. 516.

12. Warren Ripley, *Artillery and Ammunition of the Civil War* (New York: Van Nostrand Reinhold Co., 1970), pp. 249–50; *OR*, I, 46, pt. 2, p. 84.

13. During an early phase of the Yorktown siege, Hunt also had a little-publicized run-in with a Republican politico, Senator Zachariah Chandler of Michigan. Visiting at McClellan's headquarters, Chandler tried Hunt's patience with an incessant clamor about the enemy garrison, which he considered much too weak to warrant a tedious investment: "Where are the lines drawn? Where is the enemy anyway?" Finally Hunt's patience broke and he instructed one of his aides: "Capt. Bissell, take Mr. Chandler

along the lines and draw the enemy's fire!" Bissell did as told, guiding the senator so close to the rebels that Chandler's position was laced with a fearful shelling by masked batteries. The senator was not injured, though an observer found him "frightened to death," and very quiet during the remainder of his visit to the army: *Eunice Tripler: Personal Recollections* (New York, 1910), p. 144.

14. John C. Tidball, "The Artillery Service in the War of the Rebellion," *JMSIUS*, XII (1891), pp. 710–12.

15. HJH, "Report of Service, 1861–63."

16. "Opposing Forces at Seven Pines, May 31–June 1, 1862," *B&L*, II, p. 219; Lt. Col. William Hays to HJH, June 6, 1862, Tidball Papers, USMA-L; Alexander S. Webb, *The Peninsula: McClellan's Campaign of 1862* (New York, 1881), p. 104.

17. HJH, Orders 94, June 20, 1862, Records of Headquarters, Artillery Reserve, Army of the Potomac, RG–393, E–4011, NA.

18. *OR*, I, 11, pt. 2, pp. 236–37; Lt. Col. William Hays to HJH, July 7, 1862, Tidball Papers, USMA-L; E.M. Law, "On the Confederate Right at Gaines's Mill," *B&L*, II, p. 363.

19. Fitz-John Porter to McClellan, June 27, 1862, McCP-LC.

20. Clifford Dowdey, *The Seven Days: The Emergence of Lee* (Boston: Little, Brown, 1964), pp. 209 and 244.

21. Webb, *The Peninsula*, p. 151.

22. *OR*, I, 11, pt. 2, p. 238; Cullen, *Peninsula Campaign*, p. 146.

23. Fitz-John Porter, "The Battle of Malvern Hill," *B&L*, II, p. 411; Joel Cook, *The Siege of Richmond* (Philadelphia, 1862), p. 335.

24. Dowdey, *The Seven Days*, p. 325; Fairfax Downey, *Cannonade: Great Artillery Actions of History* (Garden City, N.Y.: Doubleday & Co., Inc., 1966), p. 185.

25. *JCCW* (1863-I), p. 573.

26. Samuel Appleton, "The Battle of Malvern Hill," *Military Essays and Recollections: Illinois MOLLUS*, III (1899), pp. 37–38; HJH to Gen. Rufus Ingalls, Sept. 30, 1863, Records of Headquarters, Chief of Artillery, Army of the Potomac, RG–393, E–4005, NA.

27. John Lamb, "Malvern Hill—July 1, 1862," *SHSP*, XXV (1897), pp. 213–14; J.J. Marks, *The Peninsula Campaign in Virginia* (Philadelphia, 1864), p. 292.

28. Porter, "The Battle of Malvern Hill," pp. 419–21.

29. Marks, *The Peninsula Campaign*, p. 293; William H. Powell, *The Fifth Army Corps* (New York, 1896), p. 170.

30. William W. Averell, "With the Cavalry on the Peninsula," *B&L*, II, p. 432; Daniel H. Hill, "McClellan's Change of Base and Malvern Hill," Ibid., p. 394.

31. Fitz-John Porter to McClellan, July 1, 1862, McCP-LC; HJH to Porter, July 29, 1881, Webb Papers.

32. Porter to HJH, July 26, 1881, Ibid.; *OR*, I, 51, pt. 1, p. 721.

33. "Opposing Forces at Seven Pines," p. 219; "The Opposing Forces in the Seven Days' Battles," *B&L*, II, pp. 315 and 317.

34. Downey, *Cannonade*, p. 190.

35. *OR*, I, 19, pt. 1, p. 205.

36. HJH to Thomas Gantt, Feb. 11, 1882, Fitz-John Porter Papers, USMA-L.

37. L. Van Loan Naisawald, *Grape and Canister* (New York: Oxford University Press, 1960), pp. 146, 148–49; Jennings C. Wise, *The Long Arm of Lee, Or the History of the Artillery of the Army of Northern Virginia* (2 vols. Lynchburg, Va., 1915), I, p. 276.

38. For a self-appraisal of McClellan's frame of mind when reassuming field command, see his "Antietam Campaign," ll 10–11, TS. in McCP-LC.

39. *OR*, I, 12, pt. 3, p. 693; Richard B. Irwin, "The Case of Fitz-John Porter," *B&L*, II, p. 695; John Pope, "The Second Battle of Bull Run," Ibid., pp. 492–93.

40. *JCCW* (1865-I), p. 92.

41. *OR*, I, 19, pt. 2, p. 188.

42. William E. Birkhimer, *Historical Sketch of Artillery* (Washington, D.C., 1884), p. 98.

43. HJH, "Report of Service, 1861–63."

44. Tidball, "Artillery Service in the War," p. 974; *JCCW* (1865-I), p. 92.

45. *OR*, I, 19, pt. 1, p. 205.

46. McClellan to HJH, July 30, 1863, HP-LC.

47. Naisawald, *Grape and Canister*, pp. 188 and 227.
48. Wise, *Long Arm of Lee*, I, pp. 298–99; Tidball, "Artillery Service in the War," p. 958.
49. HJH to McClellan, Apr. 5, 1864, McCP-NJHS.
50. David Fitzgerald, *In Memoriam* (Washington, D.C., 1889), p. 7.
51. Allan Nevins, ed., *A Diary of Battle* (New York: Harcourt, Brace & World, 1962), p. 336.
52. *OR*, I, 21, p. 838; Naisawald, *Grape and Canister*, pp. 241–42, 568n.
53. Richard B. Irwin, "The Removal of McClellan," *B&L*, III, pp. 103–4.

CHAPTER 9

1. *JCCW* (1865-I), p. 92.
2. Allan Nevins, ed., *A Diary of Battle* (New York: Harcourt, Brace & World, 1962), pp. 107, 114, 129, 131.
3. HJH to War Department, n.d., HP-LC.
4. L. Van Loan Naisawald, *Grape and Canister* (New York: Oxford University Press, 1960), pp. 229–30.
5. *OR*, I, 21, pp. 49, 827–28.
6. Bruce Catton, *Glory Road: The Bloody Route from Fredricksburg to Gettysburg* (Garden City, N.Y.: Doubleday & Co., Inc., 1952), pp. 21–23.
7. Ibid., p. 34; *JCCW* (1863-I), p. 690.
8. Bruce Catton, *Never Call Retreat* (Garden City, N.Y.: Doubleday & Co., Inc., 1965), p. 17.
9. William Farrar Smith, "Franklin's 'Left Grand Division,' " *B&L*, III, pp. 129–30; Nevins, ed., *A Diary of Battle*, p. 150.
10. *OR*, I, 21, p. 181; Edward J. Stackpole, *Drama on the Rappahannock: The Fredricksburg Campaign* (Harrisburg, Pa.: Stackpole Books, 1957), p. 160.
11. HJH, "Artillery Administration," *JMSIUS*, XII (1891), p. 221.
12. *OR*, I, 21, p. 753.
13. Naisawald, *Grape and Canister*, pp. 236–38.
14. Vorin E. Whan, Jr., *Fiasco at Fredricksburg* (University Park: Pennsylvania State University Press, 1961), pp. 32–33; George W. Cullum, *Memoir of Brevet Major-General Robert Ogden Tyler* (Philadelphia, 1878), p. 14.
15. *OR*, I, 21, pp. 180–82; Francis A. Walker, *History of the Second Army Corps in the Army of the Potomac* (New York, 1886), p. 146.
16. *OR*, I, 21, p. 170. The sequence of events that follows is drawn from Naisawald, *Grape and Canister*, pp. 238–44.
17. *OR*, I, 21, pp. 170 and 182.
18. HJH to C.C. Buel, May 16, 1886, *Cen*-C.
19. John H. Rhodes, *History of Battery B, First Regiment Rhode Island Light Artillery* (Providence, 1894), p. 138; *Frank Leslie's Illustrated Newspaper*, Dec. 27, 1862; Stackpole, *Drama on the Rappahannock*, p. 136.
20. James Longstreet, "The Battle of Fredricksburg," *B&L*, III, p. 75; Shelby Foote, *The Civil War: A Narrative* (3 vols. New York: Random House, 1958–74), II, p. 28.
21. HJH to C.C. Buel, May 16, 1886, *Cen*-C.
22. Marginal comments, HJH to Ambrose E. Burnside, Apr. 10, 1863, HP-LC.
23. Ibid.; *OR*, I, 21, p. 282; William Swinton, *Campaigns of the Army of the Potomac* (New York, 1882), p. 241.
24. Marginal comments, HJH to Burnside, Apr. 10, 1863, HP-LC.
25. HJH, "Battle of Fredricksburg & Passages of the Rappahannock," MS. in Ibid.; J.H. Stine, *History of the Army of the Potomac* (Philadelphia, 1892), p. 257; *OR*, I, 21, pp. 89 and 170.
26. Smith, "Franklin's 'Left Grand Division,' " pp. 133–36; Arthur L. Wagner *Organization and Tactics* (Kansas City, Mo., 1894), p. 321.
27. Catton, *Glory Road*, pp. 49–60; Longstreet, "Battle of Fredricksburg," p. 73; Whan, *Fiasco at Fredricksburg*, p. 33.
28. Catton, *Never Call Retreat*, p. 22; "The Opposing Forces at Fredricksburg, Va.," *B&L*, III, p. 145.

29. *OR,* I, 21, pp. 76–77; HJH, "On the Passage of the [Rappahannock] River on January 6th, 1863," MS. in HP-LC.

30. HJH, Journal of the Appomattox Campaign, entry for Apr. 10, 1865, in possession of Cmdr. J. Conway Hunt.

31. *OR,* I, 21, pp. 752–53; E.P. Alexander, *Military Memoirs of a Confederate* (New York, 1912), p. 314; Diary of Pvt. John K. Alloway (Battery B, First Pennsylvania Light Artillery), entry for Jan. 22, 1863, HSP.

32. Rhodes, *Battery B, 1st Rhode Island,* p. 156.

CHAPTER 10

1. David S. Sparks, ed., *Inside Lincoln's Army: The Diary of Marsena Rudolph Patrick, Provost Marshal General, Army of the Potomac* (New York: Thomas Yoseloff, 1964), p. 210.

2. *Charles Francis Adams, 1835–1915: An Autobiography* (Boston, 1916), p. 161. Hunt shared Adams's opinion of "Fighting Joe."

3. Bruce Catton, *Glory Road* (Garden City, N.Y.: Doubleday & Co., Inc., 1952), p. 95; Walter H. Hebert, *Fighting Joe Hooker* (Indianapolis: Bobbs-Merrill Co., 1944), pp. 65 and 180.

4. Ibid., pp. 177 and 183; Darius N. Couch, "The Chancellorsville Campaign," *B&L,* III, pp. 154 and 156.

5. HJH, "The First Day at Gettysburg," Ibid., p. 259; Allan Nevins, ed., *A Diary of Battle* (New York: Harcourt, Brace & World, 1962), pp. 165 and 215.

6. *JCCW* (1865-I), pp. 92–93; HJH, "First Day at Gettysburg," p. 259.

7. Hooker to HJH, Mar. 6, 1863, HP-LC.

8. HJH to Burnside, Apr. 10, 1863, Ibid.

9. Nevins, ed., *A Diary of Battle,* p. 164; L. Van Loan Naisawald, *Grape and Canister* (New York: Oxford University Press, 1960), p. 273.

10. HJH, "Artillery Administration," *JMSIUS,* XII (1891), p. 219; *OR,* I, 25, pt. 2, pp. 98, 130–31.

11. Nevins, ed., *A Diary of Battle,* p. 175.

12. HJH to the Adjutant Gen., Mar. 10, 1863, in his ACPF.

13. Hans L. Trefousse, "The Joint Committee on the Conduct of the War: A Reassessment," *Civil War History,* X (March, 1964), pp. 5–19; T. Harry Williams, "Investigation, 1862," *American Heritage,* VI (December, 1954), pp. 16–21.

14. *JCCW* (1863-I), pp. 571–72, 690.

15. Ibid., p. 575.

16. John Bigelow, Jr., *The Campaign of Chancellorsville: A Strategic and Tactical Study* (New Haven, Conn., 1910), pp. 139–53; Edward J. Stackpole, *Chancellorsville: Lee's Greatest Battle* (Harrisburg, Pa.: Stackpole Books, 1958), pp. 90–109.

17. Theodore A. Dodge, *The Campaign of Chancellorsville* (Boston, 1881), pp. 27–36.

18. This gave Hooker an aggregate of 422 cannon, thirty-eight of them in the horse artillery, forty-eight in the Reserve, the rest in the field army. See Mjr. Alexander Doull to HJH, Feb. 17, 1863, "Military Papers," HP-LC.

19. Naisawald, *Grape and Canister,* pp. 274–75.

20. *OR,* I, 25, pt. 1, pp. 246–47.

21. Ibid., p. 246; *JCCW* (1865-I), p. 89; "E.S.Allen, Aeronaut [Observation Balloonist]" to HJH, c. Apr. 28, 1863, in possession of Cmdr. J. Conway Hunt.

22. Dodge, *Chancellorsville,* pp. 32–55; Naisawald, *Grape and Canister,* p. 277.

23. Catton, *Glory Road,* pp. 184–85.

24. *OR,* I, 25, pt. 1, p. 248.

25. *JCCW* (1865-I), pp. 89–90.

26. Ibid.; *OR,* I, 25, pt. 1, p. 248.

27. Matthew Forney Steele, *American Campaigns* (2 vols. Washington, D.C.: Combat Forces Press, 1951), I, p. 169; Hebert, *Fighting Joe Hooker,* pp. 206–10; HJH to C.C. Buel, Aug. 25, 1886, *Cen*-C.

28. Dodge, *Chancellorsville,* pp. 165–208; *JCCW* (1865-I), p. 90.

29. Nevins, ed., *A Diary of Battle,* pp. 193–94.

30. Sparks, ed., *Inside Lincoln's Army*, pp. 242–43; *OR*, I, 25, pt. 1, pp. 250–51, 381, 557; Col. Charles Wainwright to HJH, Aug. 4, 1863; and HJH to War Department, n.d.; both, HP-LC.

31. *JCCW* (1865-I), p. 90; Nevins, ed., *A Diary of Battle*, p. 200.

32. HJH, "Report of Service, 1861–63," in his ACPF; *OR*, I, 25, pt. 1, p. 252; Jennings C. Wise, *Long Arm of Lee* (2 vols. Lynchburg, Va., 1915), II, p. 546.

33. Edwin B. Coddington, *The Gettysburg Campaign: A Study in Command* (New York: Charles Scribner's Sons, 1968), p. 42; Hebert, *Fighting Joe Hooker*, pp. 177 and 223.

34. G.J. Fiebeger, *The Campaign and Battle of Gettysburg* (West Point, N.Y., 1912), p. 22; *JCCW* (1865-I), p. 94; Special Orders 129, May 12, 1863, HP-LC; *OR*, I, 25, pt. 2, p. 440; Coddington, *Gettysburg Campaign*, pp. 40–41; Earl Fenner, *The History of Battery H, First Regiment Rhode Island Light Artillery* (Providence, 1894), p. 19.

35. Catherine S. Crary, ed., *Dear Belle: Letters from a Cadet & Officer to His Sweetheart, 1858–65* (Middletown, Conn.: Wesleyan University Press, 1965), p. 195.

36. *OR*, I, 25, pt. 1, pp. 252–53.

CHAPTER 11

1. Edwin B. Coddington, *Gettysburg Campaign* (New York: Charles Scribner's Sons, 1968), pp. 130–32, 209.

2. Bruce Catton, *Glory Road* (Garden City, N.Y.: Doubleday & Co., Inc., 1952), p. 257.

3. "The Opposing Forces at Gettysburg," *B&L*, III, pp. 434–37.

4. *JCCW* (1865-I), p. 448; HJH, "The Second Day at Gettysburg," *B&L*, III, pp. 290–91.

5. Frederic Shriver Klein, "Meade's Pipe Creek Line," *Maryland Historical Magazine*, LVII (1962), pp. 135 and 146.

6. HJH, "Second Day at Gettysburg," p. 290.

7. HJH to C.C. Buel, Sept. 26, 1886, *Cen*-C; HJH to Alexander S. Webb, Jan. 19, 1888, Webb Papers.

8. HJH, "Second Day at Gettysburg," p. 291.

9. George G. Meade, Jr., *With Meade at Gettysburg* (Philadelphia: John C. Winston Co., 1930), p. 95.

10. For information on artillery's part in the 1 July fighting (in addition, of course, to Hunt's "First Day at Gettysburg"), see L. Van Loan Naisawald, *Grape and Canister* (New York: Oxford University Press, 1960), pp. 338–62; Fairfax Downey, *The Guns at Gettysburg* (New York: David McKay Co., Inc., 1958), pp. 15–57; *OR*, I, 27, pt. 1, pp. 228–32; and John H. Calef, "Gettysburg Notes: The Opening Gun," *JMSIUS*, XL (1907), pp. 40–58.

11. *JCCW* (1865-I), p. 448; *OR*, I, 27, pt. 1, p. 232.

12. Meade, *With Meade at Gettysburg*, p. 96.

13. Downey, *The Guns at Gettysburg*, p. 119; HJH, Journal of Siege Operations, Apr. 16, 1864–Mar. 23, 1865, marginal comments beside entries for May 25–27, 1864, HP-LC.

14. William E. Birkhimer, *Historical Sketch of Artillery* (Washington, D.C., 1884), p. 102n.

15. *JCCW* (1865-I), p. 448; *OR*, I, 27, pt. 1, pp. 232–33.

16. HJH to Alexander S. Webb, Jan. 19, 1888, Webb Papers; HJH, "Second Day at Gettysburg," pp. 297, 299–300.

17. Coddington, *Gettysburg Campaign*, p. 336. For a wry glance at one facet of Col. McGilvery's lifestyle, see Washington Davis, *Camp-Fire Chats of the Civil War* (Chicago, 1887), pp. 284–85.

18. Warren Ripley, *Artillery and Ammunition of the Civil War* (New York: Van Nostrand Reinhold Co., 1970), pp. 164–65; Henry L. Abbot, *Siege Artillery in the Campaigns Against Richmond* (New York, 1868), pp. 152–53.

19. HJH to C.C. Buel, Aug. 25, 1886, *Cen*-C.

20. *JCCW* (1865-I), p. 449.

21. Meade, *With Meade at Gettysburg*, p. 110; Glenn Tucker, *High Tide at Gettysburg: The Campaign in Pennsylvania* (Indianapolis: Bobbs-Merrill Co., 1958), pp. 238–39.

22. Henry E. Tremain, *Two Days of War: A Gettysburg Narrative* (New York, 1905), pp. 43–44; HJH, "Second Day at Gettysburg," p. 301.

23. W.A. Swanberg, *Sickles the Incredible* (New York: Charles Scribner's Sons, 1956), p. 211.

24. Tucker, *High Tide at Gettysburg*, p. 239; "The Meade-Sickles Controversy," *B&L*, III, pp. 415–16. Sickles also wanted the Emmitsburg Road held so that his errant ammunition train might use it and thus reach him as quickly as possible: George Meade, Jr., "Notes on 5th Corps & Round Tops at Gettysburg," Fitz-John Porter Papers, LC.

25. *JCCW* (1865-I), pp. 449–50; *OR*, I, 27, pt. 1, p. 233.

26. HJH, "Second Day at Gettysburg," p. 303.

27. *JCCW* (1865-I), p. 453; Coddington, *Gettysburg Campaign*, p. 345.

28. *OR*, I, 27, pt. 1, pp. 234–35.

29. Ibid., p. 235; Downey, *The Guns at Gettysburg*, pp. 78–79.

30. James E. Smith, *A Famous Battery and Its Campaigns, 1861–'64* (Washington, D.C., 1892), pp. 10–12; *JCCW* (1865-I), pp. 450–51.

31. HJH, "Second Day at Gettysburg," pp. 305–6.

32. Michael Hanifen, *History of Battery B, First New Jersey Artillery* (Ottawa, Ill., 1905), p. 77.

33. Jesse Bowman Young, *The Battle of Gettysburg: A Comprehensive Narrative* (New York, 1913), p. 229; HJH, "Second Day at Gettysburg," pp. 306–11; *OR*, I, 27, pt. 1, p. 236.

34. Frank P. Deane, II, ed., *"My Dear Wife": The Civil War Letters of David Brett, 9th Massachusetts Battery* (Little Rock, Ark.: Pioneer Press, 1964), pp. 59–61. The most detailed account of this phase of the battle is John Bigelow, *The Peach Orchard: Gettysburg, July 2, 1863* (Minneapolis, 1910).

35. Hanifen, *Battery B, 1st New Jersey*, p. 77; Smith, *A Famous Battery*, p. 104. Here the most comprehensive source is Oliver W. Norton, *The Attack and Defense of Little Round Top, Gettysburg, July 2, 1863* (New York, 1913).

36. Swanberg, *Sickles the Incredible*, pp. 216–17. A partial list of Hunt's 2 July losses can be found in *OR*, I, 27, pt. 1, p. 237.

CHAPTER 12

1. *OR*, I, 27, pt. 1, p. 237.

2. Ibid., pp. 234 and 237; *Philadelphia Weekly Times*, May 31, 1879; *JCCW* (1865-I), p. 451.

3. Ibid., p. 452.

4. Allan Nevins, ed., *A Diary of Battle* (New York: Harcourt, Brace & World, 1962), p. 246.

5. *OR*, I, 27, pt. 1, pp. 237–38.

6. *History of the Fifth Massachusetts Battery* (Boston, 1902), p. 651; Frederick Fuger, "Cushing's Battery at Gettysburg," *JMSIUS*, XLI (1907), p. 407.

7. HJH, "The Third Day at Gettysburg," *B&L*, III, pp. 371–72.

8. E.P. Alexander, *Military Memoirs of a Confederate* (New York, 1912), pp. 418–19.

9. Jesse Bowman Young, *Battle of Gettysburg* (New York, 1913), p. 298; *OR*, I, 27, pt. 1, p. 238.

10. Fairfax Downey, *The Guns at Gettysburg* (New York: David McKay Co., Inc., 1958), pp. 123–24, 149; Edwin B. Coddington, *Gettysburg Campaign* (New York: Charles Scribner's Sons, 1968), p. 496.

11. Benjamin F. Rittenhouse, "The Battle of Gettysburg as Seen from Little Round Top," *District of Columbia MOLLUS: War Paper 3* (1887), p. 9.

12. L. Van Loan Naisawald, *Grape and Canister* (New York: Oxford University Press, 1960), p. 415.

13. HJH, "Third Day at Gettysburg," pp. 373–74.

14. Nevins, ed., *A Diary of Battle,* p. 249; Fuger, "Cushing's Battery at Gettysburg," pp. 407–8; Rittenhouse, "Gettysburg from Little Round Top," p. 10.

15. Alexander, *Military Memoirs of a Confederate,* p. 418; E.P. Alexander to HJH, June 27, 1879, HP-LC.

16. HJH, "Third Day at Gettysburg," pp. 373–74.

17. HJH to War Department, n.d., HP-LC.

18. B.D. Fry, "Pettigrew's Charge at Gettysburg," *SHSP,* VII (1879), p. 92. For other Confederates' reactions to Hunt's counterbattery barrage, see C.A. Fonerden, *A Brief History of the Military Career of Carpenter's Battery* (New Market, Va., 1911), p. 43; and R.W. Figg, *"Where Men Only Dare to Go!" or, the Story of a Boy Company* (Richmond, 1885), pp. 142 and 144.

19. *Philadelphia Weekly Times,* May 31, 1879; George R. Stewart, *Pickett's Charge: A Micro-history of the Final Attack at Gettysburg, July 3, 1863* (Boston: Houghton Mifflin Co., 1959), pp. 154–55.

20. HJH, "Third Day at Gettysburg," p. 374.

21. Downey, *The Guns at Gettysburg,* pp. 137–38.

22. Glenn Tucker, *Hancock the Superb* (Indianapolis: Bobbs-Merrill Co., 1960), p. 152.

23. HJH to War Department, n.d.; Capt. Patrick Hart to HJH, Aug. 27, 1879; both, HP-LC.

24. Nevins, ed., *A Diary of Battle,* p. 253; Gen. Winfield S. Hancock to House Committee on Military Affairs, Jan. 22, 1874, quoted in *HR 594,* May 13, 1874 (43rd Cong., 1st Sess.), III, p. 8.

25. More than twenty years after the fact, controversy arose anew over whether Hancock or Hunt had the better idea regarding use of artillery on Cemetery Ridge that hot July afternoon: "General Hancock and the Artillery at Gettysburg," *B&L,* III, pp. 385–87. For a sound analysis of the feud from a modern vantage point, see Naisawald, *Grape and Canister,* pp. 438–43.

26. Frank A. Haskell, *The Battle of Gettysburg* (Madison, Wis., 1910), p. 112; Alexander, *Military Memoirs of a Confederate,* pp. 422–23; Catherine S. Crary, ed., *Dear Belle* (Middletown, Conn.: Wesleyan University Press, 1965), p. 209.

27. Stewart, *Pickett's Charge,* pp. 184–200; Nevins, ed., *A Diary of Battle,* p. 253.

28. James Stewart, "Battery B Fourth United States Artillery at Gettysburg," *Sketches of War History, 1861–1865: Ohio MOLLUS,* IV (1896), pp 192–93; Capt. Andrew Cowan to Gen. Daniel E. Sickles, July 25, 1876, HP-LC.

29. Andrew Cowan, "Repulsing Pickett's Charge," *Civil War Times Illustrated,* III (August, 1964), p. 29.

30. John Bigelow, *The Peach Orchard* (Minneapolis, 1910), p. 38; HJH to C.C. Buel, Sept. 26, 1886, *Cen-C*; HJH to Mary Craig Hunt, July 4, 1863; HJH to Comte de Paris, May, 1877; both, HP-LC.

31. A second assault on Cemetery Ridge—actually, a belated effort to support Pickett on the part of a disorganized segment of Major General Cadmus Wilcox's infantry division—met the same fate as the more widely publicized main attack against the Federal center. See *OR,* I, 27, pt. 1, p. 240; Stewart, *Pickett's Charge,* pp. 251–52; and Naisawald, *Grape and Canister,* pp. 437–38.

32. For perhaps the only specific criticism of Hunt's handling of artillery on 3 July 1863 (proving, if nothing else, that the determined critic can find flaws in even the most faultless-looking feat of arms), see Thomas M. Aldrich, *The History of Battery A, First Rhode Island Light Artillery* (Providence, 1904), p. 219.

CHAPTER 13

1. *OR,* I, 27, pt. 1, p. 241.

2. Ibid., pp. 241, 878–79.

3. *JCCW* (1865-I), p. 455; George G. Meade to Margaret Sergeant Meade, July 5, 1863, Meade Papers, HSP.

4. HJH to War Department, n.d., HP-LC.

5. HJH to Mary Craig Hunt, July 4, 1863, Ibid.

6. Allan Nevins, ed., *A Diary of Battle* (New York: Harcourt, Brace & World, 1962), p. 250.

7. *JCCW* (1865-I), pp. 455–56; HJH to Alexander S. Webb, Jan. 19, 1888, Webb Papers; Freeman Cleaves, *Meade of Gettysburg* (Norman: University of Oklahoma Press, 1960), p. 181.

8. HJH, "The Third Day at Gettysburg," *B&L*, III, pp. 383–84.

9. *JCCW* (1865-I), p. 448.

10. HJH to Gen. A.A. Humphreys, July 26, 1863, HP-LC.

11. Humphreys to HJH; HJH to Humphreys; both, July 27, 1863, Ibid. See also endorsement on latter by HJH.

12. William E. Birkhimer, *Historical Sketch of Artillery* (Washington, D.C., 1884), pp. 316–17.

13. Nevins, ed., *A Diary of Battle*, pp. 276–77.

14. *JCCW* (1865-I), p. 449.

15. L. Van Loan Naisawald, *Grape and Canister* (New York: Oxford University Press, 1960), p. 441.

16. *OR*, I, 27, pt. 1, p. 242; HJH to Gen. John T. Sprague, Mar. 27, 1863, Gratz Collection, HSP.

17. Nevins, ed., *A Diary of Battle*, p. 286; *OR*, I, 29, pt. 2, pp. 157, 410–11.

18. Cleaves, *Meade of Gettysburg*, pp. 198–99; Bruce Catton, *Never Call Retreat* (Garden City, N.Y.: Doubleday & Co., Inc., 1965), pp. 255, 271–72.

19. Ibid., pp. 273–74; Nevins, ed., *A Diary of Battle*, p. 304; Alloway Diary, Nov. 30, 1863, HSP.

20. HJH, Journal of Siege Operations, marginal comments beside entries for May 25–27, 1864, HP-LC.

21. *New York at Gettysburg* (3 vols. Albany, 1900), III, p. 1189.

22. *HR 122*, Jan. 30, 1884 (48th Cong., 1st Sess.), p. 2.

23. HJH to "My Dear Colonel," Nov. 6, 1863, HP-LC.

24. Nevins, ed., *A Diary of Battle*, pp. 284, 286.

25. Unsigned and undated letter in Hunt's ACPF; *OR*, I, 33, p. 431.

26. General Orders 2, Jan. 15, 1864, Records of Headquarters, Chief of Artillery, Army of the Potomac, RG–393, E–4006, NA (and published in *OR*, I, 42, pt. 2, pp. 574–82).

CHAPTER 14

1. Headquarters, Army of the Potomac to HJH, Mar. 23, 1864, HP-LC; Allan Nevins, ed., *A Diary of Battle* (New York: Harcourt, Brace & World, 1962), p. 338.

2. George R. Agassiz, ed., *Meade's Headquarters* (Boston, 1922), p. 313.

3. John Y. Simon, ed., *The Papers of U.S. Grant* (c. 20 vols. Carbondale, Ill.: Southern Illinois University Press, 1967-   ), I, pp. 316, 326–27.

4. For a comprehensive roster of the Army at this period, see "The Opposing Forces at the Beginning of Grant's Campaign Against Richmond," *B&L*, IV, pp. 179–81.

5. Nevins, ed., *A Diary of Battle*, pp. 336–38; HJH to Col. Charles Wainwright, Mar. 26, 1864; HJH to Gen. Rufus Ingalls, Sept. 30, 1863, Feb. 21, 1864; all, Records of Headquarters, Chief of Artillery, Army of the Potomac, RG–393, E–4005, NA; *OR*, I, 29, pt. 2, pp. 237 and 261.

6. Ibid., I, 33, pp. 760–61; I, 36, pt. 1, pp. 284–89; L. Van Loan Naisawald, *Grape and Canister* (New York: Oxford University Press, 1960), pp. 463–65. The quote about the unpopularity of the Parrott battery is from Augustus Buell, *The Cannoneer* (Washington, D.C., 1890), p. 147. It seems a valid remark, though Buell has been revealed never to have served, as claimed, in the Federal artillery: Milton W. Hamilton, "Augustus C. Buell, Fraudulent Historian," *Pennsylvania Magazine of History and Biography*, LXXX (1956), pp. 478–92.

7. W.A. Swanberg, *Sickles the Incredible* (New York: Charles Scribner's Sons, 1956), p. 248.

8. Ibid., p. 250; *New York Herald*, Mar. 12, Apr. 4, 1864.

9. *JCCW* (1865-I), pp. 452, 456–58. Many Confederates remained long convinced that Meade was about to retreat on the evening of 3–4 July and had actually begun to do so before reevaluating his situation and countermanding the order to withdraw. Supposedly, Hunt himself corroborated this view in the late 1880s, shortly before his death; so, at any rate, reports a third-hand source, Gen. George McIver, who wrote

seventy years after the battle. See McIver to David R. Barbee, May 6, 1936, TS. in U.S. Army Military History Research Collection, Army War College.

10. *JCCW* (1865-I), pp. 91–94, 447–49, 456–58; George G. Meade to Margaret Sergeant Meade, Apr. 6, 1864, Meade Papers.

11. HJH to George B. McClellan, Apr. 5, 1864, McCP-NJHS.

12. G.H. Vaughan-Sawyer, *Grant's Campaign in Virginia, 1864* (New York, 1908), pp. 19–23.

13. *"More Than Conqueror,"* or, *Memorials of Col. J. Howard Kitching, Sixth New York Artillery* (New York, 1873), p. 124.

14. Here again it seems safe to accept at face value an observation from Buell, *The Cannoneer,* p. 164.

15. HJH, Journal of Siege Operations, May 6, 1864, HP-LC.

16. Ibid., May 9–10, 1864; *OR,* I, 36, pt. 1, pp. 286–87.

17. HJH, Journal of Siege Operations, May 9, 1864.

18. Ibid., May 10, 1864.

19. Ibid.; Nevins, ed., *A Diary of Battle,* pp. 360 and 362.

20. HJH, Journal of Siege Operations, May 13, 1864.

21. Ulysses S. Grant, *Personal Memoirs* (2 vols. New York, 1885–86), II, p. 181.

22. William E. Birkhimer, *Historical Sketch of Artillery* (Washington, D.C., 1884), pp. 86–88; H.W. Hubbell, "The Organization and Use of Artillery During the War of the Rebellion," *JMSIUS,* III (1882), pp. 405–6; *OR,* I, 36, pt. 2, pp. 840 and 882; pt. 3, p. 567.

23. Ibid., pp. 6–7, 40; pt. 2, p. 542; HJH, Journal of Siege Operations, marginal comments beside entries for May 25–27, 1864.

CHAPTER 15

1. Bruce Catton, *A Stillness at Appomattox* (Garden City, N.Y.: Doubleday & Co., Inc., 1953), pp. 131–49.

2. *OR,* I, 36, pt. 1, p. 1004; pt. 3, pp. 554–55.

3. Bruce Catton, *Grant Takes Command* (Boston: Little, Brown, 1969), pp. 274–76, 280–94.

4. Allan Nevins, ed., *A Diary of Battle* (New York: Harcourt, Brace & World, 1962), p. 426.

5. *OR,* I, 33, pp. 880–81; I, 36, pt. 2, pp. 191–92, 320, 373, 484–85; I, 40, pt. 1, p. 278. For details about the Coehorn, see Warren Ripley, *Artillery and Ammunition of the Civil War* (New York: Van Nostrand Reinhold Co., 1970), pp. 59–60.

6. *OR,* I, 36, pt. 2, pp. 843–44; I, 40, pt. 1, p. 655; pt. 2, pp. 488 and 552.

7. HJH, Journal of Siege Operations, June 27, 1864, HP-LC; Gen. U.S. Grant to the Army of the Potomac, June 27, 1864, in Hunt's ACPF (and published in *OR,* I, 40, pt. 1, pp. 210 and 284).

8. Nevins, ed., *A Diary of Battle,* pp. 436–38. In 1883, Hunt noted ruefully: "It is a great pity than they [Grant's siege plans] were spoiled by not making the operation a *unity* under the Chief of Art. and of Engineers, and a *Director of siege,* instead of carrying water on both shoulders by giving each corps commander control of his own front and thus causing the heads of the Engineers & the Artillery to try to serve two masters—and with the usual result!!": HJH, Journal of Siege Operations, marginal comments beside entry for July 9, 1864.

9. David S. Sparks, ed., *Inside Lincoln's Army* (New York: Thomas Yoseloff, 1964), p. 317; Nevins, ed., *A Diary of Battle,* p. 509.

10. HJH to Gen. A.A. Humphreys, July 18, 1864, Records of Headquarters, Chief of Artillery, Army of the Potomac, RG–393, E–4005, NA (and published in *OR,* I, 40, pt. 3, p. 318.

11. Ibid., pp. 350 and 367; John Gibbon, *Personal Recollections* (New York: G.P. Putnam's Sons, 1928), p. 254.

12. Joseph Gould, *The Story of the Forty-Eighth: A Record of the Campaigns of the Forty-Eighth Regiment Pennsylvania Veteran Volunteer Infantry* (Philadelphia, 1908), p. 212; Henry Pleasants, Jr. and George M. Straley, *Inferno at Petersburg* (Philadelphia: Chilton Co., 1961), pp. 46–51.

13. Ibid., pp. 66–70; Catton, *A Stillness at Appomattox,* pp. 221–24.

14. HJH, Journal of Siege Operations, June 29, 1864; *OR,* I, 40, pt. 2, pp. 199, 514, 528, 532, 593, 615.

15. Ibid., pt. 1, pp. 285–87; pt. 2, p. 600.

16. HJH, Journal of Siege Operations, marginal comments beside entry for July 9, 1864.

17. Ibid., July 17, 1864; L. Van Loan Naisawald, *Grape and Canister* (New York: Oxford University Press, 1960), pp. 509–10.

18. H.L. Abbot, *Siege Artillery in the Campaigns Against Richmond* (New York, 1868), p. 23; Robert B. Sylvester, "The U.S. Military Railroad and the Siege of Petersburg," *Civil War History,* X (September, 1964), pp. 311–12; *OR,* I, 40, pt. 3, p. 219; I, 42, pt. 3, p. 277.

19. Gould, *Story of the Forty-Eighth,* pp. 213–14.

20. HJH, Journal of Siege Operations, July 17, 1864.

21. Ibid., July 28, 1864; Gould, *Story of the Forty-Eighth,* p. 215; *OR,* I, 40, pt. 1, p. 96.

22. Ibid., pp. 110 and 281; Nevins, ed., *A Diary of Battle,* pp. 448–49.

23. George R. Agassiz, ed., *Meade's Headquarters* (Boston, 1922), p. 197. A copy of Hunt's meticulous instructions, July 29, 1864, is in Dreer Collection, HSP.

24. Pleasants and Straley, *Inferno at Petersburg,* pp. 104–14.

25. Ibid., pp. 119–24; Freeman S. Bowley, "The Petersburg Mine," *California MOLLUS: War Paper 3* (1889), p. 5; Nevins, ed., *A Diary of Battle,* pp. 444–45.

26. Gould, *Story of the Forty-Eighth,* p. 216; Catton, *A Stillness at Appomattox,* pp. 244–45.

27. E.B. Bennett, comp., *First Connecticut Heavy Artillery* (East Berlin, Conn., 1890), p. 20; W.H. Stewart, "The Charge of the Crater," *SHSP,* XXV (1897), p. 78; *OR,* I, 40, pt. 1, p. 96.

28. Nevins, ed., *A Diary of Battle,* p. 449.

29. Catton, *A Stillness at Appomattox,* pp. 245–52; Bennett, comp., *First Connecticut Heavy Artillery,* pp. 20–21; *OR,* I, 40, pt. 1, p. 659; pt. 3, pp. 687 and 715.

CHAPTER 16

1. Pvt. James Mitchell, Third New Jersey Light Battery, to David Mitchell, Sept. 2, 1864, U.S. Army Military History Research Collection, Army War College.

2. The Hunt-Hancock feud of Sept. 9, 1864 can be followed through several letters and telegrams in Records of Headquarters, Chief of Artillery, Army of the Potomac, RG–393, E–4005, NA, as well as through Hunt-Hancock correspondence, Sept. 17, 28, 1864, and Col. B.F. Fisher to HJH, Oct. 23, 1866; all, HP-LC. Much printed material on the subject is in *OR,* I, 42, pt. 2; see especially pp. 571, 759–60. The second, more minor conflict between the two men is covered in Ibid., p. 832.

3. Ibid., pp. 849 and 895; HJH to Gen. Seth Williams, Sept. 17, 1864, Records of Headquarters, Chief of Artillery, Army of the Potomac, RG–393, E–4005, NA.

4. David S. Sparks, ed., *Inside Lincoln's Army* (New York: Thomas Yoseloff, 1964), p. 420; Allan Nevins, ed., *A Diary of Battle* (New York: Harcourt, Brace & World, 1962), p. 477.

5. For a thorough overview of the fighting on all fronts, Sept., 1864–Mar., 1865, see Bruce Catton, *Grant Takes Command* (Boston: Little, Brown, 1969), pp. 326–432. The quote by Col. Lyman is from George R. Agassiz, ed., *Meade's Headquarters* (Boston, 1922), p. 275.

6. Nevins, ed., *A Diary of Battle,* pp. 479, 500, 500n.

7. William H. Powell, comp., *List of Officers of the Army of the United States from 1779 to 1900* (New York, 1900), p. 389; James M. Bugbee, ed., *Massachusetts Society of the Cincinnati* (Boston, 1890), p. 274.

8. *OR,* I, 42, pt. 3, p. 1095. For purposes of seniority, the brevet was antedated to July 6, 1864.

9. "The Opposing Forces at Petersburg and Richmond," *B&L,* IV, p. 590; *OR,* I, 46, pt. 1, pp. 659–61.

10. Bruce Catton, *A Stillness at Appomattox* (Garden City, N.Y.: Doubleday & Co., Inc., 1953), pp. 335–36.

11. Nevins, ed., *A Diary of Battle,* pp. 503–4; *OR,* I, 46, pt. 1, pp. 174–75; pt. 3, pp. 113, 120, 150, 174, 174n.

12. L. Van Loan Naisawald, *Grape and Canister* (New York: Oxford University Press, 1960), pp. 530–31.

13. Catton, *A Stillness at Appomattox,* pp. 346–58.

14. *OR,* I, 46, pt. 1, p. 663.

15. Ibid., pp. 661–63; HJH to Thomas Gantt, May 8, 1888, HP-LC.

16. HJH, Journal of the Appomattox Campaign, Apr. 7, 1865, in possession of Cmdr. J. Conway Hunt.

17. HJH, "Third Day at Gettysburg," *B&L,* III, pp. 373–74. The best source of information on Hunt's activities immediately before and immediately after Lee's surrender is his MS. journal, cited above. Unfortunately, it is a badly scrambled record, for he scrawled (and even this seems too elegant a term to describe his spidery script) in it wherever he could find ready space, regardless of chronology. To maintain proper order, his diary should be read in this sequence: entries for Apr. 9, Mar. 7, Mar. 8, Apr. 10, Mar. 10, Feb. 10, Apr. 19, Apr. 20, 1865.

18. Ibid., Apr. 15, 1865; *OR,* I, 46, pt. 3, pp. 788 and 810.

19. HJH, Journal of the Appomattox Campaign, Apr. 18, 1865.

20. For further information on this obscure court-martial, see Albert G. Riddle, *Arguments for Defence in the Case of the United States vs. Colonel Louis Schirmer* (Washington, D.C., 1865).

21. *OR,* I, 46, pt. 3, p. 1027n; Catton, *Grant Takes Command,* pp. 490–91.

22. Nevins, ed., *A Diary of Battle,* pp. 524–29; Joshua L. Chamberlain, *The Passing of the Armies: An Account of the Final Campaign of the Army of the Potomac* (New York, 1915), p. 332.

CHAPTER 17

1. HJH to Asst. Adjutant Gen., Army of the Potomac, June 1, 1865; Special Orders 280, June 5, 1865; both, HP-LC; *HR 212,* Feb. 3, 1886 (49th Cong., 1st Sess.), p. 3; *OR,* I, 46, pt. 3, pp. 1254–55.

2. Ibid., I, 47, pt. 3, p. 679; I, 48, pt. 2, pp. 680 and 1111.

3. James E. Sefton, *The United States Army and Reconstruction, 1865–1877* (Baton Rouge: Louisiana State University Press, 1967), pp. 3–16.

4. James M. Merrill, *William Tecumseh Sherman* (Chicago: Rand McNally, 1971), p. 335.

5. Edwin C. Bearss and Arrell M. Gibson, *Fort Smith* (Norman: University of Oklahoma Press, 1969), p. 309.

6. HJH to Gen. William T. Sherman, Feb. 21, 1866, Sherman Papers, LC.

7. HJH to Capt. J.T. Smith, Sept. 22, 1865; HJH to Gen. John Sanborn, Jan. 11, 1866; both, Records of Headquarters, District of the Frontier, 1865–66, RG–393, E–4754, NA.

8. Sanborn to HJH, Jan. 9, 1866; Capt. W.H. Wood to HJH, Feb. 1, 1866; HJH to Mjr. Silas Hunter, Feb. 7, 1866; Hunter to HJH, Feb. 24, 1866; all, Ibid., E–4756.

9. HJH to D.H. Cooley, Jan. 3, 1866, Ibid., E–4754; Matthew Gray to HJH, Feb. 8, 1866, Ibid., E–4756.

10. HJH to Cooley, Jan. 3, 1866, Ibid., E–4754; Chief Comm. of Subs., Fort Smith to HJH, Dec. 11, 1865, Ibid., E–4756.

11. "Citizens of Western Arkansas" to Andrew Johnson, Feb., 1866; Chief of Chocktaw Nation to HJH, Apr. 24, 1866; both, HP-LC.

12. HJH to George B. McClellan, Sept. 29, 1867, McCP-LC.

13. Capt. John Flick to HJH, Feb. 2, 1866; Mjr. Silas Hunter to HJH, Feb. 24, 1866; both, Records of Headquarters, District of the Frontier, 1865–66, RG–393, E–4756.

14. HJH to Sherman, Feb. 21, 1866, Sherman Papers.

15. William E. Birkhimer, *Historical Sketch of Artillery* (Washington, D.C., 1884), p. 378.

16. HJH to McClellan, Dec. 13, 1867, McCP-LC. For Upton's reaction to Hunt's claim, see Peter S. Michie, *The Life and Letters of Emory Upton* (New York, 1885), pp. 211–12, 216.

17. For a light-handed discussion of the practical value (or lack thereof) of brevet rank in the latter stages of the Civil War, see August V. Kautz, "How I Won My First Brevet," *Sketches of War History: Ohio MOLLUS,* IV (1896), pp. 363–64, 364n, 373.

18. HJH to McClellan, Sept. 29, 1867, McCP-LC.

19. Russell F. Weigley, *History of the United States Army* (New York: Macmillan Co., 1967), p. 273; John M. Schofield, *Forty-Six Years in the Army* (New York, 1897), p. 426.

20. Birkhimer, *Historical Sketch of Artillery,* p. 186.

21. Ibid., pp. 288, 288n; Report, Jan. 16, 1867, Records of Proceedings, Artillery Board to Determine Calibre and Proportion of Rifled Guns for the Armament of Fortifications, 1866–67, M–619, R–470, E–369E–1866, NA.

22. Asst. Adjutant Gen. E.D. Townsend to HJH, June 26, 1867; HJH to Townsend, July 16, 1867; HJH to Sec. Edwin McM. Stanton, Feb. 10, 1868; copy of charges and specifications vs. Gen. Lorenzo Thomas; all, Military Papers, HP-LC.

23. HJH to Col. Henry Knox Craig, July 17, 1867, HP-LC.

24. HJH to Craig, Nov. 15, 1867, Ibid.

25. HJH to McClellan, Sept. 29, 1867, McCP-LC.

26. HJH to Craig, Apr. 9, May 14, 1868; both, HP-LC.

27. HJH to Thomas Gantt, Nov. 1, 1886, Ibid. For a "Z" communication typical in content and style, see *A&NJ,* June 12, 1875, p. 8, col. 1.

28. William Sturgis Thomas, *Members of the Society of the Cincinnati* (New York: privately issued, 1929), p. 82. A list of all organizations to which Hunt belonged is included in his last will and testament, dictated Mar. 12, 1883, HP-LC.

29. William E. Birkhimer, "Henry J. Hunt, Class of 1839," *Twentieth Annual Reunion of the Association of Graduates, U.S. Military Academy, West Point, New York (June 12, 1889)* (West Point, 1889), p. 83.

30. James C. Bush, "Fifth Regiment of Artillery," in T.F. Rodenbough and William L. Haskin, eds., *The Army of the United States* (New York, 1896), p. 397.

31. Ibid.; David Fitzgerald, *In Memoriam* (Washington, D.C., 1889), p. 12.

32. *A&NJ,* May 8, 1886.

33. Fitzgerald, *In Memoriam,* p. 12.

34. William L. Haskin, comp., *First Regiment of Artillery* (Portland, Me., 1879), pp. 253–54.

35. *Report of the Secretary of War* (Washington, D.C., 1874), I, p. xxviii; *HR 592,* May 13, 1874 (43rd Cong., 1st Sess.), p. xi.

36. *HR 594,* May 13, 1874 (43rd Cong., 1st Sess.), III, pp. 1–4, 7–8.

37. HJH to Sherman, Feb., 1880; HJH to Comte de Paris, May, 1877; both, HP-LC.

38. HJH to Sherman, Mar. 9, 1880, Sherman Papers; HJH to Alexander S. Webb, July 4, 1881, Webb Papers.

CHAPTER 18

1. *New York Times,* Feb. 17, 1889; HJH to Thomas Gantt, July 25, 1888; Mjr. Carl Berlin to HJH, Aug. 21, Oct. 28, 1888; Berlin to Gen. J.P. Hawkins, Oct. 21, 1888; all, HP-LC. See also copy of codicil of last will and testament of Henry Knox Craig, Ibid.

2. HJH, Last Will and Testament; HJH to Craig, Sept. 10, 1874; HJH to Gantt, Nov. 21, 1884; all, Ibid.

3. *HR 122,* Jan. 30, 1884 (48th Cong., 1st Sess.), p. 4; *A&NJ,* Oct. 2, 1886.

4. Post Returns, Charleston, S.C., Nov., 1876–Apr., 1879, M–617, R–199, NA; James C. Bush, "Fifth Regiment of Artillery," in T.F. Rodenbough and William L. Haskin, eds., *The Army of the United States* (New York, 1896), p. 398.

5. James E. Sefton, *United States Army and Reconstruction* (Baton Rouge: Louisiana State University Press, 1967), p. 186.

6. John Hope Franklin, *Reconstruction After the Civil War* (Chicago: University of Chicago Press, 1961), p. 210; Hodding Carter, *The Angry Scar: The Story of Reconstruction* (Garden City, N.Y.: Doubleday & Co., Inc., 1959), p. 223.

7. Robert Selph Henry, *The Story of Reconstruction* (Indianapolis: Bobbs-Merrill

Co., 1938), pp. 568–69; William B. Hesseltine, *Ulysses S. Grant, Politician* (New York: Frederick Ungar, 1957), pp. 409–10.

8. Sefton, *United States Army and Reconstruction*, p. 248; Francis Butler Simkins and Robert Hilliard Woody, *South Carolina During Reconstruction* (Chapel Hill: University of North Carolina Press, 1932), pp. 509–13.

9. Manly Wade Wellman, *Giant in Gray: A Biography of Wade Hampton of South Carolina* (New York: Charles Scribner's Sons, 1949), p. 271.

10. Ibid., p. 272; *A&NJ*, Jan. 20, 1877. Information on Mayor Cunningham, Marshal Wallace, and Chief Hendricks is drawn from letter to author from Ms. Martha Matheny, South Carolina Historical Society, May 30, 1975.

11. James Morris Morgan, *Recollections of a Rebel Reefer* (Boston, 1917), p. 350.

12. Ibid., pp. 350–51; Alfred B. Williams, *Hampton and His Red Shirts: South Carolina's Deliverance in 1876* (Freeport, N.Y.: Books for Libraries Press, 1970), p. 371.

13. F.A. Porcher, "The Last Chapter of the History of Reconstruction in South Carolina," *SHSP*, XIII (1885), p. 62.

14. Walter Allen, *Governor Chamberlain's Administration in South Carolina* (New York, 1888), pp. 445–87; *A&NJ*, Jan. 20, 1877; Robert M. Fogelson and Richard E. Rubenstein, eds., *Mass Violence in America: Use of the Army in Certain of the Southern States* (New York: Arno Press, 1969), p. 29.

15. Inspector Gen. R.B. Marcy to Sherman, Nov. 21, 1876; Gen. E.D. Townsend to Sherman, Jan. 10, 1877 (see also Sherman's endorsement on same); HJH to Townsend, Jan. 20, 1877; Judge Advocate Gen. William M. Dunn to Townsend, Feb. 12, 1877; Townsend to Sherman, Feb. 12, 1877; all in Hunt's ACPF.

16. *New York Sun*, Jan. 12, 1877. Hunt's report is printed in full, p. 3.

17. Sec. Cameron to Chief Clerk, War Department, Jan. 17, 1877 (and note Mjr. C.L. Best's endorsement), HP-LC.

18. Capt. William A. Courtenay and officers and men of the Washington Light Infantry, Charleston, S.C., to HJH, Apr. 22, 1879; HJH to "Gentlemen," May 5, 1879; TSS. of both, courtesy Cmdr. J. Conway Hunt.

19. Hunt's earliest mention of severe headaches is in HJH to Isaac I. Stevens, June 16, 1852, Stevens Papers.

20. Of Hunt's surviving children, Conway (1861–1947) became a renowned civil engineer, helping to construct Washington's Union Station, the Q Street and William H. Taft Bridges, and other capital landmarks. Presley (1871–1910) launched a pioneering career as a psychiatrist, in residency at Washington's St. Elizabeth's Hospital— where he met a violent death at thirty-nine at the hands of a deranged patient. John (1874–1950) matriculated at West Point but failed to graduate. Entering the Army from civil life, he rose from private to full colonel, being decorated for gallantry in the Spanish-American War and closing out his career after World War I as prison commander on Governors Island, New York, where he guarded the celebrated draft-dodger, Grover Cleveland Bergdoll. Hunt's daughters enjoyed somewhat less prominent careers: Maria (1862–1938) became a State Department employee; Julia (1867–1954) was a worker in Herbert Hoover's post-World War I economic relief effort for Near Eastern Lands and later in other bureaucratic posts; and Jane (1875–1921) was a White House secretary. Curiously, only John, among the half-dozen children of Hunt and his second wife, married—and he died childless.

21. *A&NJ*, May 8, 1886; A.A. Hoehling, *The Jeannette Expedition: An Ill-Fated Journey to the Arctic* (New York: Abelard-Schuman, 1968), pp. 173 and 188.

22. *Roster of Troops: Department of the South, Commanded by Col. H.J. Hunt, 5th Artillery* (Washington, D.C., 1883), pp. 3 and 5; Bush, "Fifth Regiment of Artillery," p. 398.

23. R.P. Thian, comp., *Notes Illustrating the Military Geography of the United States* (Washington, D.C., 1881), p. 95; Post Returns, Newport Barracks, Dec., 1880–Sept., 1883, M–617, R–847–8, NA.

24. HJH to McClellan, Nov. 8, 1877, McCP-LC.

25. *New York Times*, July 3, 1884; George F. Howe, *Chester A. Arthur: A Quarter-Century of Machine Politics* (New York: Frederick Ungar, 1957), pp. 251–52; Thomas C. Reeves, *Gentleman Boss: The Life of Chester Alan Arthur* (New York: Alfred A. Knopf, 1975), p. 384.

26. *HR 212*, Feb. 3, 1886 (49th Cong., 1st Sess.), p. 1; circular, HJH to The

President of the United States, Dec., 1881, courtesy of Cmdr. J. Conway Hunt; Frederick A. Virkus, ed., *The Abridged Compendium of American Genealogy* (7 vols. Chicago: Marquis Co., 1925–42), VI, p. 423.

27. HJH, Annual Report, Department of the South, Sept., 1883, Records of Headquarters, Department of the South, 1868–83, RG–393, E–4091, Sub–E–254, NA.

28. War Department to HJH, Sept. 14, 1883, in Hunt's ACPF; Remarks of Lt. Col. H.C. Corbin, Sept. 14, 1883, copy in Ibid. For Hunt's reply to the testimonial speech of his subordinates, see Orders 59, Department of the South, Sept. 18, 1883, copy in HP-LC.

CHAPTER 19

1. This once sumptuous home (built c. 1840) is now the Phi Sigma Delta house on the campus of George Washington University.

2. *HR 78,* Dec. 10, 1883 (48th Cong., 1st Sess.), p. 1; Fairfax Downey, *The Guns at Gettysburg* (New York: David McKay Co., Inc., 1958), p. 258n.

3. *HR 122,* Jan. 30, 1884 (48th Cong., 1st Sess.), pp. 1–3.

4. HJH to anon., n.d. (c. 1884), HP-LC; James Morris Morgan, *Recollections of a Rebel Reefer* (Boston, 1917), p. 351.

5. HJH to C.C. Buel, May 26, 1886, *Cen*-C; HJH to Francis W. Dawson, Apr. 4, 1888, Dawson Papers, Duke University Library.

6. Downey, *The Guns at Gettysburg,* p. 259n.

7. George F. Howe, *Chester A. Arthur* (New York: Frederick Ungar, 1957), p. 252; Lt. Col. E.M. Hudson to Mary Craig Hunt, May 25, 1889, HP-LC.

8. For facts about later attempts to revive Hunt's pension bill, see *HR 212,* Feb. 3, 1886 (49th Cong., 1st Sess.), and *HR 3824,* Apr. 24, 1888 (50th Cong., 1st Sess.). For Hunt's congratulatory letter to his old colleague, see HJH to Fitz-John Porter, July 4, 1886, Porter Papers, USMA-L.

9. *A&NJ,* Mar. 6, Sept. 11, Oct. 2, 1886; *New York Times,* Sept. 9, 1886; HJH to Thomas Gantt, Sept. 30, 1886, HP-LC.

10. *A&NJ,* May 8, 1886; "In Memoriam: Lines to the Memory of Lt. Henry J. Hunt, U.S. Navy," Ibid.; HJH to Thomas Gantt, Sept. 30, 1886, Ibid.; *San Francisco Weekly Bulletin,* Feb. 13, 1889.

11. *Washington Evening Star,* Feb. 11, 1889; HJH to Board of Commissioners of Soldiers' Home, June 17, July 6, 1885, Records, Office of the Governor, U.S. Soldiers' Home, Washington, D.C., 1885–89, RG–231, E–1 and 7, NA; HJH to War Department, Feb. 12, 1885, in his ACPF; Paul R. Goode, *The United States Soldiers' Home* (Richmond, Va.: privately issued, 1957), p. 132.

12. HJH to Thomas Gantt, May 16, Aug. 18, 1885, HP-LC.

13. HJH to Gantt, Mar. 18, 1886, Ibid.

14. HJH to Gantt, Feb. 22, 1886, Ibid.

15. HJH to Gantt, Mar. 11, 18, Apr. 15, 1886; all, Ibid.; *A&NJ,* June 19, 1886.

16. Ibid., May 8 and 15, 1886; HJH to Gantt, May 6, 1886, HP-LC. In Oct., 1888, Harry's widow, Blossom, remarried, this time the bride of Hughes Oliphant (Princeton '70). The couple had three children of their own, two sons and a daughter.

17. Clipping of unidentified California newspaper, Mar. 29, 1889, in HP-LC.

18. HJH to Board of Commissioners of Soldiers' Home, Oct., 1885; HJH to Gen. P.H. Sheridan, Dec. 22, 1886; both, Records, Office of the Governor, U.S. Soldiers' Home, RG–231, E–1 and 7, NA.

19. HJH to Board of Commissioners, June 17, Oct., 1885, Ibid.

20. HJH to Thomas Gantt, May 16, 1885, HP-LC; *The Society of the Army of the Potomac: Report of the Sixteenth Annual Re-union at Baltimore, Md., May 6 and 7, 1885* (New York, 1886), p. 6; HJH to Fitz-John Porter, July 4, 1886, Porter Papers, USMA-L.

21. HJH to R.U. Johnson, Nov. 7, 1885, *Cen*-C.

22. Manly Wade Wellman, *Giant in Gray* (New York: Charles Scribner's Sons, 1949), p. 272; Clifford Dowdey, *Death of a Nation: The Story of Lee and His Men at Gettysburg* (New York: Alfred A. Knopf, 1958), p. 359n.

23. HJH to R.U. Johnson, Mar. 25, 1887, Mar. 14, 1888, *Cen*-C.

24. HJH to Johnson, May 14, 1887, Feb. 25, 1888, Ibid.; HJH to Thomas Gantt,

Oct. 10, 1887, June 19, 1888, HP-LC; HJH to Francis W. Dawson, Apr. 4, 1888, Dawson Papers.

25. Attending Surgeon, Soldiers' Home, to Adjutant Gen., Mar. 2, 1889, Records, Office of the Governor, U.S. Soldiers' Home, RG–231, E–7, NA; *Washington Evening Star,* Feb. 11, 1889; *New York Times,* Feb. 21, 1889. Beyond his name, rank, and life dates, no inscription adorns Hunt's grave in the cemetery of the Soldiers' Home. Apparently he wished it that way: "As to my epitaph, I think I shall forbid one, then there will be no lies told": HJH to R.U. Johnson, Nov. 16, 1886, *Cen*-C.

26. *Washington Post,* Feb. 12, 1889.

27. Hunt's Pension File, in his ACPF; *New York Times,* Feb. 17, 1889; *HR 2688,* Feb. 27, 1889 (50th Cong., 2nd Sess.), p. 2.

28. General Orders 14, Headquarters, Department of the Army, quoting War Department eulogy signed by Sec. Endicott, Feb. 12, 1889, copy in Hunt's ACPF.

29. *A&NJ,* Feb. 16, 1889.

Selected Bibliography

NOTE: Space limitation precludes listing the almost four hundred printed sources consulted during the preparation of this book. Many, if not most of these, have provided material incorporated in the text and thus are to be found in footnote citations. The bibliography below lists only the manuscript sources and unpublished records drawn upon in research.

MANUSCRIPTS

Abbot, Henry L. Papers. Gratz Collection, Manuscripts Department, Historical Society of Pennsylvania (Philadelphia, Pa.).

Alloway, John K. Journal, 1863. Manuscripts Department, Historical Society of Pennsylvania.

Barry, William F. Papers. Gratz Collection, Manuscripts Department, Historical Society of Pennsylvania.

Dawson, Francis W. Papers. Manuscripts Department, Duke University Library (Durham, N.C.).

Duncan, James. Papers. Manuscripts Section, United States Military Academy Library (West Point, N.Y.).

Files on Civil War Ordnance. Headquarters Library, Gettysburg National Military Park (Gettysburg, Pa.).

Hanson, Joseph Mills. "A Report on the Employment of the Artillery at the Battle of Antietam, Md." Headquarters Library, Petersburg National Battlefield Park (Petersburg, Va.).

Hazlett, James C. "Field Artillery on the Gettysburg Battlefield." Headquarters Library, Gettysburg National Military Park.

Humphreys, Andrew A. Papers. Manuscripts Department, Historical Society of Pennsylvania.

Hunt, Henry J. "Journal of the Appomattox Campaign." In possession of Cmdr. J. Conway Hunt, USN Ret'd. (Washington, D.C.).

————. Letter of April 12, 1861 to General Braxton Bragg. Manuscripts Department, U.S. Army Military History Research Collection, Army War College (Carlisle Barracks, Pa.).

————. Papers. *Century* Collection, Manuscripts and Archives Division, New York Public Library (New York, N.Y.).

————. Papers. Dreer and Gratz Collections, Manuscripts Department, Historical Society of Pennsylvania.

————. Papers. In possession of Cmdr. J. Conway Hunt, USN Ret'd.

————. Papers. Manuscripts Division, Library of Congress (Washington, D.C.).

————. Papers. Manuscripts Department, New-York Historical Society (New York, N.Y.).

Hunt, John Elliott. Reminiscences. Local History Collection, Toledo-Lucas County Public Library (Toledo, Ohio).

McClellan, George B. Papers. Manuscripts Division, Library of Congress.

————. Papers. Manuscripts Department, New Jersey Historical Society (Newark, N.J.).

McIver, George W. Letter of May 6, 1936 to David R. Barbee. Manuscripts Department, U.S. Army Military History Research Collection, Army War College.

Meade, George G. Papers. Manuscripts Department, Historical Society of Pennsylvania.

Mitchell, James. Papers. Manuscripts Department, U.S. Army Military History Research Collection, Army War College.

Nichols, Emmet A. "A Survey of Field Artillery . . . Gettysburg National Military Park." Headquarters Library, Gettysburg National Military Park.

Porter, Fitz-John. Papers. Manuscripts Division, Library of Congress.

————. Papers. Manuscripts Section, United States Military Academy Library.

Reed, Charles W. Papers. Manuscripts Division, Library of Congress.

Sedgwick, John. Papers. Gratz Collection, Manuscripts Department, Historical Society of Pennsylvania.

Sheldon, Charles H. Journals. Headquarters Library, Gettysburg National Military Park.

Sherman, William T. Papers. Manuscripts Division, Library of Congress.

Stevens, Isaac I. Papers. Manuscripts Department, University of Washington Library (Seattle, Wash.).

Swan, Henry R. Papers. Manuscripts Department, U.S. Army Military History Research Collection, Army War College.

Tidball, John C. Memoirs. Manuscripts Division, Library of Congress.

————. Papers. Manuscripts Section, United States Military Academy Library.

Webb, Alexander S. Papers. Manuscripts Department, Yale University Library (New Haven, Conn.).

UNPUBLISHED RECORDS

Academic Record of Cadet Henry J. Hunt, Class of 1839. United States Military Academy Archives (West Point, N.Y.).

Appointments, Commissions, and Promotions File of Henry J. Hunt. Record Group 94, National Archives (Washington, D.C.).

Generals's Papers of Henry J. Hunt. Record Group 94, Entry 159, National Archives.

List of Demerits of Cadet Henry J. Hunt, Class of 1839. United States Military Academy Archives.

Post Returns, Various U. S. A. Forts, 1839–83. Microcopy 617, Various Rolls, National Archives.

Records of Headquarters, Chief of Artillery, Army of the Potomac, 1862–65. Record Group 393, Entries 4005, 4006, National Archives.

Records of Headquarters, Chief of the Artillery Reserve, Army of the Potomac, 1861–62. Record Group 393, Entry 4011, National Archives.

Records of Headquarters, Department of Northeastern Virginia, 1861. Record Group 393, Entry 3684, National Archives.

Records of Headquarters, Department of the South, 1868–83. Record Group 393, Entries 4091, 4094, 4114, National Archives.

Records of Headquarters, District of the Frontier, 1865–66. Record Group 393, Entries 4754, 4756, National Archives.

Records of Headquarters, Fifth U. S. Artillery, 1861–63, 1869–83. Microcopy 727, Rolls 33, 34, National Archives.

Records of Headquarters, Second U. S. Artillery, 1839–61. Microcopy 727, Rolls 10, 11, 12, National Archives.

Records of Headquarters, Third U. S. Artillery, 1863–69. Microcopy 727, Roll 21, National Archives.

Records of Office of Governor, U.S. Soldiers's Home, Washington, D. C., 1885–89. Record Group 231, Entries 1, 7, National Archives.

Report of Proceedings of Artillery Board to Determine Calibre and Proportion of Rifled Guns for the Armament of Fortifications, 1866–67. Microcopy 619, Roll 470, Entry 369E-1866, National Archives.

Report of Proceedings of Board to Regulate the Number and Calibre of Cannon to be Mounted in the Permanent Fortifications of the United States, 1861–62. Microcopy 619, Roll 95, Entry 355E-1862, National Archives.

Report of Proceedings of Board to Revise the System of Light Artillery Tactics, 1856–57, 1858–59. Microcopy 567, Roll 600, Entry F10-1859, National Archives.

Report of Service of Henry J. Hunt, 1861–65. Record Group 94, Entry 160, Volume III, Sub-Entry 36, National Archives.

Index

283